for tudor on your
birthday
14. 2. 19
... a perspective on Brexit?

HOW TO BE
EUROPEAN

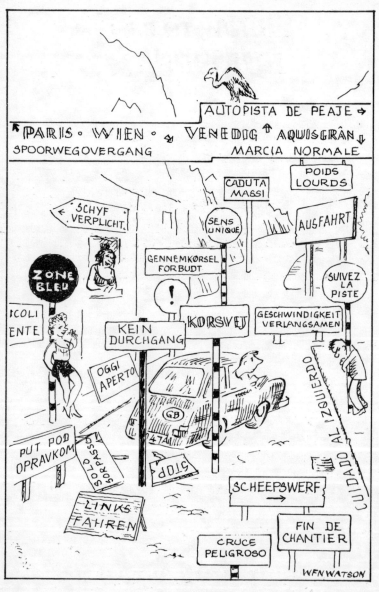

Travellers' Joy

HOW TO BE EUROPEAN

Compiled by E. O. Parrott
and edited by Noel Petty

Illustrated by W. F. N. Watson

SIMON & SCHUSTER

LONDON·SYDNEY·NEW YORK·TOKYO·SINGAPORE·TORONTO

First published in Great Britain by
Simon & Schuster Ltd in 1991
A Paramount Communications Company

Simon & Schuster Ltd
West Garden Place
Kendal Street
London W2 2AQ

Simon & Schuster of Australia Pty Ltd
Sydney

A CIP catalogue record for this book is
available from the British Library
ISBN 0–671–71055–9

Typeset in Palatino 10.5/12.5pt by
Falcon Typographic Art Ltd, Edinburgh & London
Printed and bound in Great Britain by
Billing & Sons Ltd, Worcester

W. F. N. Watson first had illustrated humorous articles and cartoons published during his thirty years' Regular Army service.

Since he retired, his maps, historical illustrations, humorous verse, prose and artwork have appeared in thirty books. From 1977 to 1988 he was question-setter for the television programme University Challenge, and also wrote for other television programmes.

CONTENTS

ARE YOU READY FOR 1992?

As the Year of the Single European Market approaches, many public figures can be heard lamenting Britain's unreadiness for the challenges it will bring. Large sections of industry, they tell us, are oblivious of both the commercial opportunities and of the competitive threats; among the general public, confusion reigns.

There is a paradox here, for in our travels about Britain, as we shall see, we have found everywhere a goodwill and enthusiasm for the concept of being European – albeit not always well-directed. What was missing, it seemed to us, was a sound textbook for the apprentice European. This book aims to supply that need.

Our team of correspondents has therefore been despatched all over Europe, sending back reports on places and people, on customs, cuisine and culture. The aspiring European, if he applies himself diligently, should be able by the end of this book to claim common citizenship with Mozart, Molière and Michelangelo; to be, in short, a European.

First, however, we would like you to take a little time to complete a brief questionnaire. Keep a record of your answers so that, when you retake it after you have finished the book, you will be able to see how much more European you have become.

1. Is 1992
   a) a heavy-metal rock band from Newcastle?
   b) a new telephone code for London?
   c) when trade barriers drop all over Europe?
   d) a recently-discovered novel by George Orwell?

2. Is the Single Market
   a) a cut-price dating agency?
   b) the promotion company behind the Eurovision song contest?
   c) another plan for re-developing Covent Garden?
   d) a simpler way of selling goods and services in Europe?

Cut-price Dating Agency?

3. Is the EEC
  a) a patent sting-relief, particularly effective against wasps?
  b) a poisonous food additive used to colour soft drinks?
  c) Steven Spielberg's latest film about an endearing alien?
  d) a way of encouraging European trade, so that Spanish onions end up in Scunthorpe while Stilton cheese gets to Strasbourg?

4. Did Britain join the EEC in
  a) 55 B.C. (a result of the Roman invasion)?
  b) 1066 (After the Battle of Hastings)?
  c) 1815 (as part of the Romantic Movement)?
  d) 1973 (as a last resort)?

5. Did Britain join the EEC for
  a) cheap wine?
  b) a chance for Mr Heath to broadcast in French?
  c) a new outlet for rioting football fans?
  d) the amusement of lots of civil servants who thought the shuttle to Brussels would have more style than the 8.05 from Godalming?

6. Is Britain's biggest benefit from the EEC
  a) easy shopping trips to French hypermarkets?
  b) an influx of scantily-clad foreign language students?
  c) a reduction in the number of civil servants on the 8.05 from Godalming?
  d) the chance for lots of magazines to print quizzes like this?

7. Is Mrs Thatcher's attitude to Europe
  a) hatred: because Mr Heath got all the publicity by getting us in?
  b) contempt: because it's all foreign?
  c) envy: because *their* Royals take the back seat?
  d) superiority: because they're not British?

8. Is Mr Major

    a) pro-Europe because all the best Plazas in Spain are named after him?

    b) nostalgic for bread and circuses?

    c) prepared to take whatever action is appropriate if and when the right circumstances occur, always bearing in mind and paying due regard to ... ?

    d) confident because neither Herr Kohl nor Monsieur Mittérand can tell a leg-break from a googly?

9. Is the Labour Party's attitude one of

    a) nervousness because Mr Scargill has been seen reading 'Say It In French'?

    b) uncertainty about whether to ally itself with the Christian Socialists, the Socialist Democrats, the Democratic Christians, or the Scottish Episcopalians?

    c) embarrassment about having to take the Internationale seriously?

    d) hwyl?

10. Is or are Brussels

    a) a night club founded by Bertrand Russell?

    b) a fruit or a vegetable?

    c) a perfectly harmless town in Belgium that wasn't hurting anybody?

    d) the place you wouldn't start from if you were trying to get to Strasbourg?

11. Will the Channel Tunnel

    a) flood?

    b) enable rabid squirrels to race over from France and infect our household pets?

    c) increase demand for ladies' underwear at all branches of Marks & Spencer south of the Thames?

    d) ever be finished?

12. Do most people in the EEC speak
a) French?
b) loudly?
c) loudly, *and* wave their arms about?
d) English, in desperation?

EEC-SPEAK

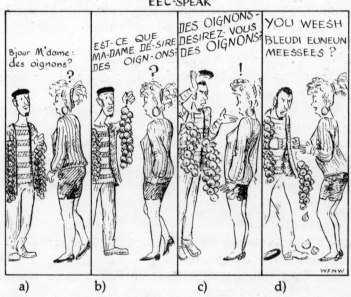

a)   b)   c)   d)

13. Finally, should we celebrate 1992
a) with a year-long street party?
b) with champagne?
c) with a bang?
d) with a whimper?

So how European are you?

If your answers are mainly a)s you obviously haven't a clue what's happening around you but enjoy life and parties. So, why not get over there and take a look at what Europe's up to.

If you've ticked more **b)**s than any other letter you don't know much either, but have got a good eye for nubile young Europeans, and probably own a dog. Don't use him as a excuse for not going over there – the kennels can open tins of dog food just as well as you.

If most of your answers are **c)**s you take a more detached view of the Single Market. You've heard of it, but you'd rather it stayed 'over there', and that the Channel Tunnel remained a castle in Spain. Try harder!

If you've totalled more **d)**s than any other letter, please keep your views to yourself. We're in this up to our necks and the last thing anyone wants is people like you blowing the gaff on the Emperor's new clothes. Please.

D.A. PRINCE

EUROPAEANS

The first thing the aspiring European should note is that Europe is no longer to be defined in terms of continental shelves, land masses or tectonic plates; it is now an Ideal. Before we descend to the particular, therefore, the Eurostudent should spend this first chapter contemplating Europe as a whole, in all its simultaneous unity and diversity.

Bliss it is to be alive now,
Euro-dreams at last come true,
Never year so hyped and hoped for,
Hail to Nineteen-Ninety-Two!

See the Famous Twelve in concert
Entering the Promised Land,
Merging in the Single Market
Euro-visionaries planned.

Whom Commerce hath joined together
Let no politicians part,
Trade does more than wishful thinking
To give Europe a new heart.

From the Wash to the Aegean
Hidebound attitudes are shed,
We must learn that Britain's moat is
Not the Channel but the Med.

This *annus mirabilis* now
Ushers in the Age of Gold;
What new hopes lie round the corner?
What else does the future hold?

What ideas will sprout from Brussels,
Chunnelling beneath the Straits?
Shall we soon be jingling *écus*
In the new Eunited States?

Critics may complain that there is
Less incentive now to roam,
See no point in foreign travel
When Abroad is just like home.

Banish all such petty carping,
Let the banners be unfurled,
And the trumpets sound a welcome
To our Brave New Euro-World!

STANLEY J. SHARPLESS

Cultural Stereotypes Rule O.K.

In Spain the path of Time is never straight;
It arches like a tropical banana.
The Spaniard's motto is 'Procrastinate:
Neglect today what you can do *mañana'*.
In Italy men brashly stare and lurk,
Their hands plunged deeply into trouser pockets.
Invisibly, their fingers are at work,
As though to prise their gonads from their sockets.
The Germans' love of discipline and order
Is world-renowned, as is their record score
At crossing some adjacent nation's border
With nothing to declare but total war.
The French extort the foreign tourist's francs;
By nature they are grasping, mean and rude.
They grab all they can get, and give no thanks
(Although their chefs create fantastic food).
Cuisine in Belgium doesn't count for much
(The Belgian joke is chips with everything),
While Luxembourg clips coupons and the Dutch
Are squeaky-clean and decent but lack zing.

The Scandinavians are clean as well,
Although the magazines they print are dirty.
They pay high rates of tax. They ski like hell.
They suicide. They're mostly under thirty.
Our European partners – what a soup:
The blond, the swarthy, soap- or garlic-scented,
Nasal and guttural, a chequered troupe,
Quite alien to us. And quite demented.

BASIL RANSOME-DAVIES

A European Alphabet For Absolute Beginners In 1992

A's for Albania, Marx's last mate,
B is for Belgium, a rather small state.
C is for Cyprus where Greeks fight with Turks,
D is for Denmark where Hamlet's Ghost lurks.
E is for Eire where snakes are unknown,
F is for France and the wines of the Rhône.
G is for Germany, now all in one,
H, by analogy, stands for the Hun.
I is for Iceland with geysers and cod,
J is for Jersey where money is God.
K is for Knowledge of new things to eat,
L is for Luxembourg, Justice's seat.
M's for Monaco, the playground of lords,
N is for Norway that's riddled with fjords.
O stands for Offshore and oilwells awash,
P is for Poland and *Solidarność*.
Q's for the Queerness of Boche or of Frog,
R's for Romania with orphans to flog.
S is for Spain where crooks live in peace,
T is for Turkey, but watch the police.
U's for United, which one day we'll be
V is for Vatican, Peter's Wee Free.
W's for Wales, where guards follow a goat,
X is the Cross that we use when we vote.
Y's Yugoslavia, a racial mish-mash,
And Z is for Zlotys and other strange cash.

JOHN SWEETMAN

Hail to Europe

In between the steppes of Russia
And the northern herring pond,
To the south of arctic hush, a-
Bove the Nile and lands beyond,
Here is Europe, the receiver
Of all different types of race,
Nordic cool to latin fever,
Clout teutonic, celtic grace.

So, all European nations
Stand together side by side,
Leave behind all confrontations
Let your aims be unified,
Set aside all trade embargoes,
Regulate your subsidies,
Build up mountains from your cargoes
Higher than the Pyrenees.

Where Napoleon and Nelson
Fought to gain supremacy,
Let us fight for nothing else on
Land which is forever free.
Where de Gaulle with gallic humour
Made a point by saying 'Non!'
Let each EEC consumer
Thrive on affirm-ation.

Where the British stooped to conquer
Then puffed up with their success
Made the Chancellor a plonker
Keeping out of EMS,
Let each treasury be willing
To accept the Eurosnake,
Subjugating franc and schilling,
Pound and deutschmark to its shake.

Let no rancour taint your dealings,
Never show self interest,
Think about the others' feelings,

Never say your Country's best.
Dampen patriotic fever,
Sublimate all native pride,
Take all measures to achieve a
Europe that's solidified.

Spreading, growing ever greater,
Let your numbers swiftly swell,
Till your members can create a
Strong invincible cartel.
Closer, ever closer blending,
Melt all lines of sovereignty
Till the world knows it's contending
With the glorious USE.

KATIE MALLETT

EUROPLACES

In this chapter we aim to give a taste of some of the places in Europe that the novice European should see first.

The Costa del Sol

Say goodbye to your tantrums and tension:
From the day you're receiving a pension
   You can have a long hol
   On the Costa del Sol
With pleasures too many to mention.

Say hullo to the blonde on the pillion
And the bottles of booze by the million;
   I'm sure that senescence
   Can beat adolescence
In painting the city vermilion.

Say goodbye to your Qses and Pses;
For a greybeard can date whom he pleases;
   And then if he's lucky
   She'll say he's a Ducky
And welcome avuncular squeezes.

Say hullo to the sun and the beer, oh!
You can pose to the world as a hero,
   And no one will boo you;
   At least, if they do, you
Can turn down your deaf aid to zero.

PAUL GRIFFIN

I fear I cannot paint you without rancour
The Costa Brava and the Costa Blanca.

PAUL GRIFFIN

Rome

The Vatican, the Vatican
we wandered there and back again
from Via Julius Caesar you
turn right and you are at it then;
the marketeers are everywhere
you pass them by, and Peter's Square
is to your right and through the gate
you find the fountain and you're there.
The guards in fancy dress stand by
(they carry weapons, God knows why)
but don't waste time go on until
the Sistine Chapel takes your eye.
A rapid glance will quickly show
the famous Michelangelo
preoccupied with lots of nudes,
you heave a sigh, and off you go.
Museums, chapels, painted crypts –
the oohs and ahs assault your lips,
fantastic to have been and seen,
but now you're set for other trips.
(Forget the bloody fish and chips!)
The Spanish Steps you've got to view,
the Trevi Fountain beckons you,
get on the metro, no great feat,
and see the Colosseum too.
There's Trajan's Column, goodness me
It's time to travel to Capri . . .

FRANK McDONALD

The Loire, with its famous chateaux
Is attractive as far as it geaux,
But, compared with the Seine,
I would firmly maineteine
It's a second rate dreine – and it sheaux!

MICHAEL FOSTER

In Venice it's hard for a tramp
To set up an overnight camp,
For St Mark's Square submerges
Each time the tide surges,
And the streets are exceedingly damp.

KATIE MALLETT

The tower of Pisa keeps leaning
A bit more each season, this meaning
That soon it will lie
Parallel with the sky.
(Which will make it more easy for cleaning).

KATIE MALLETT

In Père Lachaise Cemetery

For wormy circumstance, try this:
Stroll down the titled avenues
Of Paris's necropolis
And count the corpses where they lie
In family sarcophagi –
Expensive, gothic, bleak
And sheltering an underclass
Of bristling, feral cats who streak
Like radar blips across the grass
From all invading shoes.

Apollinaire, Bizet, Colette,
David and Eluard: the names
Encode a marble alphabet
Of French – of European – art,
Though dimmer bones, too, play their part –
A strangely mingled crew:
The duellist of little skill,
A mad philosopher or two,
And buried mediums who still
Drag out their occult games.

The corner for the Commune dead,
A wall-flanked wedge of quiet terrain,
Is history's ground, for where you tread
Was where a different future died
In rituals of fratricide . . .
Elsewhere, scrawled signs read 'Jim':
The raver's gravestone is the place
Their arrows lead to. Yes, it's him,
A chipped, graffiti-smeared stone face.
The children are insane . . .

Now contemplate the Déco sphinx
That guards the tomb of Oscar Wilde.
There, *hubris* went before a jinx:
He mocked the ways of boring pseuds
With Anglo-Saxon attitudes

And paid, in spades, the price.
Should old Britannia boldly go
To swell the party, break the ice
And join him in a *fine à l'eau*,
Will he be reconciled?

BASIL RANSOME–DAVIES

A Villanelle from Tuscany

Just fancy launching boats from here –
  Real boats, I mean, not pedaloes!
They've changed the beach of yesteryear.

Put down that empty can of beer:
  Someone will clear it, I suppose.
Just fancy launching boats from here.

No lonely dips these days, my dear;
  ICES FOR SALE, the notice goes.
They've changed the beach of yesteryear.

Old fishermen and nets and gear
  Were there, where tubby ladies pose;
Just fancy launching boats from here.

Some tiresome birds beyond that pier
  Would nest where all that housing grows:
They've changed the beach of yesteryear.

The locals hate the atmosphere;
  Efficiency gets up their nose.
Just fancy launching boats from here:
They've changed the beach of yesteryear.

PAUL GRIFFIN

Fancy launching boats from here!

The Brandenburg Gate

Oh, Brandenburg, for long the gate to hell,
The living death of deprivation's curse
Before the wall around you swiftly fell
To let the hungry millions traverse
The border to democracy and wealth,
Unfettered by the communist ideal,
And not by exercising midnight stealth
But freely walking through. How do you feel,
Isolated after many years?
Now just a monument to Prussian power
And symbol of a severed nation's tears
You may well ask, in glasnost's shining hour
As by your side graffiti's ugly spore
Spreads Wogan's name, 'Is this what freedom's for?'

KATIE MALLETT

In the Catacombs

'Are any actual corpses buried here?'
the American asks with middle-aged persistence.
The youthful English guide is growing weary
of his charge's baseball-capped resistance
to information given three times already.
'There've been no bodies here for centuries,'
he reaffirms, his voice crisply steady.
The American shakes his head, screws up his eyes.
'No corpses. Gee. What in hell's this place for?'
Fists thrust into pockets, he strides unbent
where centuries of pilgrims knelt to adore.
Traipsing past emptied tombs I am content –
albeit the saints and martyrs aren't at home:
in August this is the coolest place in Rome.

TOM AITKEN

The Ariège

The tourist maps display a blank
Where no one goes to tan or ski;
A weathered, hidden Arcady
As hard and natural as a plank.

The houses in the mountain cloud
Have walls the shade of fishes' scales;
Above the nimbus, waymarked trails
Web out to spread the hiking crowd.

A village Sybil whispers how
A summer swarm of men on bikes
And cars and cameras and mikes
Obscured the pasture from her cow.

'The age of speed' – what she was taught
Was simply that what touches fits.
Her grandson lives in Biarritz,
As distant as an astronaut.

It doesn't pay to stay and farm,
The slopes assume an altered face
Of barns with baths and parking space
Whose *maquillage* is rustic charm.

Sheep ramble on the forest floor,
As lifeless as an ammonite,
Where conifers conceal the light.
The lorries grind. The chainsaws roar.

Tough Spanish loggers fell the pines
And cart the cut wood off to Spain,
Which trucks it back to France again
As standard furniture designs.

What special sense of wonder crowns
This chain of peaks that irrigate
A shallow, green collection-plate
And power its money-coloured towns?

BASIL RANSOME-DAVIES

On Being Lost in Venice

I'm sure we crossed this bridge not long ago.
We turned out of that brick-built colonnade
with plaster medallions, set oddly low,
studding its walls. And then we must have made
for the spire of the church we're hoping we might see
along this fondamenta, through that square
beyond the grim-faced statue and those three
small shops. The spire's in view, right there,
behind the locked-up, gaudy-with-posters block
which could be flats. We went that way last time.
Let's try through here, startling this warbling flock
of scavenger pigeons. An archway, low. Green slime
edging the water. This time . . . surely . . . ? No!
I'm sure we crossed this bridge not long ago.

TOM AITKEN

Munich

In Munich there's held every year
A knees-up with brewed atmosphere,
Where chaps dressed in leather
Keep dancing together –
They SAY they're just there for the beer!

KATIE MALLETT

Florence

A maiden aunt visiting Florence
Might view with a certain abhorrence
Nude statues galore
With parts to the fore
Which art, she'd maintain, never warrants.

KATIE MALLETT

Drawbacks of the Mediterranean

One curse of the Mediterranean
  Is a longing to plaster and paint,
To put on a wing, or a floor, or a thing
  That might be a garage, but ain't.
No building they start's ever finished;
  With all the improvements they do
You're constantly baffled by pieces of scaffold
  When you're trying to get into the loo.

There are curious insects in Italy,
  And specks in the salad in Crete;
The average walker in Rhodes or Majorca
  Will be stung from his head to his feet.
There's a noisy mosquito in Cyprus
  That drives you near out of your wits;
How did Aphrodite get out of her nightie
  Without being bitten to bits?

But the Med has a magic that conquers:
  The ointment is more than the flies;
When the sea is all sheeny and ultramariney
  It's a sight for the sorest of eyes;
And the sun on the thyme and rock roses,
  The olives and carobs and vines,
The air oxygenic, Hellenic, Edenic,
Make the whole place so scenic and non-neurasthenic,
  That the critic is lost and resigns.

PAUL GRIFFIN

APHRODITE
KALLIPUGOS

Paris

A fellow, by name Gustav Eiffel
Had an urge, that he just couldn't stifle,
To build a huge pylon
With steel by the mile on –
The ultimate souvenir trifle.

KATIE MALLETT

Your Questions Answered:

Q. Why was France originally called Gaul?
When early tribes inhabited what is now known as
France, they imported with them the habit of smoking
pungent tobacco-sticks, known as 'Gauloises'. Because
of this notorious tendency, the region was christened
'Gaul'. The modern name 'France' derives from the
franc, or coin, which was used (ironically enough!) to
purchase the Gauloises. Later still, the coin gave the
language of the Gauls its proper name – *lingua franca*.

Q. Why are the Benelux countries so called?
The word derives from Latin, *bene* (good) and *lux* (soap),
and refers to the obsessive cleanliness of the denizens of
Luxembourg, Belgium and Holland. In these countries,
the streets are scrubbed daily at dawn, schoolchildren
wash their faces three times during a school day, and
all milk is specially filtered by a local preacher, or
pasteur.

Q. Why is Holland known as The Netherlands?
Because the literal translation, The Nether Regions, was
felt to be liable to cause offence.

Q. What is the importance of The Hague?
The Hague is where World War I finished and was
named after Douglas Hague, the British commander. It
is where croquet is played with the traditional croquet
potatoes. The Orange Order is decided upon there. It
is where the International Jurists sit. There are twelve of
them, and they can be called up any time to decide on
important legal tussles – for instance whether a Bourbon
is a biscuit or a drink, whether spanking should be permitted if the child consents, whether you can wear

. . . the traditional croquet potatoes

a mini in the Midi, and vice versa, whether masochists
have the right to self-determination, who the Saar of
Germany is, whether the Côte d'Azur is blue, whether
Britain should return the dominoes stolen by Lord Elgin,
and if it is safe to wash in the Paris Basin.

*Q. What is the origin of the phrase 'Rome was not built in a
day'?*
This interesting old saw refers to the cartographical
problem of *suburbia ex pande*, that is, that it is impossible
to chart the growth of a city because, as soon as the
chart is made, it is obsolete. And yet the original
Rome WAS built in a day, by itinerant Picts and shov-
els. Ramparts were thrown up, villas constructed, a
hot bath installed, all within one frantic twenty-four
hour period. Unfortunately, this original settlement
was near the outskirts of modern Bordeaux, owing to
a misunderstanding about specifications. It was subse-
quently rebuilt near Palermo, Nicosia, Glastonbury and
Baden-Baden before work began upon the current site.
Hence also the saying 'All roads lead to Rome'.

BILL GREENWELL

EUROCORNERS

In a short book such as this, the Eurostudent cannot expect to cover the full panorama of all that Europe has to offer, and we will inevitably spend much of our time in those countries which are both the most prominent and the closest to Britain. However, we must not forget the host of smaller or more peripheral countries which also form a part of our rich heritage. This chapter is devoted to them.

Albania!

There's a corner of the Med that's been forgotten,
It's on the Adriatic, north of Greece,
A place I've never been to, but one day soon I mean to
Take a ticket and indulge this odd caprice:

I've got a mania for Albania,
I can hear it calling from afar,
It's cut off from the West,
That's why I like it best,
And no one there's allowed to have a car.
Albania, Albania,
My Baltic Ruritania,
I'll get zanier and zanier till I'm there;
Oh, how I'd love to jog
Through the land of ex-King Zog,
And consummate this long-range love affair!

STANLEY J. SHARPLESS

Finland

A curious country is Finland:
It's a mixture of thick land and thin land,
  For all round the coast
  Is where the land's most,
While the water is plentiful inland.

PAUL GRIFFIN

A Dream of Portugal

When I was just a little lad of not much more than ten,
Our geogger teacher told us things that seemed quite
    useless then.
But still one fact stays with me from those days of chalk
    and talk:
The chief exports of Portugal are port, sardines and cork.

A little later on in life I learned the ways of Trade,
Of billion pound computer deals; how power plant is
    made.
I thought it then a trifling thing beside such vast machines
To deal in merely cork and port and Portuguese sardines.

But now in riper years I see that all is vanity;
The finest things we find in life, though not exactly free,
Are not high-priced technologies, but things less dearly
    bought,
The simple things, like Portuguese sardines and cork
    and port.

One day to Portugal I'll go, and on some beach I'll walk.
Beside the sea I'll eat sardines, and slowly draw a cork
To wash them down with crusted port, and find out what
    Life Means.
In Portugal, the land of cork, and port, and tinned
    sardines.

NOEL PETTY

Turkey-in-Europe

It's no longer a gamble
To visit Istanbul
Or gaze at the hills of Gallipoli.
You can visit the Black Sea
By boat or by taxi
And soak in it, African hippo-ly.

You'll be wanting to hear
Of Mersin and Izmir
With their temples in groves of acacia,
But through no fault of mine
We're drawing a line
At the Bosphorus, boundary of Asia.

It's Europe, I'd mention
That holds our attention
And Asia must stay unexpressed,
So, after one starry-
Eyed gaze at Scutari,
We must turn our face back to the west.

PAUL GRIFFIN

Your Questions Answered

Q. Is Monaco in the Common Market?
This is a very tricky question indeed. Monaco is a sovereign state, run by the Grimaldi family who used to star in the circus. However, Monaco is very friendly with France, and France, of course, is part of the Common Market. Monaco probably *will* join one day but, during the War, the Germans attacked their capital, Monte Casino, and broke the bank. This, I am afraid, has not been forgotten.

Q. Is Andorra a country? What is it like?
Yes and no. Andorra *used* to be a country, but it no longer exists, having been swallowed up by France in a sudden *coup d'état* in the 1960s. This was not good news for its main industry which, as with many other small

countries, is stamps. It is mainly famous for its Andorra goats, out of which so many famous coats have been made. Andorra had no language at all, which of course made the region unspeakable – hence the takeover.

Q. Is Liechtenstein in Europe?
Indeed it is. This tiny country has been made famous by Robert Maxwell, who keeps his money in it. It is a very small country indeed, consisting as it does of one large building with a series of signs announcing 'Passports', 'Cashier', 'Foreign Transactions', 'Customer Advice Services Management Supervisor' and 'Exit'. The shopping is limited. Although it is not formally in the EEC, it is thought to own most of it.

Q. Where and what is San Marino?
You do not need much Italian to translate the name of this wonderful little country. Literally, it means 'Holy Sea' – a phrase most curiously misspelt in Britain as 'Holy See'. In other words, it is where the Pope (who presides over Europe's most tiny state, the Vatican) goes for his summer holidays. Set amidst glorious sands before a pellucid azure sea, San Marino offers friends and Romans everywhere a fresh, new, inspiring and frankly mystical experience. We cater for small children and also grandparents too! Come and see our fantastical stamp collection, or simply sit back and soak up the atmosphere. See the famous Stanley gibbons! [This answer was paid for by the San Marino Tourist authority.]

Q. Is the Isle of Man in Europe? Who is the Dame of Sark?
The Isle of Man *is* in Europe, like all the Channel Islands – Guernsey, Jersey (where the sweaters come from), Ynys Mon, Wight, Mull, Lindisfarne, Scilly, and Dogger Bank. All of them have their own police force, and have revived the ancient fertility custom of 'birching', which is very jolly.

The Dame of Sark is an entirely imaginary figure. 'Sark' is just a place in a famous poem by Lewis Carroll called 'The Hunting of the Sark', which concludes that 'A Sark was a Boojum'. Possibly 'Dame' arises from the corruption of Boojum into *Begum*, or 'mportant woman'. Incidentally, this is the origin of the Northern expression 'Eee ba gum' – i.e. 'Dear mother of the family'.

BILL GREENWELL

EUROLIT

One of the most effective ways to become European is to read the works of English language writers of the past, who have always been enthusiastic travellers.

English Writers in Europe

English writers, like many other artistic types born on these shores, commonly live as far as possible from their place of origin. Most of them go no further than Europe, though Robert Louis Stevenson popped up in the South Seas – strictly on medical grounds, of course – and anyway he was a Scot.

It is surprising what grounds can be discovered for going to the most heavenly place one can imagine: in the thirties a whole batch of writers went to Spain, ostensibly to interfere in a war; Browning pleaded his wife and his father-in-law as an excuse for settling in Italy; and Byron explained to the Countess Guiccioli he was there to avoid scandal. I am not sure what Shelley was explaining – perhaps that he was looking for Byron.

Even Isherwood's plea that he was in Germany to be a camera was less than the truth, which is that these writers went where they wanted to go because they wanted to go there. We who manage fourteen nights bed and breakfast in a half-built tower block on a dirty grey beach once a year, have long gazed in envy at the writers in their villas, high above our mean affairs: Paddy Leigh Fermor in Southern Greece, Larry Durrell in the Midi and, earlier, Noel Coward on his Alp with Robert Graves perched on a crag in Majorca.

Perhaps the day will come when we too sit in the friendly sun by our swimming pool, sipping Pernod and passion fruit, writing immortal lines about the beauty of the country to which nothing on earth would persuade us to return.

'Meadows of England, shining in the rain!' wails James Elroy Flecker, fresh from a swim in the Bosphorus. 'Oh, to be in England, now that April's there!' sobs Browning, between gulps of Campari.

In reverse, continental writers hardly ever settle in this wonderful England, unless they are genuinely in fear of their lives. No one suspects Karl Marx of a sentimental passion for the British Museum Reading Room.

European literature does not need England; but clearly, without Europe, English literature would cease to exist. There would be nowhere to write it.

PAUL GRIFFIN

It is tempting to wonder how some of our writers might have responded to the Europe of 1992.

Abroad Thoughts from Home

(Br*wn*ng)

O to be in Europe
Now '92 is there,
And waking up to Europe
Means we're totally aware
That our tariff bars and Customs posts
Will soon be dead as ancient ghosts
As the Single Market shows us how
In Europe – now!

And '93 – what then will follow,
What more can fall, or Europe swallow?
Look, where the franc and lira, pound and mark

Rub shiny shoulders, and o'er-weigh the pocket,
'Til Euro-travellers, fumbling, loud remark
If common coinage comes, they will not mock it.
A policy some view as – not with rapture! –
The first fine hairline fracture.
And though the EC's rough on member states
Who, out of line, oppose its stern dictates,
Its bureaucrats, Brussels' grey-petalled flower,
Will smooth each gaudy diff'rence with their power

D. A. PRINCE

Euro-Cargoes

(M*s*f**ld)

Gleaming silver monster on a long-haul flight path,
Forty thousand feet above the Alpine snows,
   With a cabin full of rich men, first-class travellers,
Waking up to bubbly from a long, cool doze.

Scheduled flight from London, zooming out to Germany,
Serving mostly Seltzer and a light Moselle,
   With a cabin full of yuppies, British and American,
Checking on their briefing for the next big sell.

Battered little Boeing, heading into Malaga,
Working at a profit for a cut-price line,
   With a cabin full of school kids, housewives, burglars,
Getting pretty squiffy on the free white wine.

PAUL GRIFFIN

Ode on the Dawning of the Single European Market

(McG*n*g*ll)

At last – 1992!
The year about which there's been such a hullabaloo.
After a lot of difficult negotiations
No fewer than 12 different European nations
Now form a Single Market, stretching from the silv'ry
     Tay
As far as Greece, which is quite a long way.
Henceforth travelling on the Continent will be so easy
The idea need no longer make one feel queasy.
With over 300,000,000 customers at our door,
We should be able to export a lot more,
And so become a good deal better off,
A prospect at which it would be foolish to scoff,
Though with all this new competition there is no doubt
We shall certainly have to pull our fingers out.
What a good thing Britain joined the EEC,
Otherwise I don't know where we should be.

If Scotland had been counted separately, as it should
     have been,
Instead of 12 countries there would be 13,
However, that is something which for the moment we
     must shelve,
So to be going on with, let us give 3 cheers for the 12!
As for what will happen next, who can say?
We shall just have to live from day to day.

STANLEY J. SHARPLESS

A Tourist's ABC

(Al*r*c W*tts)

An Altrincham art-class, awfully arrayed
Bravely by Baedeker besiege Belgrade.
Couriered coachloads camera-clad come,
Diligently detailing Danube's drearest dome.
Every entablature eager eyes explore
For friezes, fillets, foliate finials four.
Great gadrooned gables gawping gazers greet –
Homesick, hotelbound, hating humid heat.
Illyrian ices? Incipiently ill
Jane jostles Justin, Jeremy jogs Jill.
Kitschiest keepsakes Kulturkinder kid,
Like 'local' leadware ('Longton' labelled lid!).
Many mugs mint Marks, market merchants muse.
Nightmares nag news-nuts, (nobody needs news).
Optional outings oldsters overtax;
Puny pickpockets pinch purses, passports, packs.
Querulous questioners, quintessential queues,
Rustic restaurateurs refunds refuse.
Sliwowicz sampled, Serbian sights surveyed,
Thirty tired trippers taste the tourist trade.
Uplift unforgettable? Urlaub unsurpassed?
Varied vacation – vistas very vast –
Well, wasn't wet, (was Watchet, Windsor, Wells?) –
Exotic excursion – experience excels –
Yes, Yugoslavia! Youngsters, yachtsmen, you
Zealots zoom Zadarwards – Zounds! Zagreb Zoo!

GAVIN ROSS

Death in the Discotheque
(H*m*ngw*y)

There are people who will tell you otherwise, but if you wish to study the art of *juliganismo* you should visit Torremolinos. I have seen the fights in Madrid and Cordoba, but there it is done with a lack of passion and, afterwards, a feeling of shame. Because there is no serious intention to damage, the element of physical danger is absent. Also, often the fighters are not drunk enough or else they are too old. But in Torremolinos there is always the danger that comes with cheap wine and the presence of many young, violent people. It is important that much wine be drunk because, although many are sick, the art cannot be performed with the brain, and if you are a an intellectual with a deficiency of the male parts *juliganismo* is not for you and you should stay away.

The fighters spend many hours in ritual preparation so that the action commences late, but for the *aficionado* this time is not boring. You can tell much about the fighters from their preparation, such as that the one who drinks too quickly, and may seem truly aggressive, has no stomach for the bodily harm and extensive destruction of property that are the special beauty of *juliganismo* and will not, later, assault anyone but instead will utter sexual insults to young women. There is an art to the uttering of sexual insults, but it is a stale and empty art, like the paintings of David Hockney, and there is no sense of threat to it. Really, anyone can do it.

In the Disco-Bar Wham in 1983 the Essex Pistols fought with a classical rigour for seven hours and sent twelve people to hospital, including a Guardia Civil. There were serious mutilations and, I believe, a severed jugular, though I am unable to swear to this on account of the vomit. It is hard to see details when your head has been vomited on, and some do not like the vomiting part, though without it there is only a sterile formalism and no test of nerve. Dave Dork, the Wanstead boy who fought five seasons in Torremolinos, one with a ruptured spleen, would vomit on himself. The smell was formidable, the vomit and the unwashed clothes and, sometimes, double incontinence, all that and the lack of air, the loud music, the furniture disintegrating, everything a blur, a panic, and, invariably, cries of pain.

Then too, the police would intervene, not in a pedantic fashion to restore order, but to hit, themselves, the fighters who were attacking one another and, after the intervention, the police, so that the violence was general. Of course the police had the advantage, as they were less drunk and did not have to stop all the time to vomit, but art is not a matter of fair play and besides it is sad. I do not think I have seen anyone as sad as Dave Dork. His sadness was of a great depth and after he met the woman he was sadder and I knew he would never be any good again.

BASIL RANSOME-DAVIES

WFNW

The Isles of Greece

(B*r*n)

The isles of Greece, the isles of Greece
Are now within the EEC,
And Homer nods and rests in peace
When Brussels-based bureaucracy
Decrees the wine-dark sea should take
The status of a wine-filled lake.

D.A. PRINCE

Duty Done

(P*m A*r*s)

I thought I'd write one of me poems
In praise of the EEC,
But it's turning out rather different
From what it was meant to be;
I can't feel enthusiastic,
'Cos there's one thing bothering me.

I'm afraid that the Single Market
Is going to be a flop;
So far as yours truly is concerned,
It's really not much cop.
(And you won't get me through the Tunnel
With all that water on top).

The thing that'll stop me going
On those cheap-day shopping sprees –
And though it hurts me to say so,
It's the fault of the EEC's –
They're actually going to do away
With the cut-price duty-frees.

What's the use of going
To the Calais Super-Marché

If you can't bring back cheap plonk and cigs
In the good old-fashioned way?
You might as well shop at Tesco,
At least, that's what I say.

No more need to wonder
What the cross-Channel fare is.
No more Brie and Camembert
And cream from those nice French dairies.
Calais is written on my heart
Like it was on Bloody Mary's.

I'm staying put next Christmas,
Deaf to the family pleas,
No more trips to the Continong
Though they beg on bended knees;
I'll splash out on some Gucci shoes
What I save on me duty-frees.

STANLEY J. SHARPLESS

Grantchester Reversed

(Br**k*)

. . . God! I will pack and take a train
And travel Europe once again.
The EEC's one group I know
Where common-passported I'll go:
And Brussels sprouts in every heart
A love of bureaucratic art,
And European pulses beat
At new directives on spring wheat.
The French appease their bourgeois dreams
By lavish dining at Maxim's.
In Italy society's café-er
Except when threatened by the Mafia.
While Eire men know just what sin is –
A publican who waters Guinness.

Each man in Portugal's José
And only sups Mateus Rosé.
The Spaniard talks a lot of bull
And tipples by the wine-skin full.
The Luxembourgers are a bunch
Who close the country down for lunch.
In Holland there is none so erring
As he who does not swallow herring,
While gallant Belgium shows us ways
To smother chips with mayonnaise.
The German diet's wurst and torte:
Their sugary wines resemble water.
Of Denmark there's no notice taken –
Their sole concern is slicing bacon:
And Greeks, the latest in the arena,
Wash down their sorrows in retsina.
Touring the EEC goes jammily
Now we're all one big Euro-family,
And every instinct bids me stir
From Cambridgeshire and Grantchester,
From sludgy mead and reedy fen
To ramble Europe once again.

D.A. PRINCE

Euro-if

(K*pl*ng)

If you believe the French are rather charming,
If you're convinced that Belgium is unique;
If you find Germans wholly unalarming,
(If you adore the language that they speak);

If you regard the Danes as quite exciting,
If you think every Greek a decent chap;
If Luxembourg to you seems most inviting,
(If you can even find it on a map);

If you deem all things Dutch to be exquisite,
If you admire the Irish for their style;
If Italy to you seems worth a visit,
If Spain and Portugal you don't revile;

If, be they chic or perfectly plebeian,
To hobnob with these nations makes you glow,
You'll be a quintessential European,
And possibly the only one I know.

RON RUBIN

Albert Goes to Paris

(M*rr**tt *dg*r)

One weekend, young Albert Ramsbottom,
  'Im as ad trouble wi' lion,
Took a notion to travel to Paris
  To look at that tower built of iron,

It seemed that 'is teacher 'ad told 'im
  About Common Market and such
And said: 'Now we're all Europeans
  It's right that we should keep in touch.'

So as it were young feller's birthday
  They packed up and straightaway went
On a ferry from Dover to Calais
  On sightseeing pleasure 'ell-bent,

But when they clapped eyes on the marvel
  That yon clever Eiffel 'ad made
Father Ramsbottom said: 'Crikey!
  That really puts ours in the shade.'

You see they were all born in Blackpool
  With its tower that's both famous and tall,
And to see summat bigger and better
  Didn't please the Ramsbottoms at all.

But 'as it 'appened, our Albert
  'Ad with 'im a lovely big set
Of Meccano 'e'd 'ad for 'is birthday,
  To play with if weather turned wet,

And inside the box were a tool-kit
  For tightening up nuts, bolts and screws –
An item that Albert was certain
  Was one 'e was going to use.

That night 'e crept out of his lodgings
  All secret and stealthy and sly,
And sneaked out to where Eiffel Tower
  Soared up in't Parisian sky

And, being a smart little nipper
  Who'd worked out just what 'e must do
He dismantled that ruddy great structure
  Down to the last nut and screw.

He dismantled that ruddy great structure

Then they stuffed it in sacks and departed
   For home on the very next tide
And halfway across English Channel
   They chucked the lot over the side.

And that's why if you go to Blackpool
   And mention the subject of towers
Folks there 'll say: 'Cop that one yonder
   It is the biggest there is, and it's ours!'

PHILIP NICHOLSON

A Song Against Europe

(Ch*st*rt*n)

When God laid out our planet,
Millions of years ago,
Britain was joined to Europe,
As fossils clearly show;
Later, upon reflection,
The good Lord thought it best
To separate us, seeing
We're different from the rest.

And so, through countless aeons,
He re-arranged the scene,
Deliberately inserting
The Channel in between,
So that God's Englishmen
Could dwell for ever free,
Securely set apart
By wog-defying sea.

Whom God hath put asunder
Let no man seek to join;
Boycott the Channel Tunnel,
And alien ecu coin!
Beware the Euro-dogs –
Dread carriers of rabies –
Ready to rush across
And bite our English babies.

United States of Europe?
The whole thing is a con
By faceless functionaries
In Paris, Strasbourg, Bonn;
Once-happy Brits are now
Betrayed by zealous fools,
We used to rule the waves,
But now they've waived the rules.

We won't drive on the right,
We won't give up our Queen;
Pardon, M'sieu – we'll stay
The way we've always been;
Here is a piece of wisdom
For every Eurocrat:
Good fences make good neighbours;
Kindly remember *that.*

No hectares and no kilos,
We love our English pound,
No garlic and no nonsense,
We won't be pushed around.
God save us from a Europe
By men of Brussels planned,
The bureaucratic nightmare
Of their Cloud-ecu-Land!

STANLEY J. SHARPLESS

A Song for Europe

(Any Eurovision Songwriter)

Pop into your travel bureau,
Everybody's going Euro,
That's where we belong;
Once you get as far as Calais
You'll find everyone so pally-
On the Continong.

(Chorus)   Cheers! *Prosit! Santé! Ciao!*
Kiss both cheeks and make a bow,
We are all *amigos* now,
Cheers! *Prosit! Santé! Ciao!*

Yoo-hoo-hoo, it's Ninety-Two,
The year when all our dreams come true,
Sing it far and wide;
Say goodbye to British phlegm, dear,
Let yourself go – be more like *them*, dear,
On the other side.

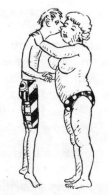

Kiss both cheeks

Cheers! *Prosit! Santé! Ciao!*
etc.

We'll go dancing cheek to cheek,
Whisp'ring love in Euro-Speak,
Happy days before us;
And wherever we may be
Venice, Brussels, Bonn, Paree,
We'll sing this Euro-chorus:

Cheers! *Prosit! Santé! Ciao!*
                              etc.

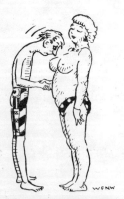

And make a bow

If there are occasions when you
Cannot understand the menu
On one of our trips,
There's no need for parley-vooing,
(That may lead to your undoing),
Ask for fish 'n' chips.

Cheers! *Prosit!* *Santé!* *Ciao!*
                                etc.

Seeing famous Euro-places,
Meeting friendly Euro-faces
Every single day,
We shall be so Euro-smitten
That when we get back to Britain,
This is what we'll say:

Cheers! *Prosit!* *Santé!* *Ciao!*
                                etc.

STANLEY J. SHARPLESS

Barcelona

*(K*pl*ng)*

From the summit of 'is column, 'ighly on-parade and
        solemn,
Chris Columbus casts 'is eye across the town,
Watchin' bands of 'appy amblers down below 'im on the
        Ramblas,
Givin' glad-eyes as they saunter up and down.
In the boozers they serve dishes 'eaped with little foreign
        fishes
What you eat with toothpicks, not with knives and forks,
And your Catalan is 'andy when it comes to swiggin'
        brandy
But most of all the 'eathen devil talks.
'E will serenade your lug'oles with the story of 'is strug-
        gles
Or the goals what Gary Lineker 'as missed.
You can bet your bleedin' kitbag 'e'll say: 'Franco was a
        shitbag'
As 'e makes a filthy gesture with his fist.
While your local colour's speakin' there's a never endin'
        shriekin'

From a fruit-machine what's perched atop the bar
And your ears are gettin' clouted by the orders bein'
    shouted
By customers 'oo want another jar.
All the racket from the traffic jammed outside is somethin'
    graphic,
Like an 'ore's 'owl when your rubber johnny's torn:
You can 'ear a thousand curses from the drivers, and
what's worse is –
Their sweaty 'ands is never off the 'orn.
What with sirens, bells and 'ooters, and the noisy kids on
    scooters,
And the poundin' from the club what never shuts,
It's a fair old ding-dong riot. Still, 'oo fancies peace
    and quiet?
All matelots are Barcelona nuts.

BASIL RANSOME-DAVIES

Dog End

(H*rry Gr*h*m)

When Uncle bought a dog abroad,
He ill-advisedly ignored
The statutes and the regulations
Governing such importations.
So Aunt and Uncle died of rabies,
Revoltingly, with all their babies.

RON RUBIN

EUROTRAVEL

There are many ways to see Europe. The simplest of all is the package holiday, bought through your travel agent.

Florence,
Wednesday.

Got here yesterday, nice digs, leave tomorrow. Do you know what, Fred, you remember that plaster statue of a nude bloke that Auntie Edie won at the Bingo, the one she kept hidden under the stairs? Well, we were just strolling out for a bevvy last night when I turned a corner and here it was in the square, large as life – well, twice as large, really – and nothing missing, if you know what I mean. They call it David here. I'm not kidding, these Italians will rip anything off.

Regards to May,
Charlie

Siena,
Thursday.

Arrived here this morning, and got quite a shock. We were just looking for the loos when we were swept into the middle of the town by a enormous crowd. Would you believe it was a horse-race? Right there in the middle, like having greyhound-racing in Trafalgar Square. Well, you know what the Italians are like, it was seething mad. The 4.15 at Newbury it certainly was not. I couldn't get a programme, not to mention a pork pie and a glass of Watneys and to cap it all they gave the race to a horse that had thrown his jockey three laps back, with no stewards' enquiry or anything. Good job I never got near a bookie.

See you—
                    Charlie

                                        Venice,
                                        Thursday.

Quite a nice place this, but dead easy to get lost, and if you happen to be on the wrong side of the road, it costs you a quid to get across. Last night we wandered into a big square with a queer-looking church at one end. We saw a sign that said Caffe Florian so I naturally thought you could get a cup of coffee for a florin. When we'd finished – nice cup, I will admit – I offered my 20p and the waiter wanted £5! I was for calling the police, but Beth thought they might be in on it, so we paid up and left. Apparently Florian is the owner and it's famous or something. What a liberty!

                    Charlie

                                        Strasbourg,
                                        Sunday.

You won't believe this, but the people here are called Alsatians. Honest, no kidding! They eat like Alsatians, too. Last night we had something called a shoe cruet, a sort of huge cabbagy mass stuffed with bacon, sausages, pork and God knows what. In the top of it they'd stuck a pink, fleshy object about six inches long. I said they wouldn't would they but Beth said oh yes they would they'd eat anything and wouldn't stop giggling. I don't know what the lads at the Arms would have made of it, but we left it well alone. The courier told me today it was the pig's tail, that straightens out in the cooking. Phew!

Cheers—
                    Charlie

Tours,
Tuesday.

Beth says that Tours is just the name of this town, but it
sounds like a smart piece of marketing to me. Anyway, we
took one of their tours – a cruise up and down the Loire.
Quite interesting, too, one or two nice brick and cement
works, several fertilizer factories and a really smart nuclear
power plant. Unfortunately they kept stopping the boat to let
people off to look at some big old houses they have dotted
around – I suppose they used to belong to the factory owners.
Still, it was a nice change from all the history.

Regards to Ned and the regulars at the 'Arms'—
Charlie

Chartres,
Wednesday.

Stopping off here on the way to Paris. Not much of a place,
I don't know why they chose it – more or less like Woking
but with a big old church in the middle. There are some
huge stone figures round the doorways, thin as beanpoles.
Beth says it's because there wasn't much to eat in the old
days, but they're supposed to be kings and suchlike so it
can't be that. I expect it was just the fashion at the time,
like the F-Plan. Still, you can see where that bloke Lowry
got his ideas from. Paris tomorrow!

Charlie

Paris,
Thursday.

Well, here we are! Beth says it's the capital of European civilization, but I can't quite see it. They do have a Marks & Spencer, I admit, but even there they haven't got any of the strong grey wool socks I like to replace all the ones I've worn out since last week. Apart from that it's mostly museums as far as I can see. We did find one you'd have liked – a permanent outdoor exhibition of plumbing, all laid out so you can inspect the welds and everything. The sign says it's the Centre Pompidou, which isn't in Beth's pocket gem dictionary, but I've worked out it means Quiet Pumping Centre, and you certainly can't hear anything.

Back Saturday—
Charlie

NOEL PETTY

A Travel Agent's Confession

Do go and see Europe whatever you do;
We can send you by minibus, hearse, or canoe;
    It's a *sine qua non*
    With wading boots on
        To see Venice in spring,
        And our Tour's just the thing
    To enjoy it before it's all gone.

They're not at all cliquey in Thessaloniki;
    They're frightfully sweet in Calais;
Though the Mafia maffick they're really seraphic
    In Sicily, *most* of the day.
    We can send you to curious coasts
        Where the law's not dictated by prudery,
    For we make a good rakeoff from people who take off
        Their pants on a beach that's for nudery.

Do you want to go French with the minimum fuss?
Or tackle the Alps from the back of a bus?
    Is your notion of peace
    Being Spartan in Greece?
        Behaving like toads
        On the island of Rhodes
    Or not very nicely in Nice?

The average tourist, unless he's a purist,
    Can survive with bad food and worse bedding,
Which is why we can face recommending a place
That we wouldn't ourselves be seen dead in.
    There are people – though where, never mind–
        It's not a great distance from Spain–
    Who pay us commission from your malnutrition;
        While for us – it's GREAT YARMOUTH again!

PAUL GRIFFIN

Torremolinos,
Sunday.

Been here three days and we're still trying to find the sea.
I think we were getting close yesterday, but we found
ourselves in between a US submarine crew and a Welsh
rugby club and had to cut back up a side street. We're
getting through a lot of Sangría, which is a kind of fruit
salad with wine in the cracks. We're still trying to work out
what you're supposed to do with the fruit. Must go now, May
wants to have another crack at finding the Med, just to say
she's seen it. Or was it the Adriatic? Anyway, as long as we
find one of them.

Regards to Beth,
Fred

Granada,
Tuesday.

Just here on a one-nighter from Torremolinos. Pedro on the coach says this is the place where they finally got rid of the moors, and it must have worked because there's certainly nothing but olive trees here now. Tomorrow they're taking us to the Alhambra, but they haven't told us what's showing yet. I hope it's in English.

Adios—
Fred

Seville,
Thursday.

A day trip this time. It wasn't supposed to be a mystery tour, but it's all mysterious to me. You know, Charlie, I don't understand this country. Down by the sea it's all bikinis and wet T-shirts, but up here where it's twice as hot they're all walking around in the streets in great black cloaks and hoods with a couple of holes for the eyes. I mean, I suppose it keeps the sun off but there must be better ways. I think there's a lot of house-moving going on too, because some of them (the blokes in black) are carting huge thrones and statues around on their shoulders. May says perhaps we came at a bad time. Still looking for the Med, by the way.

Home Saturday, in time for the snooker,
Fred

NOEL PETTY

*You may prefer to go under your own steam. This will enable you
to absorb more local colour on the way.*

It seems very soon everyone'll
Be taking the train through the Chunnel
To go continental,
Though traffic through Kent'll
Be jammed up like sand in a funnel.

KATIE MALLETT

The ferry
Ain't merry;
The hover's
A bovver;
Flying
's too trying.

The tunnel, I hope,
will offer more scope.

D.A. PRINCE

What a Relief!

Underneath the waves you'll find me
On the way to France by train,
All me former fears behind me –
Tum no more seized up with pain.

Even standing in a station,
I can spend a penny when
Europe is me destination –
And uncross me legs again.

Vacuum-powered an' teflon-coated
Loos on chunnel trains have tanks.
To our comfort they're devoted
Now – for this relief, much thanks.

MARGARET ROGERS

Some Useful Continental Road Signs

France

Pierres Tombées:	Bistro ahead
Zone Bleu:	Red-light district
Virages sur 6km:	Feminist commune ahead

Poids Lourds:	Pilgrimage in progress
Priorité à Droite:	Go ahead, you're in the right
Bétteraves:	Go on, let your wife drive for a bit
Fin de Chantier:	No Singing Past This Point
Nids de Poules:	Caution: Poultry Nesting
Passage à Niveau:	New Road

Spain

Salida de Fabrica:	Light Lunches To Order
Autopista de Peaje:	Drunken Drivers Will Be Fined
Cruce Peligroso:	Religious Processions Ahead
Obras:	Topless Bathing Permitted

Despacio:	Post Office
Centro Urbano:	School of Deportment

Germany

Ausfahrt:	Atmospheric Pollution
Ein Bahn:	EEC grain store

Kein Eingang:	Entry to pig farm
Links Fahren:	Sausage Lunches
Geschwindigkeit Verlangsamen:	By the Time You Have Finished Reading This Notice It May Already Be Too Late To SLOW DOWN

Italy

Veicoli Lenti:	Car Hire
Solo Sorpasso:	Caution – Luciano Pavarotti ahead
Marcia Normale:	This is a probably a message to the Mayor from his mistress, and should be ignored
Transito con Pneumatico da Neve:	Inflatable military dinghies in transit

The Netherlands

Inhalen Verboden:	Toxic gas alert
Spoorwegovergang:	Snail crossing
Niet parkeren:	Mind your own business

Belgium

Schyf Verplicht:	You are in a Flemish-speaking area. Do not attempt O-level French beyond this point

NOEL PETTY

A Load of Boules

While driving through a small French village, I came upon
a strange sight. On a piece of rough ground, a group of men
were taking it in turn to toss large steel balls at a small white
one. I stopped the car to watch and, seeing my puzzlement,
one of the group approached me to ask, in very good English,
if he could help.

'What are you doing?' I asked.

'That will take time to explain and it's a very hot day. Let's
retire to somewhere more comfortable.'

He indicated an estaminet across the road. We trooped
across, followed by his companions and a few villagers who
were now taking an interest. I ordered a round of drinks for
them all and settled down to hear my new-found friend's
explanation.

'Have you not heard of the deadly Mediterranean Spitting
Spider?'

I confessed my ignorance.

'Then you are very lucky. You English think there are no
dangers in our countryside, but many fall victim to this
creature every summer. We are Spitting Spider extermina-
tors. They live in holes in the ground, rather like Trap-door
Spiders and if an enemy approaches, they pop out and spit
their venom as far as five metres, and then pop back in again.
We are expert at finding their colonies, which we mark with
a white ball.'

'I didn't notice any holes', I said.

'No, they are well disguised. That's why we need the
white ball.'

'And I didn't see any spiders.'

'Good; now you realise the dangers – they are so quick!'

'But after you had aimed all your balls at the spiders, wasn't
it dangerous to approach the colony, as I saw you do?'

'No, the impact of the balls frightens them and makes them
hide in their holes for several minutes, so we have time to
count the victims.'

'And how many victims have you caught today?'

'Only one.'

I had to be on my way so I thanked my informant and left them all to finish their drinks. As I departed, vowing to avoid the hidden risks of straying from the road, and if I did, to watch out for the little white balls, I heard the sound of distant laughter.

How good it was that these brave men found such pleasure in this public-spirited and dangerous pursuit.

ARTHUR P. COX

In the hills near the city of Parma,
You can camp in the field of a farma
Who is somewhat aloof –
But there's milk on the hoof,
And his wife is an absolute charma!

MICHAEL FOSTER

Bottoms Up!

One stormy night in Austria, near the Brenner Pass
A climber of our party fell down a deep crevasse.
We watched him go with horror, and shed a silent tear.
It really spoilt our evening; he was carrying the beer.

FRANK RICHARDS

How We Brought The Camping Gear
From Ghent To Aix

I sprang to the tent-flap, and Doris, and Bea;
I gargled, Bea gargled, we gargled all three.
'Are we there?' cried the twins as we folded the tent,
'No we're not,' I replied. 'We're at some place called
  Ghent,
And the sooner you're dressed we can all be away
To the place where we're aiming to be, which is Aix.

We'd arrived on the six o'clock ferry, you see,
My missus, the twins, Auntie Doris and me,
Intending to camp by the end of that day
At a camp site we'd heard about just outside Aix,
But the darkness came on, so our first night was spent
In a rather damp turnip-field somewhere near Ghent.

We asked at the tourist place which way to go.
'To Aix?' said the lady. 'I'm sure I don't know,
But set off for Paris, that's always the best,
And then when you're round it I think I'd suggest
You follow the Autoroute signs to Marseille
Then turn left at Lyons and ask there for Aix.'

We set off at once in the bright morning air
The twins calling every few miles, 'Are we there?'
With Auntie D. prodding me: 'Keep on the right!',
I motored all day and I motored all night
Till, just as the lady had told us it should,
At length into Aix the car shuddered and stood.

We asked at the tourist place where was the camp,
While poor Auntie Doris recovered from cramp,
But the gentleman said, in his frenchified twang,
'Non, non! Quel dommage! C'est ici Aix-les-Bains.
I'm sure what vous cherchez is Aix-en-Provence.
Nous fermerons now, so bon soir et bonne chance!'

'Which way do we go, though?' 'Vous turn round,'
  he said,
'Retournez a Lyons, then make pour le Med,

Go straight sur le main Autoroute du Soleil,
And that should deposit vous plumb into Aix.'
We drove through the night again, ragged and worn,
And entered our second Aix just before dawn.

As soon as the tourist place opened at ten,
We asked for the Camping all over again.
I saw by his face that the prospect was bleak:
'Hélas! Je regrette that the place that you seek'
– I saw Bea and Doris get ready to scream –
'Is the Island of Aix in Charente-Maritime.'

'Go back up the Autoroute – ne pas despair –
You'll soon find the great Autoroute des Deux Mers.
Just follow the signs to Toulouse and Bordeaux,
Then ask at Niort for the best way to go.
The place that you seek is a little remote,
But find La Rochelle and you'll soon get a boat.'

'Are we there?' cried the twins. 'No, not quite,' I replied,
As I bundled them up with Aunt Doris inside.
I could see that the axis of Doris and Bea
Was starting to blame the whole journey on me.
I got it all day and then all night as well
Till we saw the Atlantic and hit La Rochelle.

We asked, when the tourist place opened next day,
If our campsite was there, on the Island of Aix.
I could feel Auntie Doris's breath on my neck
As he flicked through his Carnets des Campings to check.
'Monsieur, I'm afraid – are you feeling unwell? –
The Aix that you want must be Aix-la-Chapelle.'

'You'd better go North East to Paris, that's clear,
It's always the best way to start out from here.
Then North on the Autoroute, turn right at Ghent'
– I coughed at this point to put Bea off the scent –
'Then left round Liège, the map's quite explicit,
And roll into Aix, you can't possibly miss it.'

I sprang to the saddle and started the car.
'He's told me the way and it doesn't sound far.'

But we drove through the night without sign of our goal,
And through the next day, paying toll after toll,
Till, just as the second day started to darken,
We stopped by a notice: WILLKOMMEN IN AACHEN.

'That's enough!' said Aunt Doris, and started to weep.
'That's it!' muttered Bea, and turned over to sleep.
'Is this it?' cried the twins. 'Is this it? Are we there?'
'No, we're not,' I replied, and was starting to swear
When I looked at the notice and gave a great yell:
'Look – Aachen – see – formerly Aix-la-Chapelle!'

We asked at the tourist place. 'Yes, that's the site,
Just park over there by the tree on the right.'
'Are we there?' cried the twins. 'Yes, we are,' I said,
  'Yes,'
'Let's run up the tent,' I said, flushed with success.
Then paused. 'Better not. It'll make too much work:
First thing in the morning we sail from Dunkirk.'

NOEL PETTY

Continental hotels have the usual range of facilities.

No Finn
Will scauna
Sauna
Unless
He lacks Finnesse . . .

MICHAEL FOSTER

Protest to Continental Hoteliers

I am an ancient traveller
Who stoppeth at your inn
Where hot & cold awaiteth
But I'll not come again.
For there are no plugs
In your marble baths
To keep the WATER in!

ARDA LACEY

Helpful Notes From A Greek Hotel

1. Peoples of all manners use this hotel. You are welcome to it.
2. Guests are beseeched to empty chambers before midday, as new arrivers wish to fill them.
3. Before to possess guests for yourself in the Restaurant, to kindly obtain adhesion of the Receptionist.
4. If you wish to make a party in our rooms, the Manageress will make herself agreeable.
5. Our shop is open to show you things Greek people do except on Mondays.
6. Not to keep your valuables, but to give them away to the Manageress.

PAUL GRIFFIN

The Lorelei Rock Hotel

The River Rhine is a very popular and picturesque, – though uphill – route to Southern Germany, with many good hotels on the way. For attraction, none can compare with the legendary Lorelei Rock. A centuries old castle (or Schloss to the locals), it is situated high above a bend in the river.

Hidden by immense cliffs, the hotel would be difficult to locate were it not for its singing group, who spend all day performing at the water's edge. Calling themselves 'The Sirens', they are readily audible from several kilometres and their particular style called 'Rhine whine', like bagpipes, is better heard at a distance. At close range, though, they change to greetings of: 'Hello Sailor!'

There is always space for your boat, however big. The novel introduction of underwater moorings gives the nautical equivalent of a multi-storey car park. The age of some of the boats in the lower strata indicates the popularity of the hotel as a retirement home.

The Lorelei Rock Hotel is one of the chain, employing only female staff, operated by Valkyrie Hotels Ltd. Our correspondent was uncertain about their duties, which seemed to include all-night room service, but was pleased to note that the chambermaids had dispensed with the apron and coal-scuttle uniform of the parent hotel in Bavaria.

Among the many amenities are two wells, appropriately known as A and B. In keeping with their wish to cater for all tastes, the management have not overlooked the requirements of teetotallers, so the A-well (A, of course, standing for 'abstainer') contains water flowing in from the river. This appeals more to the connoisseur than the purist, for it has a characteristic and unforgettable flavour. The B-well supplies beer, and is a great attraction during the spring *bierfest* when the guests can become, as they say, B-well *schlossed*.

Your correspondent found only one general complaint about the Lorelei Rock Hotel. Every guest said that his bed was damp.

ARTHUR P. COX

Sightseeing should be high on your agenda; information for tourists is freely available.

Chaton-Sur-Mer
Michelin Map 51 4 – Pop. 1069

Set amid flat, marshy terrain a short distance from the Belgian border, Chaton is no longer 'sur mer'. Mostly devoted now to the assembly of light electrical components, it was completely razed in both World Wars. As a result, its architecture is unusually homogeneous. The main square features the low, angular buildings in grey cement typical of the rapid rebuilding programme of the late 1940s. The drain-grids, spared by repeated bombardments, are unusually bare and plain in a style popular under the Third Republic. In the town hall may be seen a signed photograph of Clement Attlee.

Church – Funds for the new Protestant church (1951) included a donation from the mayor and corporation of Watford. In gratitude, the head of a stag was carved by the local sculptor Guillaume Carbonade and placed in the porch. One of its antlers was damaged in a gale in 1960.

Mont du Diable – At the southern end of the town, this hill rears 20m over the surrounding countryside. In clear weather, the vista from its summit includes the Belgian villages of Houtem and Laisele.

Pan Museum – *Open from 10 a.m. to noon and 3 to 4 p.m. June-October, admission: 10F.*
The museum, housed in a former bicycle shop, holds a collection of almost forty pans of the flat, circular type used for making *crêpes*. Some are of local origin, the remainder gathered from a variety of sources in north-eastern France. To the left of the shop entrance used to be an enamel Peugeot sign: traces of the screw holes are still clearly visible.

Vallée de la Boue – *5km/3 miles to the west. Leave Chaton by the D55. At the Beaux Jours garden centre turn left on to an unmetalled road. Park by the EDF sub-station. 8 minutes walk to river.*

Now largely dry thanks to the area's irrigation needs, the Boue was once a vital waterway, giving access by boat to the Canal de la Basse Colme. It is now an important wildlife habitat. Newts regularly breed there and it is used by the Société Ornithologique de Chaton. There is a legend that those who cross the footbridge barefoot will enjoy happiness and good fortune.

                                        BASIL RANSOME-DAVIES

A Returning Tourist Explains Greek Architecture

I'm pretty sure this is right, because I wrote it all down here, straight from the mouth of the guide who showed us round.

Greek architecture happens (usually) in ruins on top of pretty bumpy little hills where the coaches won't take you. A cropperless is what they call most of these hills, which is obviously a joke, because falling over is exactly what you can expect to do, either over stones on the track or over the solid mass of tourists who are on the way down while you are on the way up, or vice versa.

More often than not these ruins are temples, consisting of rows of pillars and not much more, and apparently it's terribly important to get the kind of pillars right. I think it's something like this:

1. Euphoric – zooms straight up into the air and is then severely flattened.

2. Tonic – rises rapidly to the top and then fizzes over the edges.

3. Cornucopian – stuffed solid all the way up and then bursts into fruity bits.

A name which makes rather more sense is a carryalid, which is a pillar in the shape of a woman with a flat bit on top.

Then there are sometimes bits above these pillars with carvings and so on: the artystage supports this artistic bit, which is jestingly known as the squeeze because of the crush of indistinguishable figures with bits broken off here and there. A largish bit chopped out of an old wreck in Athens is known as the Bulgin' Baubles and can now be seen in the British Museum. Some of these temples have a sort of triangle above all this – it's called the impediment, as it stops the building going up any further – quite a good idea, really.

There's seldom anything of interest or indeed anything at all inside these buildings, except tourists, but sometimes you find a bit in the middle with a few extra pillars which, though it doesn't look like one, is called the cellar. The Greeks liked to see their gods (or perhaps their priests) well supplied with booze and this was the most sacred bit of the temple.

That's the essence of it, anyway.

MARY HOLTBY

Some Practical Hints for Streetwise Tourists

Italy
Each church provides candles for an impromptu bar-
becue.

Custodians in Italian churches will occasionally challenge the dress of lady visitors. The correct response
is to remove the offending garment and place it as an
'offering' before the nearest statue.

JOHN SWEETMAN

Germany
The German people welcome donations, however small,
towards the rebuilding of the recently destroyed Berlin Wall.

D.A. PRINCE

Belgium
Don't forget to take the family for a nice bedtime drink
in old dockside Antwerp, where the coffee shops are
all clearly marked and the friendly waitresses sit in the
windows to welcome you.

YVONNE REID

If you find one of the roadside lacemaker's cushions
unattended, this is an invitation to try your skill. See if
you can take the pattern a bit further!

NOEL PETTY

France
Every block of flats maintains its own prostitute in a flat
beside the main entrance.

D.A. PRINCE

If the wine-waiter asks you to taste the wine, it is correct
to spit it out. You then ask him to pour with the word
'*Merde*', a truncation of '*Maitre d'*.'

NOEL PETTY

The Netherlands

All bicycles are state-owned, and free for the use of everyone.

NOEL PETTY

Britain

The Queen entertains paying guests to afternoon tea on Saturdays. To make a booking, slip a £20 note into the fist of the guardsman on duty outside Buckingham Palace.

Any London taxi-driver will be happy to advise on alternative bus routes.

D.A. PRINCE

Spain

The deck-chair attendants can be identified by their odd patent-leather hats. Ask one to set you up a chair – the service is free.

When entering the Spanish customs area from France, you may sell your surplus francs by calling out 'Viva Franco!' This will ensure you instant attention.

NOEL PETTY

Your Questions Answered

Q. *Where would you advise travellers to go if they want to see the really important sights?*

Take the train first to **Lille**, where they manufacture the unmentionables, and then on to make **Aix** while the sun shines. Then travel south to **Avignon**, to sail in the famous punt, before crossing the Pyrenees and aiming for **Castile**, where they make the soap. Drop in at the tuneful town of **Guantanamera** on the way. Then it's off to **Faro**, which was the cradle of Egyptian civilisation, believe it or not, and up to **Gama**, where Vasco came from. Cross Spain and Portugal from your list!

Sur le Punt d'Avignon . . .

Fly across the Med to Italy, where a trip to **Bologna** will show you how to make that fabulous thick sauce, and a walk along the **Sabine mountains** will thrill you with its notorious local crop, rapeseed. I always go to **Ferrara**, where the racing cars are built; and no Italian trip is a complete without looking in on **Umbria**, where umbrage is cooked. Now on to Greece.

Greece is full of history: **Sparta, Olympia, Corinth, Necropolis, Drama, Peninsula, Roussos, Athos, Porthos** and **Aramis** all await you. The islands are delightful: my favourite is **Patmos**, named after a racing driver (**Stirlimos**, another so-named, is close by). Drink the **raki**, the **saki**, the **khaki**, and visit the tombs of Byron, Rupert Brooke and Keats, who is buried in an urn.

I hold no candle for Germany, but you must visit the power station in **Mainz**, and visit the HQ of the Scouting organisation in **Baden-Powell**. You could visit **Schleswig-Holstein** and try to answer the famous Question there, I suppose, but only on the way to Denmark, where the apples of **Zuider** are tasty, and the family spirit is alive in **Aarhuus** ('our house').

Now, down to Luxembourg, where there are far too many impressive places to list here, and then on, on to Belgium, where I recommend the port of **Liège** (where the princes came from, as in 'My Liege') and its 'ostend', or East End, where the Belgian Cockneys live. Holland next, and **Rotterdam, Amsterdam, Blastandam** and all the other sea-defences will ensure a 'dam' good time.

Scurry quickly to Ireland, go the long, long way to **Tipperary** (the road is frightful), visit the flutes in **Galway**, and sample the cooking in **Ovens**, near Cork. Then home to Great, Great Britain.

Q. What sports are popular in Europe?
Well, funnily enough, darts is very popular all over Europe, although the French have a quick version of it called ***vingt et un***. The French and Belgians play a game called ***boules***. All over both countries you can find the locals carrying their characteristically colourful set of plastic balls, which they throw in sandpits, or on a beach if they've got one. The Italians love guessing games, and there is a party special, popular with children, in which special *ravioli* is passed round

and nibbled, the winner being the one who guesses the contents correctly. It's called **pasta parcel**. But really, they play all the same sports as we do – cricket, snooker, Aunt Sally, Rugby League.

Q. What about bullfighting?
This is a very sensitive issue. As you know, the Spanish like to watch swordsmen (*pointilista*) waving a red cape (*flamenco*) at a bull (*pamplona*). When Spain joined the Market, this had to be kept off the agenda – a little unfair, since we had to give up hare-coursing, fish-baiting, pig-sticking and many other ancient English pastimes when we joined. A shocking film was circulated in Spain to dissuade the Spanish from continuing their dreadful hobby. It starred Sir Thomas Steele, and was entitled *Thomas the Toreador* (a *toreador* is the title of a man who cuts off the bull's ears). Unfortunately, the Spanish are a very musical nation, and there was a slightly catchy song in the film – all about cruelty – called *Uno pamplona blanca,* which went straight to the top of their hit parade. Nor does it help that writers like Ernest Fitzgerald, who wrote *For Whom the Bull Toils,* wrote about the killing so enthusiastically.

Q. Where can you ski?
Yoghurt.

BILL GREENWELL

EUROSEX

*This is a topic which few guide books deal with at all adequately.
We believe that in 1992, the time for coyness is past. The following
pages indicate something of the rich variety of practices to be found
in Europe.*

A tumescent young man from Gerona
Had a long and extraordinary boner.
I have met those who say
That it reached all the way
To the Plaza Real, Barcelona.

A couple residing in Dreux
Grew bored with coition *chez eux,*
So they fucked on the floor
Of the café next door:
Évidemment, folie à deux.

In Munich the Man of the Year
Will have drunk twenty litres of beer,
Sung a military song,
Farted loudly and long,
And molested young girls from the rear.

In Sweden the way to have sex
Is to interface stomachs and necks
While contriving to look
At a medical book
For the right sets of muscles to flex.

There was a young blood of Turin
Whose penis was frightfully thin,
And when placed inside
His attractive young bride
Felt less like a prick than a pin.

Though their diet is Gouda and ham,
The Dutch practise sex from the pram.
They enjoy it so much,
Those inscrutable Dutch.
Yeah – play it again, Amsterdam.

A chef and a waitress in Nîmes
Struck up a *liaison intime*
She enjoyed *soixante-neuf*,
For the chef's *langue de boeuf*
Was renowned from Cap Ferrat to Rheims.

An athletic *señora* from Ronda
Once fellated her mate on his Honda.
It was oh-so-sublime
That he urged 'One more time!'
But to do it again was beyond her.

There's a rumour that men in Toulouse
Have a thingamajig about shoes,
And I hear that the brogue
Is enjoying a vogue –
It's the wing-tips that make them enthuse.

A shipyard apprentice from Bremen
(A city world-famous for he-men),
Incautiously busting
His condom by thrusting,
Submerged his fiancée in semen.

In the better-off suburbs of Bruges
The men are not built at all huge,
Which accounts for the wives
Leading lesbian lives
In their sable and diamonds and rouge.

BASIL RANSOME-DAVIES

EUROCUISINE

Good food and drink is at the root of Continental European Culture, and it is important for the would-be European to acquaint himself with its main features.

Do it yourself: A Bluffer's Guide to Euro-Gastronomy

From 1992 onwards we will, in the interests of international co-operation and profit, ceaselessly entertain European visitors in our homes.

So what do we serve them? The patriotic answer might be 'ordinary British food', but the poor sods probably get most of their meals from MacDonalds as it is. Perhaps it would be best to make the foreigner feel at home. The conscientious host will therefore mug up a few basic ethnic menus. This is simple and cheap and, since showing willing is an effective form of blackmail, will repay many times over such little trouble and ingenuity as is required.

Basic ingredients (suitable for all EuroCuisine):

1. Last week's loaf with the mould scraped off.

2. The collection of dried herbs in little jars someone gave you as a wedding present.

3. The stock cubes you bought after your last visit to Italy – when was it?

4. An onion.

5. A head of garlic.

6. Bottles of your favourite wines from each country. Drink the wine yourself, then make your own refills using a kit from your neighbourhood chemist. If you do not draw the corks in the presence of your guests it might almost be argued that no actual deception is involved in this practice. DO NOT use white wine bottles from Austria since everyone will assume they have been topped up with anti-freeze. The fact that this has not been done for some years makes no difference: food fads die hard.

Alternatively, you can fight back with our own regional esoterica.

The essence of Scottish Cuisine is that familiar ingredients (handfuls of oatmeal aside) turn up under exotic names. A checklist is appended.

Howtowdie with Drappit Eggs:	Roast Chicken with Poached Eggs
Forfar Bridies:	Steak and Suet Pies
Inky Dinky:	Cold Beef with carrots, warmed in gravy
Clapshot:	Mashed Potatoes and Parsnips
Colcannon:	Sophisticated Bubble and Squeak
Kailkenny:	Creamy Bubble and Squeak
Rumbledethumps:	Bubble and Squeak with Chives
Skirlie:	Fried Onion with Oatmeal
Cloutie Dumpling:	Fruit Dumpling cooked in a Cloth

TOM AITKEN

French Wines

Dear Sir, as requested,
I've carefully tested
The wine-growing systems of France;
I've been in the cellars
With numerous fellers
And left not a vintage to chance;
For I've tasted chateaux
From all parts of Bordeaux
And quartered the Burgundy fields;
I've staggered through oceans
Of talk with negociants
On corking and cuvées and yields.
Of grapes, the Merlot,
Chardonnay and Pinot,
The Cabernet, Syrah, Gamay,
Are all in a mess
In my mind, and to guess
Which is which I can't possibly say.
But leave me alone
With a Beaune, or a Rhône,
And I promise it won't go to waste;
You can tell me it's classy,
Or lengthy, or grassy,
That it's pétillant, placid,
Good-tempered, or acid;
You can say that it's oaky,
Or spicy, or smoky,
Or a bit of a brute
With masses of fruit,
But the truth is, I just like the taste.

PAUL GRIFFIN

Croissantry . . .

The croissant is defined as a flaky, crescent-shaped bread roll made of a yeast dough similar to puff pastry, and it is the staple form of the Continental so-called breakfast in France. The same alleged meal, which scarcely dents, let alone breaks, the fast of the Britisher who normally requires cereal, eggs, bacon, toast and marmalade to perform that function, may, in other European countries, consist instead of cake or biscuits, even, in Holland, of bread and cheese. But definitely in France, you pays your money and you takes your croissant.

It is sometimes seen to be eaten dry, especially by young women hurrying to work and breakfasting as they go along. By more leisured classes or earlier risers it is taken at table, buttered, jammed, honeyed or whatever. But the method most commonly seen of a morning in the restaurant is by 'dunking' (from the town of Dunkerque, or vice versa). The croissant is held by one curved end or horn, while the other is 'dunked' (gently dipped) into the outsize French breakfast-cup of *café-au-lait*. In non-French hotels, where cups are smaller, a cereal-bowl is often used, both for drinking from and for dunking in. *'Après-dunke'*, with an adroit twist of the wrist in a clockwise or off-break direction, the soggy portion is brought up to engage with a sharp downward snap of the teeth. The importance of speed, timing and accuracy in this manoeuvre cannot be overemphasised: too long in the liquid and the dunked end becomes so coffee-logged that disintegration sets in, so that on being raised it belly-flops obscenely and messily back into the cup. The same occurs if the off-break is performed too slowly; while if too fast or with poor control, the inept croissantier or his neighbours, may well receive a full toss in the eye.

Despite intensive research, it is not possible to establish a reason for the French preference for this meagre breakfast or petty day-journey as they rightly term it. It is assumed to be possibly in the interest of either economy or time-saving, vide street consumption described above; or perhaps to permit semi-starvation by noon to be advanced as a credible excuse for the normal French luncheon interval of three or four hours, comprising a solid and leisurely repast plus time to spare for a couple of hours chez the chère amie. Whatever the reason, it certainly does not seem to be personal taste or lack of appetite, judging by the whole-hearted way in which Gallic guests in international hotels are seen at the buffet to undergo an enthusiastic, instant road-to-Damascus

Obscene belly-flop back into the cup

conversion to a grande alliance of 'English breakfast' of bacon, eggs and tomato; German *frühstuck* of *schinkenwurst*, rolls, butter, fruit and cereal, and Dutch *ontbijt* of breads, cheeses, cakes and cold ham. It is not known whether on returning to La Patrie they revert to frugal croissantry or continue to breakfast *à la Perfide Anglais*.

W.F.N. WATSON

. . . And Other Breakfasts

Some years ago I discovered the French Railways English breakfast. It was served in the cooking pan – anything else would have been impossible. You cover the bottom of the pan with rashers of bacon and break two eggs on them. The bacon is then fried until done, leaving the eggs almost uncooked, a result which cannot be obtained in any other way.

A technique from the Balkans which has taken many years of development, perhaps since the days of Homer, is Greek Toast. You find a large flat rock and at daybreak, cover it with slices of bread. At midday you turn over those which have not curled up enough to roll into the bushes and the final slightly sun-burned results are collected up at sunset to be served for breakfast the next day. The wild birds do not eat the toast first because it is far too hard for their beaks. Note how many species of the region have bent ones. This is solely due to Greek Toast.

ARTHUR P. COX

Claret

Chateau Talbot, Chateau Palmer, Chateaux Canon and
    Belair,
  Not to speak of Chateau Margaux, great Latour, Gruaud-
    Larose,
Lovely names for lovely liquor, purple, secretive and
    spare,
  Vapourizing on the palate, leaving scents and afterglows.

Rich and ripe they leave St Julien, St Emilion, Haut-
    Médoc,
  Travel out to spread their riches even to the dullish
    Brits;
Hard-faced dealers pay the needful, fill their cellars, turn
    the lock –

This is something called investment, making people lose
their wits.

Lost in cellars till the market soars to prices few can pay,
Decent claret is for no one till its price is out of reach.
Here's a glass. A tenner for it? Now I know why people
say:
'Bring the plonk out, Uncle Raymond, let's go picnic
on the beach!'

PAUL GRIFFIN

Let's Not Halt Awhile

More than anywhere else, France is a country in which you
may take pot luck in restaurants with reasonable confidence.
However, there are exceptions – and not only those places
that have loud signs in English, attract plenty of Americans
or specialise in *nouvelle cuisine*. Here is a generic guide to the
less than truly wonderful.

The Past Glories
It will be an attractive building, often ivy-clad, with a name
like *La Chope d'Or* or *L'Hostellerie du Roi*. The menu is designed
to resemble a parchment scroll, and is very extensive. There is
a superabundance of waiting staff crisply dressed, sporting
an aloof professional air. The deficiencies are in the kitchen,
however. You will be urged to sample the *menu gastronomique*,
twice the price of the standard *prix fixe*. All its most interesting dishes carry heavy supplements. Wine probably starts at
80 francs at bottle; for this you will not get much more than a
vin de table. Also, the menu is deceptively long. Mostly, it is
different sauces. These are floury, and spooned on in thick
dollops they disguise the questionable quality of the meat or
fish. The delight expressed by the manager when you pay
the bill is from the heart.

The Fresh Start.

This out-of-the-way hotel-restaurant is going places, or so the madman who owns it has decided. His non-stop talk is peppered with the word *dynamisme*. Try to address him in French and he will assume you are German and tell you of the time he worked in Trier. He is prone to bursts of song as he races about with a rattling tray. He offers snacks, including a sort of ploughman's lunch, the *assiette randonneur*, and a few easy-cook hot dishes. He has arranged pony rides for the kids. He rents out bicycles. In the evening he plays English pop music and barbecues *merguez*. Having bought a run-down joint at a knock-down price, he is applying the entrepreneurial *dynamisme* which he is convinced France, and especially the Midi, needs. He knows everything and does everything except leave his customers alone.

The Third Age

Gentlepersons *en retraite* flock here for the bland, watery food which they trust not to disturb their fragile digestive systems. The dining room is faded, without colour. Even the staff seem anaemic. You feel sinful ordering wine, because no one else is drinking it. Instead, the grey, elderly people who only communicate in nods and brief murmurs will be drinking mineral water. There is a bottle on each table, though not one will get finished. The faint, tinkling noise in the background is Richard Clayderman, an endless loop of him. In the lobby sits a pile of out-of-date retirement magazines, each packed with advertisements for specialised cures at spa towns. You begin to hope that no one will actually die *in situ*, and feel relief when their cars roar away like fighter planes. The atmosphere of painstaking, low-key politeness, is a strain, and when you go, you still feel slightly hungry.

The Take It Or Leave It

Nothing wrong with the food here – when you get it. The restaurant seems warm and welcoming, and the menu looks good and well-priced. The problem which you cannot realise until it is too late, is that the small family who run the place are all drunk and engaged in a deep quarrel with one another. The daughter does not want to wait table. She wants to be at the movies with her boyfriend, and her attitude lets you know it. The father tears frenziedly between kitchen and dining room, shouting unintelligibly. The mother is getting defiantly pissed at the bar and flirting with anyone who calls in for a casual Pernod. Intimidated by all the mysterious passion, you put up, helplessly, with the wayward service. You may get away by eleven if you're lucky. If you're even luckier, the bill will have been miscalculated in your favour. It may just be worth it if you're in a mood of humorous detachment.

BASIL RANSOME-DAVIES

A Report on Spaghetting

Mastery of the mysteries of Spaghetti Function was observed to be of a generally low standard and haphazard in approach. Four main methods were noted, as detailed below.

a) *Britischer*s and Germans, after fairly ineffectual efforts to cut up the spaghetti, then forked or spooned it into the mouth, which left numerous untidily trailing ends. These were then sucked up to rendez-vous with the rest of the mouthful, invariably leaving one long and refractory tube to be either hooked out with fork or finger, or drawn up into the mouth like an anchor-chain disappearing into the cat's-eye, or a serpent into a drain. The Britische approach, it should be added, often began with a forlorn attempt to deal with this arcane substance as though with a macaroni pudding.

b) The *Méthode Française* was via the Baden Bend, without preliminary chopping, which looked not like one disappearing snake but an entire reptile family, and noisily hissing.

c)   An alleged mode recalled by one committee person, of the trailing ends being trimmed off with scissors at lip-level by the spaghetteer or by a waiter, was traced to a film of the late M. Charlot Chaplin, and was not observed in practice.

d)   The Britkinder method was similar to b) above, with spoon, fork, knife and fingers employed even more untidily.

Spaghetting   Jugged Hair

e)   The Italian Connection involved the holding of the spoon in the left hand, while the fork in the right was plunged into the tangled skein. This, supported by the spoon also, was raised and lowered a distance of some 20 cms several times to free it from the main jumble, after which the fork, pressed into the bowl of the spoon, was remorselessly rotated to wind the skein on to the fork in an oval ball as of knitting wool. This was then inserted into the mouth leaving seldom more than one short, disconsolate end to be vacuumed à bord. This adroit process was then repeated until the whole was consumed.

The recommendation of the Committee is that spaghetting
be avoided by those non-Italians who are not virtuosi of the
Italian Connection.

W.F.N. WATSON

A Fragrant Libel

You wrote of Burgundy when it was Claret!
  What other libel can compare to this?
What Queensberry wrote of Wilde? What Mr Barrett
  Wrote of Elizabeth when he came to miss
    His erring daughter?
      If you should come to dine
      You'll not again have wine;
    I'll give you water.
And yet . . . perhaps you lost your sense of smell,
  And I'm uncharitable. Even so,
You must have been without your taste as well:
  It's rare for all one's faculties to go
    At one fell swoop.
      Besides, as I recall,
      You found the wherewithal
    To praise the soup.
No, it's quite clear the best that you deserve
  Is burgers, chips, and shandy in a garret;
For you insulted France, and had the nerve
  To write of Burgundy when it was Claret.

PAUL GRIFFIN

Diary Of A Wine Writer

The following is an unedited extract from the diary of a well-known wine-writer on a tasting trip to the Bordeaux region.

Monday
Woke at 6. Marvellous morning, delicious air, soft and perfumed. Jogged twice round the parc and had a quick dip before breakfast. Declined coffee despite delicious aroma. Must keep taste buds fresh. Toured Pauillac in a.m., then lunch and more tastings at St Julien. Some of the early '80s wonderfully delicate and fragrant now, and the '84s and '85s really come out to meet you.

After dinner a lecture with tastings by an organic chemist on the complexities of Bordeaux. Concluded human palate a much more subtle instrument than his spectrometers. Absolutely fascinating, though; stayed up till midnight discussing conclusions over some interesting Mouton Rothschilds.

Tuesday
Got up at 8, decided give jog a miss. Toured Margaux in a.m. with more tastings before lunch. Thought flavours a bit less sharply defined than yesterday; still, lovely stuff. In p.m. a lecture on conjectural reconstruction of pre-phylloxera taste of Bordeaux, with examples to taste. Room rather warm, fell asleep. Woke in time for tasting, though.

Wednesday
Rose at 10, just caught breakfast but couldn't manage much. Went on visit to caves north of river, St Emilion or something. Tasted some big-nosed stuff that went down jolly well, but didn't quite catch name. Cut lecture after dinner, had 2/3 brandies and went to bed.

Thursday

Slept till noon nearly. Light extraordinarily bright today. Had to wear dark glasses to go down for lunch. Fell down last flight, destroying prized Sèvres vase in process. After lunch, tastings at St Estèphe. Great afternoon – can't beat the old vino I always say. Missed dinner, watched TV in bedroom. Couldn't understand a word but pictures restful.

Friday

Got down about two. Missed breakfast, missed lunch, and missed coach to Pomerol or somewhere. Spent afternoon in bar, having private tasting of Pernods. Feeling just a bit below par. Touch of the old malaria coming on, perhaps.

The diary ends here. Being incomplete, the notes are of limited value as a guide for wine-lovers, but do offer a fascinating insight into how connoisseurs of fine wines go about their work.

NOEL PETTY

One final word of warning: like us, the Continentals have their food scares.

Hard Cheese: New Loony Cow Euro-Shock

Rumours of a severe psychiatric disorder among French cattle are causing grave alarm throughout Europe.

British farmers, permanently angry after a series of clashes with the French, are calling for a complete ban on imports of beef and dairy products from France because of 'laughing cow disease'.

But while the French government stayed silent on the matter last night, the country's milk and meat producers denounced the British demand as 'hysterical'. One said: '*Nom d'un nom*! We believe it all started because some English fool noticed a picture of a laughing cow on a packet of French cheese.

'It is all ridiculous. Our cows do not laugh, any more than British farmers do.'

But a leading British cattle breeder declared: 'There is no doubt that laughing French cows are producing cheese which our children are eating. And youngsters have been seen laughing their heads off at school.'

'Putting two and two together, we advise mothers: stick to good old Cheddar for the kiddies' sake – at least until this scare ends and another one starts.'

The Ministry of Agriculture is taking the matter seriously. It is assembling a team of cow psychiatrists – 'not an easy job,' said a spokesman – to investigate selected herds in France.

A recent opinion poll indicated that few people were seriously worried about 'laughing cow disease'. Here are some comments:

A 70-year-old man: 'Cripes, if I was a bloody French cow, or a French farmer, I'd be laughing all the way to the bank.'

A 19-year-old girl student: 'I've heard they do awful things to make those cows laugh, like they feed up those poor geese for pâté.'

A 30-year-old lager drinker: 'I wouldn't have no part of a laughing cow, no more than I'd eat frog's legs, but it's a free continent, innit?'

PETER VEALE

Your Questions Answered

Q. *What is the Common Agricultural Policy?*
This is one of the main things that countries joining the
Common Market have to agree to. Each country has to
use every bit of its resources to be able to give something
to its friends (rather like Christmas, when you come
to think of it). That means using all the land to grow
vegetables and crops – even land which is just sitting
there doing nothing, like village commons for a start. The
Common Agricultural Policy means we all agree to grow
something on any land where it will grow. Dartmoor is
expected to be a market garden by the year 2020. It will
be known as 'Heath Heath' after the man who took us
into Europe.

Q. *I have often seen journalists writing about something known as
a CAP. What exactly is a CAP?*
Every country in the Common Market has to be stopped
from growing too much food, otherwise it is just a waste
(or the people living in the country get very fat indeed).
For instance, they are very fond of goats' cheese in
France – and, before the Common Market started up,
they used to produce a ridiculous amount of it. They
had to eat it for *petit déjeuner*, *grand déjeuner*, every
déjeuner going. Now there is a CAP on goats' cheese
and the French are healthier as a result. In the meantime,
the goats have been given a new job. They are used to
graze the grass from Commons, so that other crops
can be sown. And they are also used for modelling
for stories in children's books, an awful lot of which
are about goats (*The Three Billygoats Gruff, The Lonely
Goatherd, Goat Ellut On The Mountain, The Goat Of Many
Colours* and so on).

Q. *What is a Dutch CAP?*
This is a special policy applied to Holland, where tulips
are allowed to be grown in their millions – far more than

are needed. Partly this is to disguise the really rather dull
Dutch landscape. Some of the tulips are picked to make
the famous Sauce Hollandaise.

Q. What is the Butter Mountain?
Let us first clear up the silly idea that it is a mountain,
like the Alp, made out of butter. No-one has ever taken
ropes, axes, picks and croutons and tried to climb it! It
is in fact a Health Precaution. Too much butter is bad for
you. But you cannot stop cows producing dairy goods –
indeed, in some parts of Europe, even goats and sheep
are known to produce dairy goods, something we have
managed to prevent in this country. The sensible answer
to this problem, therefore, has been to stockpile, in a
giant freezer, all the extra butter left over after each
country has been allowed its ration.

Q. What happens to the Butter Mountain? What does it look like?
   What are its advantages?
The Butter Mountain is arranged as a huge pyramid, and
is kept in a large freezer which moves between Brussels
and Strasbourg. It is constantly maintained by a team of
butter-boys and -girls, who also act as guides to those
who wish to inspect it. The Butter Mountain is very
useful. It is used to feed starving Russians (who have
no cows, and therefore no cheese, either). It is also very
good insurance against serious outbreaks of Mad Cow
Disease (*Bovrili Spinacchio Encefilato*, as the Italians call
it), and also against War, when we would need to top
up supplies. Furthermore, the Butter Mountain pays for
itself by providing all Europe's airlines with pre-packed
portions of butter – known as 'pats' after the Aer Lingus
stewards who first introduced them. This cuts the cost
of aviation very considerably.

Q. What is the Wine Lake?
This is a famous and enormous pool beneath Luxembourg, into which each Common Market country pours
some of its best vino. The resulting blend is then bottled

and sold (hence the legend 'made from the wines of different EEC countries'). Since Greece joined the Common Market, the addition of *retsina* (Greek for 'eye-opener') has made for a fascinating new flavour.

Eye-opener

Q. Are there any other stockpiles?

Yes. The Spaghetti Hoop, The Biscuit Barrel, The Hamburger Hill, The Pasta Collection, The Olive Ocean, The Rye Heap, The Maize Maze, and The Blood Banks are among the many reserve supplies upon which we may draw in times of crisis. My own favourite is the Sheep Dip, in which quantities of mutton are kept marinading in subtle blends of EEC spices.

Q. Who are the major wine-makers, cider-farmers, distillers and brewers in Europe? Where would I go to drink the proper stuff?

You can usually tell where a drink has come from by

looking at its name. For instance, there is a drink called VAT 69 which pretty obviously comes from The Vatican, vintage of 1969 (such an excellent year that we hardly ever hear of other harvests). **Sherry** sounds English, but is really French, being an anglicisation of 'Chérie', i.e. a very dear, or costly drink. It is made using water from the river Cher, which flows through the district of the same name. **Port** comes from Port Talbot in Wales, which is why it is often mixed with lemon, the Welsh national fruit. **Beer** was first made in Opladen, which is near Dusseldorf in Germany; **lager** is Spanish, and originates in the port of La Garrucha (the reason supplies are so plentiful to British holidaymakers); *Liebfrau* is not made from mothers' milk as is so often feared, but from that of cows. **Whisky?** Scotch whisky comes from Scotland; Irish whisky comes from Ireland; and Malt whisky comes from Malta. **Madeira** comes from Majorca. No-one's sure where **wine** was first made, but the likeliest places are Finland and Vinland (America – Vinland is what the Vikings called it).

Q. What about soft drinks?
That beautifully refreshing and fizzy orange drink **Tango** comes from the centre of Spain, where oranges are drunk, and roses are clenched between the teeth. There is a beautiful dance named after this popular beverage, in which the woman wears a praying *mantis*, or shawl, and *castanet* stockings. The man is called the *flamenco*, or flamingo, after the way he inclines his neck to the woman. In Crete, they dance the *hoki-koki*, and this too is a dance named after a drink – *koki*, or, as we know it, **Coke**. Eire is the source of **Sprite**, which is supposedly the drink of the leprechauns. And **Fanta** comes from Santa Cruz in Spain (where it is called Santa – our pronunciation comes from the funny way we used to write our 'S'). **Lemonade** is made in every village, town or city throughout Europe, although its strength varies. Most road signs or proper maps will give you the current

strength underneath the name (e.g. *pop* 14,534); Berlin's is said to be particularly potent.

Q. Where does bottled water come from?
This is all made in Spa. – which is short for Spain. It was in very short supply until Spain joined the EEC, which is why it used to be so expensive. There is one brown water supply which some people drink, but we do not recommend it. This is taken straight from the River Tizer in Rome, and is named after it.

Q. What is the European for 'Cheers!'?
A number of possibilities are being aired. In hotels, people tend to call **Hasta la visa**!, but most locals will soon greet you with **mana la mancha**, or (literally) 'Down the hatch'. Certainly, we would not recommend the insufferably pretentious **Proust!**

Q. Is it true that the best ice-cream comes from Italy?
Funnily enough, it isn't. The French make the finest of all the creamy delights in Europe. Legend has it that Joan of Arc was caught in a snowstorm with a cow, its udder bursting. Deftly she grasped the teats, and extracted the hard buttery substance. When local people came to see the miracle, they were overcome by its taste, and Lyons Maid remains Europe's most popular brand.

Q. What is a baguette?
A baby bague. The French use it for shopping.

BILL GREENWELL

Joan . . . caught in a snowstorm with a cow.

EUROLOOS

The enquiring European should aim to be well-prepared for the variety of post-prandial arrangements likely to be encountered.

The pre-lunch *pastis* hit the spot.
The wine was insolent, robust.
The steak, bestrewn with parsley dust.
Was tasty, tender, rare and hot.
The *mousse au chocolat* a must.
The Calva apple-rich.

So time to light a cigarette
(The restaurant abounds with smoke)
And be a debonairish bloke?
A wishful thought: the food you ate
Has stirred things up, and it's no joke,
That frantic rectal itch.

Le water is across the yard.
Where Stella crates are stacked like bricks
And someone's dog morosely licks
Its testicles. The choice is hard,
Unlike your bowels. What a fix –
Yet still you hesitate.

Sure, hesitate, but not for long
Before you wrench aside the door:
Ceramic footsteps on the floor,
A string-pull flush, and what a pong,
Like dead whales rotting on the shore . . .
At least you're not too late.

You crouch above the evidence
Of other users of the hole
In darkness, with no toilet roll,
And half-relieved, although half-tense
In case some slip of palm or sole
Should land you in the *merde*.

Omitting details, this ordeal
Can be completed with success.
Yet why's the bog a noisome mess
When elegance adorned the meal?
I asked a man in Bourg-en-Bresse,
But bugger-all he cared

BASIL RANSOME-DAVIES

The Loos of Europe

The British have lots of views
on European loos.
They say the French ones are just holes in the ground –
it's immoral and very unsound.
But for Yugoslavian Ladies and Gents
you have to choose
between Ladies' and Gentlemen's shoes –
it's just a huge emblematic shoe
that holds out hope to stressful you!

GAVIN EWART

The Loocu – A Proposal

Now that we're all good Europeans, let's get our act together
regarding coins and sexist signs at public loos.
    Let's avoid confusion. Let's not be misled by the silhouette
in trousers. Many an absent-minded woman travels in slacks.

Conversely, Scots, Greek and Albanian males may prefer to travel in kilts.

If no sign exists, other than the letters WC, this means that all are welcome. Partings of the way are generally made plain in various European languages after entry. But be prepared for the unexpected.

Some loos are free. Some require coins. There is no knowing. Therefore, be prepared to carry a bag full of loose coins of various denominations.

Perhaps there is something to be said for a common coinage, such as the ECU; a LOOCU at a fixed rate and size throughout Europe would be even more useful. No one would need to know the language, but everyone would know exactly what it was for!

ARDA LACEY

Eurograffiti From European Loos

Montmartre
Girls who drink in France, just ponder –
Absinthe makes the heart grow fonder . . .

MICHAEL FOSTER

The Vatican
Contraception is the odium of the papal.

KATIE MALLETT

Marbella
Oh to be in England now that April's there;
I must look out my wellies and my thermal underwear!

FRANK RICHARDS

Dublin

Parnell
Fell,
After having it away
With Mrs O'Shea

RON RUBIN

Paris

Girls! Leave those French *gentilhommes* in no doubt
That they jolly well can't Messieurs about.

W.F.N. WATSON

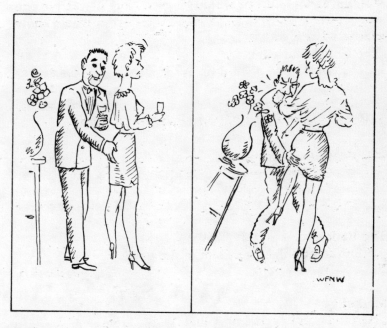

Belfast

Roared Rev Ian Paisley
Crazily:
'God
Is a Prod!'

RON RUBIN

John O'Groats
O my luve's like a red, red rose
Especially about the nose,
For the braw bricht winds of Caledonia
Gave her pneumonia.

FIONA PITT KETHLEY

Florence
The Uffizi
Is not so ritzi
's a matter of fact, it's totally naff –
Hasn't even got a decent caff.

E.O. PARROTT

The British Museum
The Greeks had a word for it – theft.

STANLEY J. SHARPLESS

Strasbourg
'We must mind our P's and Ecus.'

STANLEY J. SHARPLESS

Clermont-Ferrand
Ladies met in bistros in Paris
Are not the sort you maris.

W.F.N. WATSON

Liverpool
If we don't build a high-speed link
To the Channel Tunnel,
What benefits will come our way?
None'll.

STANLEY J. SHARPLESS

Hamburg
When you're chatting her up, a Fraülein
May adopt a rather caülein;
A Frau
Seems different, somehau.

W.F.N. WATSON

Brussels
   Oui, oui! It's that mannequin again!

PETER VEALE

London, Westminster Bridge
   Earth has not anything to show more fair;
   I cannot see a tourist anywhere.

E.O. PARROTT

Stratford-on-Avon
   To be, or not to be; that is the question
   Unless you come up with a third suggestion.

PETER VEALE

EUROSPEECH

The British are not traditionally well-versed in the languages of other nations. This need not be a cause for despair, however; a great deal can be achieved through phrase books, intelligent interpretation of foreign words and a willingness to compromise by both sides.

Let's Sprachen Deutschlisch

English Tourist: Diese ist certainlisch ein wunderbar Tafel-wein. Already ich quite gepissed feel.

German Host: Ja, ja! Wir sellen quite a lot von diese Wein zu die Englisch. Es ist 'Liebfraumilch' genommt.

E.T.: Liebfraumilch? Du kannst nicht be serious? In Deutsch-land man macht Wein von *milch*?

G.H.: (*sotto voce*) Wir haben ein richtig one hier. (*aloud*) Nein, nein, mein Herr. Das ist only ein Weinmetafor. Ein bisschen like 'Bullsblood', für example. Wein ist always von Grapen gemacht, natürlisch.

E.T.: Nicht so, actuallisch. In England wir priden uns auf unsere Homemadeweinen. Man kann of course ein Grapenkonsenträt usen, like ein Bootsweinmäkingkit für example, aber ich prefer die Ingredienten von Natur – Elderberrywein, Mangelwurzelwein, Kompostwein . . .

G.H.: Mein Gott! Und was about der Realale? Man hat mir gesagt that Englischerbier von warm Washingupwasser gemacht ist, aber up till now ich believed it nicht!

E.T. (through clenched teeth) Ha, ha! Sehr droll! Auf secondthoughts, diese Wein ist nicht so gut . . .

PETER NORMAN

Torre Pendente, or Tour Hang-ups

'The administration declines all responsibility for possible accidents and will denounce the transgressors in case of damages.' Thus, unambiguously, in an 'archaeological area'; but outside, what of the potential transgressors who find themselves in a linguistic wilderness of mysterious signs, where grim admonitions compete with grotesque allurements, puzzling advertisements and perverse announcements?

No more 'care of painture', or 'Trieste is very choreographical and scenic': we are now faced with the real thing and have to tease out a meaning as we travel. *Rallentare!* we can readily interpret as 'Get a move on', and *Continua*, 'Keep it up! but look out – down there is a crazy road (*via dotto*), and here we are warned of hazardous weather conditions: a frosty area (*rimozone*) or very thick mist (*foggia grande*). We could try the mobile canteen (*mobil servizio*) where it's possible to choose your fish (*elletrauto*), but alas! this park is for classy German cars only (*supermercato*). It might be as well to avoid the conference of windbags (*confartigianato*), and not to be so bold as to enter the loos for lecturers only (DONNE) . . .

Yet it seems that on all sides, paradoxically, we are offered a unique sensation (*senso unico*), and this vague, if intriguing, promise occasionally becomes more specific in such regrettable notices as *Antico Trullo* (old woman of easy virtue) or *Campo Sportivo* (gay goings-on). Of course we are hardly qualified to do much about these when there is emphatically no currency exchange (*banchino intransitabile*) – which equally prevents us from laying out money on crummy junk (*grotte*), a self-playing violin (*autostrada*), or a puppy-basket (*porto dogana*). Anyway, a notice in the same area warns *Imbarco* (barking prohibited) – no doubt for fear of distracting the performers in 'One Man and his Dog' (*colle del sole*).

But madness is setting in – why the badtempered butler (*crossodomo*)? Is it he whose intransigence inspired the moving legend *Parcheggio / Lavaggio* (I'm dying of thirst and I need a wash)? By now we can identify with those characters described by a guide as 'desperated pipple'; so desperated, perhaps, that in order not to 'commit all sorts of things in contrast to the dignity and respect of the places' we should betake ourselves to the *terminal regionale* – that country from whose bourn no traveller returns . . .

MARY HOLTBY

Puppy basket . . . Barking prohibited

Pronunciation Mnemonics For Place Names

A rugger fanatic from Nîmes
Once scored twenty tries in a drîmes.
When he dived for one more
He woke up, on the floor –
Things are not always quite what they sîmes . . .

MICHAEL FOSTER

There was a young lady of Nantes
Who murmured: 'I know what you wantes.
   If you asked me I would,
   And I know that I could
Procure you the plumes of my tantes.'

E.O. PARROTT

The chap in the train at St Gotthard
Turned out to be rather a rotthard
He shocked all the Swiss
By starting to piss
And using their coats as a blotthard.

GINA BERKELEY

There once was a housewife of Pisa
Who carelessly fell in the freezer.
   It's not very nice
   When your spouse turns to ice,
And disposal's a bit of a teaser.

MARY HOLTBY

Notes On The Danish Tongue

There is only one fault to find with this delightful and
enlightened tribe who, after all, have the inestimable social

advantage of having settled half England in the 11th century and ruled the whole lot for almost thirty years. Thus they provided the monarchy-loving English with one nearly-king, Sweyn Forkbeard; one Supaking, Cnut the Water-Repellant, and two shockers, Harold Harebrain and Harthacnut, both right bastards, though legally only the former could be called a proper bastard. Stacks of Eurobritish place-names demonstrate our affinity with the Danskers, so that if the name of your neck of the woods ends in -by, -thorpe or -hulme you can claim that your forebears were Vikings. It is therefore painful to state that after their thus getting off to a head start, the one Great Danish fault aforementioned, and bar to greater understanding of their ways and traits, is the Gloomy Danish language.

Cnut the Water-Repellent

It is not just the matter of the sounds they utter when talking, unintelligible and unidentifiable though they are; it's the unreasonable and baffling impossibility of picking up a tiny working smattering of it from a phrase-book, as every earnest True–Brit traveller seeks to do in order to make contact and build relationships with the natives everywhere he goes. But not in Denmark. As an example, consider a conversation with a Danish friend who had kindly arranged

a marvellous holiday for us at a delightful farm-cum-inn at
the edge of the forest on a Danish island. But, he told us, they
don't speak English. However, I remembered that the great
traveller and linguist George Borrow reckoned he taught
himself Danish simply by procuring a Danish Bible, so I
organised the following Borrovian-style dialogue:

Myself: No problem. I've often had to manage with phrase-
   books and Grammars – German, Arabic, Urdu, Dutch,
   Italian – so could you lend me a Danish Grammar Book,
   or Dictionary?
Georg: What for?
Myself: So that I can speak to the people at the inn.
Georg: You cannot speak Danish from a book.
Myself: I'm sure I can manage enough to make our needs
   understood.
Georg: You cannot speak Danish from a book.
Myself: Well, have you a book, so that I can try?
Georg: I have a dictionary. Please keep it. But you cannot
   etc., etc.
He produces a book. It is entitled *Gyldenals rde Ordbger.*
Engelsk–Dansk, and I have it beside me now as I write.
Myself: Thank you very much, Georg.
I flip the dictionary open at random. Page 114. Find a familiar
word, 'Duck (subst.)', and I point to the Danish word, which
is 'And'.
Myself: Now, this word; is it 'ah-nd' or 'and'?
Georg: It is 'eh-uh'.
[It seems that a Danish word either looks entirely familiar,
like 'and', and sounds like nothing on earth, or looks utterly
daunting, like 'børnehjælpsdag' and sounds oddly familiar –
'bairn-helps-dag', and means just that – Help the Children Day.
But mostly, like 'tandlægevæsen sygeplejerske' (Dental Nurse,
if you need one), it's as impossible as it looks; and I don't know
about G. Borrow and his Bible, but I reckon Georg was nearer
the mark; you cannot praje Dansk from a bog.]

W.F.N. WATSON

Vile as the pun, I dare to utter it –
That Yugoslavian tongues must all be split
How else could people speak or understand
The names of towns and islands in their land?

Porec, and Krk, Ljubljana and Lyubinje,
Grke, Hvar, Cenj, Skopje, and Trebinje,
Vrsac and Vrbas beat your tongue, I'll bet,
And so do Plevlja, Gracac, and Mljet.

Beyond Dubrovnik, Yugoslavia ends,
And black Albania unknown miles extends;
Then, where green Corfu lifts her northern peak,
Let tongues relax, for all the names are Greek.

PAUL GRIFFIN

Eating Out In Greece

The Greeks' ancestors taught us to be free,
With every town its own democracy;
Now their descendants hear the song they sang
And, feeling free, let all the rest go hang.
One Greek, one point of view, entire, unique;
Were two identical, they'd not be Greek.

This applies to everyone and everything in Greece that
has not been internationalised. But outside the cities and
package hotels, the Greek Tourist Authority has imposed a
sort of uneasy conformity on restaurants and tavernas. In
consequence, they all display a notice something like this:

'By this Order is necessary expose ourselves promi-
nently in Restaurant.
At often, persons of the Town shall visit Restaurant to
make inspexion all bodies in labor and to check tacks
on dishes.

All ofering dishes contain 15% tacks and 10% for them
in labor.
By this writen upwards we become Place of Licence
under Act of Public Dirtiness.'

My rich uncle rightly commented on one of these notices:
'Who would have expected to see "licence" properly spelt
in so remote a place?'

But there is another reason why Greek restauranteurs more
or less conform. It is simple and overwhelming. They have
no food.

What they do have is menus: vast and entrancing folders,
with every dish under the sun listed in Greek and a language fondly thought to be English. Some items are easily
deciphered:

Roast Lamp
Smacked Xam
Eal Catlets

Others become clear only as one masters the language:

Kalamaris
Kotopolo
Galatopourekko

But some are completely opaque:

Fried gazoil
Arico jumpers
Oppijops

Little of this is actually available. Ever since the Turks
departed, leaving a confused memory of intolerable oppression and a marvellous cuisine, amiable chaos has reigned.
Turkish coffee survived till the Cyprus Troubles, when it had
to be renamed Greek Coffee; then everyone thought: 'What
the hell?' (in Greek: 'What the Hades?') and drank a liquid
universally called Nes. Under the Hellenised menus lurks the
memory of real Greek food: bread and olives, sheep's cheese,
a pile of beans or whatever grows in a poor dry soil, and, with
luck, a chunk of lamb once a week.

PAUL GRIFFIN

Useful Phrases For Travellers

On the ferry to Ostend

Toegang: Football supporters
                              through here.

Spui: For use of passengers in
                              rough weather.

E.O. PARROTT

Germany

Aufsprungdurchtechnik: State-of-the-art flick-knife
Deutschland uber alles: German beer is best
Guten abend: Gone round the bend
Nicht wahr: Pyjamas

MARY HOLTBY

In Italy

La donna è mobile: The wife's got the car.

PETER VEALE

WFNW

Via Dolorosa:	Unmade-up road

E.O. PARROTT

Literati:	Refuse collector

SUE SAXBY

In Spain
Auto da fe:	Fairy cycle
Por favor:	Do me a favour and be Mother

MARY HOLTBY

In France
Bidet:	June 4, 1944
Boulangerie:	Down with underwear
Je pense donc je suis:	I live on immoral earnings
Esprit de corps:	Embalming fluid
Café au lait:	Spanish coffee hits the spot
Route nationale:	Carrot
Plus ça change, plus c'est la même chose:	I'll have my change, if it's all the same to you
Poule de luxe:	Jacuzzi
Autres pays, autre moeurs:	If someone else is buying, I'll have another drink
Cache-sexe:	Prostitution
Nom de Guerre:	I am a photographer
Alimentation:	Islamic philosophy

BASIL RANSOME-DAVIES

Folie à deux:	Schizophrenia

LIONEL BURMAN

Défense de cracher:	Buffers
Biftec:	Third degree
Interpol:	A parrot's funeral

ARTHUR P. COX

Avoirdupois:	Do have some peas

E. O. PARROTT

Hors de Combat: The colonel's little bit on the side

Tour de force: Police outing
KATIE MALLETT

La vice anglaise: Black & Decker workmate
GEORGE SIMMERS

Film noir: You left the lens cap on
TIM BEECHAM

Ménage à trois: A very small zoo
BEN FRANCIS

Déjeuner sur l'herbe: Vegetarian meal
MONICA RIBON

Tant pis: Auntie's drunk
GERARD BENSON

Homme de lettres: Postman
PASCOE POLGLAZE

Belle laide

Belle laide:	Good in bed
Crie de coeur:	Bow-wow!
Amour propre:	Missionary position
Suivez la piste:	Follow that drunk
Belle esprit:	Scotch whisky

PETER VEALE

Après moi le deluge:	I pulled the chain and look what happened!

MARY HOLTBY

Lament

Now that we're all European
'Ow I wish that I'd stuck at me French,
Me name might 'ave been up in neon
If I'd not been a bone-idle wench.

I'd 'ave wowed 'em in Paris twice-nightly
Wiv me witty an' wise Eurospeak,

In Athens 'ave shone just as brightly –
'avin' picked up a smatterin' of Greek.

The fellas 'd all 'ave chucked roses,
The girls 'd'ave all been green-eyed,
An' I'd 'ave been snapped in louche poses
For magazines sold Eurowide.

But the nights when I should 'ave been doin'
French 'omework, I'm sorry to say,
I was courtin' me downfall an' ruin
By makin' a good deal of 'ay.

So I'll never be toast of French caffs, nor
Yet of the smart set in Rome;
P'raps, like Wordsworth, I'll look at the daffs more
An' learn to speak proper at 'ome!

MARGARET ROGERS

Your Questions Answered

Q. Where do European languages come from?
To understand this, we have to go right back in history to the time of the dinosaurs and the pyramids. At that time, there were very few people indeed in Europe, apart from a few cavepersons, who spoke only in a grunting 'language' called **Trog**. It wasn't until Europe was invaded by the speaking peoples of India, Persia and Mongolia, that people actually began to talk amongst themselves in what we would nowadays recognise as words. The first word known to have been spoken in Europe is *Ecce*, and there are still some parts of Lancashire where this prehistoric greeting is used. Most of the early conversation concerned killing and dying, since everybody ate meat and most people died young.

Q. Is this why dead languages are so called?
Yes. There were two dead languages which sprang up: **Latin** and **Greek**. They are very similar, and together form the basis of nearly all the languages spoken today in Europe. However, this is not always obvious, because linguistic variation occurs. This is because different tribes needed secret codes in which to communicate their private ideas. The Germans, for instance were known as 'the salt of the earth' by the aristos in Rome (the first capital of Europe). The Latin for 'salt of the earth' is *terra saxa*, and the wilder common people came to be known as Saxons as a result. The Saxons invaded Britain (which is why we sound German when we have 'flu). Some German words still survive, as in the Scots phrase 'och aye.' The German for 'high' is '*hoch*', so the phrase is really 'hi hi', or in Glasgow, 'aye aye.'

Hoch aye

There are a few tribes on Europe's fringe who continue to speak in languages derived from codes so secret that, after a while, no-one could remember what they meant, tribal elders having forgotten to pass on the meanings. One of these is **Breton**, which is spoken in Brittany. Now if you say the word 'Breton' very quickly, you should notice that it *does* sound very like 'Britain'. This is why, on a clear day, Bretons can understand Welsh language speakers (Wales used to be called Small Britain before Great Britain existed). There is also **Cornish**, which is unfortunately a dead language now, although you still buy their famous clotted cream at Poldark Tregarras, their ancient capital.

Q. Are there any other fringe languages?
Yes. The most famous is **Basque**. This unusual language has given the rest of Europe many words, including *basket, biscuit, busker, tabasco,* and *basically*. Some think it is even related to Cornish (think of *The Hound of the Baskervilles*). **Lapp** is another very mysterious language, and is thought to derive from the need to speak very slowly and carefully because in Lapland, it is always snowing, and usually dark. **Gaelic** speakers were driven out of Gaul into the west of Ireland and the North of Scotland by those Latin aristos.

Two other strange languages are **Mafia**, which nobody talks about talking, but is thought to be spoken in Sicily, and **Geordie**, which is spoken on the banks of the Tyne by moving the *geor* (jaw) in a peculiar way.

Q. *Will there ever be a single language spoken throughout Europe?*
Yes, indeed. There are already plans for a Common European Linguistic Tongue (or **CELT**) to be in place shortly after the turn of the century. Ifa ich geçälle amt to spooken uno bitte du yon tjŒngk, ich thönck yu vilt llykelly undistini mio verbos widŒt mochâ dificilité. Actually, this is a simulation, but it is very like the sort of thing they are planning. Essentially Europranto (as it will colloquially be known) is an attempt to get back to the basic language spoken before all these secret codes confused everything.

Q. *What language do they speak in Belgium?*
Congo.

BILL GREENWELL

EUROCUSTOMS

One of the pleasures of European travel is the festivals. How the tourist's spirits lift on entering a European town to find the shops already closed in preparation for the fiesta! Here are some festivals uncovered by our correspondents.

The Festival Of The Farmers, Northern France

Nowhere in Europe is the contrast between city and country more marked than in France, and the Festival of the Farmers, which can take place at any time of year, is the countryman's traditional way of reminding urban folk of the agricultural heritage upon which they all depend.

The Festival takes many forms, but the element common to them all is the symbolic bestowal of agricultural produce upon the city-dwellers by the farming community. They may, for instance, distribute a thousand tons of turnips outside the Ministry of Agriculture as a token of thanks for the consideration they have received in the past and anticipate in the future. At another time the citizens at large may receive the gifts, as for instance when large quantities of mature cabbage are spread liberally throughout one of the fashionable shopping streets. Sometimes motorists are the beneficiaries, as when sheep carcasses are heaped on the roads approaching the city.

The Festival is not confined to Paris, however, or even to France. Tourists arriving at the Channel ports may find a welcoming cordon of tractors denoting that the Festival is in progress there. The Farmers in their picturesque

blousons and berets, may be good-humouredly overturning
egg-trucks in their eagerness to ensure that tourists rushing
for the autoroutes linger awhile in the country regions. A
particularly imaginative climax to one Festival 'happening'
was the presentation of a live cow to the EEC Commissioners
on the top floor of their headquarters building in Brussels.

All this, of course, is recognisable as a basic fertility rite,
and is doubtless of considerable antiquity. Some authorities
believe that after the French Revolution, when the Church
was separated from the State, the farmers, deprived of
the opportunity of paying tithes, assuaged their guilt by
making the people the recipients of their bounty. In fact,
the Festival may be much older even than this; the incident
of the Brussels cow, elevated as it was both physically and
hierarchically, suggests that the Festival may have its roots in
a form of Hinduism imported by the Indo-European migrants
in the 15th century BC.

Be that as it may – and it must be admitted that these
theories are somewhat speculative – it need not cramp the
enjoyment of the Festivities by the tourist with an eye for
local colour. The farmers will usually pose for your camera,
and may even wave their farm implements at you. If so,
don't be afraid to greet them in their own language, praising
their countryside with a cry of *'Paysan!'* (literally, 'Healthy
Country!') or perhaps *'Ventre Bleu!'* ('May the Breeze Blow!').
You will be assured of a warm response.

The Festival Of Le Grand Départ, France

Many visitors to France about the end of July are puzzled to
find a step-change in the pace of activity around them. They
have been enjoying the extraordinary peace of the French
countryside, the amazingly uncluttered roads, the villages
with no sign of life; when suddenly, as at a pre-arranged
signal, the roads are full of perspiring families in overloaded
cars of all types and sizes, hurrying dangerously in all
directions. What can have happened? A nuclear accident,
perhaps? An extra-terrestrial invasion?

No. It is merely the festival of Le Grand Départ, which takes place annually on the first Saturday in August. It looks like a pre-arranged signal because it *is* a pre-arranged signal. On this day, by ancient and hallowed tradition, it is necessary for all French people to be somewhere else. Nor is this simply a desire to be near to the sea brought on by the warm weather, for visitors to the seaside are quite likely to be greeted by notices on hotels and restaurants advising them of the 'Fermeture Annuelle'; the proprietors have departed for their own somewhere else. City dwellers depart for the coast, coastal dwellers depart for the countryside, and country-dwellers depart for the towns.

The festival clearly ministers to some deep primitive instinct, perhaps harking back to the time of the Visigoths, or some other nomadic occupants of the country that is now France. However that may be, this is one festival which is not recommended for tourists. The French like to keep this one for themselves, and to venture out with GB plates showing appears to invite volleys of '*le klaxon*', though to be fair it is not always easy to tell at whom these warnings are directed. All the same, it is a good weekend to spend with a couple of dozen Simenons.

The festival only lasts for the weekend, after which the movement is absorbed into the Campings and Plein-Airs until the corresponding weekend four weeks later, when the whole process is repeated, or rather reversed. The nomadic urge has then been sublimated for a further year.

The Festival Of The Lagelouts, Costa Brava, Spain

Spain has long played host to a variety of ethnic cultures. The Romany and Moorish civilizations both took root here many centuries ago and flourished in the hospitable Spanish sunshine. Of more recent origin, though equally obscure, is the annual Festival of the Lagelouts, which takes place each year in August along the Costa Brava.

The Lagelouts descend on the coast apparently guided only by oral tradition, much in the way that Gypsies congregate at horse-fairs. Nobody knows their place of origin, and the Lagelouts themselves don't seem to know where they have come from, how soon they are going back or, for that matter, where they are. An old local superstition even has it that they descend from the sky. Linguistic studies have detected a predominantly Northern European influence in their speech, and it has been suggested that their language is a relation of English, albeit a poor one. As with Bretons and Cornish people, there is a persistent tradition that the Lagelouts and the English can make themselves mutually understood, though when one listens closely to the Lagelouts, this is difficult to believe.

The Festival itself has no organised sequence of events, being essentially orgiastic in character. In this it may owe something to the Dionysan and Bacchic traditions of the ancient world, though the Lagelouts themselves know nothing of this, at least at the conscious level. One Lagelout I questioned did say he thought it was 'All fickin' Greek' to him, but it would be unwise to infer too much from this remark. A more likely origin might be found in the Orcadian mid-winter celebration of 'Up-helly', the Lagelout's mid-summer counterpart having become by a simple process of euphony, 'Out-belly'.

Nevertheless, it is clear that Lagelout culture exhibits many of the most enduring features of primitive cultures found throughout the world. Sun-worship is an important element, even to the extent of merging into self-mutilation, as though the Lagelout is engaged in self-preparation as a burnt offering. An element of ritual cleansing is also present, as evidenced by the drinking of large quantities of liquid matter, which, since it is promptly regurgitated, clearly has a function more purgative than nutritive. One further aspect of Lagelout behaviour over which anthropologists are still puzzling is their unique custom of competitive copulation.

Lagelouts keep a tally of their 'score' during the festival, though investigators suggest that many of these 'scores' are unreliable, not to say plain impossible.

Unreliable Scores

However, it is not as a dry academic study but as a colourful piece of pageantry that the tourist can best appreciate the Lagelouts. In their exotic costumes – vests blazoned with strange messages, tri-coloured loin-pieces with their characteristic ethnic design, hair either rampant or cropped out of existence – they are unmistakable. If you follow them, at a safe distance, you may be privileged to hear their tribal chants: 'We ate not in um forest', for instance, harking back to who knows what primeval deprivations; or that fierce yet haunting song marking the rite of passage to manhood, 'You'll never wear cologne.'

There are those who would seek to 'civilise' the Lagelouts, to bring them into the modern world. To me, though, they represent an echo of less complex times, before the world was embroiled in such fiendish complexities as computers, space probes, and joined-up writing.

The Festival Of The Coro Dell'Alba, Rome

When visiting foreign countries, particularly when we are on
holiday and in a relaxed mood, it is tempting to start the day
a little later than usual. Visitors to Rome should try to resist
this urge, at least on one or two occasions, for they run the
risk of missing one of Rome's most spectacular sights and
sounds, the *Coro dell'Alba*, or dawn chorus.

The Italians are an impetuous and life-loving people, and
the return of daylight after the hours of darkness awakes
in them an echo of the old festivals of Primavera, the
celebration which used to accompany the return of Spring.
The *Coro dell'Alba*, however, is a thoroughly modern affair.
All over Rome the citizens, full of joy, jump into their cars
or straddle their scooters and set out for the city centre.
Gradually the roads and streets fill up until the entire city
seems to be a mass of gaily-coloured vehicles. When the
point is reached at which no further progress is possible and
all the vehicles are stationary, the many-timbred horns, or
'*trombe*', begin to be heard, rising to a massive crescendo.
The resulting sound, ascending above the city's ancient
monuments, swirling and echoing round the Colosseum and
the great dome of St Peter's, is something no tourist can ever
forget.

The Festival Of The Air Traffic Controllers

This is one of the truly international festivals of Europe,
transcending all national boundaries, for the Air Traffic
Controllers are an international brotherhood. The festival
usually takes place in the summer months, in late July
or August, though it can sometimes happen quite sponta-
neously at other times such as April or late December.

The Air Traffic Controllers are a secretive cult, and their
arcane rituals are jealously guarded from the eyes of people
outside the order. They are, however, a charitable foundation

whose purposes are to shield the traveller from harm in the tradition of St Christopher. It is necessary for them, therefore, to reimpose the purity of their discipline from time to time, and this is the reason for the festivals. At these times the Air Traffic Controllers go back to the fundamentals of their beliefs, reasserting the primacy of the Book in everything they do. For the duration of the Festival all their words and deeds are dictated by absolute adherence to the literal text which holds the key to their faith, and which no outsider has seen. At the end of the festival the Air Traffic Controllers emerge renewed and rewarded.

Naturally, the lay traveller may be occasionally inconvenienced by the festivals, but he may rest assured in the knowledge that the renewal of faith is in the direct interest of his travelling safety. Indeed, it can be claimed that safety is outstandingly high at festival times, for not only is the Air Traffic Controllers' vigilance at its height, but many would-be travellers have their safety secured by ensuring that the part of their journey which involves actual movement through the air is avoided altogether.

The Ceremony Of The Blessing Of The Imports, Poitiers, France

France, although lacking the ceremonial splendours associated with a Royal family, has, nevertheless, a number of fascinating and rewarding traditions in its more ancient cities. One of the most interesting is that which takes place every day in the Customs Centre at Poitiers in Western France: the Ceremony of the Blessing of the Imports.

The goods to be blessed are brought to Poitiers – which is some distance inland – by road, but are not technically on French soil until they have been inspected, blessed and cleared. Each item, which may be a Japanese video-recorder or a Taiwanese microwave oven, for instance, is brought before one of the *douaniers*, who scrutinises the box with great care and reads details from the the accompanying papers aloud to the assistant *douanier*. Then, flanked by two assistant *douaniers*, he turns smartly and walks with measured tread to the other end of the Customs shed, a distance of some two hundred metres. He halts before the chief *douanier*, salutes, and says, 'Video 5657349 inspected and approved. Permission to release requested.' The chief *douanier* stands, draws his sword and returns the Douanier's salute; and bows his head in symbolic granting of the request. The *douanier*, still flanked by his two assistants, then processes back to the other end of the shed and pronounces the Video-recorder free to enter the Republic of France. The whole ceremony, which takes little more than ten minutes, is then repeated for the next package.

The ceremony has its origins in a more turbulent past, when it was necessary to protect the French people from the importation of undesirable items such as New Zealand butter or hydrogen bombs. Nowadays it remains as an interesting survival of days gone by. It is generously sponsored by French manufacturing companies to ensure that the gentler ways of the past are not entirely forgotten.

The Berlin Wall Game

The Berlin Wall Game is quite unlike the famous Eton Wall Game in that it involves the actual destruction of the wall. This is necessarily a slow process, however, and the tourist anxious to catch a glimpse of this picturesque custom can be assured that it is likely to continue for many years yet.

It can be seen at any time in most stretches of the wall, but is particularly active at the weekends, when large numbers of Berliners gather with picks and other small implements to chip away pieces of the wall. These are then taken away to their homes, which in every case are furnished with equipment for embedding the fragments in clear plastic, and printing presses for printing Certificates of Authenticity. The embedded fragments are then sold internationally, and it seems entirely possible that the wall will prove to be large enough to provide such a memento for every desk and mantelpiece in the world. In this respect the wall may eventually take on a significance similar to that of the True Cross, fragments of which were such a staple of international commerce in the middle ages.

Although the Wall Game can be regarded as a competitive sport, there is no formal declaration of a winner. Among the adherents of the game, however, any player who has accumulated a million marks from wall-related activities is accorded considerable respect. For this reason the Wall Game also has a deep economic and political significance; for the East Berliner travelling West, it is his first glimpse of the miracle of how the market economy works for the universal benefit of mankind.

NOEL PETTY

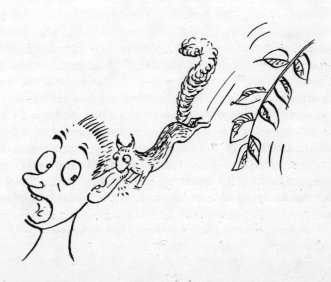

Your Questions Answered

Q. Where does Santa Claus live?
As you can probably see from his name, Santa Claus
was originally Spanish (think of Santa Cruz), but he
is a TRUE European. His reindeer are from Iceland, but
their names, Doner (Greek), Blitzen (German), Bambi
(Dutch) and Prancer (English) show just how Euro-
politan Santa is. In some countries, his name has been
corrupted over the years until it has become 'Saint
Nicholas' or 'Father Christmas'. These kinds of changes
come about because we all speak in slightly different
dialects, and they are just part of the rich tapestry that
comprises our continent. As for where Santa lives, it
is no secret that he lives at the North Pole, which is in
Denmark.

Q. Who is the patron saint of Europe?
St Alban, chosen by Brussels because he has his head
in his hands. In Britain, he is sometimes known as
St Hemel of Hempstead, although it is not known
why.

Q. What is the Orthodox church?
Basically, this is a very ordinary church, very plain,
with no steeples, flying buttresses, frescoes, vestries,
pantries, fonts or anything like that. In fact, it's just an
'orthodox' building. It could be a bus station, or even
a beach-hut. Orthodox churches do not worry about
prayers, hymns, holy water or doctrinal disputes. They
just get on with it, although there is one rule, which is
that priests must wear black and grow beards. You can
find an orthodox church in Greece (the **Greek Orthodox**), Belgium (the **Walloon Orthodox** and the **Fleming
Orthodox**) and also in Liverpool (the **Liverpooldox**).

Q. What are the national costumes of each country?
The Spanish wear a whisk at the waist known as a
Spanish Fly; the Germans wear a hat with a feather

in it, known as a **Deutsch Cap**; the Greeks wear a tunic called a **Hella**, but only on feast days (the rest of the time they are locked away upstairs – 'Hellas – from the Attic'.) The Italians dress for emphasis in **Italics**, beautiful togas which slope from left to right. The British wear shirts and trousers called **Separates**.

Q. *What are the national dances?*
The Irish dance the **Jig**. The British dance the **Morris**. The French dance the **Citroën** (in which oranges and lemons are pressed). The Germans dance the very graceful **Benz**. The Spanish and Portuguese dance the **High Sierra**. The Italians dance the **Fiat Uno**. And the Greeks dance the **Domestica**.

Q. *What are the most famous dishes?*
Contrary to public belief, the French do not subsist entirely on but frogs and snails. Their national dish is ***crapaud dans le trou***, which I believe is very scrummy. The Spaniards eat ***cordobes***, or bully beef. Danes eat

bacon in butter; Greeks eat *feta*, the hooves of local goats. Germans usually eat *brot*, a fish. In Italy, *pisa puddini* is very popular with locals and tourists alike. The Irish serve a wonderful dish of potatoes stewed in Guinness and scrag juice, known locally as *shebeen*.

Q. What are the national instruments?
In Greece, the principal instrument is a **bazooka**, which is played throughout the day, but never on Sunday. The Italians have many instruments – the **cello**, the **viola**, the **cornetto**, the **piano**, the **forte** and the **diminuendo**. Germans are famous for the **handel**, a barrel-organ, and for the **gato**, a Black Forest speciality. The Belgians play percussive instruments like the **hergé** and **tin-tin**. Dutch folk play the **windmill**, heard to great effect on their National Anthem, the 'Hollandaise'. The Spanish play the **olé**, a thin reedy pipe, and the French play the **cor anglais**.

Q. Will Europe ever have a king or queen?
Really, this is a family matter for our queen. You may not realise this, though there is a royal family in every country in Europe, though some of them got bored and handed in their crowns many years ago. In Holland, the royal family goes shopping on bicycles, and the King of Portugal wears a funny hat and tells ribald stories on street corners. The locals salute their royals, but nothing more. They are all related to each other, and to our Queen, who is related to herself in fifteen different ways. Her as-it-were unemployed cousins are known in Debrett's as 'cousins once removed' (like King Constantinopoulos of Greece). Probably King Charles III will be crowned monarch of the continent next century.

BILL GREENWELL

EUROCULTURE

The aspiring European should be well acquainted with his cultural and historical inheritance. This is a very wide field to cover and should be taken gradually. Here are some of the salient points to get you started.

The culture of the Ancient Greeks
  Unites all Europe, so it's said;
And yet how rare it is one speaks
  Of all those celebrated dead;
For Agamemnon, Paris, Helen,
Find little place in Tring or Welwyn.

If you discuss the goddess Hera,
  Compare her lightly with Astarte,
You'll not make conversation clearer
  In any pub or sherry party;
Legends are dead where life is hectic,
Material, and dialectic.

Better recall those other Greeks,
  Fathers of science and research:
So leave Demeter as she seeks
  Persephone by beech and birch
For Archimedes, bath towel round him,
Who ran the streets and cried: 'I've *found* him!'

It's true the gods were far more flighty;
  They loved their triangles of love:

Hephaistos once with Aphrodite
  Netted poor Ares from above;
But this has lost its power to stagger us:
For triangles, we need Pythagoras.

And as for nets, why, let us give
  Our thoughts to Eratosthenes
Whose justly celebrated Sieve
  Possesses virtue that can please;
For in a way that outlasts time
It shows which numerals are Prime.

Pierian Muses, sink your breath
  Into your fountain's deepest basement;
Galen will certify your death
  And Archimedes your displacement;
For now, when verse is in request,
Euclid's name will be addressed.

Farewell then, nymphs of trees and springs;
  Farewell to you, O Cytherean;
Let ancient scientists be kings –
  They too were born in the Aegean:
Theirs the uniting culture sent
To countries of our continent.

PAUL GRIFFIN

Lost Marbles

When Britain and Greece and the rest
Put full market links to the test
Will the Greeks count the cost
Of the marbles they lost
Or think they are jointly possessed?

KATIE MALLETT

Though the Venus de Milo is armless
She's nevertheless far from charmless.
   Even chiselled in stone
   Her erogenous zone
Is highly suggestive, if harmless.

STANLEY J. SHARPLESS

History Repeated

One day, in a field near Pompeii,
Edward lay with his girl in the hay.
When Vesuvius erupted
She cried out: 'Get up, Ted –
I don't want to get stuck this way!'

E.O. PARROTT

The Romance Of The Rose – An Insight

Some European countries consider that they possess indig-
enous cultures, and it seemed important at this stage to
understand them. I therefore wrote to an educated French
lady, asking if she would explain one of their great poems of
the Middle Ages. This was her reply:

You demand me that I describe the intrigue of the
grand French poem of middle age: 'The Romance of
the Rose'. It necessitates first that you comprehend
figures of metaphor. When the poet visits the Garden
of Funny Laughter it does not concern itself nor with
poet nor with garden. It is the life that is figure.
   After deities disporting, one bud of rose has spotted

itself to our man, in a basin where jets of water propel themselves. He sees not the bud but as in a mirror. The rose is figure of dame. Our poet wishes to arrive at her, but he is interfered with by personages not truly personages: Ashamedness, Boss, Incorrect Seeming, Thinkful, and Jealousness.

Cupidon shoots at him flitches and depends our man to him. His advice how to penetrate? One must find servile female and corrupt her with winepot.

But jealousness becomes constructor and undertakes battlements in surround of the desired. Alas! no penetration!

Not all there, is what to comprehend of these figures, of the dames, of the belief, of the society; but that which rests gives much severity.

PAUL GRIFFIN

A Very Early Tourist

At King Arthur's court, bold Sir Lancelot
And Queen Guinevere used to dance a lot,
  They both got so zealous
  That Arthur grew jealous,
So he sent Lancelot off to France a lot

STANLEY. J. SHARPLESS

When Giotto
Got blotto
His sense of perspective
Became defective.

RON RUBIN

I learned in an art class
That G.A. Beltraffio
Copied his master,
Adhered to his style.

His master, da Vinci,
Said: 'That's enough flattery –
Imitate somebody
Else for a while.'

BRUCE E. NEWLING

'That's enough flattery . . .'

Christopher Columbus
Wasn't much good at rumbas,
But as for his samba –
Caramba!

RON RUBIN

Airily-fairily
Madame de Maintenon
Made the remark, 'After me comes the flood'.
Did she foresee, maybe,
Ultraclairvoyantly
Guillotines dripping with upper-class blood?

BASIL RANSOME-DAVIES

M. Guillotin made his Rex ex.
He divided, and ruled, either sex.
　His capital cutter
　Would slice, as through butter,
Pierres from their Robes, and their nex.

BILL GREENWELL

As Asia is the source of copra,
A coconut derivative,
So Italy's the home of opera:
It really hits them where they live.
An ultra-extroverted nation,
Their attitude is 'play it loud',
And calm, reflective contemplation
Is not for them. They like a crowd.
While *Rigoletto* or *Aïda*
May blow their minds in Rome and Florence,
I'd rather sit and quietly read a
Mucky book by D. H. Lawrence.

BASIL RANSOME-DAVIES

Clattery, battery,
Ludwig van Beethoven
Banged on the keyboard, re-
Gardless of clef;

Some thought his music was
Superterrestrial,
Others said crossly: 'The
Man must be deaf.'

MARY HOLTBY

Although Louis Pasteur
Was an obsessive voyeur,
He'd much rather watch the fermentation of cheese
Than strip-tease.

RON RUBIN

Said Gaugin, inflamed by *vin sec*:
'Paris gives me a pain in the neck.
  I'm off to Tahiti
  Where the girls are more meaty;
I've nothing Toulouse but Lautrec.'

STANLEY J. SHARPLESS

You cannot hope to warp or twist
The vision of a Dadaist,
Who turns into subversive jokes
What makes good sense to normal blokes.
Why bother to unhinge his brain?
The man's already quite insane.

BASIL RANSOME-DAVIES

'I can't make out what that is,'
Complained Matisse;
'Is thasso?'
Replied Picasso.

GERARD BENSON

The Stalinisation of Albania
Was a sort of a mania
Of Enver Hoxha.
He was a terrible old coxha.

PAUL GRIFFIN

O, Mann!

Niminy-piminy,
Gustav von Aschenbach
Sighs for a stripling
As seaward he slips;

Torn by this touch of the
Extracurricular,
Takes to cosmetics and
Hands in his chips.

MARY HOLTBY

Observe this photograph of Munich:
The *Führer* in a well-cut tunic
And Chamberlain demure beneath
His spectacles, moustache and teeth.
A European love affair!
Yet all too soon the happy pair
(So fickle is the human heart)
Discovered they were Poles apart.

BASIL RANSOME-DAVIES

higgledy-piggledy
Cinéma vérité
Took the approach of a fly on the wall
With the result that its
Cinematography
Captured the essence of nothing at all

BASIL RANSOME-DAVIES

Hoitily-toitily
Victor Emmanuel
Told Mussolini, 'I'm ending our fling.'
As a result of his
Impetuosity
Italy now has no Duce or King.

BASIL RANSOME-DAVIES

From the land of the sild and the brisling
Came a venomous traitor called Quisling.
Does he know that his name
Is a symbol of shame,
In the hell where he's currently sizzling?

BASIL RANSOME-DAVIES

Your Questions Answered

Q. Is there a connection between the Common Market and the Eurovision Song Contest?

Yes. A long and proud one. An early winner of the Song Contest was the Copenhagen songstress, Dana, for instance. The Spanish entry by Massiel won the competition with a song written entirely in French ('*La la la, la la la*'). The French singer, Lulu, once won the competition with a wonderful ditty about the likely consequences of excessive consumer expenditure upon the exchange markets, a number called 'Boom Bang-a-Bang' which had a profound effect upon EEC thinking. There is something surprising, perhaps this question hints, at the fact that Morocco, Israel, Turkey and Yugoslavia, amongst others, are involved. Well, all one can say is that, if they are not 'in Europe', they SHOULD be, and they are bound to join the Common Market one day soon. So the Eurovision Song Contest is always looked upon as a very forward-looking, even prophetic institution. That is why one perennial loser is a spoof country called 'The Ostrich' '*L'Autriche*') – it's Europe's way of telling the world that we should not stick our heads in the sand.

Q. What is the cultural capital of Europe?

Most emphatically, **Venice**. This is the haunting city where such classics as *Don't Look Now, Death In Venice, The Sea, The Sea* and *The Riddle of the Sands* were set. There is nothing like wandering its narrow cobbled streets with the local guides, the gondoliers, singing their merry songs. There is the beautiful Cathedral of St Mark, with its cheerful *campanile* and her pigeons flocking to meet you. There is that wonderful cloth shop, the Harris Bar, where tweed is woven before your very eyes. This is where the Doge ruled, where the Venice Glass hangs beneath the Bridge of Sighs, where the Venice de Milo was found, where blinds were invented, and where Ruskin sat eating the local delicacy – stag, or *venison* as we know it. A city that should be on *everyone's* itinerary!

BILL GREENWELL

. . . flock to meet you . . .

EUROCRATS

The administrative centres of the EEC, in Brussels and Strasbourg, have sometimes attracted unfavourable comment from uninformed sections of the British press. The good European will ignore this; one has only to look at the work of these bodies in detail to see that it is solely for our benefit.

A Contract For Fish Sticks

It is not true that life in the EEC is more complicated than it used to be. To prove the point, here is part of the new, simplified form of the contract required by those people who wish to purchase fish sticks. These contracts may be signed, witnessed and ratified in the presence of a member of the EEC legal department at most supermarket check-outs. What could be more straightforward than that?

MEMORANDUM of Agreement made this . . . . . day of . . . . . 19.. between . . . . . (hereinafter called the purchaser) of the first part and . . . . . . (hereinafter called the vendor) of the second part.

WHEREBY it is mutually agreed as follows respecting an item of comestibles required by the said purchaser and at present known as 6 FRY-UP FISH STICKS, hereinafter referred to as the goods.

1. The vendor shall during the legal term defined by the sell-by date provide the purchaser with the goods at a price not greater than . . . . . .

2. The vendor may offer the goods at a discount which may (or may not) vary between 15% and 3% of the recommended retail price at any moment up to and including a valid check-out, which shall be defined by the point mid-way between the entrance to the check-out channel and its exit. A check-out shall be deemed to be valid when a check-out person is in attendance at a till.

2a. A check-out person shall be identified by a plastic lapel badge which may (or may not) bear the name or identification of that person. The check-out person shall be considered to be in attendance at a till when seated and signed on by a supervisor. (See EEC form SM/003/5 for regulations governing relations between supervisors and check-out persons.)

2b. The purchaser hereby agrees not to enter into conversation with a check-out person.

3. The purchaser hereby warrants to the vendor that the said goods shall be referred to only as FISH STICKS and not as FISH FINGERS or by any other name regardless of the fact that such a name may contain the word FISH.

4. The vendor hereby agrees to consume the said goods on or before the sell-by date. The consumption of the goods shall only be deemed valid when completed by the named purchaser or by other persons referred to by name in clause 17c.

N.J. WARBURTON

Lingua Franca

'If only we spoke a common tongue', I sighed,
Brooding over the European map;
'We've got one already', the Brussels man replied,
'In daily use. We call it Eurocrap'.

STANLEY J. SHARPLESS

Food for Thought

When the animal's dead
And they've cut off his head
And the rest has gone off for its quartering,
   You will see at your feet
   A mass of 'Green Meat' –
For that's what they call it in Slaughtering.

   We in Feeds are not fools:
   We know all the rules
Which forbid using Green Meat for food,
   So we send it away
   To a firm near Marseilles
On whose business we never intrude.

   I can't undertake
   To say what they make;
If I asked them I doubt if they'd tell it;
   They're all part, you see,
   Of 'Hans Gartner A. G. –
Eurocake, Eurograin, Europellet!'

   The meal we import
   Is a very good sort
Sent from Gartners, just south of Treviso;
   It's a quality feed
   Of a kind guaranteed
By a paper that swears it to be so.

   In your magazine, please
   Don't speak of disease;
Think of each Euro-state as a partner;
   This affair's made our boss
   So terribly cross.
You'd like him. His name is Hans Gartner.

PAUL GRIFFIN

Harmonisation of Breathing

In spite of strenuous government denials, there is a very strong rumour in Brussels that, following on from the Euro-standards applied to air pollution, the lung intake of every adult individual is to be graded, on a scale from one to ten. (Children under the age of 18 will be exempt from the grading, which it is thought will eventually result in a new air tax). A fully grown 6 foot, 16 stone weightlifter is thought to have a lung capacity of 9.62 litres, to put him at the top of the scale at ten, whereas a small-boned woman would have a capacity of only 3.1 litres at the rating of one.

First to receive the grading (by means of an external valve device) will be the members of the Europarliament, followed closely by each country's representatives in the home parliaments.

Members of the British Parliament are said to be worried about the effect of hot air on the dials, and have demanded a recount.

Meanwhile, electronic measuring device manufacturers are secretly getting ready for the new regulation, under cover of making pumps for central heating systems.

The Green Party have expressed an interest, stating that tax rebates should be available for those compelled to breathe polluted air.

KATIE MALLETT

Though Euro-MPs want it *their* ways,
They seldom agree which are fair ways,
    But their comings and goings
    In various Boeings
Are a wonderful boon for the airways.

PAUL GRIFFIN

From the Office of the European Commissioner for Culture.

AN ORDER OF SERVICE FOR A MEETING TO PLAN AN EXCHANGE VISIT BETWEEN THE CHOIRS OF ANY TWO TWINNED TOWNS IN EUROPE

When any such visit is to be planned, the committee of the host choir shall gather around the dining table of The Chair, who shall be of either gender and shall for many years have maintained a relationship of bantering distrust with The Conductor.

The Chair shall ask whether anyone has heard from Donald, who is supposed to have collected brochures extolling the beauty of the locality from the Council Offices and there shall be negative, humorously irritated murmurings from those present.

Then shall The Chair say:
DEARLY beloved, forasmuch as it is two years since we visited n or m, it has come to pass that the choir of n or m is to pay us a return visit.

The People shall respond,
Oh God, not again!
OR:
Doesn't time fly, is it really two years?
OR:
Heavens, I've been meaning to write and thank Françoise and now she'll be here before I get round to it.
OR:
Just when I've got the builders in.

The Chair, smiling tolerantly, shall continue,
Whereas two years ago we sang Elijah with the choir of n or m in the cathedral of n or m, now it shall come to pass that they will join with us in doing Messiah in the great squash court at the sports centre.

And The People shall respond,
I enjoyed Messiah – the first hundred and fifty times.

OR:

The squash court brings on my hay fever.

OR:

Can they sing English well enough?

OR:

Is Ian conducting, or their man?

And the Chair shall say,
Their man, it is his turn.

And with one voice the people shall say,
It'll go on all night.

And The Chair shall say,
Verily we are not here to talk about music, for unless we get down to planning a programme there will be a vain and sanguinous shambles. There remaineth a scant five weeks before the Itinerary must be typed and photocopied and sent to n or m, and ere that time shall have elapsed we must book the coaches and any other transport which may be deemed meet, fix the reception with the Mayor . . .

The people shall cry,
Those awful long speeches!

The Chair shall implacably continue,
. . . and decide who shall be responsible for the food.

And The Conductor shall intervene thus,
May I point out through The Chair that I shall expect two full rehearsals each week unto the time of the visitation so that we may most certainly and confidently show them that we are a better choir than they are.

And Some One shall say,
We can sing Messiah in our sleep.

And The Conductor shall riposte,
Yea, verily, and doth it sound like it!

Amidst laughter The Chair shall remark,
Witty as ever Ian. But we must renounce light and foolish pleasures. What dost Thou, Treasurer, have to say?

The Treasurer, in a voice rich with years of cigars and cautionary speeches, shall declare,
These international high jinks always go over budget. If this one runs true to form the sinking fund will sink out of sight.

And The Librarian shall muse,
I suppose we do have to invite them.

And The Chair shall say,
The invitation was given formally at the end of the post-concert dinner at n or m two years ago. Verily, if we renege, World War Three will erupt. Forasmuch as they will arrive on the Friday Night in two batches according to when they can get off work, we shall meet them, take them to our several homes and give them a good meal.

And the Deputy-Treasurer shall say,
They fed and watered us well last time.

And The Chair shall say,
Exactly my point, brethren. It behoveth us not to let the side down.

And the Publicity Person shall say,
Fridays is my Origami class.

And the Chair shall say,
Dost thou believe in International Goodwill? Then must Thou renounce all private convenience. Saturday morning there shall be a rehearsal of all the choruses . . .

And the Treasurer shall interpose,
With or without orchestra?

And the Conductor shall respond,
Can we afford it with?

And The Treasurer shall state,
No.

The Chair shall continue,
. . . Saturday afternoon shall be free with the proviso that if the morning goes badly we shall rehearse again. The Concert

is in the evening. That looks after Saturday. Sunday night is the Mayoral Reception. Which leaves just that day to fill up.

The Federation Person shall say,
They took us sailing on Lake n or m.

And The Secretary shall say,
I enjoyed that. The buffet was smashing.

And The Publicity Person shall say,
What about the canal?

And The Treasurer shall say,
We can't crowd them on to a public boat and a special hire will cost a bomb.

And the Federation Person shall say,
We have to push the boat out sometimes. As it were.

And The Chair shall ask,
Would the Council give us a grant, do you think? Seeing it's a twinning project.

The People shall laugh hollowly.

The Librarian shall say,
It will probably rain. It usually does.

And The Chair shall say,
It rained when we were on Lake n or m, remember. I was quite pleased. I didn't feel so bad about our weather.

Then shall The Chair smile brightly, say that much useful progress has been made and declare the meeting closed.

TOM AITKEN

Eurobaffled

The E.R.M. fills all my dreams,
The ECU haunts my nights.
I spend my hours of fitful sleep
In frantic fiscal flights.
From deutschmarks to the gallic franc,
And lira to the schilling,
I try to fathom out what's what
(Mind weak, though spirit willing).

But really, all I want to know,
When all is said and done,
Is what my pound coin will be worth
When the Eurograb's begun.

KATIE MALLETT

Must I alone ask it:
Why in a basket?
What have matters monetary
To do with punnetry?

MARY HOLTBY

Your Questions Answered

Q. Why is The Common Market so called?
Because it replaced an organisation called The Common Wealth. There is a great deal of confusion about this. Joining the Market did not mean that Britain lost its Wealth, merely that it had to share it with others. Of course, the others have to share what was formerly *their* Wealth with us (which, if you think of Germany, is not too bad).

Q. What is The Treaty of Rome all about?
Probably you are thinking about The Treaty of **Frome** (an easy mistake to make). Frome is a Somerset village in which the locals struck a bargain whereby they could make a new cheese, in honour of the Common Market, which was a mixture of French Brie and Danish Blue. (The cheese is soft and sticky, like Brie, but with tangy blue bits in it.) The locals got permission, but their original choice of name, **'Fromage'**, had to be turned down when it was discovered that there was already a little-known French cheese of the same name. It is now called Lymeswold, after a local farmer, and very nice it is, too.

Q. What does the European Parliament do?
This august institution lies at the Common Market's heart, and takes care of all the political matters. For instance, it has to decide where each country's borders lie, how many political parties there are, and who should sit with whom when they're discussing important issues (like Borders). This is not easy. For instance, the word 'Liberal' means something very different in each country. The European Parliament has to sort out the Right-Wing liberals from the Left-Wing Liberals, and that takes patience. The Parliament also has to pass Laws, for instance that only Britain could call its Ice Cream 'Ice Cream' where everyone else had to call it 'Vegetable Fat'. Perhaps this example shows

you just how important the European Parliament is. It also does a lot of food tasting, which is vital for our health.

Q. What is an EEC Commissioner?
Commissioners are appointed to see if any countries are committing crimes which break European Laws. Europe has its very own court, the European Court of Human Rights, and the commissioners make sure that no country is committing a Wrong. After all, you can't have a proper European country filling its prisons with innocent victims, as in South America. So when, for instance, Spain applied to join the Common Market, the commissioners went straight round and said 'That's enough of this Inquisition business', and they had to stop it there and then.

Incidentally, commissioners are known by the country from which they come. Ours is called Sir Lion Britain, and is the son of the very famous Vera Britain.

Q. What is the Common Fisheries Policy?
There are several rules which govern fishing in Europe. For instance, Luxembourg is entirely forbidden to send out fishing-boats, because it has no border with the sea. There is a minimum mesh size, so that sprats, tiddlers, sticklebacks, dolphins and other small fish are not hunted to extinction (this is where the phrase 'net catch' comes from; gross catches are entirely against the rules). There was some resistance to this Policy at first, especially in those states where they had been using sprats to catch mackerel, but the sprat is now thought to be safe. The prawn cocktail is the only small fish that trawlers are allowed to hunt, since it is so popular, and a quick look inside every European restaurant will confirm that there are plenty to go round.

Entirely Forbidden

Q. What is 'The Snake'?

The Snake (or, to give it its full name, the European Monetary Snake) is the way money is kept in order inside the Common Market. In Brussels a large wicker contraption (the so-called Basket of Currencies) is hung from the ceiling of the central counting-room. In it there are special compartments, each of which is filled daily with one mark, one franc, one peseta, one 10p and so on. At eleven o'clock, and on the hour until teatime, news is flashed to Brussels about how much money is being spent in every European country. If (for instance) Germany is spending more than everyone else, then a small weight is added to the German compartment, and a note is made of the fact. Then, and this is the clever bit, a small weight is added to all the other compartments, so that all the currencies are equal, news of which is sent to all the exchanges, *cambios* and *wechsels*.

It is called 'The Snake' because the person who puts in the weight is known as an 'adder' (in France the official is known as *le chevalier*, a play on *ajouter* (to add) and *jouter* (to joust) – just one more example of

how rich and diverse our senses of humour are in the
European Community.)

Q. Will Europe have its own currency one day?
After no end of argument between the member states,
this question has now definitely been decided. Every
single country will have an **ECU** (European Cash
United) – *ecu* actually *means* money in France, so
this is indeed a happy coincidence. In Britain, the
ECU will be known as a *'pound '*, in Germany a *'mark '*,
in France a *'franc '*, in Italy *'lire '*, in Spain a *'peseta '*, in
Greece a *'drachma '* and in Ireland a *'doubloon '*. The
others are still deciding, although Belgium is believed
to have opted for the **'poirot '**.

Q. Will we all have to measure things differently in Europe?
Of course. But there is no need to be afraid, because
other countries will have just as much difficulty adopting
some of our measurements (it is a rule that we have
to share things out fairly). Although we will have to
use 'avoirdupois' to weigh our vegetables, this will
also tax the Greeks who naturally wished to use Troy
weights. Besides, some of the changes are not nearly as
mysterious as they seem – **hectares** is just an anagram
of **the acres**. It would be nice if we could do this with
all measurements, but **inches** is an anagram of **chiens**,
and this might well lead to some confusion!

Q. Will we get rabies when we join the Single Market?
Rabies is carried by the continental bunny, the **rabit**,
and it has sometimes been known to spread through
contaminated lettuce. In Europe, however, the main
party is called The Greens, and they hope to have it
under control soon.

Q. What is the French agricultural policy of 'remembrement'?
I forget.

BILL GREENWELL

EUROCHARGE

All over Britain 1992 fever is beginning to stir, as all sections of society prepare.

The book world has not been slow to rise to the challenge of Europe. It has, however, had some hard thinking to do about its usual lines of best-sellers. How can these be made more European? How, in particular, can the Royal Family be made to fit the bill?

Here are some extracts from a few of the forthcoming Euro-friendly titles soon to be found in our bookshops:

Diary of a European Country Lady

June 4th ... Tea and crumpets after a gruelling day under the lights filming our Christmas message. We can't remember it taking so long before. Probably because we had to repeat the whole thing in a succession of the most throat-wrenching languages. Really, we felt as if we were trying to spit our tonsils out half the time. We hope the translation people have done their job properly. We have no idea what we were saying most of the time but some of it *sounded* rather rude.

June 11th ... A sweet little toady from Euro-channel came round with what he called the 'rushes'. It all sounded awfully urgent. P went off in a huff and wouldn't watch. He says he doesn't hold with talking to wops, frogs and the like. It's all right for him, though. He doesn't have to 'front the show' and can get by with standing around with his hands behind his back and looking faintly bored.

We don't mind being monarch of a complete country but to be a monarch of one *part* of a community is really spreading royalty rather too thinly in our opinion. After all, our country is very good at royalty. And royalty, we feel, is something we can offer to the rest of Europe. Must make a note of that for next year's broadcast. (We did suggest to the toady that it might be 'cut in' this year but he would say nothing but 'No way'. Apparently they'd have to trim something off the Christmas message of the EEC Commissioners and it would take till Easter to work out what.)

June 15th ... We have had a chat with the family and they've come up with some jolly good suggestions which might help to make Europe a kingdom rather than a mere community. D says community does sound so *common*. The Common Market, full of commoners. She can't really believe that that is what our subjects *really* want. (Good, coming from her, we thought.) The PR suggested that we might dabble in a little export business. Some countries in Europe have never had a proper monarch of their very own, she said. Or, as we pointed out to her, they have somehow managed to lose them. Anyway, we have plenty of spares and perhaps we ought to be prepared to loan some out on a long-term basis. E is young but could probably rule a smallish country quite nicely and wouldn't be missed terribly ...

The Royal Adventures of Dibby the Dago

Hallo. It's terrifically easy to write a book for kiddies and to prove it I've whizzed a few off for you. They're all about the Euro-thing and they're bags of jolly fun too. If you know a kiddie why not get hold of it and read it one of these wonderfully original yarns, OK? As well as Dibby the Dago, there's Fudgie the Frog and Kobbo the Kraut. There might be a few more too when they let me know what the other Euro-places are. Well, that's enough from me, so on with the

exciting story of Dibby and how he comes to fancy a sweet
little thing called ... Chuddy, I think it was. Or Cruddy.
Anyway, here goes –
    'One day, as Dibby was bobbing along ...'
    (This is probably enough to give a flavour. Ed.)

A Vision of Europe

During one's travels in Europe, one has been appalled at the
absolute bloody awful state of buildings in some European
countries. (This includes ours, one has to say.) Bits of stone
lying about all over the place in Athens, ugly great iron
contraptions sticking up in the middle of Paris. That kind
of thing. Absolute bloody disgrace. You might think that
that's what you want but, one can assure you, you don't.
Not really.

    This is why one is starting a 'Prince's Vision of Europe'
Fund and top of the list is that ghastly monstrosity in Pisa.
Not only does the thing look like a stack of fastfood pizzas
(hence the name, very probably) but it's also not even up
straight. Bloody shoddy workmanship, no two ways about
it, and it ought to be put to rights ...

                                        N. J. WARBURTON

1992 On the Newsstands

Editorials from a selection of magazines and newspapers

Women's Weekly
1992 is just around the corner. But that doesn't mean we'll
all have to put garlic into our homely cottage pies, and
olive oil on everything. Europe is more than just strange
foreign food and people with dark eyes who wave their
arms about when they talk. In the next few weeks we're

going to look at what 1992 means to *Women's Weekly* readers, with serious articles on European knitting – the latest yarns: Crumpets and crêpes – tasty tea-time treats from Cremona to Cleethorpes: and short stories set where the language is Romance. All you need to know about Europe from your favourite weekly.

Cosmopolitan

1992 – and the barriers are down to Europe's hottest men. With easier travel you can have a lover in every EEC state and still run your London-based company. Worried about your stamina (and who wouldn't be with all Europe asking for it!)? Follow Cosmo's 5-day Euro-diet, and you'll be ready for anyone – anywhere.

Amateur Gardening

1992 won't spell the end of clematis wilt, carrot fly, or clubroot, but will give us a chance to swap 'tips and wrinkles' with gardeners across the Channel. When the fences come down you see more of folk, and can pick up some handy ideas. In next week's issue the French show us they know their onions, and our eesi-pull-out supplement is on Dutch ways with cabbage. Will calabrese crop in Catalonia? Does deutzia do well in Dusseldorf? Can buddleia blossom in Bari? Look in next week's Euro-number and find out.

Psychic News

1992 is knocking on our doors: everywhere poltergeists are preparing for the onslaught and spirits are summoning up their spectral beings. Language is no barrier in the spirit world, neither are walls or doors. Next week: Gubbio and ghosts – a spirit-hunter speaks out; Belgian banshees and French phantoms – a re-appraisal; Gremlins in the Gobelins – the undead of the Uffizi corridors.

The *Sun!*
Wotcha!
1992 – and it's HELLO to hell-raisers across the Channel.

With everything free 'n' easy, Britain can let it all hang out, Continental-style.

Nothing to pay and nothing in the way – as cheeky Cheryl shows us on Page 3. Ooh-la-lady!

The *Financial Times*
1992 marks the completion of the EC internal market, propounded in the SEA of July 1987 and good news for GATT, UCITS, the EEIG and the ECU, although the EMS was starting to falter this week with the latest reports from IDIS.

D. A. PRINCE

Union Jack

To The Editor,
The Times

Dear Sir,

In planning for the understandable celebrations which will take place all over Europe next year, I fear that one most important factor may be overlooked. Our national flag – I refer to the good old Union Jack – is going to be hoisted in a lot of European towns, and in my experience these foreign Johnnies seldom manage to get it the right way up. The consequences, of course, could be disastrous, with any British motorist who happens to be passing dashing into the local Mairie or Stadthuis to try to find the fire that needs putting out or the person who needs rescuing.

May I diffidently put forward my solution to this problem? We should take a leaf out of the book of the chaps who export crates of goods abroad. If we were to amend the flag by the addition of a black umbrella in the centre, it would not only eliminate errors of this type, but also enhance our national standard with a potent symbol of our culture.

Yours faithfully,
Col. G. G. Pharthingale (retd.)

NOEL PETTY

WfNWatson)

WHICH Trading Bloc?

Extract from a Consumers Association Special Report

1992 – and trade barriers are down in Europe, for better or worse.

How is the EEC wearing after 25 Years? Is it still good value for money? We looked at its performance, and asked: Is Euro-citizenship still our Best Buy?

The EEC provides adaptable living space, and is easily extended to accommodate a growing family. Starting in 1957 with six living modules, it now has twelve. Surveyors found some ties weaker than we would like (Brussels has yet to concern itself with the standards of ties between countries) 'though the 1960s problem of subsidence in the French corner has largely been overcome.

Although the overall boundary line is untidy – a problem

caused by unco-ordinated bolt-on components – we still liked its flexibility and adaptable profile. But the shape remains a problem: it's not aerodynamic, and no one in our survey could draw an outline map of the EEC. We think Brussels should remedy this and give the EEC a stronger visual identity for consumers: at present consumers identify too closely with their own unit-area (country) and this is a structural weakness that could lead to rusting.

Sadly the EEC is not proving as economical as we'd expected, and the running costs are now prohibitive. A current average of ten tonnes of photo-copier paper per discussion document, and 2002 million expenses-claimed miles per resolution is too high, while housing costs (Brussels and Strasbourg) have risen above inflation levels.

The road-holding qualities of the EEC remain good, but it is slow to corner, often taking several years to negotiate a simple ruling. Speed has never been its top selling point – and zero-to-Single Market in 25 years is not impressive. And while it provides a comfortable ride for bureaucrats in cushioned seats, it offers far less comfort for passengers, particularly in the back seat. It is notoriously lax on child restraint (see *Rod, Pole or a Good Hiding?* Feb., 1990).

Because the EEC has no competitors we feel consumers are deprived of the right to exercise their consumer choice: once locked in to the EEC it is difficult to get out. We'd like the Monopolies Commission to look into this, and especially at some of the more restrictive practices – VAT, for example. But uniformity has advantages – you can now get Diet Coke in Delphi, and Cornettos in Cordova as a result of our recent campaigns.

Does it give value for money? We rocked the boat 6,000 times by putting this question to over 6,000 EEC staff. While we couldn't find anyone to give a firm answer to this question we did learn that a working party of 3,000 economists, and 5,000 support clerical staff (excluding translators) using 2,000 photo-copiers, are currently investigating this issue, and hope to present an interim report in 2002.

D.A. PRINCE

*Even in the small country town of Mughampton, every organisation
and individual is playing a part.*

*An extract from the minutes of the Europeanisation Sub-Committee
of Mughampton Borough Council, in Room D of the Town Hall.*

THE CHAIRMAN, in his inaugural address, reminded members that the Council foresaw vast changes in the British way of life in 1992. Britain would become more European, and Mughampton wanted to be in the lead. A large number of projects had been suggested, some of which were already well under way, and this special committee had been set up to supervise these, and initiate many more. It was an exciting brief, and he was proud to have been chosen to lead the team.

MRS RENÉ HEAVYSIDE asked if his selection had anything to do with his being in the same Masonic Lodge as the Chairman of the Council, but was ruled out of order.

THE SECRETARY reported upon some of the existing projects:

a) The public's response to the introduction of some continental dishes to the Meals on Wheels Service was disappointing. Several clients had broken their dentures on the pizza, and the *escargots* had given rise to a particularly strong protest. However the Committee would be pleased to learn that Meals Assistant Mrs Marcia Palmer would be leaving hospital next week. The Meals van was off the road at present, for two days, whilst bortsch was removed from the petrol tank.

b) Mr Frederick Gudge, owner of 'Fred's Place' on the Mughampton By-Pass, had written to say that he had been forced to discontinue his Continental Breakfast, owing to a lack of interest on the part of his customers in the long-distance transport industry. A lorry-driver, 'Big Jim'Oakes, was to appear in the Magistrates' Court

Meals on Wheels

next week charged with assault on Mr Gudge and the
wilful destruction of 179 bottles of brown sauce and 98
bottles of tomato ketchup. The fire brigade had had to
be called to rescue Mr Gudge from the café roof.

c)   Mr Rummage had returned from an investigative visit
to Denmark with a view to extending the range of
magazines and other literature on sale in Mughampton.
More samples than anticipated had been obtained, and
the necessary extra funds had been despatched to
Copenhagen.

COUNCILLOR RUMMAGE said he was grateful for
the assistance of an ad hoc reading sub-committee
recruited from the Mughampton Rugby Club. An offer
of further assistance from the ladies of the WI had been
turned down, as the present sub-committee had more
than enough volunteers.

THE MUGHAMPTON OPERA HOUSE PROJECT

THE CHAIRMAN said that this was the most ambitious project to date, but the Council had become aware that many continental cities of any consequence had at least one Opera House, and Mughampton could not allow itself to remain a cultural desert. Councillors Mrs Lydia Bellows and Mr Jolyon Jollyboy were even now on a fact-finding tour of Europe. At present they were in Salzburg, and intended travelling on to Vienna, Milan and Monte Carlo, where, it was understood, there might be opera houses for them to visit.

E.O. PARROTT

From the Mughampton Sun

MARBLES MISHAP

Mughampton's marbles team failed to play its scheduled fixture at Chaton-sur-Mer because its marbles went missing. The players, in the charge of Euro-trotting Councillor Jolyon Jollyboy, were said to be 'in high spirits' at the ship's bar on the crossing to France, and during some heavy horse-play the star player, Reg Froth, had his trousers pulled off. When he got them back the team's marbles, which had been in his pocket, could not be found. On arrival at Chaton the team was offered substitute *billes* to play with, but declined on the ground that these might have been 'doctored'. This accusation infuriated the Frenchmen, and the Mughamptonians beat an ignominious retreat. On their return home, Councillor Nathaniel Muffin, who had refused to go on the trip said: 'I could have told those Frogs at the start that this lot had lost their marbles anyway.'

PETER VEALE

Mughampton Gnome Works Staff Committee

Minutes Of Extraordinary Meeting Of Sub-Committee On 'Project Europe'

Present:
J.B. Clatworthy – General Manager (Chairman)
F.H.C. Harcourt-Jones – Marketing
Miss J.W. Johnson – Design
P.K. Prodwind – Production
F.P. Smoothie – Personnel
F. Tonks – Paint Shop Convener
Mrs S. Wilkinson – Secretary

1. Introduction
Mr Clatworthy welcomed everyone to the first meeting of the sub-committee. He made no apology for starting with a short speech to stress the need for the sub-committee to exercise real vision, to raise its sights above the mundane matters which had sometimes bogged down the Works Committee in the past. The task before the sub-committee now was part of the historic mission to weld together a great continent, and Little Mughampton Gnome Works should not be found wanting.

2. Administrative Matters
Mr Tonks pointed out that in the Works Committee minutes which had set up the sub-committee his name had appeared after that of the Secretary, who was not in fact a full member of the sub-committee, but only an observer and reporter. Mr Clatworthy regretted the oversight. It was agreed that the correct sequence of names should be that of the Chairman, followed by the full members in alphabetical order, followed by the Secretary.

3. Europization
The Chairman outlined the history of the Company, which, though illustrious, had hitherto been confined to its native shores. The opportunity of Europe was now wide open,

and he invited those present to start the proceedings with
a brainstorm on how the Company's product range might
be Europized for 1992.

After a false start, it was explained by Mr Smoothie to
Mr Tonks that it was implicit in the idea of a brainstorm
that laughter at other members' suggestions was inhibiting
to the creative process. Mr Tonks promptly apologised to
Mr Prodwind and the session resumed, yielding the following
ideas for further evaluation and scrutiny:

Germany
Mr Harcourt-Jones expressed the view that little modification
would be required for the German market, since garden
gnomes were culturally based on Bavarian traditions anyway.
He cited the legend of Snow White and the Seven Dwarfs in
support, which led to a brief reminiscence of his childhood
by Mr Clatworthy. Mr Tonks' suggestion of the addition of
a small toothbrush moustache was thought not to be in the
spirit of 1992.

France
A Gallic gnome was not thought to present too much of
a problem. Miss Johnson believed that a modification of
the mould to flatten the peaked hat into beret form would
be quite feasible, and Mr Tonks said that the Paint Shop's
resources were up to the job of a striped sweater. There was
some doubt about whether Mr Prodwind's idea of placing
a small frog under the toadstool would be received in
a properly good-humoured spirit, and Mr Harcourt-Jones
undertook to do additional market research in the area of
French humour.

Spain
Miss Johnson's idea of using the cultural icon of a matador
was welcomed enthusiatically. The addition of a cape would
be no problem, and the gnome's tunic and trousers could
be painted as a multi-coloured 'suit of lights'. Mr Tonks
expressed severe reservations about the demands that this
would place on the Paint Shop, but agreed that resistance
might be overcome by a new agreement on overtime rates

and skill-related payments. Miss Wikinson intervened at this point, saying that as an animal rights supporter and vegetarian she could not condone the use of this symbol. Mr Tonks then asked, on a point of order, whether Miss Wilkinson was entitled to express an opinion. Mr Smoothie explained to Mr Tonks that, since ideas only were being expressed, Miss Wilkinson's contribution should be accepted, and to Miss Wilkinson that no action would be taken without full consideration of the sensibilities of employees.

Portugal

This was acknowledged to be a difficult one. The only lead which was produced came from Mr Clatworthy, who reminisced about an aunt of his who had been stung by a Portuguese Man of War while bathing at Westcliff-on-Sea. Miss Johnson expressed doubt about the feasibility of converting the familiar mould quite so radically as to produce a convincing replica of a jelly-fish, and Mr Harcourt-Jones was not hopeful of a ready acceptance of such a product in Portuguese markets. He was not sure whether the Portuguese accepted ownership of this species; as he put it: 'For all we know they may call the things English Men of War over there.' Further research was called for.

Denmark

The initial idea of simply painting the gnomes to resemble Danish Blue cheese was thought unappealing. However, the Hans Anderson connection was thought to have considerably more potential, gnomes not being readily distinguishable from trolls, goblins etc. At a pinch, therefore, it was agreed that the existing models would serve very well. A suggestion from Mr Prodwind that the mould be modified to incorporate something which he swore he had seen on open display on news stands and novelty shops in Copenhagen was hastily terminated by Mr Clatworthy, who agreed that Mr Prodwind could go into detail on another occasion when certain members of the sub-committee were not present. It was, however, unlikely to be adopted.

Greece
No overpowering image of Greek connection thrust itself
forward. Mr Harcourt-Jones, however, recalled from his
military days that the Greek soldiers, when in full dress
for guards of honour, were in the habit of wearing a kind
of wide white skirt, with a sort of tasselled cap not unlike
that worn by the standard gnome. This in turn prompted
Miss Johnson to remember the Scottish campaign of 1962,
when a new mould was made of a gnome wearing a kilt
and playing bagpipes; she believed the mould was still in
a store cupboard. The campaign had foundered on the
difficulty the Paint Shop had with tartan, but of course
that question would not now arise. Mr Clatworthy expressed
great gratification at this juxtaposition of ideas, since this
was exactly how brain storming ought to work. Mr Harcourt-
Jones undertook to find out what a bouzouki was, and check
on its bagpipe-convertibility.

Ireland
It was generally agreed that Ireland would present no difficulty; the existing gnomes would simply be painted green
and make very presentable leprechauns. Mr Clatworthy
expressed a view that the addition of a clay pipe held upside
down would enhance the attractiveness of the figure further;
but after listening to Miss Wilkinson's objection about the
discouragement of smoking and Mr Prodwind's warning
about the fragility of small projections in plaster figures,
conceded the point.

Belgium
Several members of the sub-committee had visited Brussels,
and all seemed to recall one symbol in particular, that of
a well-known statue of a small boy in the act of relieving
himself. Mr Clatworthy said that this was a very delicate
area, and the Company must be mindful of its reputation.
We lived in liberated times, it was true, but that section of
the public which formed the prime buying-group for the
garden gnome was not necessarily ready for this kind of
thing. Miss Wilkinson, to some members' surprise, expressed
the view that there was nothing to be ashamed of in the

display of a natural bodily function. Encouraged by this view, Mr Clatworthy gave the go-ahead for 'Project Le Gnome Pis'.

Luxembourg

No member of the sub-comittee could recall meeting a Luxembourger. Mr Harcourt-Jones, however, asserted that Luxembourg used to have a Grand-Duke and very possibly still had. Until anything more inspiring came forward, therefore, Miss Johnson was authorised to proceed with designs incorporating a Ducal crown into the Gnomal hat.

The Netherlands

Miss Johnson said that Dutch traditional dress would not present major difficulties. The standard gnome already had sizable feet, due she believed to the influence of the late Miss Enid Blyton and her protégé, Noddy. The conversion to clogs would therefore be relatively simple, and baggy trousers would complete the picture. A suggestion that the toadstool be converted to a windmill was made by the tea-lady, Mrs Grommet, who happened to be present, but the problems of execution in this case were thought to be more severe. At Mr Clatworthy's request, Mr Prodwind's offer to describe a number of objects he had seen during a recent visit to Amsterdam was adjourned *sine die* in view of the limited time available.

Italy

Mr Harcourt-Jones wasn't sure whether the Italians went in for gardens very much, but proposed wrapping the gnome in a toga. Although superficially attractive, the idea was thought to be insufficiently modern for the spirit of 1992. An alternative suggestion of a papal crown was also rejected both for the same reason and because of Mr Smoothie's fears of possible charges of insensitivity. The most appealing idea was that of setting the gnome on a scooter of the Lambretta type, which Mr Harcourt-Jones believed still flourished in the Italian cities. The idea was enthusiastically supported by all members except Miss Johnson, who had reservations about the design problems.

Summary

Mr Clatworthy thanked everyone for the remarkable flow of ideas which he had witnessed. He recalled the time when his father had founded the factory, fifty years ago. Little had he thought then of the glittering international future that was now opening up. He was expanding on this theme when several members of the sub-committee remembered urgent appointments and the meeting was adjourned.

NOEL PETTY

Language Teaching – A Protest

To: The Editor
The *Mughampton Sun*

Dear Sir,

I am concerned about recent developments in the teaching of languages in our schools.

Whilst I am not against a certain amount of language tuition as part of a child's education, I learn with horror that my daughter, who is taking her GCSE at Mughampton Upper School, has been asked if she would like to do an exchange visit with a French girl, spending three months living with a French family, in France, where she would be expected to speak French all the time.

So far as I am aware, the teaching of French at school was never intended to prepare people for speaking the language. Of course, a knowledge of catering terms in French can come in useful in some restaurants, and when travelling in France one should be able to hold one's own with waiters, ticket collectors, gendarmes, and other such persons. But all educated French people speak English, and surely, they are the only ones a really nice girl need spend her time talking to.

As English people, we ought to be proud of our magnificent language, and continue to use it everywhere we can. Going into Europe should not mean a lowering of our standards, or 'going native'.

Yours etc.,

Gladys Muffin (Mrs)

E.O. PARROTT

To: The Editor,
The *Mughampton Sun*

Dear Sir,

I want to disagree most strongly with your recent correspondent who claims that you can't get a decent cup of tea anywhere on the continent.

Last year my husband and I went on a coach holiday for the over 60s to five European countries in eight days. Or it might have been eight European countries in five days. My memory is not what it was. About the third day we stopped for toilets on the E15 (why do they call all their roads after additives?) between Hamburg and Hanover and saw a Robin Reliant just like the one we used to own which was stolen. You hear a lot about cars being thieved in England and sold abroad so we asked the driver who was under the bonnet where he had bought it. He told us he got it through the *Exchange & Mart* from a man in Chislehurst so that was alright. Anyway, the driver who turned out to be a Mr Wheeler had a gadget which he plugged into the cigarette lighter in his dashboard and dangled the twirly bit on the other end into a teapot. We were soon all enjoying a good strong cup of Brooke Bond Divi.

So you can get a good cuppa in Europe after all. Mr Wheeler says he goes motoring on the continent every year so readers who like a good cup of Rosie Lee should look out for him. Apparently he spends a lot of time brewing up in car parks waiting for Europ Assist.

Yours faithfully,

Gladys Small (Mrs)

V. ERNEST COX

... good strong cup of Brooke Bond Divi ...

Mughampton Women's Institute

From the minutes of the Sub-Committee for Europeanization:

Mrs Heavyside reported on the 'Beautiful Mughampton' campaign. She and other members had been to Switzerland on a week's tour, and had been impressed by Swiss standards of cleanliness. They were determined to make Mughampton as neat and pretty as Basle or Lausanne, and would stop at nothing to achieve this aim. Each member would be responsible for galvanizing her immediate circle into action:

1. Mrs Amalia Trench and the Mughampton Horticultural Society were undertaking floral decorations and, with the aid of a Council grant, proposed to line the streets with tubs of flowers, bulbs and shrubs, and to strike an original note, unusual receptacles were being sought. Mr Fred Boot had offered an old hip bath which he had recovered from the canal, and old Joshua Boot had turned

up trumps with an original Victorian pig trough – a real find, Mrs Trench had said.

2. Mrs Doreen Stillworthy had persuaded Messrs KLEEN-ABRIX to donate a quantity of their product for cleaning pavements, walls and front steps, and this had already been distributed to all except the inhabitants of Guy Lane, who had refused point blank to use it as they said it would destroy the many unique pieces of mural and pavement art with which this area abounds.

3. The Art Department of Mughampton College of Further Education, together with High Street shopkeepers, were designing banners with symbols denoting the various trades and professions, under the Arms of Mughampton. This was still at the drawing-board stage.

4. Mrs Ruddle had been asked to approach Mr Ruddle with a view to cleaning up the Station. He had admitted that it was a bit grubby, but he did not want to upset old Mr Porter, the porter, as he was getting on now, and tended to wait for a strong wind to blow the dust away. Mrs Ruddle had said she would persevere with this.

E. O. PARROTT

More from the Mughampton Sun

SHOVE OFF

An attempt to restore Mughampton's sporting reputation in the French resort of Chaton-sur-Mer has ended in failure. A shove-ha'penny team from the Tattooed Arms arrived in Chaton ready to play the locals; but before the board could be set up at a seafront hotel, a European monetary official dramatically appeared. He declared that the contest would be illegal, since it involved a coin which had not been in use for some years and would never again be part of European currency. Both teams angrily pointed out that the game was played with counters, not actual halfpennies. But the bureaucrat insisted that the law was clear. Anglo-French accord was established when both teams attacked the official. Baton-wielding gendarmes finally restored order. No charges were made against the Mughampton men, but they were put on the boat for home.

PETER VEALE

Report On The 'Ooh La La! Mein Signor, Por Favor' Competition at Mughampton's Safegate Supermarket

Competitors for our prize of a weekend for two in Gay Paree were asked to identify the nationality of typical Europeans in pictures printed on the labels of our own-brand toilet paper. To decide between all-correct entries, the tie-breaker was to write not more than ten words beginning, 'I fancy a weekend in Gay Paree because . . .'.

First, the pictures. The gentleman in the spangled suit waving his cape at a charging bull was from . . . yes, sunny Spain! An impressive 30% of you got this one right, though I sympathise with those who thought he was from India, where these animals are also held in high regard. Next, the girl with the ice cream standing in front of the leaning building. A tricky one this – some of you thought it was from Japan after an earthquake, but remember, it's still in Europe. Over 20% guessed correctly that she was Italian. Then the jolly fellow in the clogs with the windmill behind. No, he wasn't from Oldham, he was a Dutchman, or I'm a Dutchman. Get it? Well, 19% of you did. And finally a really tough one, the gent in the beret and hooped shirt with the onions round his neck. Some of you thought they were swedes and went for our Scandinavian friends, but the right answer, which 15% of you got, was French. The object behind him was meant to be a clue, but some people thought it was Blackpool Tower and got confused. Sorry about that.

So to the tie-breaker. First our apologies both to the gay community, who threatened us with the Advertising Standards Authority when it transpired that the prize was a straight weekend; and also to the Citizens' Vigilante Group, who thought just the opposite. Honestly, don't blame us, we're not in charge of the English language. Also, we should have made it clear that the partner in the 'weekend for two' would have to be supplied by the winner.

We were puzzled, too, by the entry which read, '. . . because it makes the cow so happy,' but we finally worked out that the entrant had got confused between this one and last week's one on our milk ('I always drink Safegate's Milk because . . . it has that spicy continental flavour.'). After disqualifying a few for sending in identical entries, we gave the second prize (a fresh baguette) to Mr Mayling, for his telling '. . . because Safegate is an excellent company on which one can rely in every way', but felt it didn't quite have the precise appositeness required to win the prize. So the weekend goes to our overall winner, who, somewhat disappointingly, asked to remain anonymous and to have the tickets sent in a plain brown envelope. The winning line was, '. . . because an "eiffel" of the girls there keeps me "seine".' Congratulations, Mr Polewheel!

NOEL PETTY

The Chunnel for Mughampton

To: The Editor,
Mughampton Echo

Dear Sir,

We are continually reading in our newspapers, and seeing on television, reports about the difficulties experienced by the Channel Tunnel Company in finding a suitable place for a terminal on the British side of the Channel. The people of Kent seem to be very selfish. Does not this, however, represent a wonderful opportunity for Mughampton to show its European spirit and offer itself for this purpose? It is surely not too late to extend the tunnel from Dover to the old South Mughampton gravel pits, where the excavations already made would be a good start. And how wonderful it would be for our Continental friends to emerge from their journey in the heart of England's Green and Pleasant Land, to a nice welcoming cuppa at Mrs Bastable's Tea Rooms!

Yours, etc.

P. Wickens (Miss)

Our transport correspondent writes:
Full marks for creative thinking, Miss Wickens, and the warm-heartedness of your sentiments does you credit. I have mentioned your idea to the Channel Tunnel Company, but they rather feel that Mughampton, situated as it is some ninety miles from the coast, would present them with a number of difficulties which could not be easily overcome. As you may know, they are working to a rather tight budget. They did pause in their labours, however, to ask me to convey their warmest thanks for your thought.

NOEL PETTY

Your Questions Answered

Q. What is Britain most famous in Europe for producing?
Britain has always been famous for its coal, ship-building, oil and tourist industries, although times do change, and new industries spring up all the time. Only a few years ago, for instance, the 'burgher' was a dish which was exported from Calais – as those of you with GCSE History will know. But now Scotland has taken over the making of this popular dish, which it sells as a **Big Mac**, after its maker, the former cider-farmer, **Apple Mackintosh**. The Big Mackintosh, unlike its French cousin, is designed for indoors. Britain currently exports more tourists than anyone else, but we are looking to redress this balance in time for the opening of the Channel Tunnel (or **Chanel Tunnel**, as the French call it, after its major sponsor). At present Britain is therefore engaged in building hundreds of holiday houses in rural England and Wales, all white, thatched, and with roses round the door: the so-called **'cottage industry'**.

The Burgers of Calais

Q. What do the other countries in the EEC make?
Eire produces peat, and also bogs (I'm afraid that they
were first to invent them, long before **Looe** and **Flushing**, who also claim to be the original manufacturers).

. . . before Looe or Flushing.

France is famous for its **pâtisserie** (pastry), **pharmacie**
(agriculture), **boutiques** (cobblers) and **magazins** (literature). Italy makes pasta, the main ingredient in Cornish
pasties and the drink 'pastis' amongst other things. It
also makes **spaghetti**, **ravioli**, **zucchini** and **deli**, the spicy
and rather peculiar food you can buy at special shops
throughout the continent. Greece produces olives, with
or without stones, and sometimes in a hybrid form with
red pepper. It is thereby also the chief oil producer in
the Common Market, and the Community's chief representative in OPEC. Portugal manufactures **algarve**, a
famous cloth, not unlike linen. Denmark is best known
for its butter, its bacon and its enormous dogs (bred to
be mountain rescuers in the Swiss resort of St Bernard).
Belgium produces two national commodities – **phlegm**,
a gluey substance, and **walloons**, which are like balloons,
only bigger. Holland makes Lego, although it is also
known for its light industry, manufacturing hundreds

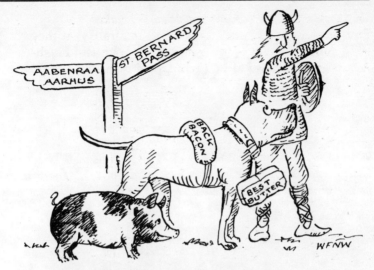

Denmark is best known for its
butter, bacon and enormous dogs . . .

of bulbs. Germany makes **Frankfurters** and **Hamburgers**
and mattresses (**Vorsprung**). Spain is known throughout
Europe for its television, which is beamed all over the
EEC from its headquarters in Granada. For many years,
the monarchists overthrown by Franco produced the
programme which I am told Britons know as *Coronation
Street* from an illegal broadcasting station, never discovered by the Generalissimo. And Luxembourg is famous
for its **radio**, and its special 'white noise' touch of
authenticity.

Q. Where did the duvet come from?
Bedfordshire. It replaced the Scandinavian ice-sheet.

BILL GREENWELL

EUROBRITS

We have been concentrating our attention in this book largely on Continental Europe as seen by the British Europhile. But how should he see himself? This chapter offers a brief guide.

The British

Oh, no-one hates being British like the British.
Take your liberal, educated Brit.
His heart is sadly torn, that the fact of being born,
In this island guarantees he'll be a shit.
His hatred of his nationhood's deep-seated,
He throws up when he sees his flag unfurled;
Oh no-one hates being British like the liberal British –
We're the worst bloody country in the world.

This trait is not in-bred in Anglo-Saxons.
Americans will boast of being Yanks,
And if you mistake Canadians for being anything but
  Canadian,
They are the last to give you any thanks.
New Zealanders quite relish being New Zealanders.
Australians, God knows why, are pretty proud
Of their suburban trim to the outback's rim –
At least they tell you so, and very loud.

But those who got their ancestors exported,
Through poverty or penal servitude,
Find an antipathy in being what they're forced to be,
And on the subject of their origins, are rude.

. . . ancestors exported . . .

And they scrutinise their character to pieces,
And on themselves, they practice Cultural Crit.
Oh no-one hates being British like the British hate being
  British.
Your liberal, educated, travelled Brit.

Italians dance and sing at being Italian,
French savants endure being very French,
Being Swiss is total bliss to the average Swiss,
Being Danish doesn't cause the Danes to blench,
But take your open-minded, thinking British;
On themselves, they'll call down every curse.
We're utterly obscene, lowest that's ever been.
No-one else could ever have been worse.

Belgians are quite happy being Belgian,
Swedes aren't ashamed to say that they are Swedes,
Spaniards think they've made a gain in being citizens
  of Spain,
Poles think the Poles the finest of all breeds.

Germans have got used to being German,
They're living down their recent past, a bit,
But for a drench of guilt that would make a forest wilt,
Go to your liberal-minded Brit.

The middle-class, *Guardian*-reading Briton,
Likes abusing his own country best.
Americans are more open and much more freely
   spoken;
Italians are surely better dressed.
The Greeks are nicer, friendlier and kinder;
The Irish have much the greater charm;
For tolerance and such, we're beaten by the Dutch;
Greenlanders have done the world less harm.

Iceland has much the nicer weather;
Russians don't keep trains in such a fug;
Yes, the whole world's full of hate for the British state,
We're one and all so bloody pleased and smug.
At outdoor cafes you will often find them,
World-Service listening, with exported beer:
'The country would not alter, so now I live in Malta
I find them much less insular right here.'

'I tell you,' they say, tearful and vehement,
'We're passionless, superior and cold.'
Yes, the sun never sets, on where a Briton frets,
How awful his country was of old,
How horrible it was to have an empire,
How pathetic, to have an empire lost,
How only the short-sighted are by Europe undelighted,
When for so long they have been US-bossed.

Oh no-one hates being British like the British,
A cosmopolitan Briton, you can trust,
To rate his television, with snorts of deep derision,
And constantly he's full of self-disgust.
Oh no-one hates being British like the British;

Our country, it really is the pits.
Our police always unlawful, our food so bloody awful.
No-one hates being British like the Brits.

REM BEL

Left Behind Blues

So, mum, you're on the Costa Brava!
(You might as well have gone to Java)
Thank you for your note: 'I've gone.
Leave the central heating on.
Help yourself to gin and It:
I think I've left a tiny bit.'
As always, you're above all mothers
In your tender care for others.

Come back, mum, and bring with you
Bottles of that Spanish brew.
I know my words aren't any use:
You've the necessary juice
Where you are; and you'll be wise
To stay until the swallow flies.
Swallow? Swallow, did I say?
So I will, if that's the way.

If I could only find by art
Some Costa Brava of the heart,
Transcendental Meditation
Might ease my urge for emigration.
As it is, Mum, since you're there
And I can't afford the fare,
I'll give the gin another go –
Winter's hard in Walthamstow.

PAUL GRIFFIN

A Short Guide To British Towns

Bath
A city founded by the Romans who were obsessed with cleanliness. It was brought into prominence in the 18th century by an influx of beaux, initiated by a member of the local constabulary, PC Wren, who introduced Beau Geste into the area. Others included Beau Brunel who invented a card game called Iron Bridge, and Beau Ogden Nash who designed the Pump Room, a favourite stopping place for motorists.

Beaux play Iron Bridge in Bath

Birmingham
This has many surprising features including Bournville, a village constructed entirely out of chocolate, and a hazardous road junction made of pasta.

Cambridge
A university centre associated with many famous people, including Francis Bacon, who always insisted that his name was Shakespeare, and Isaac Walton who made the momentous discovery that if you let go of an apple it will hit the floor.

Canterbury
Noted for three things: bells, lamb and tales. The origin of
the tales springs from a priest, Samuel Beckett who habitually
loitered in the cathedral. When asked the reason for this he
turbulently replied, 'Oh, I'm waiting for God.' Henry II,
who could not stand turbulence, had him martyred. About
two hundred years later a tour operator, Cheerful Charlie
Chaucer (who was notoriously bad at spelling) organised
trips from London to Canterbury. The tales (which are of a
salacious nature) were told to while away the time in traffic
hold-ups on the A2.

Cardiff
This is the capital of Wales and its most hallowed building
is a pub, 'The Cardiff Arms'.

Coventry
Considering the number of people who have been forcibly
sent there over the years its population is not as large as one
might imagine. It has never completely recovered from the
famous ride taken by Lady Godiva who constantly refused
to visit a hairdresser. When asked the reason for this she
replied 'I've got something to hide'; a remark that has puzzled
scholars for centuries.

Edinburgh
A beautiful city known affectionately as 'Auld Cock-a-
Leekie', the home of the kilt, sporran and haggis. A notable
thoroughfare is the Royal Smile, named in honour of the
Duke of Edinburgh. Film lovers should not miss Hollywood
House which was once the home of James Stewart.

Glasgow
An impressive place with a tendency to revolve on Saturday
nights.

Liverpool
For many years it had a tenuous association with shipping,
but it was not until the sixties that it suddenly sprang to fame

when it was subjected to a plague of beetles. These insects became so much a part of the lives of the inhabitants that they grew resigned to them and even gave them affectionate names: Jack Lemmon, Rex Harrison, Charlie McCarthy and Harpo Marx.

London
The Tower of London is a medieval fortress where, for hundreds of years, the sovereign had awkward politicians beheaded. There is at the present time, a strong movement to revive this practice.

St Paul's Cathedral was designed by Sir Christopher Robin who always insisted on complete silence when he said his prayers there.

Westminster Abbey has inspired more than one poet to remark on the number of tombs it contains. These apparently embody the remains of those Londoners who, according to Dr Johnson, got tired of living there.

Piccadilly Circus is dominated by a statue of the god, Enos, which symbolises the country's tradition with the salty ocean surrounding it. Along with Leicester Square, Piccadilly is a useful jumping-off place for those wishing to visit Tipperary, but be warned: it's a long way.

Newcastle
The foreign visitor must be prepared for the revelation that an English dictionary is of little use in these parts. The two most noted names here are Geordie and his wife, Hinny, to whom constant reference is made. Newcastle is close to Hadrian's Wall, which was built by an over-optimistic Roman Emperor to stop the Scots coming into England – a project that was doomed to utter failure.

Oxford
It would take up far too much space to enumerate all the famous and learned people connected with this beautiful city, but one worthy of note is the dancing pioneer, William Morris, who is even better known through his younger brother, Morris minor, and his daughter, Minnie.

FRANK RICHARDS

Conversation Pieces

Why do the British keep Royals?
They're priced beyond valuation.
They're useful objects to their subjects,
By being subjects of conversation.
When the hassle of living in London falters,
And the state of the roads and the rails,
There's always the corpulent Duchess of York,
The filiform Princess of Wales.

The British talk about gardening.
Though now herbs in patio pots,
Replace the failures of their dahlias,
And the clay in those long narrow plots.
But how to trellis the walls can pall,
And setting of slug traps slump;
Then the Princess of Wales is a mad anorexic,
The Duchess, pleasantly plump.

A Briton's never a slave of course,
But he's his Bank Manager's liege,
The Briton's a vassal in a mortgaged castle,
Which high interest rates besiege.
So when he starts on how the price he paid's doubled,
Or how he's tied to a subsiding dump,
Contend that the Princess is sexily svelte,
The Duchess, an overgrown lump.

The British have always gone travelling,
The rich, to avoid paying tax,
The poor go on an all-paid-package,
In order to get pissed in packs.
You will see both classes queueing at kiosks,
Buying tabloids in Jersey and Greece,
For the latest on the Princess' diet,
And what makes the Duchess obese.

Could Britain ever be a Republic?
What interest could anyone find,
In a Mrs Wales's slender hips,
And Sarah York's big behind.
Meat for discussion, already on ration,
At the office, in pubs and clubs fails,
Without the fat on the Duchess of York,
The lean on the Princess of Wales.

REM BEL

EUROWARNINGS

How To Remain Completely Unaffected By Abroad

When in **Amsterdam**

DO NOT visit the red light district. Its alliance between lust, commercialism and cosy domesticity (crudely shouting or furtively sidling men assessing naked girls knitting behind lace curtains in comfy front rooms) may induce disturbing reflections on sexuality and social mores.

DO NOT go anywhere near the canals. You will be bitten by midges.

When in **Cardiff**

DO NOT attend a rugby match at the Welsh National Stadium. It is always best to tread carefully when fundamentalist religion is on the agenda. Welsh crowds know in their deepest hearts that their national side is never fairly beaten. Sometimes, through cheating and the incompetence of a referee appointed from the ranks of the aurally and visually handicapped, a visiting team may be awarded more points, but such mishaps should not be thought of as a Welsh defeat. The outsider, by definition impartial and measured in judgement, will keep all comment to himself. Indeed, if he retains the wit he was born with, he will cheer loudly in the Welsh interest. Should impartiality preclude this subterfuge, he will make an excuse, *pianissimo*, and leave. Even so, he may be pursued by small swarthy men, who will belabour him with muddy-rooted leeks and shout abuse rendered almost musical by its unparalleled liquidity of vowel. Indeed, if matters really do come to a head they may burst into unaccompanied choral song, which is worse.

When in **Castiglione del Lago**
Do NOT travel to the islands of the lake, where the Rosemary is six feet high, abandoned chapels and castles are redolent of people and times unknown, and jolly Italians picnic and dance dappled by shadows in the olive groves. You will be bitten by midges.

When in **Copenhagen**
Do NOT ride the Big Dipper in the Tivoli Gardens. To be flung spear-like to within inches of a solid wall, to be snatched away in an Immelman turn; to climb and plummet vertically within one breathless, terrified giggle; to cling to a retaining bar, your torso parallel to the solid, blurred Danish earth which hurtles past inches below in horizontal parallel: these

are experiences to test the most sanguine of men. Danish sadism (remember the rape and pillage which accompanied their visits to our own peaceable land!) is such that you are mad to endure them twice.

DO NOT make a pilgrimage to the Little Mermaid. This tiny, isolated statue, pensive on its plinth in the sea, its back turned on the ferries and their mournful lowing as they leave for Malmo, is a melancholy work, inspired by a fairy tale of Hans Christian Andersen, whose morbidly acute personality did not remotely resemble the avuncular zany portrayed by Danny Kaye in the eponymous film. In some seasons of the year it may be warm enough for you to be bitten by midges.

When in **Edinburgh**

DO NOT visit the castle on a fine afternoon in August hoping to catch a sundrenched panorama of the stern romantic city. Let stained, hill-clutching Old Town buildings straggle down Canongate to Holyrood; let New Town stand serene in its Georgian order beyond Princes Street: in the minutes it takes to achieve your coign of vantage, a thick, concealing mist, will fall, clinging to buildings and people, penetrating the stoutest, warmest facade. You might as well be in Glencoe in February, so muffled and so sinister is the scene. A piper tuning up in some invisible courtyard below is all you need to complete your saturation in that Caledonian mysticism which comes so readily to the Athens of the North.

When in **Konstanze**

DO NOT stroll by the lake or along the blue peaceful Rhine. You will be bitten by German midges. And there are too many tulips, to say nothing of the cabbages.

When in **Madrid**

DO NOT lunch at L'Hardy's downstairs. There is nowhere to sit while you browse on the *tapas* (olives, tiny fritters and meatballs) and sluice on the endless sherries, madeiras and manzanillos which are available for the London price of a slice of sticky pizza.

Do NOT dine at Botin's. Someone there will be wondering which was Hemingway's favourite table. The roast sucking pig (*cochinillo asado* – be warned) is addictive. And wine at under a pound a bottle is very bad for you.

When in **Naples**
Do NOT visit Pompeii. Some guides will prevent your wife or other female companion from seeing the naughty statues and paintings and you will be subjected to a feminist tirade for the rest of the day.

... some guides will prevent your wife
or other female companion from seeing ...

When in **Oban**
You will be bitten by midges.

When in **Paris**
Do NOT visit the Louvre. Crowds of ignoramuses, who block your view of the paintings – especially the Mona Lisa, which, to make matters worse, does its simpering within an Eichmannite protective glass booth. The collection at large consists principally of works by artists who were French or lived at some time in France. It has, therefore, only parochial interest.

Do NOT walk on the banks of the Seine. You may see topless sunbathers, or variously paired lovers engaging in acts better confined between four walls, if attempted at all. There are odours of exotic foods and even more exotic cigarettes. If you don't smoke yourself you will be bitten by midges.

DO NOT walk up the Rue St Denis. Ingenious arrangements of buckles and straps, the working gear of the young women – some not so young! – who ply their trade there, will induce troubled ponderings on the follies of mankind. Worse, any inadvertently over-attentive gaze will be construed as the go-ahead for commercial negotiations.

DO NOT go anywhere near, let alone up the Eiffel Tower. When it was first built, Parisian intellectuals took troublesome and lengthy detours to avoid seeing it. Today their eyes-off stance remains the only only one possible to those who care for architectural sense and decorum. The thing lacks human scale, is visually out of sympathy with its surroundings and is constructed in soulless iron.

DO NOT eat casserole of guinea fowl and drink *vin ouvert* in a cheap Seine-side restaurant. You might go native, raise your glass to dull care and engage vivaciously in wide-ranging philosophical debate without so much as a stammer of British reticence.

DO NOT travel on the Métro. You will infallibly get lost and arrive late. It is not because the system is unclearly arranged or badly sign-posted, nor because trains are irregular or infrequent. *Au contraire*: the welcoming Art Nouveau entrances, the wide, airy, uncrowded platforms, the clean, elegantly curving tiled walls and the apt decorative displays at individual stations all combine to induce a disorientating feeling that you are not in a transport system at all. Rather, you have found a spot for withdrawal, a place of meditation, detached from the bustling purposefulness of the city a few feet above your head.

DO NOT visit Montmartre. You have seen it all already in reproductions of impressionist paintings.

DO NOT visit the Gare d'Orsay. To have so much of the art of the nineteenth century under one (high, glazed) roof is to risk indigestion of the senses.

Do not visit Versailles. The absurd, pretentious architecture will make you feel that the French Revolution was necessary, and this has become an unfashionable view.

When in **Switzerland**
Do not venture into the streets. Their spotlessness will make you feel grimy.

When in **Vienna**
Do not look for the beautiful blue Danube. What you will find is brownish and non-descript. You will be bitten by midges.

Do not walk around the Ringstrasse exclaiming delightedly at the variety of architectural periods exemplified by the buildings. They are all fakes, run up in the mid-nineteenth century.

Do not eat potatoes made of marzipan or elephants made of meringue. The idea is kitsch and disgusting.

Do not visit Grinzing to drink the new season's wine in the lively backyards of the *heurigen*. The wine tastes innocuously delicious and comes in half pint mugs. You may get drunk and start to sing. Besides, the waitresses wear laced, extrusive bodices, rendering the entire enterprise replete with moral risk. And you will be bitten by midges.

Do not lift up sewer covers hoping to hear mysterious echoes of Harry Lime's zither or see the orotund ghost of Orson Welles. Police will blow whistles at you.

Do not ride on the big wheel in the Prater. Orson Welles isn't up there either and the view is of a railway marshalling yard.

Do not listen to small groups of men in green jackets and with feathers in their hat bands playing valveless horns. Their repertoire of fanfares will put you in mind of hunting, fighting and other unacceptable pursuits.

Do not gaze at shop windows displaying candles or hats.

In Grinzing . . . enterprise replete with moral risk . . .

Either will induce gloomy, envious meditations on the evils of conspicuous consumption.

Do NOT shop in the Flea Market. You will infallibly buy something you could have got more cheaply at home.

Do NOT go to see the Klimts and Schieles in the Belvedere Palace. They are erotic and disturbing.

Do NOT walk on any paving stone which looks more than forty years old. It may have been hewn by slave labour in Mauthausen, the death camp up the river.

When in Venice

Do NOT ride in a gondola. You will be ripped off and may have to endure songs rendered fortissimo, in Italian, a few feet above your head. You will be bitten by midges.

Do NOT go to the Scuola di San Rocco to see the cycle of Tintoretto's paintings on the life of Christ. Even on hot days the building is cool. In winter you may actually shiver. To preserve them the paintings are ill lit. They hang high on the walls. A clearer, less neck-ricking perusal is obtainable in any of the books of reproductions which are available at reasonable cost.

Do NOT eat the ice cream. It is not manufactured to British standards and there is a worrying possibility that you might enjoy it exceedingly.

Do NOT eat uncooked salads. They may contain dandelion leaves and other perils too horrific to list in a publication designed for the nervous. See also above, under warnings about ice cream.

Do NOT drink coffee at Florian's or Quadri's in the Piazza San Marco. An extortionate bill is the least of the competing perils. Paunchy, exclamatory Americans, shutter-rattling, miya-samaing Japanese, otiose, lumbering Germans and vehement, gesticulating Italians gabble in their various patois. Chairs scrape on the pavement. Crockery clatters on metal tables. The bands of the two establishments overlap:

The Barber of Seville counterpointing 'Yes, Sir, That's My Baby'. Chimes thunder from the towering campanile. Gobbling pigeons and screeching gulls wheel and mass, their curving kamikaze dives targetting any unattended foody fragment. The flicker and rustle of wings is a background susurration, growing at intervals to a pulsing rush which obliterates all other sounds. Guides, rallying straggled parties, wave brightly coloured umbrellas, clap their hands and utter undecodable cries. Add to all these auditory and visual stimulations the whispering ghosts of a millenium of political and social turbulence and you will be lucky to escape without a severe headache. This may be the world's drawing room, but the guests are ill-matched, clamorous and too many.

DO NOT visit San Francesco del Deserto. You have to travel first to the island of Burano, where, amongst the variegated cottages of the fisherfolk, the main street features a communist headquarters. Then you must hang about on the waterfront until a monk from the monastery happens to appear in his motor boat. You must negotiate a fare with him. Once on the island, after a twenty-minute trip across one of the emptiest parts of the lagoon, you will find the total silence curiously unnerving.

When Returning Home
Do, when asked whether you enjoyed abroad, intone with a judicious chuckle: 'Travel broadens the seat.'

TOM AITKEN

SARKHAN

*William J. Lederer
and Eugene Burdick*

SARKHAN

McGraw-Hill Book Company
NEW YORK   TORONTO   LONDON

A KAMIMA, INC. PUBLICATION

FOR E.K., JR., *editor, peacemaker, patient manager without whose 21,000 miles . . . ;* FOR E.P.S., *who generously helped us start;* FOR M.G., *who skillfully protected us from ourselves.*

W.L.
E.B.

Contents

x   *Contents*

Authors' Note

This book is fiction. When we began writing it, our objective was to produce a novel which, we hoped, would excite and entertain as well as inform its readers.

Almost all of the action takes place in Southeast Asia (where both of us have had considerable experience). During our extensive travels people kept asking us the same questions: "Why does the powerful United States get kicked around, humiliated by weaker nations? How is this possible? Where are America's talents?"

For over a year we spent many nights discussing and arguing about the answers to these questions. What were the causes of America's awkwardness and failures? How could they be remedied?

If *Sarkhan* gives the reader a few hours of entertainment, we are glad. If it also awakens him and even makes him angry, we will have achieved our purpose. The book has a broad foundation of fact; and the facts of our times, if told truthfully, are adequate cause for anger.

William J. Lederer
Eugene Burdick

Aptos, California
June 1965

A Trail in the Jungle

Tuc, the Communist from Sarkhan, trotted through the jungle, wearing only a pair of dirty shorts. He was hungry, but he enjoyed the sensation. He would wait another hour before eating. In a small bundle tied to his shoulders were a singlet, sandals, political cartoon books, a map case, five religious pamphlets, and a fortune in Sarkhanese rupees.

Tuc was so lean that his major muscles stretched against his skin, the large arteries bulged tautly on his calves and arms. He was average size for a Malay-stock Sarkhanese, a few inches over five feet. His black hair was close-cropped. His fingers had scores of tiny scars, the sure mark of the fish-gutter. The two middle fingers of his right hand were missing, lost when he was seventeen and a grenade he was making had exploded in his hand. A comrade had bound his hand, Tuc had borrowed a grenade from someone else and had thrown it with reasonable accuracy at a squad of Chiang's forces.

Tuc's face was usually composed and always unrevealing. His subordinates avoided him unless sent for. After leaving him they felt exhausted, strained. His curt orders seemed impossible, but they must be met. Somehow they usually were.

Although the trail was masked by the overhanging jungle, it was hot and moist, the heat of midday spilling down heavily. Tuc prided himself that at forty-five he was able to travel as fast through the jungle as the youngest recruit in the People's Army. He noted with pleasure that there was almost no sweat on his wiry body. Sweat was the sign of the beginner, the soft city person. People who lived long in the jungle soon found their bodies sweating less and less. Water was too scarce.

He dwelt for a moment on yesterday's executive council meeting at the Hotel Metropole in Hanoi. When the conference was

over, Ho Chi-minh had complimented him on his work in
Sarkhan.

"You fought the long war here for nine years and have been
organizing the liberation of Sarkhan for ten," he had said. "It is
worth it. Just as they recall Chou En-lai as a former librarian
who freed China, you will be recalled as the fish-gutter who
liberated Sarkhan."

It was a lavish compliment; and it had been spoken before
Communist leaders of nine nations, representing over half the
world's population. It had come from the senior Communist in
Southeast Asia. Ho Chi-minh needed no trappings or ceremony
to identify him as the leader. His simple uniform carried no insignia. Even though he spoke slowly in a voice which was barely
a whisper, men listened with total absorption to the lean old man.
Ho Chi-minh, the Premier of North Vietnam, was as serene as an
ancient saint, languid in physical motion, yet his black eyes glit-
tered with energy, and his wispy gray beard was the beard of the
classic Asian grandfather.

Then the meeting had broken up. The man from Sarkhan had
been taken by light plane to a small village not far from the Sarkhanese border. He had slept for a few hours, then had been off
through the jungle. He analyzed the Hanoi conference as he
moved along the old path cut through the thick foliage. Every
one of the leaders—except the Russian representative who had
remained silent—had agreed on his plan for Sarkhan. They furthermore had agreed that the offensive should begin immediately.

He jumped over a log and stopped to take a bearing. Without
knowing precisely how, he concluded he was just inside the
Sarkhanese border. He had traveled through jungle so much that
his mind unconsciously always calculated his position by the sun,
by familiar trees, by the speed at which he moved. He had seen
too often the disaster that struck a person or a platoon of men
who lost, for even a few seconds, the sense of position. He knew
where he was and he knew where he was going. The junction of
three trails was only a mile ahead. He had told his four comrades
to meet him there at 1300. It now was 1222.

He moved off the trail and into the brush. His eyes darted

from the ground up the tree trunks. Quickly he collected two tubers, three bird's eggs each the size of a golf ball, and a handful of ants gorged on honey and stupefied.

He squatted on the edge of the trail, where he could see in both directions. He ate slowly, not tasting the food. He had had a fine meal last night at the Metropole, a very Asian meal, including bird's nest soup from Soochow. Tuc smiled, recalling how the hotel had changed since the French had been driven out. Formerly no Asians were allowed in. The Metropole had been the place where the French officers brought the choicest of the slim prostitutes, drank the best of France's champagnes, and caroused until they had to go out and die at places like Cao Bang, So Lo, and Dien Bien Phu.

Now the Hotel Metropole was austere, the food simple, and the lounge filled with bored Russian technicians, quiet Chinese consultants, and a stolid "observer" or two from Belgrade or Warsaw.

Tuc wondered how long it would be before the Ritz Hotel in Haidho, the capital of Sarkhan, now loud with fat, white tourists, would become like the Metropole. Not long, he thought.

He would now move in Sarkhan. For a moment Tuc felt like an instrument of history. Then, deliberately, he wiped the thought out of his mind. He had seen men fall victim to the bourgeois sense of pride, the secret belief that they were powerful as individuals. Always they had ended by acting on the basis of their own importance rather than on the conditions that prevailed or the objective to be attained. Last night Ho's brilliant General Giap had admitted that his first attempt at major battle against the French had been a mistake caused by pride, an exaggerated notion of his own personal skill, and an over-estimation of the competence of his North Vietnamese troops. He had boasted that he would capture Hanoi before Christmas. In the vain effort to fulfill his boast he had lost 6,000 men. He had been surprised by the French use of napalm bombs and the fright of his own men. After that General Giap had never again permitted his ego to distort reality. Revolution called for selflessness, utter and complete.

Tuc finished eating, got to his feet, and immediately started off

down the trail. He would never make Giap's error. Confidence in
one's ability should never be allowed to become arrogance. One
must always move within the realm of the possible.

He came to the junction of the three trails at precisely 1300.
Four men stepped out of the jungle.

Years before Tuc had picked his provincial lieutenants carefully. Nam Tho, an intense young man from the northeast region, was only twenty-five but already he had ten years' experience in the movement. He came from a wealthy Haidho family
and had a burning hatred for white men. When the boy was fifteen, Tuc had unobtrusively and subtly begun his indoctrination. Five years ago he had been sent to teach in a public school
in one of the large northeast towns. His weakness was his unfa-
miliarity with the stubborn, clannish ways of the small villages.
Nam Tho could only learn this by experience. Already he had
acquired the look of the dedicated man who works with a desperate zeal. It amused Tuc that Nam Tho was so embarrassed by his
gold tooth, a sign of the bourgeois background, that he compressed his lips when he smiled. But Tuc would not allow him to
replace it.

The other three were older and without the intellectual potential of Nam Tho, but trustworthy, and they did their jobs
well. Cham was forty, tall for a Sarkhanese, handsome, his Mon-
goloid eyefold so slight he might have passed for Eurasian. The
eldest was Luki at forty-three, barely five feet tall, but with the
proportions of a Japanese *sumo* wrestler and a reputation for
mindless cruelty when aroused.

The fourth man was in Sarkhanese army uniform. He was Major
Phong, an intelligence officer attached to the Sarkhanese General
Staff in Haidho. He was of peasant stock, shrewd and durable, his
face impassive. Tuc had met him in Korea where they were both
volunteers fighting against the Americans. Phong was so skillful at
languages that he could shout insults at the Americans in almost
perfect slang. Tuc had arranged for Phong to be sent back to
Sarkhan where he got a position as interpreter with the Department of Defense. He soon was commissioned in the Army and rose
to the rank of major.

"Welcome, comrade," Luki said. "Welcome to the Central Committee of the Sarkhanese Communist Party."

Tuc permitted himself a grin. This was a joke they shared. The five of them were not only the Central Committee, but the only members of the Party in Sarkhan, a tight cadre that controlled dozens of "fronts" and trade unions and youth groups. Except for these five not one person in the apparatus considered himself a Communist. Most of them had never heard the word. They thought of themselves as patriotic nationalists. The Communist Party was outlawed in Sarkhan.

Now they squatted at the junction of the three trails in a circle of tamped-down grass.

"Hanoi agrees with our evaluation," Tuc said abruptly. "Not completely, but in general." He briefly told them what had occurred in Hanoi at the executive council.

"We have discussed these things often," Tuc said. "The only big change is that the signal for the first riot against the American Embassy will be the bombing of the Monastery of Buddha and Mohammed by a plane with American markings. It should be in about six weeks. Are there questions?"

They all shook their heads.

Tuc opened his pack and handed them samples of the new propaganda that had been prepared in Hanoi. Later the literature would be reproduced in Haidho. Tuc stood up, slapped his hands on his thighs and said, "We will meet in ten days, at the usual place."

They separated, each leader trotting down the trail toward his own region. Nam Tho, the young one with the gold tooth, looked back at Tuc. He hesitated, wishing that they could have talked longer. The time of testing was close and he was not sure.

2

A Small Riot

At 7:15 A.M. Edward Coldstream was meeting a plane at Haidho International Airport. He was reading the extra of the *Far Eastern Star*. The entire front page told about the destruction of the Monastery of Buddha and Mohammed, Sarkhan's most holy building, in the isolated mountains near the North Vietnam border. It had been bombed by an American Air Force plane. Coldstream knew the building well. It was clearly marked and the only large structure in miles. No military aviator, no matter how untrained, could mistake the famous place.

The Pan American jet had just landed. Squinting into the sun, Coldstream watched the big plane taxi toward the wooden terminal building with its red pagoda-like roof. The plane bumped hard on the hand-lain granite blocks of the long runway. Long years at sea had taught Coldstream how to look into the sun—as the wrinkles alongside his gray eyes showed. He moved toward the gate, with the walk of a man in good physical condition. His posture had been acquired at the Naval Academy long ago. A life at sea had kept him lean until he retired from the Navy. Since then his South East Asia Trading Corporation, with headquarters in Haidho, required his traveling about the Orient on steamers, junks, on foot and horse.

He was waiting for Thaddeus McCauley, professor of Sarkhanese Studies at Cornell. This was McCauley's eighth trip to Sarkhan, and he always stayed at Coldstream's house when in Haidho. This time he came to study the royal succession and coronation customs of Sarkhan. Prince Lin, the heir apparent, would be crowned on the 15th of November, just two months away. On that day old King Diad would abdicate in accordance with the Royal Astrologer's instructions. Few Westerners understood the astrological influence, but two former kings who had not abdicated on the predicted date mysteriously sickened and died. This would be the first abdication and coronation in over half a century. McCauley planned to study the ritual; and his friend Prince Lin had promised him access to everything.

When McCauley came down the ramp, Coldstream noticed with amusement that he wore the same old black wash-and-wear suit. It was crumpled and bulging with papers and pencils, and McCauley's short dumpy body moved in it as though he had to grunt with each step. He needed a shave. McCauley was only forty-two, yet he looked much older than Coldstream, who was forty-nine.

The two men met casually, even though they had not seen each other for over a year. Coldstream held up the front page of the *Far Eastern Star*.

"Tad, have you heard about this? One of our planes bombed the Monastery."

McCauley read the headlines. "What does the Embassy say? Was it really one of ours?"

"I don't know. This is the first I've heard. We'll stop at the Embassy on the way back. You have to check for mail anyway."

A Sarkhanese officer wearing the shoulder-marks of the Palace Guards approached and saluted. "Professor McCauley?"

"Yes."

"His Highness, Prince Lin," said the officer, "requested me to welcome you, his old friend, back to Haidho. Prince Lin is looking forward to meeting you next month when he returns from meditation."

He handed McCauley a thin envelope, saluted, smiled, and departed.

"Tad, I really resent the slick way you get around," Coldstream said. "You're a born conniver. Do you realize you're the heir apparent's only foreign friend and intimate? You arrive and are greeted by a colonel in the Palace Guards. The majority of the professional diplomats here have never even met the Prince. If you really tried you could probably be invited by King Diad himself to one of his famous wine-tasting ceremonies."

"Eddie," McCauley said, glancing at the note, "this is from Diad. I have been invited to a royal fol-de-rol—to the ritual of sampling the palm wines of Sarkhan. Very private, only His

Majesty and me." He paused, grinning. "Should I go, Buan
Suang?"

Buan Suang was Coldstream's Sarkhanese name. It literally
meant "Cold River." McCauley used it when he joked with his
friend.

"Damned right you'll go. But first Taja will have to press that
burlap bag you're wearing," Coldstream's expression sobered.
"What of our little business? Did you get something in the mail
from me?"

McCauley patted a thick manila envelope. "The documents?
They're right here. You mentioned picking them up in villages all
over Sarkhan? Well, they all come from the same printing press.
But let's discuss it at the house. I want to hear what else has been
happening."

"Plenty," said Coldstream. "You can help me piece it together."

"Last week," said McCauley, "our intrepid Secretary of State
briefed the press. He said everything in Sarkhan is just great."

In Coldstream's jeep they bumped along the gravel road north
to Haidho. McCauley looked at Coldstream and laughed. "When
I spoke to Cogswell on the phone yesterday he claimed you have
a nose like General MacArthur. An eagle beak. And it's true!"

Coldstream said, "And it was Cogswell who said that from the
top of your skull down you're the spitting image of Fiorello La
Guardia. That's also true."

"The *Washington Post* ran an editorial on Cogswell last week.
Said he has more influence on the President than any other non-
government person. I spoke to him on the phone yesterday, also.
He said you were to keep the reports coming."

At 8:15 they reached Royal Square in the center of Haidho. As
always its dimensions impressed Coldstream. It was a quarter mile
on each side and had been built as a parade ground. The Royal
Palace flanked it on the north; the American Embassy was
diagonally opposite; next to the palace was Sarkhan University.
The remainder of the space around the square was occupied by
the only modern office buildings in Haidho. One of them was
Coldstream's.

The Embassy guard recognized Coldstream's jeep and passed

them in. In front of the Embassy, newsboys were shouting the news of the bombing of the Monastery of Buddha and Mohammed by the American Air Force.

While McCauley went to the visa section to look for mail, Coldstream stopped at the press office. There were only a few local stringers on hand. The large influx of journalists was not expected until early November, in time for the coronation. The young Public Affairs Officer, Jerome Klein, was talking: "It's impossible! An American plane didn't do it. But I'll be honest with you. We have nothing but Radio Hanoi's account. If you prefer to wait in your offices or hotels, I'll phone you the moment we have anything more."

"Radio Hanoi? What in hell do you mean?" asked a deformed gnome of a man in a wheelchair. He could not sit up straight because of his hunchback. His voice was high-pitched and he seemed upset. "You're an American aren't you? Goddamn it, you know bloody well no American plane bombed that Monastery. It's a Communist trick. Why don't you say so?"

"Mister Coit," said Klein patiently. "We have queried CincPac, Washington, the Air Force, and even the Seventh Fleet. We're working on it. No one has replied yet. The only information we have came from *your* newspaper and that was a quote from Radio Hanoi."

"I'm a newspaper man," said Coit. "I've run the *Haidho Gazette* for a long time. I must print news from all sources. But you, goddamn it, should be giving us the American point of view. And you stand there saying you don't know anything, for Christ's sake."

"The moment I have facts I'll let you know."

"I'll see the Ambassador about this," said the hunchback, wheeling his chair out of the room.

When he had gone Coldstream said, "Mister Klein, does Coit always give you that hard a time?"

"I try to understand him. A man with his disability and pain has reason to be irritable."

"Marcus Coit has been like that for fifteen years," Coldstream said.

"I guess," continued Klein, "he feels a sense of power in Sarkhan. His newspaper influences the Embassy. They think if an American writes it, it must be factual."

"And he causes you trouble."

Klein smiled. "There's an old Chassidic saying: 'If the devil wants an assistant, he gives a man both pain and power.'"

Coldstream left. He was impressed with Klein's candor. He didn't lie to the press. When he didn't know the answer, he said so. Klein worked hard to know what was happening in Sarkhan. He looked like a cocktail party boy, dark and dapper, but Coldstream knew him to be a worker.

McCauley waited in the rotunda. Shielding his eyes, he pointed out through the large open doors and across the square. "Look."

From Sarkhan University a crowd of students walked in the direction of the Embassy, a few of them carrying signs still too distant to read.

The students walked across the square in twos and threes, laughing and talking. The long erratic line stretched out about a quarter of a mile. When the leaders reached the Embassy's main gate, Coldstream and McCauley could read their signs. The message seemed innocuous enough: "PLEASE, WE TALK WITH AMBASSADOR BROWN?"

"About five hundred students," said Coldstream. He paused, then added, "Strange."

Embassy staff members came to the rotunda to see what was happening. An excited gate guard took off in the direction of the Ambassador's office. Another closed the main gate, looking uncertainly over his shoulder.

Outside the gate the students stood quietly. Only those carrying the signs moved about through the crowd.

"Someone has herded them over," said McCauley. "Most of them seem to think it is a lark, and damned few can even read the English signs they're carrying."

Ambassador Brown, tall and angular, and now slightly flushed, came quickly into the rotunda, accompanied by the Sarkhanese guard. When the Ambassador reached the glass doors, Coldstream said, "Good morning, sir."

"Morning, Coldstream," he said in a nasal New Hampshire twang. "Oh, hello, Professor." He came over to shake hands. Then he turned to the guard.

"Open the gates and let them in."

Coldstream said gently, "I'd suggest you keep them out, sir. In Asian eyes the United States Ambassador deals with no one but the foreign minister."

Ambassador Brown, his rectangular face expressionless, said "Thank you, Coldstream." Then, turning again to the guard, he said, "Unlock the gates and let the students in."

The guard went to the gate, unlocked it, and pointed toward the Embassy steps.

The students, surprised, stood in small groups, embarrassed. Then one man carrying a sign urged a few reluctants inside and within a few moments nearly the whole group had entered the grounds and was walking toward the Embassy steps. They stood there, silent and respectful.

Ambassador Brown went out. He stopped at the top stair, smiled at the students, then slowly bowed in a deep Sarkhanese ceremonial greeting.

"They are supposed to bow first," McCauley said, "all of them as a group, before the Ambassador even recognizes them. He's embarrassing them."

The students did seem startled. Some looked at the ground. One of the leaders, older than the others, spoke in English. "It is generous of you to speak with us, Mister Ambassador Brown."

"What can I do for you young gentlemen?"

Two newsboys had come in with the students. One of them walked toward the Embassy shouting, "American Air Force bombs Sarkhanese holy temple!"

The leader of the students said, "Mister Ambassador, we came to ask why your Air Force bombed our most sacred monastery."

"I can assure you that no United States plane bombed the Monastery. Our radar had all of our planes clearly located."

The spokesman said, "Do you believe, sir, that Prince Ngong, the editor of our paper, the *Far Eastern Star*, is a liar?"

McCauley whispered to Coldstream, "That question is a classic

Marxist dialectic double bind. No matter what Brown says now, he will offend."

Ambassador Brown hesitated, then said carefully, "The account of the bombing comes from a Hanoi news broadcast, which is Communist propaganda. Of course, Prince Ngong, the editor, is not a liar. He merely reported a story, indicating its source."

The students lost their embarrassed look and listened intently. Those who understood English interpreted for the others.

"Your Excellency," said the spokesman, "naturally as students we have an interest in accuracy. That is why we are here. Now, sir, you believe that our leading newspaper, the *Far Eastern Star*, is an outlet for Communist propaganda. That is what you said."

"No! No!" said Ambassador Brown.

"Your Excellency, our most revered and holy temple has been destroyed by your warplane. Why, we do not know. We ask you about it and you tell us it is only Communist propaganda which our leading newspaper has spread. Sir, we came here with respect, hoping to get honest information, not to be insulted..."

Another newsboy, with a later edition of the paper, ran up, shouting, "American bombs kill fifty-three Sarkhanese priests at holy monastery."

A new tenseness seemed to weld the student group together.

The Ambassador smiled. His hands tugged nervously at the bottom of his jacket. His cool New England poise was ebbing.

"The poor son of a bitch has been boxed in," said McCauley.

Ambassador Brown said, "Gentlemen, I am talking with you as a friendly gesture, at your request..."

"The truth! What is the truth?" shouted a student in the rear.

Ambassador Brown said, "I assure you that not a single American bomb has touched Sarkhanese soil."

"What is your proof? Give us proof!"

"Gentlemen, I have just spoken to General Hajn, your Minister of Defense. He is sending an investigation committee to the monastery to get the facts. I have already received assurance from my government that no United States plane was even in the air when the monastery was bombed."

"Your government also denied the U-2 flights! Your government also denied the presence of Chiang Kai-shek troops in Burma. Give us proof!"

Ambassador Brown said, "Gentlemen, your own government will make a statement later in the day and give you the proof you need. Thank you for coming to see me. You are always welcome here." He waved at them, bowed, and turned into the Embassy.

"As retreats go, that was a pretty fair one," Coldstream said.

The newsboys began shouting again, only now it was "Americans killed Sarkhanese!"

The student leaders, the ones carrying the signs, took up the slogan, "Americans killed Sarkhanese!" They yelled it, moving their signs up and down in unison and stamping their feet.

Within minutes all the students were chanting, "Americans killed Sarkhanese!" and stamping their feet in a thunderous rhythm.

The leaders dropped their signs, put their hands on the hips of men in front of them and began to snake-dance. The rest followed, stamping and chanting in a long frenzied line.

To Coldstream this was an old picture. He remembered the student snake dances which finally had denied Eisenhower access to Japan in 1957, the frenzied students of Saigon who had crumpled U.S. policy, the passionate and determined youths who kept every South Korean government unstable. For the first time that day he felt a profound uneasiness. Near him, the spectators in the Embassy watched, their mood something between amusement and rising anxiety.

The students snake-danced around the flagpole. The leaders suddenly broke off, grabbed the halyards and lowered the American flag. A gasp went up from the Embassy personnel. There was a moment of silence as the students tried to unfasten the flag.

Then a squad of helmeted U.S. marines carrying submachine guns doubled-timed around the corner of the building. Their officer, a captain, shouted an order and the Marines started toward the pole.

The Ambassador shouted, "What do you think you're doing?"

"Stopping the riot, sir."

"Goddamn it. You stay here. Do you want an international incident?"

"Sir," said the Marine, "if we shoot two bursts over their heads the riot is over." He spoke with authority. "They'll run for cover, Mister Ambassador."

"Get back. Return to your barracks."

"Sir, those bastards are tramping on the flag . . ."

Coldstream stepped up. "Mister Ambassador, I suggest you let the Marines retrieve the flag . . ."

Ambassador Brown said with rage, "Captain, get your Marines to the rear of the Embassy. And you," he added, turning to Coldstream and McCauley, "kindly remember that I am the Ambassador here."

By now the students were snake-dancing out of the Embassy compound, dragging the United States flag in the dirt behind them.

On the steps of the Embassy, Ambassador Brown, tall and lanky, suddenly hunched protectively, like a large animal cornered and looking around for help. He turned to the Embassy Counsellor.

"Sometimes you have to pay a high price to save lives and keep control of events."

His voice begged for assurance.

3

The House above the River

The monsoon rain had started again. Coldstream and McCauley rode from the Embassy in silence. Both had experienced riots before. McCauley had watched the Indonesians tear down the American flag at the U.S. Embassy in Djakarta.

"Tad," Coldstream finally asked, "what do you think about Brown?"

McCauley did not respond. He sat erect in the jeep, unmoving. The rain splattered in, wetting him. Outside it came in long lashes of gray which bent the palms, made green, soft waves along the grass of the Royal Square and snapped buds from aging flowers.

"It doesn't add up," Coldstream went on.

"It adds up," McCauley said sharply. "It adds up perfectly. Brown is another nice amateur diplomat spending a pleasant couple of years in a country he doesn't understand. He's a decent guy who's doing the best he can, and he thinks he's doing well. He'll go home with decorations, a scrapbook of pictures, a silver tea service from the King. And he'll leave disaster behind."

"I'm not sure it's disaster yet," Coldstream said.

"You ought to be sure," McCauley said bitterly. "Ed, you know damned well that was a rigged riot. I don't give a damn if it was a little one, its pattern was unmistakable: A bunch of kids who *thought* they were on a lark at first. Then they found themselves pushed into action, bewildered and embarrassed. They found themselves yelling, chasing Marines around the corner and trampling on the U.S. flag. I don't care whose flag or whose marines, Ed." McCauley paused. He swiveled his head and glared at Coldstream. "And you know what I mean."

A huge vine ripped loose and in a beautiful troubling splash of green moved across the road.

"You think it's the same old thing again?"

The only Sarkhanese on the streets were ricksha pullers and

17

noodle hawkers. They wore enormous hats and capes made of thatched reeds. There was nothing, however, to protect them from the chill gusts of the southwest monsoon. The ricksha men were peasants who had come to the city and who could find no other jobs. After a few years they had knotty, purple varicose veins on their muscled legs, and many developed tuberculosis and suffered from malnutrition. The city drew them, yet there they died young. Ricksha pullers were the patient ones, conserving every ounce of energy, standing like statuary until the approach of a potential passenger turned them loud and persuasive.

"I know it's the same old thing," McCauley said, patting the thick manila folder under his arm. "Ed, you sent this stuff to me to analyze. Pamphlets, petitions, throwaways, posters, announcements of meetings. They came from all over the country?"

They were in the waterfront area now, passing the Bandor Corporation's big wharves, and Coldstream geared down the jeep. "I tried to make it a cross section. My people found them even in the mountain villages. It's all new in the last few months. That's why I wanted your opinion."

"Whoever wrote these pamphlets has done first-class research on the ethnic, religious, and political background of Sarkhan. It's all printed on the same kind of cheap paper, on the same press. The character for 'people' on every piece of paper here has the same small defect at the bottom. But the job is effective. It is superb—if you're a Communist. The subject matter skillfully plays on things the Sarkhanese have almost forgotten."

"Almost forgotten?"

"This propaganda was done by someone who knows and understands the old feuds of Sarkhan, and who wants them brought up to date and started again, but in Marxist-Leninist terms—without once using the term Marxism." McCauley stretched and yawned. "This propaganda is beautiful in a dirty way."

"Can you find out who wrote them? Who printed them? Who distributed them?"

"Yes. All I need is a good magnifying glass and a page of print from every printing press in Sarkhan."

"Every printing press in Sarkhan?"

"Every one."

They followed the winding road along the Tirriwongi River. The river was wide here because a mile to the north it was joined by the mighty Sekong.

When they reached Coldstream's fish-packing plant, he parked his jeep. Dozens of Sarkhanese were scaling and gutting fish to be dried out and boxed for shipment to inland areas.

A thin man, almost emaciated, with two fingers missing from one hand, supervised the unloading. Behind him was an efficient complex of moving belts, sprays, glittering knives, and small brown men wearing blood-splattered gowns.

Coldstream waved, and the supervisor loped the length of the yard, stopped in front of Coldstream, and gave a good-natured salute.

"How goes it, Tuc?" Coldstream asked.

"OK, boss," said the man. He looked at McCauley and nodded. This was not the professor's first visit to the wharf.

"You enjoy your vacation last month?" Coldstream asked.

Tuc had fish scales up to his elbows and he picked at them while he looked at the two men and then back at the workers.

"Good time," Tuc said. "I saw my family in the north."

The jeep chugged up the steep road to Coldstream's house.

"I saw Tuc by the Embassy gate as we drove out," McCauley said.

"Tuc, the manager of my fish plant?"

"Yes. Who could mistake that hand?"

"He's a Communist," said Coldstream. "Only he doesn't know I know he is."

"A Communist?"

"Or at least a Communist front man," Coldstream said. "You know how it is here. There are the signs of a Communist organization in Sarkhan, but they are misty. I get information from my people, but it's hard to add up. The front groups have the usual names—the Sarkhanese Liberation Union, the Sarkhan Student Union, the Sarkhan Political Union."

"Have you nothing concrete?"

"A couple of tons of reports. I have a list of people whose actions show Communist behavior. But I can't link them. And then, some are nicknames or aliases."

"That's the way it will be until the Communists have taken the place over," McCauley said harshly. "Hell, they never call themselves Communists until they are solidly in the saddle. It's only then the people hear about socialism and Marx. Up until that time it's 'throw the white man out' or 'end colonialism' or 'forward with Sarkhanese nationalism.' But I still don't understand why you took Tuc into the plant if you know he's a Communist or a follower or whatever he is."

"The Communists try to put one informer in every big organization. Tuc's mine. He's easy to identify; now I know whom to watch. Also, he is one hell of a fish-gutter."

"How can you be sure?"

"I put one of my bright village boys close to him and Tuc invited him to join some group. They call it the Sarkhan National Front and they meet in the loft of the packing plant a few nights a month. Tuc asked my permission. It sounds more like a choral group than a political organization. My village boy is not sure yet what they're supposed to be doing. But he says Tuc hasn't mentioned the word 'Communist.' "

As they approached the house, Coldstream looked at his watch.

"The Peking broadcast starts in a minute and a half." He pushed down on the accelerator.

The house on top of the hill was impressive. Coldstream still took pleasure in it every time he came home. Below, the great rivers joined. They had, over the centuries, carved out a white granite cliff that jutted up almost four hundred feet. Coldstream's house on the summit was exquisitely Sarkhanese. It contained no metal in its construction, not even nails. The cooking stoves were stone, the kitchen pots were the famous blue clay vessels of the Nordomii district near the Vietnamese border. The plumbing pipes were terra cotta and the faucets fashioned from ceramic, glazed a deep blue. The windows were made from light amber Haidho glass—a glass so rare that at least two ancient invaders had laid seige to the city just to obtain it. In the whole house there were only two non-Sarkhanese things. One was Taja's wardrobe, partly Parisian, and the other was a four-inch-thick steel door which secured Coldstream's basement office.

Coldstream hurried through the long living room, on the way waving at a man lying on the native sofa. "How are you, Xinh?"

In a weak voice the man replied, "Better, Buan Suang. I must tell you . . ."

The Sarkhanese was gaunt and his eyes were disproportionately large. His left shoulder and left side were heavily bandaged and Coldstream noticed the dark red of dried blood through the bandages.

"We'll be up right after the broadcast, Xinh," said Coldstream.

They hurried down circular stairs to the "vault." The room gleamed with radio equipment and filing cabinets. Large maps of Sarkhan, Southeast Asia, and China covered the walls.

Coldstream switched on a radio and set the tuning dial.

"They'll be on in twenty seconds." He put his hand on a small metal box near the radio and smiled at McCauley. "Something new since you were here last. This gadget is my pride and joy. Made it myself. It is an induction recorder. It helps cut through the static."

"Do you get useful information from the broadcasts?" asked McCauley. "Isn't the hot stuff all in code?"

"It's mostly in plain language—Chinese usually—and for me it's all hot stuff. Hell, it keeps me in business! If I get hints of a border raid, I order my river craft away from that area. Or I'll move the merchandise from my trading post. How do you think I got my people out of New Guinea in 1962 and out of the East Coast of Malaya in 1964? That's why all my ships and trading posts have radios and keep regular schedules with me. Also, when Peking is going to dump soy beans, pigs' bristles, tung oil, or cheap cotton prints, I know whether to sell short or change destination."

Coldstream turned the dials impatiently. "Peking should be on now."

He looked at the large ship's chronometer on the wall, then at his wristwatch. "My watch is five minutes fast." He couldn't suppress his annoyance. Any inaccuracy irritated him. He was aware of McCauley's mocking smile.

Coldstream picked up a leather pouch. "You want something more serious than that riot to worry about? Look at these."

Opening the leather pouch, he dropped eleven bullets into McCauley's hand.

"Tad, during the last few weeks my people took these bullets out of eleven headless bodies floating down the rivers from the north. Five of them are U.S. Army forty-five caliber and the others are of Russian manufacture. Can you guess who the dead men were?"

"No games, please, Buan Suang."

"They were Buddhist priests and Moslem religious leaders—all from the northern provinces."

"How do you know?"

"By their clothes and amulets."

McCauley shook his head in surprise. "There haven't been killings or beheadings of leaders since the religious wars of six hundred years ago! Do you associate this with the riot?"

Coldstream shrugged. "Yes, but I don't know how. It's just that too many troubles are beginning at the same time. Young men coming back from 'up north'; bodies in the river; tax collectors being killed; an upswing in nationalism; rumors about 'white man's exploitation'; provincial newspapers turning against the government for vague reasons; the formation of all these new groups with patriotic names but ambiguous objectives. And there's Xinh upstairs. We'll talk to him later."

"Does Cogswell know about these things?"

"Only in general. I thought we could send Cogswell a joint report in the next few days."

The metal door of the vault clicked open. Coldstream and McCauley watched the woman enter. She was not beautiful, but handsome, and very graceful as she moved. She might have been forty, but she might have been ten years younger. A short line of smallpox scars disfigured her right cheek.

McCauley walked to her, reached for her hand, and said, "Taja." He bowed, and kissed her hand, suddenly quite serious. Unconsciously he pulled his shoulders back and his stomach in. "You are more beautiful than ever."

"And you, as ever, are flattering me," Taja said, speaking English with a slight French accent. "It is good for both of us to see you. When you are not around, Edward becomes bored because he has no one to talk to. And I have no one to flatter me."

"Then the men of Sarkhan should be shot," McCauley said smiling, "like common dogs."

Coldstream smiled at Taja. Her beauty was always reflected in the eyes of others—even rumpled, clumsy McCauley who, to Coldstream's knowledge, had never taken time enough from his Sarkhanese studies to look at a woman seriously.

"Taja, did you hear about the riot and the flag?"

"Yes, Edward. It made me ashamed."

"What do you make of it?"

She looked at them directly. "Some of those students knew the flag would be pulled down several hours before it happened."

A crackling noise came from the loudspeaker. A voice spoke in Chinese, but it was not clear. Coldstream turned the dials, but he could not eliminate the static.

"Excuse me," he said, plugging in the earphones. Then, totally absorbed, he muttered, "I'm getting it now," and turned away from others.

The Chinese propaganda broadcasts helped Coldstream keep up his fluency in the language. He had learned it almost twenty years ago when, as a Navy commander, he had been assigned liaison officer to the Chinese Red Army. That was when Coldstream first started having difficulties with the State Department. He had written a long report predicting that unless checked politically the Communists would throw Chiang Kai-shek out and would try to take all of Southeast Asia. He had recommended somewhat unusual methods to stop the Communists: the U.S. had to go into the villages and reach the people politically and economically while they kept the enemy at bay with guns and tanks. But he couldn't get anybody outside of the Navy to consider the report. The U.S. Embassy in Chungking had forwarded it to Washington, disapproving its every recommendation.

Since coming to Sarkhan, Coldstream had practiced cautiously what he had learned in China. On his plantations he had established schools and taught basic sanitation and health. But the instructors and nurses were from the local villages. Once the people were educated and well fed, he found that they soon devised ways of protecting themselves from marauders and from corrupt officials.

McCauley had for many years observed what he called his friend's "be-kind-to-the-Gooks" program with a mixture of sardonic humor and grudging respect.

Now Coldstream removed the earphones and switched off the radio.

"The Peking news says oppression among the working class in Sarkhan is so brutal that there was a spontaneous riot of protest at the American Embassy."

McCauley said, "Can't they think of any fresh ideas?"

"Neither can we," Coldstream replied.

Taja interrupted. "Xinh has been waiting anxiously all morning to see you. I've applied compresses and his bleeding has almost stopped."

They left the vault and returned upstairs to the living room.

The Sarkhanese on the sofa opened his eyes as they approached, and smiled.

"The doctor says Xinh should not talk much," said Taja.

"I feel better," Xinh said. "And it is important that you hear. I have a few more names for your list, Buan Suang."

"You paid dearly for them, Xinh."

He began to talk slowly, breathing deeply between sentences.

4

Xinh's Village

Xinh Guyen, the manager of Coldstream's trading station in the small village of Boa Binh, had just walked into the company's *godown* to warm up the radio transmitter. It was almost time for the evening schedule which linked together all Coldstream's stations in Sarkhan.

For two thousand years little had changed in this isolated region. To the north, the big loop of the Sekong swept past the village. The cliffs on the other side had markings indicating the river's various heights.

It would soon be dark and at this time of day there was no wind. The fishing boats, propelled by long sweep sculls, approached the spidery docks. Fishermen who had already moored their crafts stretched their nets out to dry. The river was swift at this time of year. The nets had to be mended daily.

Near the *godown* were the three dozen houses which made up Boa Binh, small coconut-thatched cubicles raised eight feet off the ground by *takhian* logs. Each year during the monsoon the Sekong overflowed. The villagers retreated to their elevated houses while the water poured over their fields and rice paddies, depositing rich, black silt from the north. But now the river had receded some and the earth was merely moist. Pigs rooted under the houses, snouting about for bits of papaya, mangoes which had grown too old, and bits of dropped rice. Skinny chickens pecked at the pigs and darted off with almost invisible prizes. No one in Boa Binh or anywhere in Sarkhan dropped rice carelessly. It was always an accident. Food was so important it was almost deified.

Just beyond the last house was a small temple, and Jan Ti, the young new *bonze*, was sweeping the steps.

To the east and west of Boa Binh the jungle pressed close, dense, immensely high, almost impenetrable in places. During the daylight hours the villagers harvested the jungle. A source of

25

food, it could also be a source of death from snakes, collapsing trees, an occasional tiger, a horde of white ants. During the daylight the people of Boa Binh knew how to survive in the jungle, and they considered it a friend. But at night most Sarkhanese were wary of the jungle. After dark, evil spirits came out of the earth and from the trees, whispering and howling. The spirits' dank odors sometimes drifted into the village from the west forest. At night Sarkhanese took refuge in their elevated houses.

Xinh felt uneasy. The normal night sounds of the village were missing. Children moved slowly and had stopped chattering. The adult talk, which always became lively as the rice was cooking, was absent. Tonight, he knew, there was a new danger in the jungle. Xinh had been born in Boa Binh. He had left it for only six years out of his thirty-two to go to school in Haidho and after that he had gone to work for Coldstream's organization. Xinh never displayed his education in front of his friends in Boa Binh. He wore the same clothes they did, worked with the same rough, cracked hands.

Sometimes Xinh felt isolated from his own village. Partly it was his education, partly it was because he worked for the white man Coldstream, and that set him apart. The trading station was, after all, the only innovation in Boa Binh in the memory of living man. Xinh was respected, but the villagers knew not quite where to place him.

Two old men were playing chess on the *godown* veranda. One of them was his father, Tien, the village chief, a wiry little man whose movements were now handicapped by cataracts. His left eye was sightless and his head was cocked to the left as he studied the white ivory men on the board. With annoyance, but no self-pity, he would curse softly when his lack of coordinated vision caused him to push over a chessman. But his bad eye did not diminish his strength or authority. He had absolute obedience from his six grandchildren and the respect of everyone in the village since first he had been elected thirty-seven years ago.

The other man was Bok, a few years older than Tien, the village herbalist, astrologist, and palmist, and Tien's favorite chess partner.

"No one stirs in the village," Xinh said casually, closing the door to the radio room. His schedule was not for twenty minutes. "Do we have trouble?"

Tien shrugged. "Maybe trouble, maybe not. One of the boys out trapping mongoose saw four strangers with guns walking toward us."

"How long ago did the boy return with that news?" Xinh asked.

"Ten minutes ago, no more."

Xinh glanced around again. In ten minutes everything in the village—all the bustling activity—had stopped. The people had withdrawn to the thin protection of their huts.

"These are strange days," Bok said. "Men with guns coming from the jungle."

"There have always been hunters in the jungle," Xinh said. He was probing for information.

"But they were not strangers nor did they carry the new little machine guns," Tien said, glancing up at his son, his head cocked at an angle.

Four men came out of the jungle, ten yards west of the trail. They had avoided the clearly marked path, Xinh knew, to prevent ambush. They moved with the fluid, cautious advance of hunters familiar with the rain jungle. One man in front, two men behind him, like the sides of an arrowhead, and the fourth man following, barely visible, waiting to see what would happen in the village. The men carried Sten guns.

The advance point of the patrol moved directly toward Xinh's *godown*. The fourth man followed them, but in a peculiar manner, flitting from one side to another, seeking protection from a rock here, slipping behind a *peepul* tree there, and while the other three had slung their guns over their shoulders, he held his belly-high, with one hand on the magazine, the other on the trigger.

The three men stopped in front of the *godown*. Xinh looked around but could not see the fourth. They were professionals of some kind. Xinh recognized the one walking behind the leader. He was a thin, bespectacled man who had come to Boa Binh eight months ago in a small boat. He was a skilled carpenter and had asked Tien if he could stay in the village for a few days. He would, he said, work for his food.

Tien had welcomed the man and given him an empty hut. The carpenter had busied himself about the village, offering to help strengthen older huts or do whatever required a good carpenter. To his obvious surprise he found that the village already had two carpenters trained at the local school which had been founded by a loan from Coldstream. He then interested himself in the medical problems of the village, saying he had had some practice in first aid. He had a small kit of medicines in his boat. Tien had pointed out to him that Xinh, his son, was also trained in medical help and had a supply of medicines which the villagers had bought themselves. Yaws, malaria, *tajh* fever, and cholera had been eliminated from the village several years ago. Oddly enough, this information had seemed to irritate the carpenter. He had wandered about the village aimlessly for another week, talking to the younger men. He talked of strange things—Sarkhanese independence, the threat of "white man's exploitation," the glowing future of Sarkhan when it was "no longer dominated by outside forces." The young men had joked with him, not quite understanding what he meant, but feeling he was a friendly and unknowing man.

The carpenter had spent many hours in Xinh's store, talking with Xinh about the folly of the village becoming indebted to the South East Asia Trading Corporation. Xinh had pointed out that the village was not indebted to anyone. In fact, every family in the village had, for the last few years, saved at least a few rupees. Almost all of them owned their land or were in the process of buying it from the "absentee" landlord.

The carpenter had left suddenly one morning, unhappy and sullen. Now he had returned, carrying a gun. He had returned a stranger.

The two old men continued their game. It would be undignified to appear curious. The hands of the old men hovered over the pieces.

The first stranger, a man in his mid-twenties, spoke: "Old men, we have come to call a meeting of the village and bring news."

He was taller than the others and when he smiled, which was frequently, he showed a gold tooth. There was a strained friendliness in his voice. "We are friends. My name is Nam Tho, and I come from the north."

Tien acted as if nothing had happened. He glanced at his chessmen, clucked his tongue, held a piece up, and deliberated. Then he sighed and showed what his strategy was. Bok snorted, the friendly noise of a man who knows he has lost the game. They began to group the pieces again as if the strangers were not present.

"We have come to call a meeting of the village and to inform everyone of important news," Nam Tho repeated, a slight confusion on his face.

The carpenter whispered in Nam Tho's ear.

"In other villages we have come as friends, as helpers," Nam Tho said. "We have helped to repair huts, to heal the sick. We have paid for what we ate. But in this village you are dominated by reactionaries. You will not listen to reason. You hold back from helping the people's cause." His voice trailed off.

Tien nodded at his opponent to make the first move, then he surreptitiously studied the man who called himself Nam Tho. A gold tooth meant he was from a wealthy family. He also had the more deliberate accent of a city man. His hands were not nicked and scarred like those of a peasant or worker. Obviously he did not understand the village customs. The hesitancy in his voice indicated he was nervous. But for a city man he had moved skillfully out of the jungle. For that he had been well trained.

"We have come to be helpful. If you force us to be persuasive, we will be so," Nam Tho said.

Neither man seemed to hear his warning.

"Call a meeting immediately, old man, or someone will die." Nam Tho addressed the command to Tien.

Tien looked up, almost wearily.

"It is our custom, stranger, that the village has a meeting only after I, the chief, am satisfied that the reason fulfills Buddha's three requirements: Is it necessary? Is it true? Is it kind?"

Nam Tho shifted his feet and his smile vanished. "Old Chief, I will kill *you* if you do not call the meeting." There was a break in his voice and to mask it he deliberately raised the Sten gun. "The days of superstition are over. These are new days. Better days. Now call your people."

Tien moved a knight, sighed, and looked up.

"I cannot call my people unless I approve the business of the meeting," he said. "If you wish to kill me, you can do so." His voice had the authority of a man accustomed to command. His head at an angle, the better to look squarely into the eyes of Nam Tho, he directed, "but do it quickly if you are to do it."

Nam Tho's hands trembled slightly and Xinh knew this was the first time he had been this close to killing a man. Xinh also knew that his father would die. Nam Tho had been trapped by his own arrogance, his own uncertainty. Clearly, he did not want to kill Tien. He had been bluffing because he did not know about villagers. But now Nam Tho could not reverse his decision. Xinh could not intervene. His father would forbid such an intervention, which defied the tradition of the village.

Nam Tho moved his gun. The barrel wavered for a moment, then steadied. He made no effort to aim. It was not necessary. The first slug caught Tien with his hand holding a knight, his wrinkled and knobby fingers clenched as if he were choking the piece, its head protruding desperately. The second slug smashed into the middle of Tien's chest. Tien moved to complete the play, but instead he rolled slowly backward, curled his legs up tightly against his chest, and fell sideways.

"Call the meeting, old man," said Nam Tho, glaring at Bok. "You are now the chief. I have appointed you. Now call the meeting—or you will be dead like your friend."

Bok warily stood up, his legs unfolding gracefully, his back straight and his posture easy. First he spoke softly to Xinh. "Your father would have won," he said gently. He turned then to Nam Tho. "You cannot make me chief," Bok said. "Only the people of the village can do that. It is their task."

"It is not their task any more, Village Chief. Now it is the task of the People's Movement to tell the villagers the truth. The time of ignorance and superstition is over. Call your people together. We have important truths to tell them. And we need help from those who love Sarkhan. Now hurry!"

Bok stared. Nam Tho moved his feet again, but still the old herbalist said nothing.

"The times, old man, when you could play lackey for the imperialist powers in your village are over," Nam Tho said, his voice shrill. "Call the village together."

Bok slowly, deliberately, shook his head.

The carpenter muttered at Nam Tho. They would gain nothing by arguing. Either kill the old man or get someone else to call the meeting.

"Old man!" Nam Tho's nerves were tightening. "Are you crazy? I tell you, call the village to a meeting!"

A voice behind him said, "I will call the villagers. It will be easier that way."

Nam Tho had started to raise his gun. He moved woodenly, lowering his arm, a look of vagrant disappointment on his face.

It was Jan Ti, the Buddhist *bonze*, who had spoken. He had walked down from the small pagoda.

Cupping his hands, Jan Ti shouted, "Oh, people of Boa Binh! Assemble here for an important meeting." He walked down the street shouting.

In five minutes every man, woman, and child of Boa Binh stood outside the veranda of the *godown*. They stood in three ranks.

Nam Tho addressed them. "Fellow Sarkhanese, this is an important day." He swung his gun muzzle down. "Today all of you of Boa Binh will be joining hands with the other villages of Sarkhan to restore your rights and to assert the independence of our ancient Sarkhan ways."

The people of Boa Binh, perhaps eighty-five of them, stood quiet and impassive. Looking at any individual face one would have imagined its owner deaf. Collectively they seemed not to be listening.

Nam Tho's expression did not change, but his finger drummed on the magazine of his gun. Xinh knew then what his father had recognized earlier, that Nam Tho lacked experience in dealing with the sometimes maddening quiet of the Asian peasant.

"Twenty years ago your taxes were five rupees per hectare and five rupees for head tax," Nam Tho said, speaking too loudly. "What are they now?"

He pointed to a man about thirty years old who was standing at the front of the crowd.

"You. What were your taxes last year?"

"I do not remember."

"You do not remember your taxes?" Nam Tho exclaimed. "You must be a very rich man!"

A few of the villagers laughed, the flat Asian laugh that carried no humor, and then they were quiet again, staring straight ahead.

"Does anyone remember what his taxes were last year?"

No one stirred. Finally the hand of Jan Ti, the young man wearing the saffron robes of a Buddhist *bonze*, was raised.

It was then that Xinh remembered about Jan Ti. He had left the village for a year to "go north" to learn a trade. When he came back he could read and write. He brought a knapsack of comic books which showed the history of "New China." The comic books had been popular with the illiterates and the children in the village and gradually had been handled into shreds. Two weeks ago Jan Ti had taken up his year of service as a Buddhist *bonze*. He had shaved his head, begged for food, and meditated in the one-room Buddhist temple. Recently he had distributed pamphlets throughout the village, which disturbed the older devout people in the predominantly Buddhist community. Xinh had sent one of the pamphlets to Coldstream.

"The tax per hectare is now fifteen rupees and the head tax is twenty-five rupees," Jan Ti said in a clear voice.

"There," Nam Tho said in a flatly affirmative voice. "Now you see what is happening. The people of the village are helpless. Our taxes go up but the money all goes to the capitalists, like the American who owns this *godown*. And our government is a prisoner of American militarists who will push Sarkhan into war so that America can make profits."

The villagers did not respond.

"For many years China and Vietnam were oppressed by white colonists. But times have changed. The Americans, French, and British have been thrown out. Now we Sarkhanese must liberate ourselves. It will not be easy because the capitalistic leeches have their beaks deep into Sarkhanese flesh. We must make sacrifices and struggle and work hard. Do you understand?"

Still the villagers stood expressionless and silent.

"This district has the honor of being the first to be organized for liberation. We must liberate Sarkhan, we must free King Diad and Prince Lin from the grasp of the white man. The Liberation Committee welcomes your help. We ask for four volunteers who will come with us."

The villagers avoided Nam Tho's eyes.

"Four volunteers, step forward! Do not be frightened by rumors of the Viet Cong—that contemptible phrase by which the running dogs of capitalism label the people's movement. We work only for liberation. If they call us 'Sark Cong,' we will take pride in the name."

No one moved.

Nam Tho walked over to the first man. He was twenty and married a month. Pointing his finger, Nam Tho said, "You are the first. Step forward and volunteer."

The man neither moved nor answered.

Now it was almost dark. Nam Tho cried, "You are afraid of the capitalists and traitors! You are slaves!" He pointed to the body of Tien. "You see what happens to those who collaborate with capitalists."

Jan Ti said quietly to the villagers, "It is wise you listen."

"You are not the elder!" said Xinh angrily.

Abruptly Nam Tho raised his gun, swung around, and squeezed off a single shot.

Xinh felt the slug explode in his left shoulder, jerking it violently. He knew he was not fatally wounded. Nam Tho had not wanted to kill him. He had wanted him to survive as a reminder of terror. Xinh fell slowly to the floor. Then the pain came, a jolt at first, then in red waves. He lay still, pretending to be dead.

Jan Ti, the *bonze*, took charge. He walked down the line of villagers and tapped four young men.

"These will volunteer," he said. "We must stop the killing and work for liberation."

The four young men stepped forward.

"Good," said Nam Tho, lowering his gun. "I knew from the start that Boa Binh was a village of patriots."

The strangers ordered the four volunteers to get their bamboo

A-frame back packs. Ignoring Tien's body and that of his son, they went into the *godown*. On the first A-frame they put a fifty-kilo bag of rice. The second they loaded with canned goods and ammunition and the five rifles from Xinh's rack. On the third they lashed the portable transmitter-receiver radio, and on the fourth the company's papers and money and ten pairs of shoes.

The strangers headed for the dark jungle, moving the volunteers ahead of them.

"At night, sir?" said one of the volunteers.

Nam Tho laughed. "What is your name?"

"Suttka, sir."

"Suttka, the jungle at night has been the friend of the Viet Cong and now it will become the friend of the Sark Cong. We used the night to defeat the French, later the Americans. Now hurry, my four new friends. We must be at camp before morning."

At the edge of the jungle Nam Tho turned and shouted, "Within a week we will return for more supplies. See that they are ready!"

"*Vissentari!*" answered Jan, the *bonze*. In Sarkanese the word means "liberation."

Xinh did not move. His bleeding had lessened. He knew that Jan Ti would not approach him until daylight. He would not wish to risk the old Sarkhanese superstition that if one comes close to a dead man at night, the dead man might steal the spirit of the living.

For an hour Jan Ti was in the *godown* looking at the merchandise. Then he turned out the Coleman lantern and departed.

Xinh tried to move. His left side hurt so much he knew bone had been splintered. Inching along on his right side, he crawled the seventy yards to the river, and pulled himself into the company's small *huatze*. He loosed the line, and the *huatze* floated downstream in the swift current. It was not until Xinh was well down the river that, painfully, moving slowly and using only his good arm, he started the outboard motor. Then he turned the *huatze* and headed toward Haidho. He wondered if he could stay conscious until he reached Coldstream's house.

5

The Fish-Gutter
and the General

The thin man with the two fingers missing from his right hand came slowly past the houses that lined the Botanical Gardens. It was one of the few streets in Haidho which was paved and had graveled sidewalks. Behind the houses was the Museum of Sarkhanese Art which Prince Lin had started. Most of the houses had once been occupied by French businessmen. Now they provided quarters for foreign consuls, ambassadors, and a few high-ranking Sarkhanese officials.

The man walked slowly, glancing at the official residences. It was early evening, but the lights from the houses cast a dim glow which reached to the street. The man took advantage of the light to pick a fish scale from his arm. He was aware that he had an odor, but only from the reactions of others. Long ago he had lost the ability to detect it. After eight hours in the fish-processing plant, digging into the small mountains of cold fish, rasping them with a scaler and then filleting them and pushing pink fish entrails into huge barrels for Coldstream's fish-meal factory on the outskirts of town—after that one did not have much sense of smell left.

Fifty yards ahead the sentry in front of Hajn's house was walking directly toward him. In a few seconds he would reach the end of his beat, would stamp his feet, come to present arms, turn, stamp feet again, and start to patrol in the opposite direction. It was a perfect Buckingham Palace performance.

When the sentry turned, the bayonet on his rifle gleaming, Tuc went flat on his stomach and slid under the hedge that surrounded Hajn's house. Inside the hedge there was a thick wire fence with a very narrow mesh. Tuc followed the hedge to the rear of the house, feeling the base of the fence with his hand. In

35

the back he found a narrow hole that looked big enough to pass a small dog. Expertly, with no sign of strain, Tuc pulled himself through the hole.

He went across the lawn quickly. He had learned years before that, in the night, a single unbroken movement was less conspicuous than a series of stops and starts. When he was in the shadow of the rear veranda he looked around. The guard had turned the corner. His posture was hesitant, he seemed uncertain whether he should take his next step. He turned and went back to the front.

Tuc squatted under an open window. Inside the room General Hajn and his guest, United States Ambassador Spratt Brown, were talking. Tuc could hear them clearly in comfortable but still somewhat formal conversation. For some reason, from their relaxed tones, perhaps, Tuc knew they were sitting down.

"Mister Ambassador, I have had my security people check the whole matter out," Hajn said. "It was intended as a prank by some of the university students. They were appalled when it misfired and some other people, non-students, I might add, got carried away and thought it was genuine."

"General, I am reassured by what you say, but I confess that it was a bit harrowing to see the American flag desecrated," Ambassador Brown said.

"As you know, we have recovered the flag. I myself will return it with appropriate public ceremony. Also, at the same time, you will be given the Order of the Royal Heart, second class. It was your coolness and quick thinking that averted bloodshed."

"Thank you, General."

How little they knew, Tuc thought. He marveled at the inability of Westerners to look hard at unpleasant things. He, Tuc, had known for years that the conversion of individuals into crowds and crowds into mobs would be a part of his life's work. Long ago he had read not only Lebon and Canetti and the works of the Western sociologists, but he had also read of the older cultures and how crowds and mobs were formed centuries earlier: Cumoni on the mysteries of the Mithra, Cusinier on Indochina, Callaway on the Amazulu, Erman on Egypt. He had read of Indians throwing themselves beneath the wheels of the Juggernaut, of Moslems working themselves into a frenzy where every male in a mob castrated himself. He had studied the long rising pitch of primitive tribes as they worked themselves into a killing mood.

But always he checked his readings against what he observed. And he tested. He had organized small protest meetings in Chinese villages, flag-waving demonstrations at Cambodian schools, bloody riots in Hanoi and Saigon. He had whipped intellectuals into irrationality...

Tuc gave an inaudible grunt of satisfaction, like a man who belches happily after a perfect meal. In Coldstream's loft, Tuc was carrying out the great sweep of theory. He was distilling thousands of years of accumulated trial and error into a neat, precise functional instrument. Tuc was forging the group into "crystals" who could control a crowd through all moods and actions, like animals in a circus. Tuc grunted again. The beautiful part of it was that not one of the group knew what was happening. They all thought they were part of a patriotic and social organization.

"General, I appreciate the gesture of the Order," Brown said. "As you know I have tried to blend our Embassy into your way of life, to make our people understand the history, religion, rituals, and traditions of your people. At the American school, our children take lessons in Sarkhanese. At the same time I have to tell you that American public opinion would be very... well, the only way to put it, is very negative toward a raid on our Embassy and the desecration of our flag."

"But it was not a raid. It was a prank that got out of control."

Even Hajn did not know the real purpose of the riot, Tuc thought. Somehow, almost against his will, the knowledge made him happy. He, Tuc, had used the riot as a test and as training for his group.

"I will tell you in confidence that I persuaded my government to tone down the affair. The American press carried almost nothing. No censorship, mind you. We Americans don't believe in that. But we had to make certain the journalists did not distort a harmless, but, shall I say, embarrassing disturbance. Fortunately, I am a good friend of Marcus Coit, who represents the wire services."

Tuc sucked his breath in from surprise. Was the American

Ambassador unaware that many native-language papers in Asia had carried the violently anti-American version of the riot, the version that came from Hanoi?

There was a pause and Tuc heard ice tinkling in their glasses. Tuc found it an attractive sound. An odd thought formed in his mind: he would like to try whisky.

"We do not, of course, believe in censorship, either, Mister Ambassador," Hajn said.

The Ambassador looked at his watch. "General, it's always a pleasure working with you." He stood up. "I've got to be off. I am giving a lecture this evening at the Royal Historical Society on the influence of Thomas Jefferson on Southeast Asia."

Their voices faded as General Hajn saw the Ambassador to the front door.

Tuc swung himself easily over the window ledge and into the room. He was a light man and his entry was soundless. His bare feet felt the unfamiliar richness of the rug. His nostrils took in the odor of whisky and cigars. He glanced at the books on the shelves, then trotted softly to a corner and crouched in the half shadow.

He had never become accustomed to the luxuries of liquor and cigars or the heavy sets of books and the other symbols of opulence in the room. He did not own a clothbound book. He had read most of what Marx, Engels, Lenin, Stalin, Mao, Chou, and Ho had written and he had committed their principles to memory, then passed the books on to others—but only when he knew they, too, would read them.

He had read more books, he was sure, than either of the two men who had just left the room, but never had he coveted them as property. He was aware of the ferocity of his pleasure in the thought. Long ago he had been convinced, at a self-examination meeting in a jungle camp, that he had a weakness toward malice. He had been wary of the sentiment ever since and had carefully indulged in it only as a luxury and only when it would be harmless—but when it might affect his Marxist objectivity he wiped malice from his mind.

Hajn came back from the door and walked to the bar. He

poured himself a drink, added soda water from a sterling silver siphon. The inscription on it, Tuc knew, indicated that it was a gift from his American colleagues at the U.S. Army Command School at Leavenworth.

Hajn sighed as he drank slowly.

From the dark corner, Tuc said quietly, "I would like some whisky, comrade."

Hajn's hand jerked only slightly. His eyes found the corner in which Tuc crouched. A shadow of anger swept over Hajn's face. Then he erased it. He turned quickly and locked the door and drew the bamboo shades across the windows.

"Tuc," Hajn said, "help yourself."

"No. I have never drunk whisky. I do not know how to make the proportions. You have had much experience. I would prefer that you did it for me," said Tuc.

The humbleness was feigned. He was giving an order.

For a moment neither man moved or spoke. Hajn, in his elegant, MacArthur-style uniform, his back to a loaded bar, standing in his own splendid living room, gave no indication of moving. Tuc, still squatting, dirty, in shorts, dangling the stained piece of cloth that Sarkhanese laborers carry as a shield from sun and rain, and as a handkerchief and a sweat rag, was immobile.

Hajn sipped his drink, but made no motion toward the bar.

"It would be a comradely thing," Tuc said softly.

It was a risk and Tuc knew it. But it was also an exploration, a small feint, to see how Hajn would react, to see if Hajn would understand the import of the request. Hajn's sense of discipline to the Party was important.

The General moved now, slowly, but with dignity, like a man who is gradually awakening to civilities. Every gesture was proper, but somewhat too slow. He went to the bar and began to mix a drink.

"Ice?" he asked.

"However yours is. However your friends drink it."

Hajn put in two ice cubes and took the glass to Tuc, still squatting in the corner.

"Comrade, I did not expect you," Hajn said. Unconsciously he started to bring up his hand and say "cheers," but stopped in mid-gesture. "Did we not decide to meet tomorrow by the wharves? It is dangerous here. I have many visitors."

"And servants," Tuc said. He shook his head. It was a sideways motion in which his chin went toward his left shoulder, then came downward and toward his right shoulder, a typical Asian gesture. It meant neither yes nor no, but implied that the person to whom it was directed should have known better than to have asked the question. It was a gesture which teachers often used in schoolrooms.

"Things happen more quickly than one expects," Tuc said. "It is necessary for us to talk now. Comrade, it was interesting, what you said to the American Ambassador."

Hajn stared at Tuc. Tuc took the stare without turning, knowing Hajn was offended that his privacy had been invaded, that someone had listened to a personal conversation.

"You must realize," Tuc said, "that there are no such things as secrets or private talk."

"Why did you not tell me about the riot?" Hajn said demandingly. "I was uncertain what the demonstration meant. Had the Americans actually bombed the monastery?"

"I felt it best not to tell you," Tuc said simply. "The bombing was arranged by our friends up north."

He looked down at the glass in his hands, the brown liquid with the strange bits of ice making patterns. "There are many things one must do without understanding."

Tuc finished his whisky. It was quite tasteless, but an aroma backed up his nose. He resisted the impulse to blink. He was disappointed. He had read the American novels where the whisky hit the pit of a man's stomach and left it soft and hot in a few seconds. The whisky was in his stomach and he felt nothing. But he warned himself to be cautious.

"Tell me about next Wednesday's meeting of the Royal Council," Tuc said. "What is the agenda?"

"Would you like to sit in a chair?"

"It's a custom I haven't acquired."

"The Council meets in four days."

"I know. You have arranged for Prince Lin to be absent?"

"Yes."

"How?"

Hajn disliked being checked on or doubted. He sipped his drink slowly so as to delay his reply. His bunched jaw muscles relaxed.

"His helicopter at the Three Mountains will stay inoperative until we wish Prince Lin to return. His radio does not work. He is completely isolated at his meditation sanctuary." Hajn paused, not wanting to ask the next question. "What is it we want done at the Council?"

Tuc found another fish scale. He picked it off before answering. "Comrade, the Council must request military aid—big military aid from the United States."

Hajn said angrily, "Do not come here to make jokes. You will recall that we had agreed that anything that strengthened the Sarkhanese armed forces would make the eventual take-over more difficult. Most of the troops will remain loyal to the Crown to the very end. The better equipped they are, the more difficult our task. And now you talk about a request for American aid."

Tuc looked into his empty glass, turned it upside down. A drop fell to the highly polished floor at the edge of the rug.

"Do you understand the metaphor of this empty glass?"

"No, I do not."

"Hajn, you spend so much time with imperialists that you think like them."

"Like an imperialist," said Hajn, "I want us to build arms in our own factories—but with the Americans financing them. You are talking nonsense."

Tuc waited a moment before speaking. He understood why Hajn wanted to scorn him and why, at the same time, Hajn could not afford to scorn him. He thought of the delicate balance between the two of them, how they served one another, how their motives would eventually coincide—or conflict. Hajn was a proud and complex man and would be a more efficient instrument if not humiliated. Tuc's voice softened.

"I thought you would grasp the implications," he said. "First, if American troops come to Sarkhan, we at once label them as white imperialists. Secondly, foreign troops always provoke incidents. Remember the American in Tokyo who shot a Japanese woman? And the American soldier who killed a Chinese in Taiwan? He would have cost the Americans the support of even the Fascist Chiang if Chiang could have turned elsewhere. As it was, he caused the American Embassy to be burned. If no incidents happen, we will make one—a child run over by a drunken soldier, a scavenger shot by a nervous sentry. Mao Tse-tung made it clear it is a necessity to provide a martyr early. American troops here will help us get a martyr quick. Understand?"

Hajn hated to nod, but he did.

"Third advantage," said Tuc, "perhaps the biggest one: Every nation which has foreign troops on its soil feels humiliated. Americans are in Germany, Taiwan, Japan, Korea, Turkey—and everywhere they are automatically disliked, just as the Fascist occupation troops were hated during World War II. Agreed?" He waited for Hajn's nod. "We can build a wave of anti-Americanism whenever we please."

"But the Americans in Sarkhan are well liked."

"The few who are here now, Hajn, but not the great bulk of them later. Look at Vietnam. The Americans there are disliked by both sides. And by the French, also."

Hajn nodded again.

"Now the fourth reason is simple," Tuc said. "The Americans will bring in a huge amount of military equipment. Much of it is useless in the jungle. But the small guns are a treasure for us. We must get them. In Vietnam we could have sent guns from the North to the Viet Cong, but at first we did not and for a deliberate reason. We wanted the cadres to strengthen their morale by capturing their own weapons. Even today most of the weapons our people use they have captured from the enemy. No more than five per cent of our equipment in Vietnam comes from the Loa Sang Party. Taking the enemy's weapons teaches the ordinary soldier a lesson in Marxian inevitability."

"I understand that," Hajn said.

"Fighting the Americans and capturing their weapons also gave us heroes. In Vietnam I used to visit the families of our men who had been killed. I would take a carbine and ask which of his brothers would take his place. If there were no brothers, I would ask a sister. And if there were no sister, the father would step forward. They would strive to give us rice; they would risk their lives. It all started with the capture of an enemy weapon, Hajn. Each American-made weapon we captured in Vietnam was a seed which grew into a platoon of patriots."

The General nodded. He hated these lectures.

"Do you think you can manage things at the Council meeting?"

"It will be difficult," Hajn answered. "American aid was mentioned at a previous Council meeting. It was turned down. It was unanimous that American arms are unthinkable unless Sarkhan is invaded. Prince Lin and the Chamberlain emphasized this. The King concurred."

"Unless Sarkhan is invaded?" said Tuc coldly. "Then we will have an invasion."

"An invasion?"

"If we need an invasion, then make one. Do whatever is needed to get the Americans and their equipment here." Tuc held his glass to the light, looking at his fingerprints on it.

Hajn said, "It is impossible. The Council will never agree."

"Comrade, it is not only possible, it is inevitable. Events can go in one of three or four directions. No matter which, we must control the situation. At the beginning, Lin is the important factor. Can you follow me?"

This time the General did not nod. He just stared at the little fish-gutter.

"First, if Lin comes back from meditation and finds that there actually is an invasion and, say, a Chinese–North-Vietnamese claim on the Northern Territory, there will be no problem. His neutralism will turn to nationalism. The Prince will react the way of Nehru, the great apostle of peace and *satragya* and non-violence: he will become a savage nationalist and ask for American aid. After the victory, he will again cling to his neutralist views. Later on, it will be simple to have a quick *coup*, declare the Prince incompetent, and take over the government. Last, if the Prince flatly rejects American aid when he returns, despite the invasion, then he will have to be eliminated in some way. That would be your responsibility."

"And the Americans will sit still and just watch?" Hajn asked harshly. "Their F.I.A. agents are here just to prevent the kind of thing you're talking about. Doctor Theobald, the Embassy doctor, is one of them."

Tuc had held up his hand to stop the General's flow of words. He felt a jab of irritation with Hajn. Maybe it was the whisky. "Hajn, don't worry about the F.I.A.," Tuc said. "They are a joke. Doctor Theobald is about as 'secret' as Richardson was in Saigon during the Diem *coup.*" Tuc laughed. Now he knew it was the whisky, but it made no difference. "Doctor Theobald has 107 agents working for him. We try to know where those 107 agents are day and night." He hesitated, then could not resist adding, "The majority of the F.I.A. agents are Sarkhanese. Sometimes, Hajn, I even originate their assignments."

Then Hajn knew, with a sudden depressing certitude, that Tuc knew everything he, Hajn, did and a lot more.

"As long as you've got that part of it under control," Hajn said and paused.

"You'll move ahead on what has to be done," Tuc said, and came up from his squat.

It was as close to a command as Tuc had ever given him.

Moving toward the veranda, Tuc said, "Comrade, nothing is impossible. You already have your foot in the door. But I warn you, Prince Lin must be kept out of Haidho until after this is over. He is a neutralist—a dreamer, they say—but strong in this one idea. He will be King in two months and could spoil everything."

"Prince Lin," said Hajn with assurance, "is meditating at the old fort near the Three Peaks. I've already told you his helicopter is out of order."

"Suppose he decides to walk back? It is said that he has experience in mountains and jungles."

"We have a detachment in army uniform patrolling between the Three Peaks and Boa Binh. Nam Tho is with them. If the Prince attempts it on foot, he will be told it is too dangerous and will be restrained."

Tuc nodded, the nearest he ever came to an expression of approval.

Hajn relaxed a little. He felt that he was giving Tuc no advantage, no opening.

The fish-gutter walked to the window and looked out. He turned.

"The whisky is no good," he said. "It upsets my stomach."

The General started to speak, but Tuc had vaulted out of the window. There was a sound no louder than a mongoose creeping, then there was silence.

Hajn stood quietly, staring at the open window. His relationship with Tuc was so delicate, so severe, so precariously balanced. He wondered how long it would endure. Generals were not trained to take orders, no matter how subtly issued, from fish-gutters.

6

A Trip Upriver

Coldstream and McCauley had spent many hours discussing Xinh's experience.

The next morning Coldstream telephoned the Sarkhanese Minister of Defense. Although they did not see much of each other, the two men had been casual friends for thirty years. Hajn had been at West Point at the same time Coldstream attended Annapolis, and the General sometimes came to Coldstream's house to listen to the Army-Navy game via shortwave broadcast. After one such occasion, Taja had remarked to Coldstream, "Edward, he is more American than you are."

"General," said Coldstream over the telephone, "you know Boa Binh?"

"Certainly. It's not far from Three Mountains. You have a trading post there."

"Something strange happened at Boa Binh ..." Coldstream repeated Xinh's account.

"So," said General Hajn. "So. I must investigate. My river patrol officer is at Konru. I'll order him to Boa Binh. He'll be there in about four days. I'll phone you when I have his report. Hokay?"

The General finished a lot of sentences with "hokay," Coldstream thought. "Fine, General. Thanks very much."

Coldstream reported the conversation to McCauley. "I can't wait that long. I'm going today. Do you want to come along?"

McCauley shook his head. "I have an appointment with King Diad. He's going to spin me some dirty yarns about the royal succession."

"You don't want to miss that, Professor," said Coldstream.

"Tad, Xinh mentioned a list. I'm curious ..."

"You're always curious. It's sort of my black book. Whenever I have definite indication that someone is either a Communist or

working for the Communists, I put his name and the evidence in
my file. For example, Nam Tho, the man with the gold tooth, the
one who killed Xinh's father."

"And Jan Ti, the *bonze?*"

"Yes, but with a question mark. One of the reasons I am going
to Boa Binh is to check on Jan Ti. Who is he, really? The ones
who go to North Vietnam for training sometimes take other
names when they come back."

Coldstream's boat looked like any other *huatze* on the river,
but it had a small, powerful inboard motor to supplement the
outboard. He was accompanied by two men who had worked the
territory for the South East Asia Trading Corporation for years.

The monsoon rains had swollen the river and turned it a deep
chocolate color. The crew was kept busy avoiding the trees and
logs which swept down with the higher waters. Coldstream sat
quietly amidship.

In a way he felt responsible for what had happened in Boa
Binh. He had always trained his trading post managers to help
the villages. They received regular shipments of schoolbooks, magazines, newspapers, and where there was no village teacher, the
managers made loans to buy lanterns and held evening classes
to teach the peasants to read. Coldstream had anticipated that one
day Sarkhan might have to go through the agonies of Korea or
Laos or Vietnam. Self-sustaining and educated peasants resisted
Communist propaganda and arguments. He had seen it again and
again in the vast sweep of Southeast Asia where his company
operated. It frustrated him that the United States aid program
had not brought practical educators to the villages.

The terrorists probably chose Boa Binh because of its compara-
tive prosperity, because of his trading post, and because of the
dedication of Xinh—in short, because it was self-sufficient and,
hence, considered reactionary. Now the village had lost its chief
and four others had "gone north.'" Still Coldstream was puzzled
at the shootings. The Communists usually picked unpopular leaders or tax collectors or moneylenders. Both Tien and Xinh had
been popular in Boa Binh. However, it was an error to believe that

the Communists never made mistakes, bad ones. But seldom did they make them twice, Coldstream thought grimly. He had seen in Vietnam and China the bodies of Communists who had committed the same mistake twice—dead at the hand of their own leaders.

Coldstream arrived at Boa Binh early in the afternoon. No one came to greet the boat. As Coldstream walked down the road which cut through the village, most of the people were in their huts. The men stood just inside their doors, their faces expressionless, although most of them had known Coldstream for years.

Coldstream walked directly to the first hut. The man in the doorway was occasionally employed as a stevedore for Coldstream's company.

They exchanged polite greetings, but the man's face was unresponsive.

"Who is the new chief?" Coldstream asked.

"There is no new chief."

"Why not?"

"Because the new chief will die like the old."

"It is unnatural not to have a chief," Coldstream said. "Soon the laws will be broken and there will be no one to punish offenders. There will be quarrels over land and property, and no one to arbitrate and say what is just. Did the men from the north paralyze you?"

"No, Buan Suang," the man said, his voice angry. "We are not afraid. The next time they come, we will be ready with arms and we will fight. No more of our young men will be kidnapped. But if we elect Bok our new chief, we fear that the enemy will kill him one way or another. None of us wish to doom Bok by making him chief. That is what we fear."

"Where is Jan Ti?" Coldstream asked.

"He is at the temple."

When Coldstream arrived, Jan Ti was trimming flowers and shrubs with a short, sharp knife.

Coldstream spoke Jan Ti's name softly. Jan Ti turned as if surprised. Coldstream knew the surprise was feigned. Everyone in the village would know about Coldstream's presence immediately after his arrival.

"Jan Ti, I hear that your friends paid a visit to Boa Binh."

"My friends, Buan Suang?" Jan Ti replied. "I knew none of them."

"I did not say you knew any of them. I said they were your friends. One can have friends whom one never sees. For example, you receive many pamphlets and cartoon books from your friends in Hanoi, but I doubt that you have seen those who sent them."

"The educational literature is free to anyone who wants it," Jan Ti said cautiously. "I do not care where it comes from. When one is a *bonze* he is responsible to educate his people."

"As a *bonze* you should also remember Buddha's First Moral Rule: 'Let no one kill any living thing.' "

"I have killed no one."

"You talked to the Communists before they came," Coldstream said flatly. "You told them that no one could volunteer from Boa Binh unless the chief was killed." Coldstream was both guessing and probing. "And you got your instructions from the Buddhist Solidarity Front. You know it and I know it. I also know who ordered it organized." Coldstream paused, waited to see if Jan Ti would take the bait and reveal something more of the Buddhist group.

"I did not talk to . . ."

"Jan Ti, do not lie to me. I have traveled much in all the countries of Asia. I have seen the face of communism many times, and the tactics. They would not employ violence against popular men in their first visit unless they had been told it was the only way possible to get recruits. They would not approach a village unless they had an agent in the village."

"All I said was . . ." Jan Ti stopped. His face showed a flicker of fear. Then his eyes clouded with the queer puzzled look that Coldstream frequently saw on the faces of Asians being interrogated. It was a defense, a drawing back into self.

Coldstream's probe had been successful. He reached out and gently pressed a fold of Jan Ti's saffron robe between his thumb and forefinger. He said, "Jan Ti, you are a Communist servant. Whether you are a Communist or not does not matter. There is something else. You have discouraged the selection of a village chief." Coldstream spoke slowly, emphatically. "But you are now to change that. You are going to call a village meeting this afternoon and urge the selection of a chief."

"That is not my responsibility," Jan Ti said, turning his head slightly. "And not yours."

"As of right now it is yours. And you are going to say that you personally guarantee the safety of the new chief."

Jan Ti laughed and pulled back slightly. His eyes had lost the unfocused quality. He shook his head in contempt.

"How can I guarantee the safety of the chief?"

"Because I am going to give instructions to one man in this village to kill you if the new chief is harmed in any way or is even taken by force from the village," Coldstream said. "You can tell your friends that if the new chief is harmed, you will die. I guarantee it."

Jan Ti's eyes went wide. He had been trapped, trapped by a foreigner whose only real power was that the people trusted him.

"What business is it of yours, you, a foreigner?" said Jan Ti.

Coldstream stared for a moment directly into his eyes, until Jan Ti moved his head and looked away. Coldstream released his gentle hold on the saffron robe, then turned and moved through the village talking to one man from each hut so that Jan Ti would not know who had been picked as his potential assassin.

At the trading post Coldstream inspected the merchandise. His two crewmen were repairing the wooden door that led into what had been the radio room. Then Coldstream lighted a cheroot and squatted Oriental style on the veranda. It was the same place where Tien, the old chief, used to squat and meditate for several hours at this time of day.

Soon he saw Jan Ti going from hut to hut.

In the middle of the afternoon a village meeting was held. A new chief was selected. He was Tien's chess partner, Bok, the ancient herbalist.

When the meeting was over, villagers drifted toward the trading post. Their mood was friendly toward Coldstream. Some of the men muttered bits of information as they purchased tobacco or fish twine or candy.

Two of them repeated a rumor that the "volunteers" had been taken to a camp uphill from the village of Dao, twenty miles up the river from Boa Binh. It sounded reasonable to Coldstream. Running from Dao up into the hills was a large stand of hardwood trees that had, for awhile, been logged by Coldstream's company. A dirt road had been cut through the trees and ended in the low foothills about fifteen miles inland. Because of the white ants, leopards, and ferocious wild boar, only hunters visited the area.

The next morning Coldstream went to Dao, a tiny village of about twenty families, whose chief did business with Coldstream. The company supplied the chief with a jeep and gasoline in exchange for the village labor that kept the road open and the logging dock in repair.

The chief, gossiping eagerly, reported that a month before, two small trucks had been off-loaded from a river boat and had been driven by Sarkhanese Army troops up the road into the hills. They had not returned; but no one in the village had bothered to investigate.

The Army was always doing strange things, the chief remarked.

Coldstream found the road uphill passable, despite accumulations of leaves and debris. At one spot a tree had fallen across but had been cut and pushed aside. Around the tree marks of truck tires still remained on the hardened surface.

Coldstream drove for fifteen miles. Gradually the road rose into the foothills. An extension had been built many miles beyond his old lumber holdings.

As he completed a difficult turn, he saw a truck blocking his way. Four men leaned against it. They wore peasant's clothes and carried rifles.

Coldstream got out of the jeep and walked toward them, smiling. "How is the hunting? It used to be good pig country."

"What are you doing here?" one of the men asked. He had a high-pitched voice with an odd accent.

"I am Buan Suang, the merchant," Coldstream said. "I have come to see if the hardwood trees are worth cutting again. A few years ago we cut here—taking out rosewood and teak."

The leader smiled, showing a gold tooth. At the same time he nodded to his men.

Coldstream heard a noise behind him and felt a numbing pain along his right temple. The truck and the men dissolved, grew small and distant, then the pain became too great and he fell into blackness.

7

King Diad the Merry

To discuss the customs of Sarkhanese royalty and succession with the King himself was a privilege which excited even Professor Thaddeus McCauley, especially since no white man ever had been inside the Inner Palace. McCauley could not resist a stab of enjoyable malice as he anticipated how news of his visit would be received by fellow members of the Orientialist Society.

The Royal Chamberlain of the First Rank escorted McCauley through the palace entrance of blue-veined Sarkhanese marble, a stone sheath about two hundred and fifty yards long, twenty feet wide, and fifteen feet high. In Sarkhanese it was called *marturri*, which means "entrance to life and death." The walls of the passageway were gaudy with murals; at the left were scenes of Buddhist hell, and at the right, scenes of heaven.

The illustrations of hell showed the punishments given for the various sins which man indulges in while on earth. The glutton was shown with his mouth held open by clamps, and with two devils forcing great mounds of food down his throat. The sinner's stomach was distended to the point where it would burst through the skin. Next was a woman who had been unfaithful to her husband. She was about to be raped by Satan who held in his hand an enormous red-hot poker. The next sinner was a gossip. Two devils were pulling his tongue from his mouth while others shouted into his ears. There were other illustrations of the violent punishment awaiting the thief, the drunkard, the cruel man. When McCauley reached the end of the passageway his escort said, "Professor McCauley, can you remember the different kinds of sins shown on the walls?"

McCauley repeated them.

"Now, Professor, can you tell me what the virtues of man are and how they are rewarded in heaven?" said the escort, stretching his hand toward the other wall.

McCauley found it difficult to recall what had been on the right side.

"It is strange," said the escort, "that people who come through this *marturri* always look at hell and the sins of man and the punishments there. They hardly ever look at heaven. Good and evil are equally available, yet man unerringly chooses evil. Is that not strange?"

Before McCauley could reply, the escort continued, "Professor, you are entering the Inner Palace. If you will remove your shoes, please."

A young Sarkhanese man-servant appeared, knelt, and removed McCauley's shoes.

"Because you are studying the customs of royalty," said the escort, "His Majesty thought it might interest you to witness a palm-reading ceremony. You will sit on the King's left, on the floor, facing the east. You must not speak or make any sound of any kind at the ceremony; and you must remain silent until His Majesty talks to you. Of course, whatever predictions the Royal Palmist makes are confidential and must not be repeated."

McCauley concealed his pleasure. He was familiar with the enormous emphasis upon palmistry throughout all of Asia, but he had never seen the reading of a palm of a head of state. He knew that the independence day of Burma had been determined by a combination of palmistry and astrology. Famous men such as U Nu and the late Marshal Sarit and Phibul Sonngran never made a major move without consulting astrologers. Whether palmistry was a science or not McCauley did not know, and he had long ago stopped speculating about it. That it was believed by uncounted millions, from coolie to king, made it worth careful study.

They were approaching two huge bronze doors. On the left one in bas-relief was Gautama, the Buddha, meditating in the lotus position. On the right door was an enormous crescent and star. In front of one door stood a Moslem priest in turban and robe. In front of the other stood a Buddhist *bonze*. The two priests turned and opened the massive doors. Simultaneously a gong within the room sounded three times.

"This is the Room of the Future," said the escort.

It was about fifty feet square. The walls and the ceiling were light blue. Painted on the azure background were suns, stars, and moons in different phases and also the palms of many hands.

"There are forty-one hands shown here," said the escort. "With one exception, each is the palm of a King of Sarkhan as it was the day he died. The one exception, the forty-first hand, is that of King Diad, and the lines in his palm have not been painted in yet."

In the center of the ceiling was a large circle with the signs of the zodiac. Sitting near the only window in the room, on a small raised platform covered by tiger skins, was His Majesty, King Diad.

The escort dropped to his hands and knees and touched his forehead to the floor. McCauley did likewise.

After the King had welcomed them, the two stood up and advanced toward His Majesty.

"I welcome you, Professor McCauley, friend of my son and scholar of my nation."

McCauley pressed his palms together and gave the traditional reply, "May your wisdom and strength ever increase."

"You are more vigorous than I thought," the King said. "I expected a frail bent man with a beard."

"The absence of a beard is because of an old American custom," McCauley said. He glanced directly at the King and smiled. "The razor blade."

The King laughed. His eyes were sharp and perceptive.

"You are a bachelor, I am told," the King said.

McCauley paused as if he had been asked a profound question. Then he nodded in mock sadness.

"That also is because of an old American custom, a dreadful custom. A man may only have one wife. I can never make up my mind which woman is the right one. In other countries it is different," he added almost to himself.

King Diad roared. He slapped his hands on his thighs. His eyes watered slightly. The Chamberlain laughed a thin and somewhat embarrassed laugh. It was a badly kept secret that King Diad had eighty-two children born of twenty-three concubines and one regal son born of his single legitimate wife—and legend made the number higher every year.

"Come, sit down beside me," the King said. "My son never told me you had a sense of humor."

"Maybe it is not humor, Your Majesty," McCauley said. "Maybe it is despair." He grinned as he sat down next to the King.

"I am glad you are writing down our customs. We pass our customs by mouth from King to Prince, from one generation to the next, but they should be in books." Diad smiled, and Mc-Cauley remembered that the King, when he was younger, had been called Diad the Merry. His face was round and jovial, the eyes had laughter lines on the sides. The corners of the King's mouth turned up and his small lips were full and lusty.

McCauley knew the old King's story. Diad the Merry had lived up to the name the astrologers had given him years ago. Ever since he had ascended the throne at the age of twenty, he had spent the holidays sipping palm wine which came in small gift flasks from every village in Sarkhan. He claimed to be able to tell the mood of the country by sipping these gifts from the peasantry. His trips to Paris between the wars were the envy of every Southeast Asian monarch. His name had been coupled with that of Josephine Baker at one time, and Marlene Dietrich had considered it a pleasure to dine with him.

But the Sarkhanese also remembered the days when the French had called him Diad the Deadly, and the Japanese had given up and abandoned the country in 1944 rather than face the relentless attacks which Diad directed at them from his jungle headquarters.

Even now, at the age of seventy-one, and eight weeks before his abdication, no one who knew Diad would imagine him as being old or depressed. He would be sipping the palm wine, talking with old friends, and, if rumor were true, playing with a three-year-old boy, who was his last son.

The gong sounded again, and Dod Di, the Royal Astrologer and Palmist, entered the Room of the Future. He was an old man, dressed in a plain blue robe. As he approached, the King stood up and stepped off the platform. Dod Di, without ceremony, sat down where the King had been. His Majesty stood, bending over, holding his hand, palm up, in front of the Palmist. As Dod

Di examined the hand, the King looked down into Dod Di's face.

They were almost the same age, each with skin like wrinkled parchment. McCauley knew that Dod Di came from a family that had read royal palms for over twenty-five hundred years. The two family lines could be traced back into the mists of early Sarkhanese history, to a day before the Sarkhanese alphabet had been developed.

"You have not eaten, nor have you washed your hands, Your Highness?" Dod Di asked. It was the ritual question which the King could remember back to his childhood.

"No, I have not eaten or washed my hands," the King said.

Dod Di, with eyes closed, bent over the King's palm. He kept his eyes closed until the gong sounded again at precisely seven o'clock. For reasons which had disappeared long ago, the palm reading of the sovereign of Sarkhan always took place at seven in the morning. No one in the castle moved unnecessarily, no food was cooked, no noise was made, no tradesman appeared until Dod Di went out through the palace gates.

"We guard your hand as the palm of the nation," Dod Di continued the ritual. "The fate of all of us is reflected there." Dod Di bent very low over the King's hand, smoothing out the flesh in the lower left quadrant of the right palm. "An infinity of new lines have appeared. They are tiny, almost invisible to the eye. They were not there a month ago. The lines are lines of confusion. They appear to me to be caused by something external. Something foreign and new."

"Perhaps the anger of our neighbors, who, I am told by General Hajn, are mobilizing and will someday attack us," the King said.

Dod Di looked up sharply. He picked up the King's other hand and, holding it very close to his eyes, he studied one area at a time. Much had happened since the first time he had examined this hand. Two wars, the hard onrush of modern times, the simple life grown complex, the confusing fighting in the countries around Sarkhan.

Dod Di's hand jerked. The King looked down curiously. Dod Di spread the flesh along the lifeline taunt.

"There has been another change," Dod Di whispered. "In all the years I have read your hand, in all of the records which the

Dod Di family have kept, running back two thousand years, I have never seen a change like this. It confuses me."

McCauley saw that Dod Di was honestly agitated.

"Will I still abdicate on the appointed day?" the King asked.

"I cannot tell, Your Majesty. That is still not shown. But before that, very shortly before that day, there is an ambiguity. It indicates that a part of you will die. I do not know what it means. I see an accident, but not death to you. I must go back and read over the old records and think about this."

Dod Di completed his reading rapidly. When he was through, he bowed his way out of the chamber and hurried down the stairs. Almost at once McCauley thought he heard the clattering of the gate. The palace came alive. Sounds echoed down the corridors.

The King turned his hands palm upward, glanced at McCauley, and said, "Come."

They moved into one of the King's sitting rooms for breakfast. The first course was mango marinated in banana wine. This was followed by steaks of ugu, the small deer of Sarkhan. While eating, the King described the rituals of the royal succession, and their origin. In all the ceremonies, the royal retinue was half Moslem and half Buddhist. This custom had originated at the close of the great religious wars of six hundred years ago. The King pointed out how half of the gardeners—half of every group and category waiting attendance on royalty—was Buddhist and half Moslem.

"Your Majesty," said McCauley, "one of the most inflexible of your traditions, I have heard, is that the heir apparent must have a two weeks' period of meditation in the months prior to his coronation."

"That is correct," said the King. "This is one of our oldest ceremonies. It dates back approximately two thousand years. Its purpose obviously is to permit the new King to acquire serenity and maximum health before the rigors of the coronation. But there is another reason, and I shall perhaps find it difficult to explain to a Westerner. If there is to be a political revolt, it almost always takes place in the month or so prior to the coronation. Perhaps it is because the reigning King becomes careless, knowing that someone else is about to replace him. Perhaps it is because his enemies believe the heir apparent, in his inexperience, will not use good judgment. But historically, it is a fact. Knowing this, we have found it an advantage to have the heir apparent away from the capital and meditating. I believe such an event today is improbable, Professor. My son, Prince Lin, is quiet but very popular. And the Army is headed, as you know, by General Hajn, whose loyalty is beyond question."

"Prince Lin, Your Majesty," said McCauley, "is world-renowned as a scholar of Sarkhanese history. Do you consider him trained for kingship?"

The King laughed and clapped his hands. When the servant approached, the King ordered some wine, which was served immediately in thimble-like containers made from jade. "Do you know which wine this is?" asked the King.

McCauley wondered that the King was evading his question. But he could not question King Diad further.

"Smell it," said the King smiling.

McCauley did and said it smelled like jasmine.

"That's what it is," said the King, "jasmine wine which is made no other place in the world except from my garden. It requires almost a ton of blossoms to make a gallon of this beautiful liquid. See how beautiful it is, how fragrant?"

"Yes, Your Majesty."

"It is one of the most intoxicating liquors known to man. It reminds me of my son, Prince Lin. Indeed, he is world famous as a scholar, as an authority on our religions. And he is a gentle, quiet individual. Not a single person in the palace can remember him ever losing his temper since he became a man. But this does not mean that he is weak and unequipped. He is disciplined. The Prince is one of the best mountain climbers in Asia. Did you know he had climbed Annapurna?"

McCauley had not known.

"He will be a good king. He will be bold when it is required."

"But, Your Majesty," said McCauley, "he is a strong neutralist. He has publicly said he does not believe in violence or military pacts or attachments with any nation at all. The world had grown small, Your Majesty. Do you think Sarkhan can exist in this medieval isolation?"

The King smiled and said, "Sometimes it takes more courage to be gentle than to be belligerent. You will learn, after my son is the King, that he will do whatever is best for Sarkhan."

At this moment another brass gong sounded.

The Royal Escort touched McCauley's elbow and said quietly, "Professor, there is a woman outside who says she must see you immediately. Her name is Taja."

McCauley felt a wave of annoyance. It must have shown on his face, for the Royal Escort added, "She says it is very important. A friend of yours is very ill."

McCauley got to his feet and bowed before the King.

"Taja?" asked King Diad. "Your friend, Captain Coldstream's woman?"

"Yes, Your Majesty."

"You must tell her that I remember her with fondness. Will you do that, Professor McCauley?"

"I will tell her. I know she recalls you with fondness."

"Only fondness?" the King said and drew a dour face. "I liked Taja. I liked her very much. And she remembers me with only fondness? That is the fate of old men."

"She never mentioned your age, Your Highness," McCauley said. He smiled again. "In fact, from her description of you I expected to find a much younger man."

The Chamberlain sucked in his breath, but the sound was drowned by the laughter of King Diad. He stood up and walked to the door with McCauley.

"I would go further, but it would make some of the gossipy women in the palace jealous," the King said. "They love to talk to Taja, but they deny me the pleasure. Ah, my young professor, it is difficult to be surrounded by so much ritual and tradition—and gossip."

Taja was waiting for him in the car.

"Tad!" she said. "We must hurry. Edward is arriving at the docks. He may be dead."

"What happened?"

"I don't know. The Embassy got a message from the Sarkhanese Army that he was hurt upriver and would be arriving soon."

"What about a doctor?"

"Doctor Theobald from the Embassy is already at the dock."

Coldstream's *huatze* was approaching the pier. The *huatze* cut in sharply, made a quick turn, and came alongside the dock. Coldstream lay on a stretcher in the middle of the boat, covered with a poncho. His face was drawn tight and had aged. His eyes were open, but the eyes did not recognize the people on the dock. He stared at some distant and terrifying thing. His lips moved and then stopped in a rigid line as if he were fighting for control.

Theobald and McCauley stepped down into the boat. They pulled the poncho back. Coldstream's trousers were filthy and stiff. He had no shirt. His hands, limp and distorted, were crossed on his chest.

"*Mentado*," McCauley said. "I can't believe it."

"Good God, what's this all about?" Theobald muttered.

Taja climbed down. She touched McCauley's arm to steady herself and slowly said, "Yes, it is *mentado*."

"He's in shock and has lost blood," said Theobald. He nodded at the crewmen. They picked up the stretcher, lifted it from the boat. Theobald added, "He needs a transfusion."

For eighteen hours Coldstream muttered deliriously. Taja never left his side. McCauley forgot to make notes of his meeting with King Diad, and smoked cigarette after cigarette, growing more disheveled and rumpled by the hour. In his delirium, Coldstream was obviously trying to wrench away from some terrible experience. And over again he mouthed, "Roshuro, Konku, Roshuro, Konku. The names. Remember the names. Roshuro, Konku . . ."

8

The Royal Council

The four days before the Royal Council meeting would be crucial. If Hajn were successful with the Council, everything else was possible. Fail there, and everything was lost. The rub was that he had to be totally successful. There was no compromise. The Council did not vote, but talked things out until there was unanimity.

The five members of the Council had been chosen in such a way that the Council represented the main elements of Sarkhanese life. If any member disagreed, there was a chance that his constituency might become disaffected. There had been numerous examples in the past where the Council had a single member who could not be won over. The issue had never been forced to a vote and the disagreement had never become public.

After Tuc had left Hajn's house, Hajn settled himself in his study. He wrote a personal description of the other four members of the Council. One thing was clear: On the subject of American aid they could never be brought to unanimity at a Council meeting. No argument or pattern of arguments made before the Council could stretch over their different attitudes. Hajn decided they would have to be approached individually.

When he had thought out how to proceed, Hajn went to bed. He could not sleep. He was irritated by the fact that he was under pressure from two sides. Tuc, in his sharp way, demanded difficult things at inconvenient times. The Council members, on the other hand, could, if displeased, recommend to the King that Hajn be removed. They all were hereditary except for Hajn. As he twisted over at the edge of sleep, Hajn wished savagely that he had been born to a Council title. He was so exposed by his common birth, so vulnerable. He always had to perform perfectly.

The next morning Hajn called Bandor, Minister of Finance, first. Bandor represented the business community of Sarkhan on the Royal Council. His father, grandfather, great-grandfather, and countless male ancestors had played the same role. Bandor was trained for it. He was familiar with both the conference rooms and banks of Geneva, the United Nations, Washington, London, and Paris.

Hajn invited Bandor to lunch at the general officers' mess and they ate in a private room. Bandor was a slight man. He wore steel-rimmed glasses and he was shy. He was mixed Moslem and Buddhist, and it was reflected in the meal Hajn ordered for him: several hot curries, chapattais, meatballs of lamb, rice, green peas in oyster sauce, and a multitude of well-cooked vegetables.

Hajn brought out the financial report which Bandor had prepared for the coming meeting. Hajn's copy was studded with pieces of paper and marginal notes. Bandor eyed it quickly as they sat down.

"I have studied the report, Bandor," Hajn said. "It is, as always, beautifully put together. Parts of it are disturbing. Very disturbing. But let us enjoy our lunch."

Bandor did not enjoy his lunch. His eyes were drawn to the notes. Hajn remained cheerful, his face going somber only when the question of national finances came up.

After lunch Hajn took Bandor out to the Royal Academy parade ground. He showed Bandor a new machine gun, the M-60, which they had just received. They had bought six and had received six as a gift from the United States. Hajn handled the gun eagerly, demonstrating its excellent qualities. It fired much faster than the old 50-caliber, was lighter, stood jungle weather better, was easier to maintain.

Bandor reached out and touched the gun. It did have a sleek, lean, deceptive look, he said. Actually he was frightened of guns.

As they left the parade ground Hajn asked if they could walk along the river in front of Bandor's dock and *godown*, and Bandor readily agreed. Hajn needed relaxation, he said. He was sorry that these M-60s would be the only equipment Sarkhan could give its small but excellent army for many years. But, he said, he understood: Sarkhan was a poor country and there was little chance of war.

Bandor's office was in a huge and very old warehouse along the riverfront. It looked rickety, but it was built of solid teak which had drawn tight and snug as it aged.

"And what of my report, General?"

"Frankly it troubles me. I understand that we have the eternal problems of a small country with an agriculture-based economy. We are the victims of the monsoon, the single crop, the rise and fall of rivers, the thinning out of the veins in the tin mines."

"What we need, Hajn, and I have said it at every Council meeting, is some sort of light industrialization that can shift rapidly to new products which figure in foreign commerce," Bandor said defensively.

"But we lack the capital, you say in your report. In short, we are bankrupt."

"We have been a little bankrupt since the war," Bandor said. "Not much, but a little. It has been U.S. and U.N. aid which have held us together. This year is no worse than any other. But because we are agricultural and there is enough to eat, our bankruptcy is not noticed." Bandor paused. "That is our problem. It is not noticed. Other emerging nations have become solvent. We remain bankrupt. We lack the capital to develop light industry, therefore we cannot export, therefore we cannot accumulate capital, therefore we cannot develop light industry."

Hajn did not respond for a few moments. He looked at the single ship which was being unloaded at Bandor's wharves. Lines of men trotted up and down gangways, coming down with boxes and bags. They were stooped going down and ran back up, unburdened, with straight backs. The dock area was small, but the needs of Sarkhan were small. There was space at each end of the dock area for expansion.

"I understand the vicious cycle, Bandor," Hajn said. "The obvious way out of it is help from outside. But, as you know, I have opposed foreign military aid whether it came from Russia, China, or the United States. We are a neutralist power. I would like us to remain that way."

"You have been consistent on this matter at Council meetings," Bandor said.

"Bandor, I lived in the United States eight years, as you know," Hajn said. "Every few years I go to refresher courses at their staff colleges. I know what goes on in Washington. Do you know what counter-insurgency is?"

Bandor shook his head but was attentive.

"In Washington they call it C.I. The idea is to put down Communist-inspired insurgency in any friendly or neutral nation around the world. Now, we think we have no Communist insurgency here. But can we be sure? There are signs of it. If we are threatened by the Communists, then we would be entitled to every sort of American aid, from radio stations to Food for Peace. Tons of supplies would flow into our country." He paused. "I am afraid that some of the Council members are leaning in that direction—just to overcome our financial difficulties. Although the burden is heavy on you, Bandor, I hope you will resist giving up our neutral position."

Bandor paused, looked sideways at Hajn. He was doing some fast arithmetic. Only seven big ships called each month at Haidho. He had analyzed the American aid programs to Thailand, Formosa, and Laos. In Sarkhan a modest aid program would increase this number to about forty-five. Bandor Wharfage, Ltd. could, he estimated, build the necessary additional docks in a matter of weeks.

"There are some residual advantages of military aid, even when the insurgency danger has disappeared," Bandor said thoughtfully. "In Formosa, Americans give a great deal of aid for educational and agricultural reforms as a sort of taper-off program. Also, a firm negotiator could insist that the Americans equip a country with its own supporting factories for such things as small-arms ammunition, spare parts for moving equipment, repair shops for electronic devices. Once the insurgency was over, those factories could give us the momentum to make the economic take-off that the American, Walter Rostow, writes so much about."

"I am afraid that some of the Council members will be thinking only of the possibility of military aid from the United States when we explain the Communist threat," Hajn said. "Also, I am not sure of the extent of the threat."

Bandor thought for a moment, then nodded. "I will write another report about advantages of non-military aid." He would lay the dock-building off to his cousins, would put the small-arms factory into a corporation in which his children would be the major stockholders. The rest he could figure out later.

"The Americans send out end-use inspectors," Hajn went on. "They are dedicated men. They make sure that the money a country receives is spent for the purposes for which it was granted. Does this not infringe upon our sovereignty?"

"Of course," Bandor said. He had heard about American aid in Laos. It had become so tangled that no end-use inspector could make sense of it, except to know that the whole thing was corrupt. "We would want the most rigorous kind of supervision of such amounts of money."

The General's face took on the deeply troubled look again. "My dilemma, Bandor, is that I still don't believe in American aid for Sarkhan. It is a matter of conscience. I am a neutralist."

Bandor exercised his most persuasive manner to convince Hajn that American aid would be beneficial. In fact, Bandor said he would introduce it for discussion at the forthcoming meeting.

Hajn left, his face studiously troubled.

Immediately after leaving Bandor, Hajn drove to the largest pagoda in Haidho. He had an appointment there with the senior monk, Noc Thick Nuy. He knew that his presence there would be reported back to Bandor.

Noc Thick Nuy, the Buddhist representative of the Council, was in his late thirties, slender, light-skinned, celibate, and highly respected. He wore a saffron robe, shaved his head regularly, and begged for his food every morning. Someone from the Noc family had been the Buddhist member of the Council since it had been started hundreds of years ago.

For two hours they talked about Bandor's report and other items on the agenda for the Council meeting. Finally Hajn said casually, "I must do a meditation soon," he said. "I have a knotty problem in the armed forces. The Moslems have for some years been doing much better than the Buddhists in the examinations for promotions. As a result, most of the senior non-coms and most of the officers are Moslems. That is entirely just, but it destroys our old tradition of equality between the religions."

Noc looked up, his wide brown eyes suddenly intent.

"The Moslems are promoted because they have better schools," Noc said. "In a modern economy one must be able to do arithmetic and write if one is to work in the government, rise in the Army, or succeed in commerce. The Moslems have a school by every mosque. Do you see a school beside each pagoda?"

"Of course not. Only an occasional temple can support a school," Hajn said. "I know the reasons for the inequality in our armed forces." He got up to leave and sighed wearily. "But it is my problem. I will deal with it."

Noc asked Hajn to sit down again. He spoke slowly and was deliberate in his presentation. He spoke of the time when Buddhist schools in Burma had been neglected and the entire economy had gone into decline. In Annam the French had skillfully ignored, and thus isolated, the Buddhist schools, and the Buddhist faith had grown weak. All Buddhists believed in religious tolerance, but there were times when political and social events could so favor other religions that the Buddhist faith faded. In Vietnam, Noc said, the Buddhists had finally had to resort to self-immolation merely to establish their rights against a Catholic dictator. In the end they had brought the dictator down.

"I, like you, General, and like most Sarkhanese Buddhists, am of the Theravada way, the way of the lesser chariot," Noc said. "We will not become involved in the external and passing world unless that world imperils our immortal souls. But what you tell me is happening in the armed forces is happening elsewhere. We must be careful not to offend our Moslem brothers, but we must also find some means to keep our people equal to them. The Moslem faith tends toward the military because they believe in *jeddah*, the holy war, while the Buddhist does not. But we must have parity in the armed forces or the earthly suspicions, the secular temptations to power, will start to make themselves felt."

Hajn said he was startled to hear the inequality was felt in other areas. He confessed he did not know what to do about the whole thing. He mentioned that Ambassador Brown, the American, had once expressed concern over the inferior education given to Buddhists. The Ambassador had suggested that if there were ever an aid program in Sarkhan that he would make sure that funds were assigned to give all mosques and pagodas a school. It was, the Amassador had said, an integral part of defense. Even to aim a mortar today called for some knowledge of mathematics.

"I told the Ambassador that we would not take such aid," Hajn said. "We are neutralist."

He went on to explore other methods of improving Buddhist education. All of them seemed fruitless. He rose, again, to leave. He apologized for burdening Noc with his own problems.

Noc walked with him to the pagoda entrance.

"General, it is the way of wisdom to explore all things," Noc said. "Few things are pure. Everything is diluted, for that is the nature of corrupt man. Perhaps you should see if the Ambassador is still willing to entertain the idea of aid. The man who holds a gun does not need to fire it."

Hajn nodded, but he did not reply. He looked troubled.

Noc watched him walk away. Here was, he thought, the only general in Asia who does not wish more arms. But he will see the Ambassador; he always sees his duty.

Sarif was the easiest. This huge muscular man, full of vitality and engaged in a dozen activities, was the senior Moslem *allama* of Sarkhan and wrote two or three articles a year interpreting the Koran for the faithful of his country.

"If Bandor thinks it is economically necessary, I think we should go ahead," Sarif said. "Hajn, your record of neutralism has been consistent. But sometimes one must be practical. I understand your reservations, but think of what might be gained from American aid. Also realize that without your support we would look ridiculous even suggesting it to the Americans! Come, Hajn, be practical, be generous, bend a bit!"

The Moslems, by dominating the small village stores and government positions, would benefit enormously by an influx of foreigners, all with money in their pockets. The Moslems were, it is true, more prosperous than the Buddhists, but they needed more—for education, for their pilgrimages, for their businesses. The Moslem was less contemplative, more a man of action. Action called for money.

Hajn pointed out several more objections to American aid, including the fact that Prince Lin would oppose it. Then he devoted an hour to analysis of Bandor's gloomy statistics. He finished with a last objection to American aid: "If we do take the military aid, we would have to provide adequate housing and facilities for their officers and men when they arrive."

The words caught Sarif by surprise. He owned the only two large hotels in Haidho. With thousands of foreigners coming in it would be wise to expand the hotels, build new ones, create a catering service.

"Hajn, your knowledge of the ways of the Americans is most valuable to us," Sarif said. "It is a great national asset. The Chamberlain sees himself as the servant of the royal family and without the approval of both King Diad and Prince Lin the proposal would fail. You must convince them."

They talked for two hours. Hajn left in a somber mood. There were still two days until the Royal Council meeting.

Sarif walked to a window and watched Hajn enter his car. A Buddhist, he thought, with the soul of a Moslem.

When Hajn came back from Sarif's, Tuc was there, squatting in the shadow beside the lamp.

Hajn glanced at him, then reported calmly.

"Everyone will go along at the Council meeting except the Chamberlain," Hajn said. "He sees himself as the person who represents *all* of the people to the King. He will not go along for a sectarian reason or for profit. He will need a real emergency. I cannot give him one. We must find other means."

Tuc did not speak for almost a minute. He wondered again at how limited Hajn's views were.

"We will give the Chamberlain a real emergency," Tuc said. "We will announce that there is a territorial dispute between Sarkhan and China, and that China has laid claim to 250 square miles of northern Sarkhan. And also, that China intends to send troops into that area along with North Vietnamese troops, who see the justice of China's claim."

"What do you mean, 'we will announce'?" Hajn said. He was tired and he was edgy.

"I mean our friends to the north will make the announcement," Tuc said, his voice slightly biting. "It will be made over Radio

Hanoi and Radio Peking. Also the Chinese Ambassador to Sarkhan will call on the Chamberlain and tell him of this claim and present proofs."

"When?"

"Tomorrow. The day before the Council meeting."

At noon of the day before the Council meeting, the Chamberlain sent for the General. The honorable Tutamik was over eighty, bent and twisted by arthritis. He had a thin beard, not more than a dozen hairs. He was unmarried and had been reared to be Chamberlain.

"General, have the Chinese and North Vietnamese moved to occupy the Northern Territory?" the Chamberlain asked as soon as Hajn walked into the room. The Chamberlain was in a rage. His anger had given him a certain lithe quality, a sudden youth. "The Chinese Ambassador called this morning and told me of their claim and left me with a folder of ridiculous proof, 'evidence' he called it," the Chamberlain continued. "Now I want to know if they have made any move to occupy the Northern Territory."

"It is hard to say," Hajn said cautiously. "My patrols have encountered a few North Vietnamese along the border, but nothing big. No Chinese troops encountered."

"Anything else?" the Chamberlain asked.

"Someone attacked Coldstream, the American trader. But it was *mentado* and that means it was probably some of our own mountain people."

"General, would not the Communists imitate the methods of our people if they moved in?" the Chamberlain asked.

"There are reports of some killings in Boa Binh village," Hajn said. "Some young men were taken away and told they were conscripts for the People's Army. One cannot be sure. I have not had a chance to talk to the people in the village and all my patrols have not reported back yet."

"I have heard enough, General. I respect your usual careful views and your determination not to be a Caesarist. But I know the Chinese too well. They are moving in their usual devious manner. But this time they must not succeed."

Tutamik rocked on his cushion, his thin old body trembling.

"I cannot take any action unless the Royal Council approves," Hajn said.

The Chamberlain looked up, his eyes baleful. "General, at the Council meeting tomorrow I will persuade everyone of the necessity for action. Have no fear of that. But will you move aggressively when given permission?"

Hajn pondered the question.

"I will try, but I must tell you in advance it is impossible," Hajn said. "The Chinese and the North Vietnamese have modern weapons. They have whole divisions ready to move. They have aircraft. We have almost nothing. That, sir, has been our policy. By being neutralist we hoped to avoid a major military involvement."

"What about the Americans? Will they help?"

Hajn paused. "To be perfectly frank, I think they would not, nor do I believe that the members of the Royal Council would approve of such a move," Hajn said. "As you know, they are bound by tradition . . ."

"One does not stand on tradition at a time like this," the Chamberlain said. "Let me handle those idealists tomorrow at the meeting. We must ask for American aid and we must get it quickly. Otherwise Sarkhan will not exist as a nation a year from today."

"And what of Prince Lin?" Hajn asked. "He is very deeply convinced we should remain neutralist."

"It makes no difference what the Prince thinks," the Chamberlain said coldly. "In a time of national emergency I can convince King Diad. And Prince Lin is not yet King, General."

Hjan bowed and retired.

The Chamberlain sat for a half hour, too angry to move. He felt surrounded by traitors, weaklings, indecision, danger. He could depend on King Diad to remember the French and react in the same decisive way toward any new invader. But what of Hajn? The man who had killed several hundred Communists when they crossed Sarkhan's border during the fighting between the French and the Viet Minh now seemed uncertain, wavering. But he was a soldier. He would know his duty when it was clearly shown to him.

"Tuc," said Hajn late that night, "tomorrow the Council will draw up a request for American military aid. I have spoken to . . ."

"The details do not interest me. Just that the aid will come."

"It will."

"There is another matter," said Tuc. "Have you heard what happened to the American meddler, Coldstream?"

"No." Hajn knew every detail. But he lied. He wanted to see how much Tuc knew.

"He came close to our transient camp . . ."

"Where the volunteers assemble before going to North Vietnam for training?"

"Yes. Near Dao village. Coldstream stumbled into it. The stupid sentries panicked. Coldstream got the *mentado*."

"*Mentado*—to Coldstream? The fools. Is he dead?"

"He is alive," said Tuc. "But the four fools—the only witnesses—are dead. Now, comrade, you must take action before Coldstream talks." Tuc stared directly at Hajn. "Mistakes can be turned into advantages. You will arrange that the National Police charge Coldstream with abusing the villagers—usury, harsh working conditions, cheating. The indignant people lost their patience and handled him roughly."

"No one would believe it. Coldstream has too good a reputation."

"It need not be proved. I just want the story in the papers. The Crab will run it in the *Haidho Gazette*. I want Ambassador Brown to know about it and report Coldstream's bad behavior to Washington. A well-placed rumor is more effective than the facts."

"But *mentado* is different from just being beaten up. It hasn't been practiced since the religious wars. It will cause talk."

"If needed, we'll start another rumor—that Coldstream, in the effort to hide the truth, inflicted *mentado* on himself."

The Bureaucrats

At seven-thirty on the morning of October third the President of
the United States read the top-secret letter from the government
of Sarkhan. It requested immediate and massive military assistance. He noted the heavy gold leaf seal which had been impressed
at the end of the message beneath the signature of the King. The
President considered what a wonderful collector's item this piece
of correspondence would be. It pleased him that it would end up
in his own private papers after he was out of office.

He looked at the Secretary of State and said, "What do you
make of it?"

"The Chinese claim of Sarkhanese territory," said the Secretary of State, "plus the rumors of Vietnamese mobilization may
have panicked the Royal Council."

"What does my Special Committee on Sarkhanese affairs
think?"

"They do not know about it," said the Secretary of State. "It
was delivered by courier only an hour ago. No advance notice.
Sarkhan seems in a terrible hurry."

The President said, "Get me the Committee's opinion. And
quickly. Cogswell is chairman. He'll give it to me straight."

In a dozen offices around Washington, D.C., the preliminaries
and the preparation began.

Jeremiah Hobson had, as usual, arrived at the Federal Intelligence Agency's headquarters across the Potomac, barely in Vir-
ginia, at 8:30 A.M., well before the rest of his staff and had gone
directly to his dining room, for their meeting.

Hobson was an old man, but it showed only in the tough,
closely shaven flesh which gathered in small folds just above his
old-fashioned collar, and the small blue veins on the flares of his
nostrils. His slenderness, plus his jet black hair, gave him the ap-

pearance of youth, tenacity, and stamina. He was six feet tall and stooped a bit, like a man who had carried responsibilities for a long time or, as his enemies said, like an experienced in-fighter who is always coiled and ready to snap off a short jab.

Now he opened a black notebook, his personal diary. At night he transcribed the short remarks to a leather-bound journal, enlarging upon what he had noted during the day.

He glanced at the list of agencies which would be represented at the Sarkhan Committee meeting later that day.

Putting the notebook on the ledge of the window he wrote:

Agencies to be represented at Sarkhan meeting 11:30 A.M. this date:
Defense
State Department
Federal Intelligence Agency
National Security Council
Cogswell, President's Representative.

He stopped reading. He crossed off every agency except Defense and State. He thought, the rest don't count.

Four men entered. They were heads of the four major divisions of the F.I.A.—Intelligence, Plans, Research, Support.

Pointing to the chairs, Hobson began speaking even before the men were seated. "The Chinese Communists are claiming about two hundred and fifty square miles of Sarkhan's territory." He paused. "What do you think?" he snapped.

None of them was willing to make the opening. Hobson was famous for his open-end questions which would become sudden traps and finally, if the issue were big enough, the end of a man's career.

Hobson was used to this kind of silent reaction.

"What could be better news? It'll shake up that neutralist, Prince Lin. It'll solidify those don't-give-a-damn Sarkhanese. And it'll make General Hajn more inclined to go along with our counter-insurgency plan." He paused. No one spoke.

"Now the bad news. The President's Sarkhan Committee is meeting at eleven-thirty. The Committee hasn't met for six months and I was hoping it wouldn't meet for at least six more. What should we do?"

There was another silence. The head of Research made a note, studied it, scratched it out, and made another.

Hobson paced back and forth. He knew what he must do. He saw clearly his patriotic duty. He was going to make the "falling domino" theory work in reverse. He had watched it the other way too often. He had seen the confusion of Presidents and the timidity of Senators and the rantings of professors help the Communists to win. Half of Korea, half of Berlin, half of Vietnam, all of China, most of Cambodia, most of Laos—each a domino toppled by the Reds, falling against another domino in a chain reaction of Communist victory. Now all that was going to change. Sarkhan would be the base.

"Sir," said the Intelligence chief. "What's on the Sarkhan Committee agenda this morning?"

"I don't know. The Secretary of State said we would get the details at the meeting." Hobson paused. "Exactly how did Hajn respond three months ago when we proposed giving him an internal security force and gradually preparing him to be prime minister?"

The chief of Plans answered, "He was cagy. He said Prince Lin has common sense enough to listen to Hajn's advice."

"Do you think State or Defense got to Hajn ahead of us?" the head of Support asked.

Hobson's expression did not change. He must get rid of the head of Support in a few weeks. I got to Hajn long ago, he thought. If the head of Support didn't see it, he must go.

"The President," said the Intelligence chief, "has just sent Prince Lin a coronation message ahead of time, declaring the U.S.A.'s friendship and all that. Inadvertently he may have weakened Hajn's position."

I've known six Presidents, some good, some bad, Hobson thought. The President had a job to do which Hobson did not envy him. For one thing he had to be a goddamn matinee idol, shaking hands and making speeches, to get elected. But why couldn't he leave this kind of international maneuvering to the professionals? Imagine, sending a message like that to Prince Lin, a pacifist, a neutralist, a weakling. He looked around the table. "Has anything happened I should know about?"

"Nothing big," the chief of Intelligence said. "In this morning's report Theobald says neither Hajn nor Bandor—the finance man—has come near the Embassy for a week."

"Something's fouled up out there," said Hobson. "I'd better personally attend the Sarkhan Committee meeting. This time it's being held at State. They may forget it's the President's Committee, not theirs. Everyone wants to cut the pie. The Pentagon boys may want to start to play cowboys and Indians too quickly."

He stared at the group, nodded, and left the room.

At 8:35 A.M. on October third the Secretary of Defense convened a meeting in his office. Those invited held the rank of assistant secretary, general, or admiral. They were heads of Naval Intelligence, Army Intelligence, Air Force Intelligence, Marine Corps Intelligence, and the Defense Intelligence Agency.

"Gentlemen," said the Secretary of Defense. "I do not know the reason for this Sarkhan meeting. Everything's been going well in Sarkhan. The only flare-up was the small riot which took place in front of the Embassy. Apparently it was only a schoolboy donnybrook. So I have no idea why the President has called the meeting."

The Marine Corps representative, a burly, red-faced general named Patrick, spoke up. "I have a small group of Marines in Sarkhan. They have reported that the riot was more than just a schoolboy beer bust. They also heard that a Sarkhanese version of the Viet Cong has been terrorizing some of the villages up north."

The Secretary said, "Thank you, General, but what you have said does not agree with the reports of the other three services." He smiled and added, "Although we appreciate the *semper fidelis* of the Corps, General."

The Marine smiled politely, but when he spoke his voice had a slight bite to it. "That's what General MacArthur thought when we told him that the Chinese were mobilizing north of the Yalu River. A hell of a lot of good Marines got killed who didn't have to."

The Secretary said softly, "I have requested Assistant Secretary of Defense Dobey to be our spokesman at the meeting today. He has my instructions. The State Department may have some diplomatic scheme up its sleeves or the F.I.A. may be dreaming of a quick cloak-and-dagger job. We in Defense must be careful not to commit our funds or manpower needlessly in Sarkhan. Not now, anyway."

At 8:40 A.M. there were three men and a stenographer in the Secretary's conference room at the Department of State. One was the Secretary of State himself, wearing doeskin gloves and a light black topcoat, his black homburg in hand. He watched the stenographer check copies of the official correspondence from Sarkhan, one copy for each participant. The copies were numbered and had to be signed for.

"Abbott, I'm going to make this quick," the Secretary said to his assistant secretary for the Far East. "I'm scheduled to take off for Geneva in half an hour. I just want to make sure, Abbott, that you understand State's policy on Sarkhan. Our policy is to hold firm. Sarkhan is neutral. It looks neutral and it acts neutral. The monarchy is secure and Hajn, who is the strongest member of the Royal Council, is firmly pro-West.

"If the Pentagon wants to send in troops and supplies, we are opposed. We also are opposed to F.I.A. undertaking any covert operations in the area. The Sarkhanese government paper here mentions an invasion build-up across the border in Vietnam. If it is real, we want to handle it with negotiations. Once we start pouring arms into an area or playing the F.I.A.'s game, the possibility of successful diplomacy goes out the window. So don't let anyone hit the panic button at the meeting today. If necessary, stall. If crucial, get me in Geneva. I'll tell you to stall some more."

The Secretary of State put on his homburg and departed.

A Meeting in Washington

At 11:35 A.M. the President's Special Committee on Sarkhan met in the Conference Room at the State Department, and it promptly came to order.

Adolph Cogswell, the chairman, stood at the end of the polished conference table. He had been chairman of the Committee on Sarkhan since it had been established by President Kennedy.

He stood at a podium. The Committee members sat. Cogswell knew that men listen to someone who stands above them. It was the traditional stance of authority. Cogswell did not use the podium to harangue. In fact, he had the reputation of speaking very little. But he liked a position of control.

Cogswell remained silent for perhaps thirty seconds after he banged his gavel.

Silence, also, was a technique. Cogswell at seventy-five was stocky and solid and usually restless. He knew his silence was a strong weapon.

As the Committee grew silent, Cogswell was suddenly aware of how many times, for how many years, for how many different Presidents he had performed similar functions.

President Roosevelt had once told Harry Hopkins, "As long as I have been President, there are only three persons who call me by my first name without embarrassment: Justice Holmes, Adolph Cogswell, and you."

Cogswell nodded at a State Department clerk who handed copies of the Sarkhanese request to each member. Cogswell stood silent while they read.

The only person Cogswell knew well at the table was Jeremiah Hobson. They were the old work-horses. Maybe too old, he thought. Cogswell and Hobson had been through the veterans' march on Washington under Hoover, the Depression, the early wild days of the New Deal, the approach of World War II, the dealings with the Russians, the McCarthy scare, the New Frontier, and just about everything else.

They had seldom agreed, but they had a respect for one another's talents. Hobson was brooding, protective, suspicious. But also decisive and vigorous. Cogswell thought some of his liberal friends were overly harsh in their criticism of Hobson. The F.I.A. director got things done, an ability Cogswell admired in anyone. Cogswell's job had been to solve problems as they rushed down on successive Administrations. His merits were openmindedness, toughness, an ability to shift targets. Neither man had ever questioned the integrity of the other.

When everyone had finished Cogswell said, "The President requests your advice. He must make a decision concerning Sarkhan. He considers that decision so important that he invited Senator Donat of the Foreign Affairs Committee to meet with us. Senator, we welcome you." The Senator, a big hulking man, nodded, smiled slightly. His presence meant the possibility of action requiring Congressional approval.

"Sarkhan has requested United States aid," Cogswell said. "The medical and educational stuff is routine. But the military request includes equipment for a sixty-thousand-man balanced army, including air and artillery. They want immediate delivery of equipment and also training by U.S. personnel. The Sarkhanese claim the North Vietnamese have mobilized troops just beyond the Tikok Mountains, troops called the Sarkhan Liberation Battalions that are really there to support China's claim to two hundred and fifty miles of Sarkhan territory. The President wants your advice—by tonight."

Jeremiah Hobson, seven years Cogswell's junior, tilted his flinty narrow face upward. "Mister Chairman," he said in his fast, metallic voice, "I am wondering if such an enormous request should not be reviewed by the Congress after study in depth by experts?" He looked at Senator Donat, who nodded faintly. "I am certain the President has considered this, but just so that we are clear, would you define the powers of this Committee, its functions and limitations. I believe it would help all of us. Especially as it's been six months since we last convened."

Cogswell reached into his inside pocket and took out a cigar case. It was black leather and well worn, and from it he extracted a dark cigar. Biting off the end, he spat it to the floor, and held the cigar high, like an exhibit at a trial.

"Jeremiah, gentlemen, this is a Philippine cigar. I do not like Philippine cigars. I prefer Havana cigars. But I cannot get good Havanas any more because Cuba is Communist," Cogswell said.

Cogswell struck a wooden match on the underside of the table and lit his cigar. He puffed three times, then blew a smoke ring, obviously enjoying each phase of the little act.

"I cannot get Cuban cigars largely because the President of the United States did not get adequate intelligence information about Cuba.

"President Kennedy did not want to be surprised again in any area of the world by intelligence failures. So he drew up a list of four crucial areas where the Communists might move history in their direction and set up special committees to study each one. We around this table are his advisors on Sarkhan."

The room was very quiet. Cogswell looked directly at Hobson.

"This Committee, gentlemen, can recommend anything it wishes to the President," Cogswell said. "And that, gentlemen, is our only function. And I have to give him our recommendation tonight. Should the United States give this military aid to Sarkhan? *We* are supposed to be the experts."

Donat broke the silence. "How much would it cost?"

"My estimate is about three-quarters of a billion dollars," answered the Assistant Secretary of Defense.

"Then won't it need Congressional approval?" asked Donat.

"Unless it comes from F.I.A.," Hobson said.

Cogswell said, "Our function is to recommend a course of action to the President, to tell him what he should do, not how he should do it." He turned to the State Department man. "What is your estimate of the situation in Sarkhan?"

Assistant Secretary Abbott pursed his lips. He slowly removed his glasses and cleaned them with a handkerchief.

"An estimate of the situation in Sarkhan?" he said. "For about the last ten years we have considered it one of the most stable countries in Asia. The Sarkhanese request for military assistance comes as a surprise. Despite the shouting, we see no immediate threat to Sarkhan, either internally or externally . . ."

Hobson interrupted in his domineering, metallic voice. "Fine, fine. But how long will Sarkhan stay that way? The Reds want that kind of real estate."

Cogswell tapped his gavel. Ignoring Hobson, Cogswell smiled. "Thank you, Abbott. Sarkhan is politically stable. Correct?"

Cogswell now turned to Hobson. "Jeremiah, what is the Federal Intelligence Agency's estimate of the situation in Sarkhan?"

"One cannot tell when the Communists will decide to attack Sarkhan," said Hobson. He shrugged. "That they will attack, I have no doubt. But when? Who knows?"

"Do we have enough people out there to make an accurate estimate?" Cogswell said.

Hobson sighed. He fingered some notes in the folder before him. He had 107 F.I.A. people in Sarkhan, including native agents. They knew what was going on. But no one in the room was qualified to evaluate the F.I.A. estimate. And Senator Donat was a possible leak to the columnists.

"We don't have enough, Mister Chairman, to be absolutely sure," Hobson said, looking up from figures he had scrawled on a pad. "We have about fifteen people and we'd like to have four or five times that many."

"Why?" Senator Donat asked.

"Senator, we don't like to be uninformed on an area which the late President Kennedy and his successors have thought critical to America's foreign posture," Hobson said. "I know, Senator, your committee has to assess the claims of a few score government agencies. I'm not making a special plea for mine."

The Senator smiled.

"Dobey, what's your estimate?" Cogswell asked.

Assistant Secretary of Defense Cyril Dobey had been the president of a network of savings and loan associations along the Pacific Coast. He was usually a Republican, but he had voted Democratic in the last two Presidential elections. Dobey could be ruthless in his business operations, so it was said, but Cogswell had found him without poise and often unwilling to take a stand.

"Of course, I can only discuss the military situation," Dobey said, a little too loudly. "We see no immediate danger, and the Defense Department forces are strategically located so as to take care of any emergencies in Southeast Asia. We are puzzled by this sudden request from Sarkhan."

Of course you are puzzled, Hobson thought. Those big thick colonels and generals of yours make an inspection of a country's military forces and don't understand what the hell is happening.

"Thank you, Dobey," said Cogswell. "Up to now the Committee is unanimous that Sarkhan is in no immediate danger. We will now proceed to the next step . . ."

"Mister Chairman, if I stay quiet, the record will indicate I agree with Defense's assumption that they can handle any military emergency that comes up," Hobson said. "No insult is meant, because this is all in the family, but the military people said the same thing about Korea, Laos, Vietnam." Hobson paused and the pause was somehow Solomon-like, gentle, persuasive, wise. He smiled at Dobey. "I am not criticizing or back-biting. I am asking us to face realities. The country that is *not* invaded or overrun may be precisely the one we should help. For in such a country there is time."

Cogswell wondered about the motives behind Hobson's approach. He seemed to be saying Sarkhan was in danger, but he was not pushing for intervention.

"Thank you, Jeremiah," said Cogswell. "Your view is on record. Now, gentlemen, what are the Committee's predictions for the immediate future of Sarkhan, say during the next two years? Abbott, would you give the Department of State's view?"

"Well, sir, that's a hard one. Every political situation is in flux. I assure you that Ambassador Brown has his ear to the ground and will let us know if the situation changes. At this moment it would be difficult for me to give a specific future blueprint.

"One thing is certain, however. We don't want to get boxed in so that we are forced to support a 'strong man' government or a *junta*. We've been stung by that in Korea, Formosa, Vietnam, the Dominican Republic, Pakistan. We'd like to take a harder look at this General Hajn. We don't want to back him if he turns out to be a Trujillo."

Abbott did not understand the "strong man," Hobson thought.

Like most State liberals, he retreated whenever the phrase was used. What Abbott and State did not understand was that they always picked their strong men too late. Pick one early, give him support, build him up, and you did not have to panic when the Communists started to shout their "Fascist" slogans.

Cogswell said, "Am I correct in concluding that the Department of State has made no estimate of what will happen in Sarkhan within the next twenty-four months?"

"Yes. I mean, no. Look at it this way. Right now the Communists are spread thin trying to concentrate their efforts in countries where there is obvious dissatisfaction and poverty. But in Sarkhan there has always been a feeling of well-being. The state is efficiently administered and the leaders are popular. The efficiency and the honesty of the royal family is already a legend in Southeast Asia. Also, Sarkhan has, geographically, the protection of almost impassable mountains on her northern border. Does that answer your question, Mister Chairman? We see no obvious signs of big trouble in the next two years. We are being asked to turn a nation of peaceable peasants into a veritable Sparta. The request is unexpected. There were no preliminary discussions or forewarnings. It has enormous political ramifications in all adjacent or nearby nations, from India to the Philippines."

Hobson interrupted again. "The Federal Intelligence Agency agrees with the Department of State on the principle that the Communists may attack any place, any time, and that we should be ready for any emergency, including Sarkhan. This is a principle which we must unceasingly drive home—to everyone, including the President."

"Mister Hobson, I agree also," Cogswell said. "Anything can happen at any time. Nothing is certain in life. I may get run over by an automobile this afternoon. Mister Dobey might get struck by lightning. Gracious, you might even be retired and replaced by a younger man." He stopped, lit his cigar. "God forbid."

Hobson looked at Cogswell. He was uncertain of him. Cogswell was tough and knowledgeable. He was the only person in the room who might sense Hobson's plans and—by his utter objectivity—ultimately block them.

"The President wants a recommendation tonight," Cogswell

went on. "Mister Dobey, what's the Pentagon's prediction for Sarkhan?"

"There are two kinds of military problems," Dobey said. "One is internal subversion or rebellion. The other is external aggression. We know there is no internal Communist subversion in Sarkhan. If there were, General Hajn would have informed us."

Hobson interrupted. "I can assure you that our people out there would have known as soon as Hajn did."

I am not learning much about Sarkhan, Cogswell thought, but the stale old lessons about the strains and tugs and petty nature of bureaucracy are certainly being confirmed.

"The only hazard, as far as Defense is concerned," said Dobey, "would be an armed attack on Sarkhan either from North Vietnam or Communist China. We have no evidence of either. Our reconnaissance planes make frequent flights over the area. If there were a military build-up directed at Sarkhan, we would know about it."

Cogswell said, "There is no evidence of an invasion from the outside now? Despite what the Sarkhanese claim?"

"No, sir."

"What he is saying," Hobson said firmly, "is that anything can happen in that part of the world."

Dobey said, "That is correct. The Communists are unpredictable."

"Mister Chairman," Hobson said, "you know I have devoted my life to telling the American people of the threat of communism. I got into this game early, just after World War I, about the time the Communists got into it. Since Lenin's second revolution in 1918, I have known what we had to face. I have not been believed. My view is a simple one: if we must arm Sarkhan, let's do it before—I repeat, *before*—the Communist thrust from the outside, or we will lose the country—and along with it, all of Southeast Asia and the Malay archipelago."

"He's right," said the Air Force Intelligence officer. He hesitated as everyone looked at him. "Well, you know we have to take a stand or ..."

The General looked up, caught Dobey's eye, and stuttered to complete silence.

Cogswell knew this was the moment, the moment he had

known so many times before, the moment of summation. He was weary of the bureaucrats, even those as shrewd and tough as Jeremiah Hobson. Most of the people in the room were thinking not of Sarkhan or the United States, but of the well-being of their own agencies.

"If I understand the situation," said Cogswell slowly, "not a single one of the intelligence-gathering agencies of the United States knows whether or not there is an invasion against Sarkhan forming in the Tikok Mountains. Why not?"

Cogswell looked directly at the Air Force general sitting by Dobey.

Hobson was bored, but he did not let his attention ease. Maybe some of the other intelligence groups had information and might let it slip. It was not likely. The trouble with these people is that they can't make the link between intelligence and action. This theoretical argument that intelligence agencies just gathered information and then fed it, like neutral pap, to the executive branch was nonsense. Intelligence led to action. That was why F.I.A. had been established.

The Air Force general coughed and said, "It's hard to say. We have no recent pictures of that area."

"No pictures? What do the planes do?" asked Cogswell.

"You see, sir, this is the monsoon season. Everything from the plateau to the other side of the mountains is covered by a low-level soup, fog and rain."

"Isn't it also true, General, that there is no camera yet developed that can take pictures through *yang* and *takhian* tree leaves?" Hobson asked. He did not even listen to the answer. So often before, at just such committee meetings, he had hacked away at the basis upon which Air Force Intelligence was gathered. Most of the Tikok Mountain rain jungle was made up of *yang* and *takhian* trees.

Hobson liked his intelligence sources with their two feet on the ground, not 20,000 feet up in the air. He was thinking about Dr. Theobald, the Embassy doctor in Haidho. Theobald had established a firm connection with General Hajn. The two of them played tennis together three times a week. Always singles. A tennis court was one of the few places which could not be bugged.

It was through Dr. Theobald that Hobson had worked out his clearly understood agreement with General Hajn. When U.S. troops and equipment came in, Hajn would have control of them. This time there would be no false "strong man" who appeared late, pot-bellied and belligerent, shouting to the crowds. The "strong man" would be the national hero, West Point-educated General Hajn. And behind Hajn? Hobson.

"Gentlemen, have any agents from the United States intelligence organizations been sent north to check and confirm this invasion threat? An American citizen we can trust?" Cogswell asked.

"Mister Chairman," said the Air Force general. "During the monsoon it is impossible to travel in those regions."

"How did General Hajn's agents manage to get information? It says here in the Sarkhanese request that there is mobilization taking place just north of the Tikok Mountains," asked Cogswell.

"They're native," said Hobson. "They know the trails and the water paths through the swamps. Their families probably have lived there for two thousand years. Leeches and malarial mosquitoes kill white men, but not natives."

"Perhaps the Sarkhanese should start a training and aid program for us." Cogswell's voice turned nasty. "It seems the Viet Cong, the Chinese Reds, the North Koreans, and now the Sarkhanese are all tougher and better trained than the Americans."

"Mister Chairman," said Hobson. "I have native agents in Sarkhan. I can have an answer on this troop mobilization within five days."

Cogswell said, "Thank you. I am certain we will be convening often. We will be happy to have that information. It is the consensus that Sarkhan is not in any real danger, although, I repeat, no American agents have been to the area of the alleged invasion. Why, then, did Sarkhan ask for such massive aid?"

"Hajn is hard-headed, Mister Chairman," Hobson said. "He is also a patriot. He must have more information. I suggest that we send a message to him through Ambassador Brown and ask for amplification."

"I agree," said Abbott quickly. "What we need is time to study the situation."

Cogswell gazed around the table. There was no further comment.

"We are heavily over-committed in many areas of the world in terms of personnel, aircraft, ships," Dobey said. "We could, of course, meet the Sarkhanese request, but it should be studied. After all, we've only had half a day's notice."

They are all ducking, Cogswell thought, but only Hobson seems to have a reason, seems sure of what he's doing. And I don't know what he has in that tough old mind of his.

"Any further comments, gentlemen?" Cogswell asked. He shrugged. "The consensus is that the President should turn down Sarkhan's request for massive military aid. You have all emphasized that your recommendations are based on Sarkhan's relatively safe and prosperous internal conditions at the moment. Gentlemen, are there any objections or additions?"

No one spoke and the meeting adjourned.

Cogswell watched the members hurry out. They can hardly wait to report back to their chiefs, he thought. Whole battalions of specialists in governmental power plays will study the statements made. Then they will figure out what is the proper way to put pressure on the President to block a competing agency. Oh yes, they would study the situation in Sarkhan—while protecting their flanks and indulging in the close in-fighting that marks the skilled Washington operator.

The only one who did not hurry out was Hobson. He repacked his briefcase slowly and precisely, the way a hunter cleans his rifle after the chase and then reloads it and carries it in a position for instant use.

Cogswell noticed Hobson's new suit. It had the simple elegance that came only from the best and most expensive tailors. Hobson wanted, Cogswell thought, to give the impression of coming from a long line of New England bankers or publishers, a family that had made its basic fortune generations ago, but still practiced an elegant thrift. But the Bond Street clothes somehow clashed with Hobson's flashy Knights of Columbus ring.

Cogswell, the multi-millionaire, put on his hat and coat. The coat had been his brother's, the brother who had been killed when he parachuted into Thailand while working for the O.S.S.

in 1943. Charles had been his twin, and the dark tweed overcoat had been Charles' favorite. Adolph and Charles Cogswell always had worn each other's clothes.

Cogswell started to help Hobson into his close-fitting Chesterfield.

"Thank you, Adolph," Hobson said. For the first time this morning, the F.I.A. director smiled.

"I'll walk you downstairs," said Cogswell, lightly putting his hand on Hobson's shoulder.

"Fine," said Hobson, locking his briefcase with a key that hung on his watch chain.

The two men did not walk down. They took the elevator. In the rotunda a guard asked them to sign out. Hobson nodded and scrawled "Hobson" in the ledger. Cogswell, in a fine, neat accountant's handwriting, slowly signed his full name, "Adolph Goldsmith Cogswell."

It was raining outside.

Hobson's black limousine waited by the curb, blocking the area reserved for taxis. It was a new Cadillac. Hobson's male secretary sat in the back. When he saw Hobson, he got out of the limousine and held the door open. Cogswell recalled that Hobson always employed male secretaries and that he had lived with his mother until she died eight years ago at the age of ninety-one. It suggested nothing to Cogswell. He had heard the usual rumors but Cogswell believed none of them. He waved at Hobson. "Good seeing you, Jeremiah."

Now the secretary got back into the car. Hobson turned and walked down the sidewalk, the car moving along slowly behind him. Cogswell knew that Hobson would walk for eight or ten blocks in the rain, then summon the car. This practice was common gossip in Washington. Whenever Hobson walked, his car always followed behind him, crawling along at three miles an hour.

The old man loves plots, thought Cogswell. They are what keeps him going. The F.I.A. chief now was a half block away. Rain dripped off his hat and onto his shoulders. Cogswell was reminded of Richelieu walking in the snow outside of Versailles just before he plotted the assassination of the Spanish cardinal.

Hobson would have been a king's advisor in the Middle Ages. Or perhaps a pope. His biography is like a combination of the lives of Richelieu, Machiavelli, and Hobbes.

Some people flashed across the Washington scene and were gone. Others built huge public reputations. Hobson was different. He moved a straight inevitable line across the power structure of the capital. Steady, sure, powerful were the words for Hobson.

His narrow face, the shock of black hair, and the slightly crooked nose helped, Cogswell thought. Hobson looked like a savior of the people, an instrument of righteousness.

The broad public had a vast admiration for Hobson. It was based on the fact that his visage, thin and courageous, had been seen in every trouble spot since Wilson was President. Not a single photograph had ever shown him smiling. He was always in relentless pursuit of America's enemies. Books, pro and con, had been written about him. His biography had also been serialized on the back of breakfast cereal packages.

It had started so haphazardly.

In 1917 Hobson had been drafted into the American Expeditionary Forces. At the time he weighed 145 pounds and was five feet, ten inches tall, slim and inconspicuous. Three months after his induction, he had taken over command of his platoon at Château-Thierry when the lieutenant had been killed and the first sergeant had collapsed sobbing. With a cool sense of tactics he reorganized his platoon, surveyed the chaos churning up in front of him, and had picked the point of German resistance that was holding back the advance. Later a member of the platoon claimed they went forward only because Hobson had told them this was the quickest way to get to the rear. They thought he was leading them on a retreat. In fact, he led them into a brutal fire fight in which his platoon came slicing in on the flank of a machine-gun emplacement and obliterated it.

Newspapers back in the States had hailed the courage of Hobson in headlines that said FILE CLERK DESTROYS TWENTY-FIVE HUNS. The notion of a file clerk, an Irish-Catholic boy from New Orleans who had worked for an insurance company for two years after leaving high school, who had lost his father when he was twelve and lived with his mother, caught the imagination of the American people. He had been given a Silver Star, promoted to second lieutenant, and then, three weeks later, had led his platoon in an almost identical performance. After the second performance he was given a Congressional Medal of Honor, promoted to major, and did not see action again until just before the war ended.

When he returned to New York there was a press conference. Hobson listened quietly to a hostile question concerning his ruthlessness. It was said of him that he "drove his men mercilessly." He answered quietly, "I thought, gentlemen, the objective was to win." Somehow this simple thought simply expressed had caught the imagination of the American people. The phrase was inscribed on dozens of American Legion halls, on National Guard armories, in textbooks, and on monuments in town squares.

In the years after World War I, Hobson moved quietly through the governmental structure of Washington. At first he was a showpiece. He had worked for the F.B.I., the Secret Service, the Attorney General's office, and three or four short-lived organizations. Usually the short-lived organizations vanished because Hobson recommended that they be combined with some larger organization. Almost always he had emerged as head of the larger organization.

Though he preached anonymity, publicity always came to him. When there was an anti-Communist *coup* in a foreign land, the public usually saw a front-page picture of him talking with the president or the general heading the *junta* the day after it all happened.

In all of his jobs Hobson had been loyal to those who worked skillfully with him. Invariably his assistants moved into whatever new organization he headed. And when a subordinate wanted outside employment because of increased financial responsibility, it was Hobson who placed him as security officer in an aircraft factory, electronics plant, or munitions industry around the country.

The dedication of his followers was almost mystical. In one of the few critical books written about Hobson the author stated, "Hobson binds his organization together by a phobic fear of 'the dangerous outsider.' Those who do not come to believe, with

Hobson, that the United States is menaced, quietly find themselves out of his organization." Hobson had been quoted as saying, "An American who is blind to these facts must be neutralized even before we go after the foreign enemy." Hobson had never denied this statement.

Hobson's living habits had changed completely since 1917. He came from a shanty-Irish background in New Orleans. His father had died an alleged alcoholic. His mother was an expert seamstress who specialized in doing the detail work on the gowns of young New Orleans ladies who were about to be married. She was not a boastful woman, but in her small home she had framed a letter from a wealthy Louisiana family thanking her for "sewing two thousand sequins to Faith's dress in the critical four days before her marriage."

Until the middle of the 1930s, Hobson had always bought cheap ready-made clothes off the racks. At an important meeting with foreign military people Hobson suddenly had realized that he looked like a foreigner. His suit had stuffed shoulders, a nipped-in waist, baggy cuffs. A foreigner actually had mistaken Hobson for a European. He had talked to Hobson in a casual manner about the bad manners of Americans, the futility of the meeting, the crassness of America.

On the day Hobson was mistaken for an immigrant, he recognized that in America fashion and appearance had to a large degree replaced the work and the success ethics. Appearance and fashion were instruments of power. Hobson learned that elegant simplicity was expensive and had to be effectively displayed. He and his mother moved from the large rundown house in the shoddy northeast section into a fashionable old brick house in Georgetown. No more did Mother Hobson bustle about with a duster. The house was complete with a competent housekeeper, a cook, and a butler.

The first visitor to Hobson's new home was a British tailor. He came with cloth swatches and a tape measure. A month later Hobson married the widow of a famous Senator. She had money, breeding, and was an official in the D.A.R. After the three-day honeymoon, they moved in with old Mrs. Hobson. Their marriage was without issue.

After fifteen minutes of walking in the rain, Hobson stopped. The limousine pulled up beside him, and the secretary got out and opened the door.

Hobson settled back into the cushions and said, "John, I want to send the following encoded message to Doctor Theobald: SEE HAJN PRIVATELY AND INQUIRE POSSIBILITIES OF SARKHAN BEING INVADED IN NEAR FUTURE.

He turned to his secretary and added, "Send that top secret, for Theobald's eyes only, and with highest priority."

"Yes, sir."

Hobson unlocked his briefcase. "Back to the office. And let me see this morning's cables."

The Small Voice

The swiftness of Coldstream's recuperation had surprised Dr. Theobald who, it seemed to Coldstream and Taja, had practically lived at the house the past week. Coldstream would talk about his experience only to Taja, and not much to her. He was still very pale and had lost weight. He had not left the house since his ordeal.

One evening a week after his experience in the hills, Coldstream was alone in his vault checking radio reports from the north. The first radio signal came five minutes before the evening schedule, which linked all of his operations in Sarkhan, came through. It was a single sentence over the regular frequency and was relayed from one of the closer stations: "The jungle yields." Instantly Coldstream turned up the volume.

Coldstream recognized the small voice. It was Bui, eldest son of Apayki, the chief of a Meo tribe located fifty miles from the plateau in the foothills of the Tikok Mountains. Coldstream had traded with the village for twelve years. No other white man ever had bothered with them. The Meos were short, stocky, muscular, silent men who lived by hunting and by combing the jungle for food. Their villages were clumps of living foliage which they wove together without breaking the stalks from the roots. A lowlander could walk through a village without knowing it.

Coldstream had sent a message to Apayki asking if he would send one of his ablest men across the border into North Vietnam to scout for signs of the rumored mobilization of troops, getting details of their uniforms, equipment, language, and numbers. With the message he had sent a small receiver-transmitter radio. Coldstream suspected that Apayki would send his son Bui, who was trained in the operation of the radio and who was the most skilled jungle hunter in the village.

99

"I am at the end," Bui said, his voice sharp and clear in Cold-stream's earphones. He spoke in Meo, a fluid dialect close to the natural sounds of the jungle, which is probably what it was de-rived from.

Coldstream paused. There was no alarm in Bui's voice but Coldstream, who had spent painful months learning the language, had never mastered its nuances. No outsider ever would. Even so, he knew something was wrong.

"The end of what, Bui?" he replied in Meo.

"The end of the hunt," Bui said and laughed. "They have caught me."

Laughter among the Meo did not always mean gaiety.

"What happened?"

"First, I will say what I saw," Bui said. "They are still a half kilometer away."

He told Coldstream how he had worked his way over one range of mountains, moving over the almost invisible trails, and as he climbed the second range, the one north of Hao, he came upon sentries in sand-bagged towers a dozen meters off the ground. It was just over the border. Each tower was equipped with a light machine gun and was manned by three men. But the sentries were not fools. The ground between the towers was mined with everything from barbed wire to spikes dipped in human excre-ment and conventional contact mines.

Even for a man of Bui's skill it had taken a few hours to work through the barricade. He was convinced that the towers were made obvious just to force an intruder into the mine field.

It had taken another hour to trot to what the sentry line was protecting—a sprawling encampment of men, spread over a few square miles. There were no tents. Soldiers slept in foxholes, wrapped up in ponchos. Each group of six cooked for itself on an ingenious stove that gave off no smoke.

It had taken Bui several hours to explore the extent of the camp. He estimated that there were about one thousand men there. About eight hundred of them were young men with the dia-lect of the lowland and delta villages of Sarkhan. The rest were older and experienced. These were the teachers—Chinese, North

Vietnamese, and a few Europeans who mostly watched and said nothing.

"They are getting closer now," Bui said.

"How did you know that some of the men were Europeans?" Coldstream asked. "Could you get close enough to them in the daylight to see them?"

Bui laughed, that soft laugh, so much like water over moss or like wind through mist-drenched leaves.

During the day, it was true, he could not move. He rolled himself in moss under the roots of a huge tree and slept. At night he crept close to the men around their smokeless cookstoves. Any place a snake could move Bui could move, and just as soundlessly. He would crawl up to a group of men, listen for a half hour, then crawl to another group.

The Europeans were moaning from dysentery. Maybe they were the Russians Coldstream had told him about, but one thing was certain—they were European. No one else moaned like that. Any Asian who moaned like that from dysentery was dead before he was ten years old.

The camp was efficient, Bui said. They did not train the Sarkhanese boys with blackboards or books. They sent them out into the jungle and told them there would be mine fields, ambushes, barbed wire, and enemies ahead. And they deliberately gave different groups orders so that they would attack one another with real bullets. Bui had seen eight boys killed in the two days he had been there. It was very fine training, Bui said. The only bad thing was the endless talking at night. In each group there was someone who talked and talked and the rest must listen, because it was clear that the talker was a chief of some kind. The only thing Bui learned from the talking was that the white man must leave Sarkhan, and the people from the north were ready to help drive them out.

"Why do you say they have caught you?" Coldstream asked. His fingers were sweating.

"Because they have dogs," Bui said in a matter-of-fact voice. "Large dogs for tracking. The second morning they let them out."

Bui had tracked the tiger and stalked the leopard. He knew what was coming when he saw the dogs. Bui had made his way back to the mine field before the first dog caught up with him. The dog jumped and fell on a spike mine and twisted over in agony, each turn grinding the spikes farther in, until he grunted and lay still.

The rest of the pack had waited when they saw the dying dog. Their trainers had taken them through a cleared passage in the mine field. Bui had run fast, sometimes on trails, sometimes through the jungles, but the dogs could run faster. He had headed for the same pass he had come over, but the dogs had forced him into a cave.

"I have been shooting the dogs and the men as they come up the gorge but now I have only a few more rounds," Bui said. His voice was unworried, steady, almost phlegmatic. "You will tell my father and my wife?"

"Yes, I will tell them," Coldstream said. "And don't worry about your wife. We will take care of her and the children for the rest of their lives."

"I will leave the radio on, but I cannot talk again," Bui said.

There was a smashing sound as Bui fired his rifle. Then a splintering which Coldstream guessed was the ricochet of return fire.

Coldstream waited, thinking of Bui's tiny wife, just over four and a half feet tall, but always with a child on her hip and carrying huge loads on her head. She had a timid smile, bad teeth, and was fond of candy.

There was the sound of strange voices on the frequency.

"He must be dead," a voice said in Vietnamese. "He is not moving ..."

Then the ripping sound of a Sten gun and the beginning of a cry chopped off.

"This time he is dead," a new voice said. "Now bring a flashlight in here and make a search."

It was obviously an officer-instructor. The man's voice was deep and he spoke Sarkhanese with a strange inflection.

"Leave the radio there," the voice said. "I'll take care of it."

Coldstream leaned forward in his chair. On the bottom of the radio there was a small ordinary-looking dial that was really a detonator. Once the dial was turned to the "on" position, it would detonate one pound of powerful plastic six seconds after the radio was picked up.

"It is a good job," the harsh voice said. "Well made. Japanese style . . ."

There was a click and then silence.

12

The American Embassy

At ten minutes before seven Coldstream was walking along the river. Though still weak, he enjoyed his exercise particularly in the early morning. Boats floated down carrying cargoes of exquisitely arranged radishes, onions, and tomatoes. A small child on the prow of a *huatze*, who had probably never seen a white man, stared solemnly at him and ran to the stern to stand by his parents.

His workmen, grave of face, made signals to him from the lower dock. When he went over, they showed him what he had expected: two more decapitated bodies that had been hooked out of the river that morning.

He did not understand fully, but obviously they were intended as a warning. The citizens of Haidho had the impression that some sort of mysterious struggle was taking place upriver.

He wondered if the American intelligence people knew more. It was unlikely. They always depended on Asians for their information. It was convenient, but it put the Americans completely at the mercy of the Asians. Superior intelligence must be gathered from many sources.

Possibly the bodies related in some fashion to the curious report McCauley had given him on the throw-aways which Coldstream had gathered from all over Sarkhan. One throw-away was distributed only in Buddhist villages, another in predominantly Moslem villages. Both were printed on very cheap paper, both skillfully written, carefully using selected quotations from the Koran and the *sutras* to attack the other religion. For over six hundred years there had been no religious conflict in Sarkhan, and mosques and pagodas were everywhere.

Taja and McCauley were in the kitchen. Taja was cooking and McCauley was over the white marble-topped table making notes from a book on Sarkhanese history that must have weighed ten pounds. Coldstream gently touched Taja's shoulder and squeezed it. The professor looked up and smiled absently, obviously trying to untangle some puzzle. Coldstream noticed that his teeth were red from betel-nut juice. McCauley enjoyed the slight narcotic effect which he described as somewhere between a cigar and a martini.

Taja was making blueberry pancakes which McCauley claimed to love and which appalled Taja. She would stare at him, unable to control her laughter, as he spread the butter and poured the sweet syrup over the pancakes.

A second time McCauley looked up at Coldstream and this time he focused. "They were talking about you last night at the Embassy cocktail party. That article in the Hanoi paper."

"Oh?"

"The one that said your village *godowns* in the Three Mountain Peaks area had been ransacked by Sarkhanese villagers protesting your capitalistic methods. You had been charging the villagers exorbitant prices and getting them into debt and were foreclosing on their farms."

"You didn't tell them about Xinh's report?"

McCauley shook his head. "I gathered that the Ambassador had cabled the newspaper article to Washington."

Taja had prepared a small chicken curry for Coldstream. She served him quietly and then said she was going to the market.

"Market?" Coldstream asked.

"Yes. This evening I will make *garammassala* and for that I need coriander." She looked at Coldstream. "Also I need gossip. They are saying strange things in the bazaar these days."

McCauley glanced at Taja's shopping list. It was written on the back of a cheap, flimsy throw-away which the merchants of Haidho used to advertise their bargains. McCauley turned the sheet over and looked at the top advertisement. Hunching over, his face close to the paper, he examined the printing with his magnifying glass.

"This was printed on the same press that put out the propaganda," MacCauley said slowly. "In Sarkhanese script it has the same flaw on the character for 'people.' 'All people of Sarkhan welcome to this magnificent sale of fine copper pots.' The character for 'people' has a little burr on the bottom of it—just like the propaganda."

Coldstream walked over and stood behind McCauley. He pointed to the lower lefthand corner. In tiny type was the name of the printer: *Haidho Gazette.*

"Coit puts out the *Gazette*," Coldstream said. He paused. "Not that it means anything."

"It means a hell of a lot," McCauley said quickly, his voice edgy.

"Tad, every newspaper in Sarkhan does odd lot printing on the side," Coldstream said. "Let's look around a bit before we jump to conclusions."

"I'm not jumping to any conclusions," McCauley said impatiently. "I'm just pointing out that the propaganda and this advertisement were printed on the same press. If I had to make a conclusion right now I'd say that Coit is being had. Good Lord, he's the most anti-Communist character in Haidho. Which, if you were running off Communist propaganda, would be just the place to have it printed."

McCauley took the advertisement and put it in the book he had been reading.

"What else do you hear around Haidho these days, Taja?" he asked.

Taja said, "There is much talk at the palace. The Prince should have returned from meditation two weeks ago. He had many appointments—including one to become the godfather of his cook's new son. The servants at the palace are worried. They don't even know where the Prince is meditating. It's been almost a month now . . ."

McCauley looked up from his pancakes. "The Prince's secretary called and canceled my appointment. That's never happened before."

The two men ate silently. Taja moved about the room unobtrusively with her extraordinary grace.

"I'll go see Ambassador Brown this morning," Coldstream said.

"You still look weak," said Taja. "Shall I drive you?"

"I'd better go alone, thank you."

"You can go into the Embassy alone," she said, taking one of his hands gently in hers, "but I will drive you."

"I feel better now," said Coldstream.

Taja moved her head slightly forward, a fraction of an inch, toward Coldstream's face.

McCauley laughed. "Taja, I wish you'd hold my hand like that."

"When you get the *mentado*, I will," she said, letting go of Coldstream's hand slowly, trailing her fingers lightly.

Fifteen years ago the United States had had only a small consulate in Sarkhan, a rented bamboo house with seventeen employees. That was the same year, 1950, that Coldstream had arrived in Sarkhan with two surplus Navy landing craft, $1500 in credit, and a briefcase full of combat decorations. In that same briefcase were his Navy retirement documents and final divorce papers.

His ex-wife's name was Spring. The name embarrassed her, so he had called her "Spri" part of the time, and "ing" the rest. She was far from beautiful, but she had a sense of excitement which spread over everything she was interested in. Unfortunately she was not interested in Asia. She knew that Coldstream was. She had told him very quietly and with a finality why they had to get a divorce.

As Taja drove the jeep across the Sekong Bridge and into the crowded streets of Haidho, Coldstream thought fleetingly of Spring. His thoughts were neutral and without regret and, as always, he was mildly amused by his own detachment.

Coldstream had agreed to the divorce. Spring had gone to Reno and then to San Francisco, where she set up a small interior decorating shop. She wrote Coldstream often and sent him books she thought he would like. Two years after they were divorced she said she was making enough money so that the alimony could be discontinued. Coldstream had sent her back a humorous letter outlining how his firm had prospered. He wanted to pay the alimony; he could afford it. She replied by cable: DEAR MAN WITH THOSE ASSETS PLEASE DOUBLE ALIMONY YOU CAN'T SPEND IT THERE. LOVE. ING.

Coldstream had doubled the alimony. He received another cable from Spring: POOR DEAR MAN. I WAS KIDDING AND YOU STILL DON'T UNDERSTAND A JOKE. SENDING CHECK BACK. PLEASE, REPEAT, PLEASE NO ALIMONY. DIG? LOVE. SPRING

He had hired Taja to be his secretary shortly after his divorce. He had heard something of her background, but it did not register. She had been one of King Diad's mistresses or concubines or something, but he cared nothing for that sort of gossip. She was efficient and multilingual.

Taja moved quietly about the office and later, about the house. She brought in maids and cleaned the place thoroughly. She instructed the laundress how to iron shirts; she improved the quality of the meals; she fired half of the old staff and put on more energetic people; she sorted his mail, but without opening his letters; she met callers and sent them away satisfied, although they seldom got to see Edward Coldstream.

Then an unusual day, a day of coincidence, came. Coldstream looked at the report of his accountants and realized that in three months he had turned the corner with his company. It was the day he had sent off that cable to Spring saying that he could afford to pay alimony.

Taja had brought him her humorous reply. He was sitting on the veranda and looking down at the confluence of the rivers. With one hand Taja gave him the cable, with the other she touched his neck. It was not, by Sarkhanese standards, an intimate gesture. When a man was tired, a woman would massage his neck—any woman.

But Taja had never done this before.

It had been an odd day. Nothing really important had happened. His ex-wife had indicated she was happy. And a woman whom he had watched for weeks had touched him.

After that life was much easier.

The inside of the Embassy rotunda was vast. In the center, at a shiny reception desk, a Sarkhanese woman slumped comfortably in her chair. She was engrossed in an American comic book, forming the words with her lips. Without looking up she acknowledged Coldstream's presence with a bored "Yes?"

Coldstream spoke gently in Sarkhanese, using the northern dialect because he saw that the receptionist had the high cheek-bones and thick hair of that area. "In Sarkhan, my friend, is it not true that even the King stands up when he meets a stranger?"

The girl jumped to her feet, holding the comic book in front of her mouth. She said in English, "May I help you, sir?"

"Where is the Ambassador's office?"

"Whom shall I say is . . . ?" Then looking for a moment into Coldstream's face, she said, "I will take you to the Ambassador's secretary."

The secretary's office was a large room with a beige carpet and an executive-type desk. It smelled of perfume and Cold-stream saw why. The secretary was spraying her hair. As Coldstream entered, she removed some earphones, placing them carefully in a desk drawer. Coldstream saw the tape recorder be-fore the drawer was shut. The wire from the recorder went under the carpet and then along the wall at waist level. Behind the secretary were two pictures, one of the President of the United States, the other of Ambassador Brown.

"My name is Coldstream," he said to her. "I would like to see the Ambassador."

"Have you an appointment?"

Coldstream looked at her with a faint turning up of the corners of his lips. He shook his head.

"May I tell the Ambassador what you wish to see him about?"

"You may send this in to him and tell him I am here," said Coldstream, handing her his card.

"He has a visitor at present . . ."

"I will wait."

He sat down on a leather chair and picked up *The New York Times*. It was the regular mail edition and over a month old. Be-hind the paper Coldstream fiddled with a small black box in his briefcase, then placed the briefcase on the table close to the wire which led to the tape recorder in the secretary's desk. Glancing into the briefcase, Coldstream saw that the indicator light on the black box was flickering. Coldstream knew then that the Ambas-sador had his conversations tape-recorded.

Ten minutes later the buzzer on the secretary's desk sounded.

The young lady moved quickly past Coldstream, opened the door to the Ambassador's office.

"Roselyn," said Ambassador Brown in a high, controlled voice for which he had become famous in New Hampshire court-rooms. "Tell General Hajn's driver to bring his car to the entrance."

"Right away, sir," said the secretary. She dialed her telephone, relayed the message to the parking attendant. She had not closed the door.

From inside the office another voice said, "Thank you for your courtesy, Mister Ambassador. And may I assure you, everything will go well at the coronation. We appreciate your thoughtful-ness. That's why everyone in Sarkhan admires you."

Coldstream recognized the second speaker as General Hajn.

"That's very kind of you, General," said the Ambassador.

"Goodbye, Your Excellency," said Hajn.

"*Tai wah khin sum koon*," replied the Ambassador.

Coldstream flinched. The Ambassador was trying the language and he was coming close. The farewell he had just given was actually the way a man says goodbye to his mistress. But the Sarkhanese were much impressed when a white man could speak any words at all of their language.

Coldstream had met Ambassador Spratt Brown only casually at the last Fourth of July reception, but had heard much about him from Taja, who knew many of the 851 Sarkhanese employed at the Embassy. Taja collected useful gossip the way a dredge sucks up sand. She considered it as one of her duties, and it was easy for her. She had access to the palace, to all embassies, and also was at ease in the marketplace.

Brown tried to conduct himself in the tradition of the Peace Corps and the New Frontier. He was the heir to a considerable New Hampshire fortune, a lawyer with a long record of public service. The entire Brown family, which included five children, took lessons in Sarkhanese, and at public functions they wore native clothes. Instead of shaking hands, they bowed low from the waist, in Asian fashion. Ambassador Brown went to great effort to be "close to the natives." He rode his bicycle around the park every morning and once or twice a week he attended the opening of a new mosque, a Buddhist temple, or a factory. He lectured at luncheons to business groups. His wife wrote a column for an American magazine in which she described Sarkhanese cooking. The local papers reprinted it. The last installment had an account of how to fry grasshoppers, serving them with corn and honey. Actually the Sarkhanese did not eat grasshoppers and honey. Only the small Chinese community relished the dish. The Ambassador had a local Chinese as his chef.

Coldstream watched General Hajn as he came out. What Sukarno is to Indonesia, Mao Tse-tung to China, Lenin to Russia, and Gandhi to India, General Hajn hoped to become to Sarkhan, he thought. With one difference: Hajn did not want to be a Diem or Syngman Rhee or Ayub. The royal family and the religious leaders in Sarkhan had more prestige and prominence. It was the prestige and tradition of aristocracy that Hajn hungered for.

Hajn had made news around the world when he surrounded several hundred Meo insurrectionists at Podeka Valley in 1961 and slaughtered them. Hajn himself had manned a machine gun, rallied his men three times when they thought they were losing, and had suffered heavy wounds. The pictures showed the dead rebels wearing hammer-and-sickle armbands. Coldstream had wondered about this at the time. He had never known the wandering Meos to have had any political affiliation.

General Hajn was a physical mutation. In Sarkhan the average male weighed 110 and was five-feet-two. General Hajn was six-feet-two and weighed 230 pounds. The Sarkhanese were slow-moving and wore gentle smiles. General Hajn had the physical vitality and alert aggressiveness of a Western executive.

As the two men came into the outer office Hajn saw Coldstream, and his broad face animated.

"Coldstream!" Hajn said, thrusting out his large hand. "How are you! We missed listening to the Army-Navy game on the radio last year."

The ebullient General turned to the Ambassador. "Of course you know my old friend, Admiral Edward Coldstream?"

"I have had the pleasure. I've heard a lot about Admiral Coldstream and his South East Asia Trading Corporation."

"Just Mister Coldstream, sir. I retired from the Navy fifteen year ago as captain. The admiral title is what we call a tombstone promotion."

"Your Excellency, take good care of him," Hajn said. "Coldstream has done much to help Sarkhan. Please, don't bother seeing me to the door."

In his office, the Ambassador pointed to a leather chair. "Please sit down." What can I do for you, Mister Coldstream?"

"Mister Ambassador, I don't wish to offend you, but I would consider it a favor, sir, if you would turn your tape recorder off? What I have to say is for your ears only."

"Tape recorder? This isn't the Kremlin, Mister Coldstream," said Ambassador Brown with a forced smile.

From his briefcase Coldstream took the small metal box with dials and pushbuttons. It had a crude unfinished look about it.

"Mister Ambassador, this is an induction recorder. It flickered when placed next to the wire running from your office to the tape recorder in your secretary's desk. Whatever was being said in your office was being taped."

"Come, now," said Brown with a chuckle. "Your electric eye must have been activated by the telephone."

"It was my intention to wipe the conversation off without listening, sir," said Coldstream, "but perhaps it would interest you ..."

After adjusting two dials a light glowed on the top of the machine. Coldstream turned up the volume.

From a miniature loudspeaker, in metallic hollow tones, came the voices of the Ambassador and General Hajn.

"Then I can assure my government ... ?" said the Ambassador's voice.

The voice of Hajn answered him. "I promise you, Your Excellency, that Prince Lin has been in a sanctuary meditating and preparing himself for the coronation. Now he has a slight cold and is resting at the Royal Dispensary."

"Thank you very much, General Hajn, for your information."

"My real reason for calling on you concerns military aid. Confidentially, the Royal Council—and His Majesty also—is distressed over the refusal of your President to grant Sarkhan military aid. One member of the Council suggested an approach either to Russia or to Indonesia. Frankly, His Majesty feels rebuffed. I had a difficult time calming things."

"General, my government cannot give military aid in the amounts you requested unless there is a danger from outside aggression."

"Mister Ambassador, the package I just gave you contains copies of our latest intelligence information, which I am sure will be of great interest to your government. Within a week, when my agents return from the border, I'll give you more. Think on it."

Coldstream shut off the recorder. Ambassador Brown picked up the metal box and examined it. "What in hell is this gadget?"

Coldstream took it back from the Ambassador and dropped the box into his briefcase.

"A recorder which works on the principle of magnetic induction. I made it myself. I use it to record radio transmissions when static is high."

"You should not have used it in my office."

"Sir, I was curious as to whether my conversation with you was about to be recorded. I found it was. It was not my intention to listen. Mister Ambassador, I suggest you warn Doctor Theobald that your conversations in the Embassy can be easily bugged..."

"Doctor Theobald?"

"Your F.I.A. chief, sir."

"I think you are making a mistake here," said the Ambassador, his voice cautious. "Doctor Theobald is the Embassy physician."

"It is common knowledge in Haidho that Doctor Theobald works for the Federal Intelligence Agency. And I suggest that you instruct him, sir, to get some lead-shielded cable to go from the microphone which is obviously in the inkstand here on your desk, back to the recorder in your secretary's office. The induction impulses I picked up are from the wire, not from the machine. It would be easy for an enemy agent to do the same."

The Ambassador started to talk, his expression serious now. "Why have you come here this morning?"

"Because I am worried."

"Captain Coldstream," said Brown tartly, "I have heard about the troubles you had with the villagers upriver. I regret your agonizing experience, but I can understand the point of view of the angry natives."

"What I am worried about is that you believe those charges of usury and exploitation," Coldstream said. "Have you ever been to Boa Binh? To Dao? To the mountain tribes?"

"I have only been here six months," Brown said. "I intend to . . ."

"Mister Ambassador," said Coldstream, "I have lived here a long time. I know this country. For the last fifteen years Sarkhan has had the normal problems of a primitive land existing in an electronic age. But the adjustments are at least beginning and we have had peace. Now, in the past few months there has been a change. I sense—though I can't prove it—that the Communists are making their move to take Sarkhan from within. From within," he repeated, "exactly as they started in Vietnam, Laos, and Indonesia."

"Coldstream, there is no internal threat," Brown said, his voice patient.

"How do you know?" Coldstream asked. He put it directly, leaving no way for evasion.

Brown reversed the question. "Tell me how you know there is one."

Coldstream took the leather pouch from his pocket and spilled the eleven bullets on the Ambassador's desk. "Each of these came from a dead man floating down from the north. Eleven men shot in the back—also decapitated. This morning we found two more."

"I didn't know there had been that many," Brown said slowly. "But even so, murdering and cutting off heads is not strange in Asia."

"In China or in Indonesia it might not be strange, but in Sarkhan it is. It has not happened here in over six hundred years—during which time Moslems and Buddhists have lived without violence. Sir, five of the dead men were Moslem village chiefs. The other six were Buddhist community leaders and *bonzes*."

"How do you know that?"

Coldstream reached into his briefcase and placed a bundle of photographs on the desk. "Observe their clothes."

The Ambassador sucked in his breath sharply as he saw the pictures of the eleven bloated and mutilated bodies.

"I took those pictures," said Coldstream, "and if you test those bullets you will find that some of them are U.S. 45-caliber, some are Russian, some are German. There is a collecting of arms from other counter-insurgency actions around the world. The murdered men were all religious. From what I have gathered from my people up north, they were the most unpopular or the most corrupt or the most severe. Such a selection could only be made from within."

"Very interesting," said the Ambassador. He looked slightly puzzled.

"The technique of causing dissension by secret murders," said Coldstream, "has been used in China for fifty centuries. This is only part of the evidence that suggests to me that China is using North Vietnam to smash Sarkhan, by internal political, religious, and economic discord. Don't forget, sir, China once indirectly ran this part of the world—that is, up until eighty years ago. Actually, her border claim has some legitimacy."

The Ambassador looked hard at Coldstream but said nothing.

"The next item," said Coldstream, "is the disappearance of Prince Lin."

"Just a minute," said the Ambassador. "Prince Lin happens to be in meditation and also has a slight cold. You just heard that from your friend, General Hajn, on that little black box of yours." He smiled tolerantly at the American merchant.

"The Prince is not in Haidho. He has not returned from his meditation, and his personal retinue at the palace has no idea where he is. The Sarkhanese are talking about it. It would be a political calamity if the Prince did not show up well before the coronation."

"What is the source of all your information?"

"I have ships and trading posts throughout Sarkhan. I receive daily reports. Also, I have friends who have access to the palace and the Royal Dispensary."

In a patient voice the Ambassador said, "I'm sure your reports are accurate so far as trade and finances are concerned. But political information is more difficult to appraise. It is much subtler, it is much more complicated. It covers a much broader scope. To gather and appraise it accurately requires the services of professionals who make it their full-time career."

"Mister Ambassador, I know that you are familiar with the activities of the Viet Cong in South Vietnam ..."

"I am," said the Ambassador.

"The incident in Boa Binh and in the nearby villages was not a protest against my business practices, as was printed in the Communist papers. The incident was the beginning of terrorist tactics by the newly organized Sark Cong, an extension of the Communist Viet Cong. I have an eyewitness to the event. The looting of my trading post was nothing. What is important is that Boa Binh is one of the six villages to the north that are having pressure put on them. Strangers come for volunteers. They demand food and shelter. Mister Ambassador, this has been the pattern in every country where the Communists came to power."

Coldstream paused. The Ambassador looked at him almost as if he had not heard.

Coldstream went on to describe the flood of radio and newspaper propaganda seeping over Asia, in a score of different tongues and dialects, suggesting that the Americans were raiding Sarkhan with planes, infiltrating with agents, introducing a new colonialism. The United States Information Service, on the other hand, was broadcasting English lessons.

"Do you think the riot in front of the Embassy was spontaneous?" Coldstream asked.

"They were just schoolboys."

"Schoolboys thirty years old. Does it not appear odd to you that the riot took place immediately after the mysterious bombing of a monastery? I have evidence that the riot was a well-planned and well-executed Communist maneuver."

"Nonsense. I personally was a witness to that event, you'll remember. I spoke to those young men."

Coldstream paused and then changed the subject. "There are rumors of an invasion near the plateau region. I know the area well. I have plantations there. An invasion over that terrain this time of year is impossible. I assure you there's no ..."

"You seem to have plantations everywhere," Brown interrupted. He sat straighter. He felt he had gained an advantage. "Might not your commercial interests distort your view of things?"

Coldstream ignored the question.

"I am concerned over why such a rumor should be started," said Coldstream. "Why should General Hajn seem worried about this? He knows that the plateau region during the monsoon is the one section of Sarkhan perfectly protected by geography and weather."

"I am not privy to the secret thoughts of General Hajn, Captain Coldstream. But I do know that he is a friend of our country, a graduate of West Point, and, quite frankly, a man in whom I place great confidence."

The Ambassador got up from behind his desk.

Coldstream knew his visit was over.

"Sir," said Coldstream as he began slowly to unbutton and remove his gloves, "I know what I'm talking about. I personally went to Boa Binh to investigate and had an interesting experience..."

The Ambassador interrupted gently. "I know about your experience. You went up there on business and the natives got angry and beat you up in a particularly ugly manner. I have a report of it here in my desk—a report from the Sarkhanese river patrol which went to Boa Binh and investigated."

"Would you like to know what really happened?"

The Ambassador shook his head.

"We cannot pry into the domestic affairs of our host country," he said. "Also, Captain, we have our own sources of information and expert ways of evaluating them."

Coldstream shrugged and stood up. "I thought I would try, Mister Ambassador," he said. "I have seen the model which Mao Tse-tung developed in China unroll in a half-dozen Asian countries. Without being able to prove it, I am convinced that the Communists have begun their first state of insurgency—political infiltration of the villages. Now they are moving to the next step. The danger is from within. Not from without."

The Ambassador hesitated by the door for a moment, then said carefully, "Thank you very much, Captain Coldstream, for your information and your offer to help me run the Embassy. I think I understand what has stimulated you to come here and be so kind. Perhaps I know things which would surprise you. For example, I am aware that you have been sending information to Adolph Cogswell, the head of the President's Special Committee on Sarkhan—a most discourteous thing to do behind my back."

"Oh?"

Coldstream was unable to hide his surprise.

Ambassador Brown gave his short pleasant laugh and said, "You wonder how I got that, eh? Well, thank you very much for stopping in to see me."

Coldstream bowed Sarkhanese style and said, "*Koom p'at ili,*" the respectful way of saying goodbye to an official.

The Ambassador returned the bow and replied with the same loving farewell he had spoken to General Hajn, "*Itai wah khin sum koon.*"

Coldstream walked down the Embassy corridors, his stomach tight with anger. With me he has used the correct expression after all. The Honorable Ambassador Spratt Brown certainly screwed me.

Half an hour later Coldstream was back at his house.

McCauley studied his friend's face for a moment and asked abruptly, "What happened?"

When Coldstream had finished describing his interview, McCauley said, "The Ambassador is a fool. An absolute ass."

"We should tell Cogswell what is happening. In detail."

"Edward, whatever you do from now on will be closely watched," Taja said. She was restless. "Remember that, please. I have never seen Sarkhan like this before. When the Japanese were here we knew exactly who was watching who, who was a traitor, who gave information, who was dependable. Today things are shifting, uncertain."

Coldstream paced up and down the room for a few moments and said, "We can send a message to Cogswell tomorrow..."

"If you send him a message, everybody in Sarkhan will know. The only way is for you to fly to Washington," Taja said.

Taja's face was smooth and unperturbed, but her long fingers twined together, pressed tight, then went limp. She had never before urged Coldstream to travel. She was afraid of his long trips, uncertain of their outcome, anxious when he was gone.

"She's right," McCauley said. "I'm not optimistic about getting much done in Washington. But it's our best chance." He grinned. "Besides, it's time I personally met this behind-the-scenes genius Cogswell to judge for myself whether he's worthy of my brilliant reports."

Coldstream eyed McCauley with surprise. McCauley usually held himself aloof from politics. Then he turned to Taja. "Taja, send a cable to our agent in Hong Kong telling him that I am coming there for ten days to buy agricultural equipment and to arrange for hotel rooms for Professor McCauley and me. Also inform the Hong Kong Historical Association that Professor McCauley will want to use their archives while he is in Hong Kong."

McCauley smiled a lazy smile and said, "That will interest the Ambassador's informer. And it will be easy for us to catch a plane from Hong Kong to San Francisco."

"Edward," said Taja, "the next plane to Hong Kong leaves tomorrow afternoon."

He nodded and left the room to pack, already five thousand miles away. Taja looked after him but did not move. McCauley watched Taja and felt the sadness in the room.

13

The Ambassador's Team

Ambassador Brown called a meeting of four men for ten that evening—Dr. Theobald, the Embassy doctor; Public Affairs Officer Jerome Klein; Thomas Johnson, the political officer; and the fourth man was Marcus Coit, the publisher of the *Haidho Gazette* and trusted advisor to the American Embassy in Haidho for many years.

The inclusion of Coit was almost a tradition. He had lived in Sarkhan for forty years. During the panic of the early days of the Japanese invasion in 1942 the American Consul had forgotten Coit, probably because Coit was confined to his wheelchair. Every American in the country had been evacuated except Coit. He had been captured by the Japanese, but seeing his helplessness they had allowed him to stay in his home. A year later he had been rescued by a band of guerrillas from the Sarkhanese underground.

The first American Ambassador to return to Sarkhan after the war had, almost as an apology but also to find out about internal conditions, invited Coit to sit in on selected staff meetings. Gradually he had become a valued advisor. Ambassador Brown suspected that Coit might be on Dr. Theobald's payroll, but he had never asked. Theobald had never told Brown the extent of the F.I.A. operation in Sarkhan.

"Gentlemen," Ambassador Brown said. "You all know Captain Coldstream. I've always thought he was one of those American businessmen who value their profits above the welfare of their country. He has interests all over Southeast Asia, and is always scurrying around. Intelligent, but harmless, was the way I evaluated him. But now I'm not so sure. He came in this morning and said some things that only official Embassy personnel should know."

The Ambassador repeated his talk with Coldstream; and with

indignation he described how Coldstream had recorded his conversation with General Hajn. "Also he pointed out that the Chinese Communist claim to the Northern Territory probably had some legitimate basis," Brown said. "The borders," he said, "are always obscure and China once ran the whole continent anyway."

He paused, only to gather his thoughts, but he glanced at Thomas Johnson. Johnson was a Southerner, a career officer, and what the Department of State calls "a seasoned man."

"He might have a point there," Johnson said. "The old borders were very fluid. The Geneva Conference did not make them much firmer. The Meo and Man tribes, for example, roamed back and forth from China to Sarkhan. They refused to live at altitudes less than 3000 feet and that made fixing the border difficult."

"That may be true," Dr. Theobald said, "but the point is that right now such a statement by Coldstream just serves the Communist cause. It's their line right now."

"That's what Coldstream remarked," Brown said.

The remark caught Dr. Theobald off balance.

"Just what did he say?" Dr. Theobald asked.

"That the Communists are smothering Sarkhan with propaganda and that we are not countering. He seemed to be saying, though not in so many words, that we are not doing our jobs."

"Mister Ambassador, one of the classic ploys of the Communists is to get us to imitate them," Coit said. For a small shrunken man he had a powerful voice. "I think Coldstream took their bait. Forget him. Let's face the hard facts. Communist China has made a territorial claim. Troops are building up across the North Vietnamese border. Those are the realities."

"Really, Mister Ambassador, I don't think we have to worry about Coldstream," Dr. Theobald said. "I have a plant in his office, a clerk. We know every move he makes. We watch a big ship operator like that because there are so many chances for espionage and smuggling." The doctor fished in his pocket, brought out a slip of paper, and put it before the Ambassador with a slight smile. "Here's his schedule for next week."

"Doctor, one of the things Coldstream said was that you were head of the F.I.A. operations here in Sarkhan," the Ambassador said.

Dr. Theobald took it easily.

"That can't be avoided," he said. "We try to keep the whole apparatus invisible, but if we have to show any part of it we show the head of mission. Once I'm identified it is actually easier for the rest of the apparatus to stay out of sight."

The Ambassador thought about that for a moment. He glanced at Coit. Coit nodded his head in agreement. The Ambassador turned back to the paper Dr. Theobald had handed him.

"Now what about this, Doctor?" he said suddenly. "Next Wednesday he's having dinner with Gordon Sarkisian, George McClaine, and Betsy Winters. All journalists. If he tells them even half the nonsense he told me, it would be on every front page in the States."

"I know all three of them," Coit said. "Old China hands. They were friends of Coldstream when he was up there. They'll just get drunk and talk about the old days in Tientsin."

"Maybe so." Jerome Klein, the Public Affairs Officer, spoke for the first time. "But unhappily they've got a lot to write about. Rumors about Prince Lin's absence are floating around the marketplaces and the bars. Also some of the upcountry people coming down to market have been talking about the village boys who are forced to volunteer. And then the bodies in the river. We can't keep stuff like that down."

"Eliminating Communist propaganda," the Ambassador said, "is part of our job."

"I concur, Mister Ambassador," the Political Officer said in his soft Memphis voice. "Klein, I've been out here for two tours. In Sarkhan the rumor is like radio or television in the States. It's a form of entertainment. And the Commies try to exploit it."

"But if the rumors are based on fact, they get hard to handle," Klein said. He had been in Sarkhan only eight months, but he had poked around in the poorer districts and hiked out into the villages. "If there really is recruitment and terrorism up north, then it looks very much to the Sarkhanese like what happened in Vietnam and Korea."

"Klein, I have discussed this with General Hajn. He assured me there is nothing to the rumors about trouble," the Ambassador said. "I see no reason to give credence to the rumors. What we have to do is diminish them."

"Precisely, Mister Ambassador," the Political Officer said. He leaned forward, his voice confidential. "We stamp them out in Sarkhan, but we report them to Washington. It shakes up the boys back there, and we get the funds and personnel we need to do the job out here. With support—I mean the equipment and the trained troops—we could put down any Communist invasion while it was still small and controllable."

"I'm still worried about one thing," Klein persisted. He was perspiring slightly, uneasy at being the new man in the Embassy yet now the center of an argument. "None of our people have actually seen this enemy build-up across the border. We get it all from Hajn."

Once he had said it, Klein knew he had made a mistake. He had offended both Dr. Theobald and Johnson, the Political Officer, both of them senior to him.

"Look, Klein, political intelligence is my job," Johnson said. "Gathering it and evaluating it. Your job is to present the best picture possible to the public."

"I'm afraid he's right," Dr. Theobald said. "We have ways of gathering intelligence which we do not even tell to the Ambassador. That is the nature of our job. Now I know that you've tramped out to a village or two and that's commendable, but it takes more than that to get the total picture."

The Ambassador stepped in. "We can't afford to meddle in internal affairs. So far as public relations are concerned you should help the journalists as much as possible, but don't give them any unconfirmed rumors. Don't rock the boat."

Klein nodded.

"Now what else is there about Coldstream?" the Ambassador said.

"I'll send you our dossier," Dr. Theobald said. "But to summarize: Annapolis graduate, rose to captain in World War II, combat decorations, requested duty in China in 1945, then resigned shortly thereafter. Shrewd, energetic businessman, built a large company which does sea transport, runs river boats, maintains trading posts, and buys and sells in all legitimate commodities. No evidence of political interest. He got himself pretty well mangled about ten days ago. Some villagers upriver took exception to his way of doing business, I think. I took care of him for a few days. He's some kind of an electronics nut. Fiddles with gadgets in his basement."

"What about that woman who lives with him?" the Ambassador asked.

"Taja is her name," Coit, the hunchback, said. "She was the King's mistress fifteen years ago, but the pox left scars on her face. The King had to turn her out. Something about the concubines of royalty having unblemished faces. Usually such a woman would leave the country. But the King and the people in the palace liked Taja. And times change. So she moved in with Coldstream after a few years."

"Anything else?" the Ambassador asked. "What about this McCauley character?"

"His dossier is spotty," Dr. Theobald said, "but it gives a fairly complete picture."

The first page in McCauley's dossier was his birth certificate. He had been born in Jammu, India, on December 11, 1923, and his birth had been registered with the American Embassy in New Delhi. He was the son of missionary parents, both of whom were physicians. When McCauley was seven, his parents moved to Cochin-China. He had been educated at a village school during the day and the Calvert correspondence course at night. He could speak English, Chinese, Hindi, and French by the time he was twelve. When the war came along, he claimed he was a conscientious objector. After that the records were thin and erratic. Later he showed up in Burma as a medical corpsman with the guerrillas and there were indications he had been dropped into Sarkhan, but the dates and purpose of the mission had disappeared.

"We interviewed some of his friends from his platoon in the Burma and Sarkhan campaigns," Dr. Theobald said. "Conflicting views. Kind of thing that drives intelligence out of its mind."

Ambassador Brown interrupted. "You've gone to so much trouble to investigate this man. Do you suspect anything?"

"He's the world's leading authority on Sarkhan," Dr. Theobald said. "He's made eight trips here. For a person like that, getting a detailed dossier is routine."

Most of the members of his guerrilla group had agreed on a few things. McCauley was the most aggressive and ruthless man in the group—if it were necessary in taking care of the wounded. One man said, "For a conscientious objector he had a terribly itchy trigger finger."

"I'm curious," said Brown. "How many persons did you interview to get all this information?"

"A lot."

"Do you do this much about everyone?"

"Mister Ambassador," said Theobald, "you should see the dossier we have on you!"

The Ambassador smiled, but it was forced.

Dr. Theobald made one final point. Professor McCauley could, if he wanted, be very influential and persuasive with a large number of uninformed people, including Congressmen and Senators. Also, he was a paid consultant for Adolph Cogswell, the head of that Sarkhan Committee and a man who had influenced Presidents.

When the presentation was over, the Ambassador stood up. "Gentlemen," he said, "official relations between Sarkhan and the United States are managed by this Embassy. We cannot have amateurs such as Coldstream and McCauley meddling in *our* affairs. Let's keep them at a distance, but at the same time watch them. I don't consider them dangerous—just nuisances, that's all."

The meeting was over. Coit hadn't quite reached the door when the Ambassador said, "Just a moment, Marcus. I'd like to talk with you alone."

The hunchback moved slowly back.

"Marcus, what do you think of the situation?"

"Spratt, we've got a hell of a lot more trouble than we bargained for," Coit said. "First, that Klein chap had better go. I'm not saying he's subversive, but he's the kind of liberal that the Communists can get to. I understand he was a speech teacher in some university before he took over this job."

The Ambassador squirmed in his chair. Coit saw the motion and smiled.

"Spratt, don't get nervous," Coit said. "Some of my best

friends are—as they say. But let's face it. As a group, Jews are more receptive to the radical line."

"Marcus, I can't fire him just for that," the Ambassador said.

"No one is suggesting you fire him," Coit said, and he had to resist showing his contempt for the Ambassador. "Just have him transferred. Tokyo is a safe place. But all this wandering around the countryside, picking up intuitions. He doesn't understand the first principle of Asian politics: policy is made in the capital."

"What do you think about Coldstream?" the Ambassador asked, eager to get away from Klein.

Coit was silent for a moment. He thought of Coldstream's lithe, athletic body. He felt a savage anger, so deep it was frightening. He remembered why he had come to Sarkhan long ago. He had made the trip to escape the perfect, tanned active bodies on the beaches of southern California. Confined to a wheelchair himself, the tanned intact bodies had built a quiet fury in him. He had wanted to escape to a place where people were shorter, moved more slowly, where he could have self-esteem. Sarkhan had been the place. The streets were crowded with people who had more loathsome afflictions than his, and the Sarkhanese did not look down on a cripple—not a white cripple who had money. The Sarkhanese were used to physical afflictions and there was no condescension in their manner toward him. The place was perfect for Coit—he had position, servants, status.

"A subversive," Coit said without hesitation. "Oh, sure he's a war hero. But isn't that a perfect cover? Why would a Navy captain want to be liaison officer with the Chinese Red Army? He spent a year and a half with Mao Tse-tung and Chu-teh, eating with them, sleeping with them, working with them."

"It might have been a good way to get intelligence," the Ambassador said.

"And get yourself brainwashed. That's precisely what happened to Coldstream. He comes back and writes a report saying that the Chinese Communists have developed a new kind of guerrilla warfare that can defeat a modern Western army." Coit writhed back into his chair and when he spoke again his hand shot out like an exclamation point. "That notion, the notion of imitating the Chinese Communist guerrillas in the jungle, is playing into their hands. In war you go all out. You don't use some half-baked idea Mao cooked up."

"Just a minute now, Marcus, Mao's tactics gave us a hard time in Korea and Vietnam."

"Because we didn't use our full strength. Suppose we had started using tactical A-bombs the first day of fighting in Korea? The whole thing would have ended right there. It's subversives like Coldstream who have distorted the whole policy of the U.S."

The Ambassador did not know a great deal about Southeast Asia, and the references to ten-year-old reports and to unfamiliar names confused him. He knew that Coit was a deeply angry man, but what he said had the intense ring of truth. Also, whether it was true or not, whatever went on in the room would somehow get back to the F.I.A. in Washington and could hurt the State Department. The Ambassador was loyal to State. Ignoring F.I.A. could get State into trouble. For a moment Brown felt frustrated. He knew very little of the intelligence which the F.I.A. gathered in Sarkhan. He understood the reasons why this was necessary, but occasionally it left him with a dangling sensation.

He suspected that Theobald often made commitments in Sarkhan without telling him about them. But, again, presumably State knew about them back in Washington where such programs were coordinated. Brown assured himself again that his job was to present the public image of the United States in Sarkhan. Period.

"What do you think we ought to do about Coldstream?" the Ambassador said.

"If I had my way, an automobile would run him down at night. Or a hunting accident could be arranged the next time he's on one of his jungle trips."

"I assume that's a joke, Marcus," said the Ambassador, "and if I may say so, not a very good one."

"When you fight Communists you've got to use their own dirty methods. I know this offends you, Spratt. So don't bother about it. American foreign policy operates on several levels and you should not be concerned with this. The big thing is to shut Coldstream up or get him out of here until after the coronation.

He's been here fifteen years. Can we do something about his passport? Arrange so he has to report back to Washington to answer questions?"

"No. His passport is in order. General Hajn says he's okay. All we want is to stop Coldstream from making a ruckus before the coronation. Shut him up."

The old man blew his nose. "Spratt, I'll tell you something that no one in this whole world knows except you and me. I have a man in Coldstream's organization ..."

"It seems that everyone in Sarkhan has men in Coldstream's organization. You have one, Theobald has one, and so does General Hajn ..."

"Perhaps," continued the hunchback. Then he changed his attack. "We can find a way to divert Coldstream. You know, screw up one of his operations. He's just opening a tin mine down in Pai-ming, about six hundred new men on his payroll. If we start a strike or a riot there, he'd have to go. It's in the mountains. There's no road and it's a four-day trip over the trail. That would hold him for about ten days anyway."

"No, Marcus, I don't do business that way," said the Ambassador. "Furthermore, Sarkhan needs tin and the Pai-ming mine is financed by A.I.D. money."

Coit grinned. "Spratt, I do believe I can help you. Yes sir, I believe I can. I just remembered. There are two hundred cases of typhoid reported in Hong Kong. And Coldstream and his slovenly friend, Professor McCauley, are going to Hong Kong for a short trip."

"So?"

"You just send a cable to the Consul General in Hong Kong that no American now in Hong Kong can travel to Sarkhan until he has had fresh typhoid shots, the new thing, the Wrigley typhoid vaccine. It takes fifteen days to give the required series."

The Ambassador smiled. "That's correct. The immigration people reported it."

"Well," said Marcus Coit, "for a couple of weeks anyway they'll be out of your hair."

The Ambassador said, "Marcus, you're a genius. Now I'm beginning to understand why the doors of the Embassy in Haidho have always been open to you and every Ambassador has sought your advice. That cable to Hong Kong is a stroke of genius. Good night, Marcus, see you tomorrow."

Ambassador Brown watched Coit propel himself down the corridor. He had been told in Washington that Coit was the best-informed American in Sarkhan, that his counsel was sound and logical. Brown recognized the hunchback's brilliance, but he wondered about his judgment. Coit was practically helpless, yet he had a strain of cruelty and hate that was almost out of control. He reminded the Ambassador of a judge at the Plymouth Colony witch trials.

A clever idea, to quarantine the two Americans in Hong Kong. But Ambassador Brown knew he was not going to send the cable. He just couldn't operate that way.

14

A Quick Trip Home

At Hong Kong just the sheer concentration of planes—Qantas, JAL, Pan Am, BOAC, Lufthansa, Philippine Air Lines, Cathay Air, Flying Tiger—gives a sense of rising tempo. The corridors of the airport have crowded shops—pearls, cameras, silk, "suits custom-made in two hours," duty-free stores where Napoleon brandy is two dollars a bottle—all of which contrasts harshly with the nearby tenements for Chinese refugees. The vitality of humans struggling shakes Hong Kong as much as the hard screech of jets taking off.

As the plane landed, McCauley finished reading the two Sarkhanese papers he hurriedly had bought at the Haidho airport. Each headlined the invasion on the *Plateau des Luminaires* and also the Chinese claim to part of Sarkhan.

"I wish Asian newspapers would give more facts and less nonsense," McCauley said. "It's impossible to tell from these stories whether the editors are just excited or the story is planted. One thing is sure, there is no invasion on the plateau. Not in the monsoon."

"You could walk troops in, but not the tanks and trucks they talk about," Coldstream said. He wished he had had time to check the story before they had departed from Sarkhan.

McCauley slept all the way to Tokyo. When they took off for Honolulu, Coldstream had two quick Scotches, a codeine pill, and a Seconal. In fifteen minutes he was asleep.

McCauley studied Coldstream's face for a moment. It was pinched and thin. The *mentado* had taken more out of Coldstream than he allowed himself to reveal. In sleep the toll showed, his eyelids were blue with fatigue. His gloved hands were placed carefully on his chest.

McCauley had met Captain Coldstream at the end of the war. McCauley had been a medic with an O.S.S.-led guerrilla band in

Thailand which fought under the direction of Pridi, the leader of the Thai underground. In August 1945 the band—ragged, malnourished, and sick—was picked up by Coldstream's destroyer. McCauley gobbled the best meal he had had in two years, climbed into a bunk, and awoke ten hours later in the destroyer's sickbay where he was told by the doctor that he had a combination of malaria and mononucleosis. As a result he stayed aboard Coldstream's destroyer for almost a month.

The Captain paid McCauley a polite visit in sickbay and McCauley had been surprised by the conversation of this stiff ramrod of a naval officer. Coldstream knew of Pridi and asked penetrating questions about how the underground had been organized, how the various groups communicated, the political future of Thailand, the basic economics of Southeast Asia, the future of things. He asked endless questions.

In their first conversation McCauley was suspicious. Three years of patching up torn bodies, of fighting, fleeing, hiding, and always being on guard had twisted him. He had a reflexive mistrust of men in uniform: for three years they had been the enemy. Also, he was irritated by the odd mixture of respect and awe which the crew had for this Captain Coldstream.

"Captain, I'm not here to give you a political education," McCauley had said suddenly. "Why don't you read some books?"

The corpsmen's faces expressed shock. The Captain remained impassive.

"Take good care of him, Doc," the Captain had said quietly.

McCauley turned in the bunk, his back to the Captain. He knew he had made a mistake. The Captain had said nothing offensive.

The next day Captain Coldstream was back, offering to send a radio message to his family.

"I don't have a family, Captain," McCauley said. "They were executed the first week of the Japanese occupation."

"We just dropped your companions off at Bangkok, Mister Mc-Cauley," Coldstream said. "They told me you have quite a temper. They also said you were something of a hero."

McCauley sighed with boredom. The Captain watched him, waiting patiently.

McCauley was aware by this time that Coldstream was far from an ordinary Annapolis type. He had a kind of poise and presence and assurance which went deeper than mere Academy efficiency.

"Captain, those sad bastards are so beat they think just staying alive for three years in the jungle is heroic," McCauley said over his shoulder. "Now a real live authentic hero like yourself..."

McCauley fell asleep.

The next day when Captain Coldstream came in he said, "Good morning, Mister McCauley, did you love breakfast?" But he said it in Chinese.

"You mean, did I 'enjoy breakfast'," McCauley replied in Chinese. Then astonishment showed on his face. "Where did you learn to speak Chinese?"

"One must do something with spare time."

"Why Chinese? That won't help you when you come up for admiral."

"Because it looks like the Chinese are going to be big, not only out here in Asia, but in the world," Coldstream said. "So I thought I'd learn how to talk to them."

Two days later McCauley was giving Coldstream lessons in Chinese. Because of his extraordinary aptitude and because his missionary parents had been moved from one country to another in Asia, McCauley had an easy fluency with languages. He was surprised at how well Coldstream had learned Chinese on his own. He was a disciplined man, McCauley saw quickly.

But though Coldstream ran his destroyer by "the book" and his manner was firm, steady, and impeccable, beneath the official exterior was a curious mixture of traits. The Captain could satirize politicians, admirals, generals, and movie stars with an ingenious mixture of acid comment and generosity. He was intensely serious about political matters, China and Sarkhan amounting almost to a passion with him.

By the end of the month Coldstream had convinced McCauley that the future of Southeast Asia would be determined by what happened in China and Sarkhan. He became aware that Coldstream was suggesting that he return to the States, go to college, specialize in Southeast Asia and Sarkhan, and become an expert "in a world," as Coldstream said, "that would demand experts in every category, sub-category, nook and cranny."

Coldstream stirred in his seat, his hands touched one another and immediately his eyes were open. He sat quietly for a moment, then glanced at McCauley, who was reading one of his interminable Sarkhanese history books.

"Ed," McCauley asked in an edged voice but without looking up, "do you really think we can kick this Cogswell into doing something?"

Coldstream did not answer at once. He was reflecting about McCauley, who was almost entirely cerebral. If he started a Socratic dialogue about action and inaction in the bureaucracy, McCauley inevitably would emerge triumphant because of his extraordinary memory and skill in dialectics and the art of verbal dispute. In intellectual matters McCauley was abrasive, sharp, almost brutal. Coldstream had long ago learned to ignore his cutting and sardonic manner.

Occasionally, very occasionally, McCauley would be presented with contrary evidence during an argument. If the evidence was solid and contradicted McCauley's position, McCauley would change his position with no loss to his ego. It left his opponents confused.

"Nobody kicks Cogswell around," said Coldstream. "Wait until you see him."

McCauley took off his reading glasses. His hands lay loosely in his lap and his face was motionless except for a slow opening and closing of the mouth and blinking of his dark brown, almost black eyes.

"I'm bored with men who've made or inherited millions, picking up statesmanship as a hobby," said McCauley. "Why don't they stick to golf and girls, like in the old days." McCauley paused. "Cogswell sends me three hundred a month, and I'm worth it. If it weren't for that retainer check, I wouldn't care if he lived or died."

McCauley had the same icy detachment that Lenin and Mao and Bakunin and Chou and Bareuf had, Coldstream thought. The professor turned murderous—all in the name of an idea; the intellectual who could walk out of a study, take command of an executioner's squad or a division of troops, like Trotsky ...

"I've never met Cogswell," McCauley went on, "only on the telephone and via correspondence. You put him on to me. After I wrote my first monograph on Sarkhanese grammar. Remember?"

Coldstream remembered it well. The now famous (in limited circles) monograph had brought McCauley a letter of praise from Prince Lin. McCauley had never been to Sarkhan—except briefly during the war—a fact he acknowledged with casual arrogance in the first paragraph of the monograph. But it was not necessary, he wrote, grammar and linguistics were a science. Man could speak forty-eight phonemes and out of these he can explore all languages. His monograph, he stated, was a demonstration that Sarkhanese was a combination of Khmer and Mandarin. In the world of linguistics this was close to a heresy, but the few rebuttals which were attempted were met by an implacable refutation from McCauley.

About that time Cogswell had started querying Coldstream about Sarkhan. Partly to relieve the pressure, Coldstream wrote Cogswell that he might find McCauley useful as an expert. A month later McCauley received his first check. Three months later he was on his way to Sarkhan.

"For an intellectual you can be pretty mushy," said Coldstream, smiling. "With no evidence whatsoever you made a judgment on Cogswell. Hell, you've never seen the man."

"I know what Cogswell is like," McCauley said, "from *Who's Who* and a clipping service. Adolph Cogswell, born March 31, 1890, so the boy is old. His father was a millionaire—in pornographic magazines, scandal sheets, and whatever would make an indecent buck. Then Adolph took over. He added scientific magazines for prestige and a political quarterly for the Washington contacts. Today his empire publishes over a hundred periodicals in seven languages. Also he had an interest in an international publications business in Asia. Estimated assets: two hundred million. He is too slick to go into politics, yet he has acquired influence through these unofficial positions. The most corrupt politicians always have stood unofficially in the background."

"Cogswell is beyond corruption."

"You are sure?"

Coldstream nodded. McCauley nodded back.

"I am a bit more scientific in my approach to the human race," said McCauley. "People like Cogswell who give advice to many Presidents must not be giving very original counsel. They are asked to serve because they know how to nourish egos. They give neutral counsel. They are never too far wrong and, above all, their advice is never disturbing."

"Wait until you meet the man," Coldstream said. "He is, as you would say, *sui generis*. They only made one like him."

McCauley grunted, closed his eyes and went to sleep.

Inside the terminal at Dulles International Airport in Washington a man in a gray gabardine uniform greeted them by name, raised two fingers to his cap, and identified himself as Cogswell's chauffeur. They were to go directly to his employer's office.

"Your luggage checks, gentlemen? Thank you. Would you like to wait in the car?"

It was rush hour in Washington. Highways were jammed, traffic moved slowly. Going by the Pentagon, Coldstream and McCauley saw streams of cars moving from the parking lots, jockeying onto the highways.

"You see," mumbled McCauley pointing to the Pentagon, then sweeping his hand over the entire Washington scene, "the government buildings are vomiting out the beggars who run the country. Homeward they fly to the things which concerneth them most, their security, their homes, their cocktails to soothe their lacerated egos."

Coldstream said impatiently, "Tad, there are decent men in government. Don't you think I was a good public servant during the half-a-life I served in the Navy?"

"You were the last of the brave ones," McCauley said. "Government is an art and it takes dedicated men who can make decisions to keep it going. Right now the system works out of inertia. I've read enough of those damned committees to know they can choke any good idea to death."

"Do you really know that much about the system?"

McCauley paused and grinned.

"No, I don't. Please stop being logical," he said. "It's the end of a long trip and I want to pontificate, not argue. So I pontificate that every successful government rests upon a people who have faith and a clear vision of a future which seems reasonable. I'm not sure we have either the faith or the clear vision in America anymore."

"And where do they have it?"

"The Viet Cong volunteers, well trained and skillfully led, fight efficiently for five or ten years on empty stomachs. Eighty per cent of the well-fed South Vietnamese troops desert. It was the same in China. Chiang's troops deserted to the dedicated Reds. Unfortunately only a hungry, scared, motivated nation is efficient today. What America needs is a bad depression. Then we'd have some true believer's again."

Coldstream laughed and gently rubbed his hands together. McCauley saw the gesture. Tomorrow he was going to make sure that his friend consulted the best surgeon in town. Their car crossed the Potomac, circled the Lincoln Memorial, and headed for Washington's northwest section. At 5:25 they turned into a basement parking lot on upper Massachusetts Avenue beneath the Cogswell Building.

The chauffeur escorted them to the top floor, past the receptionist and through a labyrinth of corridors and offices. When they got to Cogswell's office, he was standing in the open doorway waiting for them.

"Captain Coldstream, good to see you again," Cogswell said, in a flat nasal tone. "This must be Professor McCauley. I expected an older man, Professor. Somebody about my own age and speed."

Cogswell's appearance jolted McCauley. He had thought of Cogswell as a tall, gaunt, and slightly stooped man with a long-jawed New England face. This was the image that went with the telephone voice and the letters. But instead, Cogswell was short, muscular, and round-faced, and walked with a bounce. He looked like a business hustler.

Scattered on various tables were comic books, adventure magazines, paperbacks, and myriad other products of the Cogswell Publishing Corporation. There were garish magazines, with screaming titles and pictures of famous movie actors or nearly nude girls on the covers. There were a half-dozen war cartoon books with slab-jawed Americans stomping on Japanese or flying a P-38 half aflame with all machine guns going. Also there were serious magazines, scientific periodicals, and engineering journals.

Cogswell looked at his watch, said brusquely, "Gentlemen, please sit down and tell me why, as you indicated on the telephone from Honolulu, you think that Sarkhan is about to go down the drain. I hope you can do it in thirty minutes. I have another appointment at six."

Cogswell settled himself slowly in his swivel chair, put his feet on the desk, closed his eyes, and said softly, "Go ahead."

Coldstream did the talking, numbering his points.

At 5:58 Cogswell interrupted. "Sorry, gentlemen, we must stop. I have only one question. Professor McCauley, do you agree or disagree with what Captain Coldstream has told me?"

McCauley replied instantly. "Conditions in Sarkhan are worse than he has told you."

The three men stood up. Cogswell led them to the door and opened it.

"Very interesting, gentlemen. Very interesting. However, what you have told me does not jibe with the governmental intelligence. Still, very interesting. Half an hour is not enough. Can you come to my house at ten tomorrow morning?" His question was phrased as a command. "Good night, gentlemen. It was good of you to come."

The chauffeur was waiting in the hall. He took them to the car and to their hotel.

When they were alone, McCauley muttered, "We wasted the price of two first-class tickets to Washington."

"You don't think much of Cogswell?"

"I cannot associate him with someone who's been the confidant of six Presidents. I have a feeling that he didn't hear a thing you said. Not a goddamn word. He took no notes and he asked only one question. He may have become senile."

Coldstream laughed. "That's precisely what Hobson was supposed to have said when Cogswell advised Truman to fire MacArthur."

"Edward, if there's not more action tomorrow, I'm on the two o'clock plane."

"You may be on that plane, Tad, but it won't be because of lack of action," Coldstream said, smiling. "It will be because you've been kicked out of town for not being competent. Ever think of that?"

"At the University or in Sarkhan, at least I have a sense of accomplishment. I know what I'm doing. But back here among the bureaucrats I say to myself, 'Oh God, what's the use?' The most powerful nation on earth is being kicked around out there because back here we're talking and meeting and memo-ing ourselves to death."

"Save your eloquence for tomorrow, Professor. I've a hunch you may need it."

15

The Confrontation

"Cogswell has lived here for forty years," Coldstream said as their taxi pulled up to the old brownstone house in Geogetown. "He has a squash court in the back garden. Ten years ago he gave it up. Now he walks three miles a day."

Before they rang the bell the door was opened by a man who obviously was not a butler. He was deferential, but his eyes inspected them carefully and he had on a plain dark business suit.

"Coldstream and McCauley to see Mister Cogswell," said Coldstream.

"Mister Cogswell will be right along, gentlemen. Would you like to wait in the living room?"

The room was done in a style which somehow pleased McCauley. The furniture was mostly leather and well aged. A huge desk with dozens of pigeonholes stood at one end of the room. Two walls were lined with bookcases. McCauley was looking at the books when Cogswell came into the room.

He had on the same suit, necktie, and shoes he had worn the previous afternoon. But Cogswell was not as bouncy. His eyes were bloodshot and the bags beneath them were darker and more pronounced. He had the appearance of a man who had been up all night.

"Gentlemen, things have gotten a bit complicated," Cogswell said. "Much has happened since last night. I have everyone here."

"Everyone? Who is everyone?" muttered McCauley.

"The President's Special Committee on Sarkhan," Cogswell said.

"A crisis?" McCauley asked.

"You might call it that, yes. Another goddamn crisis."

Cogswell ushered them through a corridor into a large room which extended the entire width of the house. Down the center was a heavy oak table. Seated around the table were nine men, three of them in uniform.

McCauley observed that the majority of the group was at sharp attention even though seated.

The men stood up as Cogswell spoke their names. There was Senator Donat of the Foreign Relations Committee, Assistant Secretary of State Abbott, Hiller of Defense Intelligence, Hobson from F.I.A., along with his assistant, Assistant Secretary of Defense Dobey, two generals, and an admiral. They were somber, substantial men, heavy with responsibility and authority.

Cogswell nodded toward the buffet in the corner which held a silver coffee service. McCauley and Coldstream helped themselves to coffee. The cups were heavy mugs. On the side of each mug was the scene of a battle from American history. On McCauley's mug were the *Monitor* and *Merrimac*, firing bright red rounds at one another. The conference table was covered with countless rings left by the coffee cups and highball glasses of other meetings. McCauley recalled a quotation: "History is recorded on illuminated parchments with glorious descriptions of noble deeds. But history's seeds are almost always first planted in a dung of hate, greed, whisky, ambition, and fear." Was it Tolstoy, that bearded hypocrite?

"Gentlemen, we can begin," Cogswell said, sitting down at the end of the table. Cogswell changed. His tired smile vanished and his actions were more deliberate. He now had an air of cool authority.

"You all know why we are here, except, perhaps, Captain Coldstream and Professor McCauley. Let me make the explanation brief." He paused, scratched his neck, reached into the humidor for a long dark cigar. "Professor McCauley and Captain Coldstream, the gentlemen sitting around this table form the President's Special Committee on Sarkhan. They recommend to the President the decisions the United States makes on Sarkhan. At this moment there seems to be a crisis in that little land. Frankly, it is not the same emergency which you described to me last night."

"I did not even know of the existence of the Special Committee," Coldstream said.

"If you had, I would have been disappointed," Cogswell said.

"The Committee is something we have tried to keep secret. And may I warn you, anything discussed here is considered highly confidential. Please sign the paper in front of you acknowledging that you know it is top secret."

Coldstream read the paper slowly and signed. McCauley signed immediately and looked up at the others. Hobson, the Director of the F.I.A., put a cigarette in a short, filtered cigarette holder. Taking a lighter from his vest pocket, he placed it on the table. It was a solid gold lighter. On one side was a small American flag made from diamond, ruby, and sapphire chips. McCauley picked it up and read the inscription: "To Major James Hobson, Congressional Medal of Honor winner, from his buddies in the American Legion."

Cogswell held up his hand for silence.

"I consider this the most important meeting our Committee has ever had," he said. "We are trying to avoid another Bay of Pigs. Because all of you are intelligence specialists, you know who Captain Coldstream and Professor McCauley are." He paused. "I assume that all of you have read McCauley's books on Sarkhan. My correspondence with Captain Coldstream has been somewhat more restricted."

He paused again, waiting for a question. Not a face changed expression. They were so many hedgehogs, Cogswell thought irritably, waiting for someone else to ask the first question, make the first mistake.

"There are three major points Coldstream and McCauley brought up last night," Cogswell said. "The first is that Prince Lin has disappeared. This in their opinion creates a hazard and has ominous implications. Ambassador Brown in Sarkhan says that the Prince has *not* disappeared and, if he had, his absence would be of little significance."

Cogswell waited again, making sure each person had a chance to speak. Later the refusal to speak could be important.

No one spoke.

"These two gentlemen also believe that it is unlikely that Sarkhan can be toppled by an external threat. In fact they believe there is none," Cogswell went on. "They also say that the invasion rumors may be only efforts to bleed us for arms and money and the 'fringe benefits' of American aid. They say that there *is* an internal threat which is invisible and slight at this time, but which might, if America moves powerfully, use our intervention as the means to play on Sarkhanese nationalism and build a powerful revolutionary movement."

Cogswell paused again. Again, no one spoke.

"Let us handle one point at a time," he went on. "Captain Coldstream, contrary to your opinion, the Embassy says that Prince Lin is ill with a cold and is not missing. He simply has been staying indoors. You claim Lin is missing from the capital. What is your evidence?"

"Before he answers that," said Hobson, "may I ask why it is so terribly important whether Prince Lin is showing himself around Haidho or not? Assume our friends, the Sarkhanese, are being invaded by a hostile army. Why should we be concerned with this Prince Lin?"

McCauley raised his hand and Cogswell nodded. "Mister Hobson," said McCauley, "for over forty generations the family of King Diad has ruled Sarkhan. For over forty generations Sarkhanese astrologers, at the birth of the King, have predicted on what day the King will abdicate. For forty generations the Kings have abdicated on that predicted day . . ."

"Please, Professor McCauley," said the Assistant Secretary of State, "we are dealing with the harsh realities of an invasion. The subject involves legislation, guns, airlifts, military equipment of all kinds—not superstition, native hocus-pocus and mythology."

McCauley went on as if the Secretary had not spoken. "There is not a Sarkhanese who doesn't know that King Diad is going to abdicate in a few weeks. They also know that on that day Prince Lin will be crowned the forty-second king of Sarkhan. Furthermore, for forty generations it has been the custom, regardless of circumstances, that the heir apparent be seen in public in front of the royal residence every day for one lunar month before the abdication of the King. It so happens that Prince Lin has not been seen for the last fifteen days. Rumors are spreading that the Prince has been kidnapped."

Cogswell said, "Why are you so sure that Prince Lin is missing and not just indisposed?"

McCauley pulled a thick volume with a Sarkhanese title from

his briefcase. "This is the basic Book of Laws of Sarkhan. The first chapter defines the obligations of the ruling family to the people," said McCauley, paging slowly. "Ah, here it is: 'Whenever the King or the heir apparent becomes sick, he shall be taken to the Royal Dispensary where he shall be nursed by a retinue of not less than eight persons, half of whom shall be Moslems and half Buddhists. Public announcements will be made daily as to his health.' "

Jeremiah Hobson cleared his throat; it was a loud, rude sound.

McCauley gave the F.I.A. Director an amused look, then continued. "The Book of Laws goes on to describe how the guards shall be stationed and so on. Now, gentlemen, if the heir apparent, Prince Lin, is ill, then he must be at the Royal Dispensary."

In a weary tone Hobson interrupted, "Please, Professor, we don't need a lecture. We already know the Prince is at the Dispensary. The Ambassador said so. General Hajn said so."

"Just like," said McCauley, "our own government said President Eisenhower had a stomach ache when he was almost dead from a heart attack."

In the moment of silence, Coldstream and McCauley glanced at each other. They had checked the Royal Dispensary and knew the Prince was not there. But the United States intelligence service had not.

"Do you say Ambassador Brown and General Hajn are liars?" Hobson asked.

"I don't recall mentioning the Ambassador or the General."

"Goddamn it," said Hobson, "that red telephone in the corner is a scrambler. It is a direct line to our Embassy in Haidho. Let's see what the Ambassador has to say about your accusation."

Cogswell walked to the telephone, cranked a lever, and also cut in an amplifier so that everyone could hear.

"Hello," he said into the telephone. "Cogswell here. Washington, D.C."

"Brown here," came the tiny words from the amplifier. "American Embassy, Haidho. What is the decision on the request for aid?"

"Mister Ambassador, it hasn't been made yet. I am calling about Prince Lin."

"Prince Lin?"

"Yes. Does your staff know where the Royal Dispensary is?" Eight thousand miles away Brown cleared his throat.

"Royal Dispensary?" he asked. "I don't know of such a place."

McCauley walked over to the phone. Cogswell handed it to him.

"McCauley here," he said. "The Royal Dispensary is the little stone building to the right of the Inner Palace. It is surrounded by a screen of bamboo trees."

There was a long silence.

"I thought that was a temple," the small voice on the phone said.

"It is. A temple of healing."

McCauley handed the phone back to Cogswell.

"Mister Ambassador, I would like you personally to go there with someone who speaks Sarkhanese . . ."

"I speak Sarkhanese."

"I request you to go to the Royal Dispensary and ask to see Prince Lin. Inquire as to his health and give us a report on it."

"It's dinner time now for most Sarkhanese."

Cogswell said sharply, "Mister Ambassador, I don't care what time it is. Just move out and take a look."

"I'll go," said Ambassador Brown, "and will telephone you within five minutes."

"Thank you, Mister Ambassador. I will hold the phone," said Cogswell.

Cogswell sat by the red telephone, the receiver to his ear. The men around the table smoked, talked in low voices, and fished for papers in their briefcases. Eight minutes later Brown came on again.

"Hello, Brown here."

"Cogswell here. What did you find?"

"Mister Cogswell, Prince Lin is not at the Dispensary. The Sarkhanese doctors said he has been away for a month and they do not know where. They seemed concerned."

"Then he is missing."

"Yes, sir," said Brown. "Before calling you back I phoned

General Hajn. He says the Prince might have left Haidho for a meditation. It's longer than usual because of the coronation. He has requested to meditate in secret."

"Where is he?"

"I don't know."

Cogswell said, "Thank you, Mister Ambassador."

Cogswell put down the phone. "It seems, gentlemen, that Captain Coldstream and Professor McCauley are correct. Prince Lin is missing and it is of some concern to the Sarkhanese."

No one spoke. Hobson looked at McCauley, no expression on his face. If he was bothered, it did not show.

"The next point of discussion is the invasion. We should start with a general summary by one of our government people." His eyes ran down the table. "General Lindquist, why don't you sum up, very briefly, the situation in Sarkhan as you see it?"

The Air Force general's fingers moved on the tabletop as if they were assembling a sheaf of papers. He pulled his head back. He had no papers. He recovered quickly.

"Of course, Mister Cogswell," said Lindquist in his crisp and sure manner. "Sarkhan has about twenty million people, is intensely pro-West, has a ruling family and a Minister of Defense who are profoundly friendly to the United States, and a people who have proven their sympathy with democratic principles. The Communists know the only way that they can take over in Sarkhan is by a military invasion from without. Hence the current emergency."

He looked at Cogswell, shrugged his shoulders. It was an aggressive gesture, yet one of hesitation.

"Go ahead, General," Cogswell said. "I accept the responsibility for your revealing classified information."

"The first phase of the invasion of Sarkhan," said the general, lowering his voice, "began a few days ago. Advance units, about three thousand North Vietnamese troops, are now in the plateau area. They are not guerrillas. They are uniformed troops with 105-millimeter howitzers, tanks, light planes, trucks, and bulldozers. They are building airfields and logistic centers. The major invasion probably will occur as soon as the monsoons stop. And just across the Chinese border there are eighty thousand well-trained troops carrying the most modern mobile arms. It is a real emergency."

Lindquist was an able and vocal general. He had been in the business of persuading people for a long time and he was very skillful at it. Now his voice took on an urgency.

"The Reds have invaded a friendly nation. If we drop three small A-bombs on the plateau area and another three on the troop concentrations on the other side of the Vietnamese border, puff, the affair is settled . . ."

The State Department representative groaned.

The red-faced Marine Corps officer, General Patrick, frowned and said, "No affair is ever settled 'puff' . . ."

Coldstream reached for a short tube of maps from his big handbag and unrolled them on the conference table.

"General Lindquist," Coldstream said, "would you show me on this map where the invasion has taken place, please?"

The General pointed to the northeast section of Sarkhan.

The conferees huddled over the maps. The admiral said, "Where did you get this, Captain Coldstream? A very remarkable chart."

Coldstream said, "I made it."

"May I have a copy?"

"Certainly, sir. But I sent the original to Mister Cogswell in 1960."

"And I sent a copy to the office of every member of this Committee," Cogswell said quietly.

There was a beat of silence.

"Captain Coldstream, I notice that you have many Sarkhanese towns circled with little red marks, others circled with little blue marks, some with black," Hobson said. "Do those marks have some commercial significance for your vast business enterprises, Captain, or would they be of some interest to all of us here?"

"Those marks . . ." began Coldstream, but he was interrupted by McCauley.

"If you don't mind," he said, "we're getting off the subject. Mister Cogswell asked General Lindquist for a summary of the situation and may I request that the General continue."

In a low voice Hobson said, "Well, I'll be damned."

Cogswell again took charge. "The Professor is correct. General Lindquist, will you continue, please?"

The General said coldly, "I have made my summation. There is no more to say. I suggest that our two visitors now present *their* summary."

"Hear, hear," said Hobson.

Cogswell said, "Which of you two gentlemen would like to begin?"

Coldstream said, "I will, sir. My quick summation is this: You are about to have another Bay of Pigs in Sarkhan. Only instead of involving a small controllable country like Cuba, it will involve all of vast, rich, restless Southeast Asia. It will be ten times as tragic a fiasco as the Bay of Pigs."

Hiller, the small gray-haired man from the Defense Intelligence Agency, raised his hand and said, "Mister Cogswell, forgive my interrupting, but it will be just for a moment. I would like to remind Captain Coldstream and Professor McCauley that the information which they have just heard concerning the invasion of Sarkhan is top secret and there are perhaps only about fifteen or twenty persons in the whole United States who know of it at this moment. If this information gets out, either to the American public or to the Asian nations at this moment, it may endanger United States plans. I know we can depend upon you."

Coldstream and McCauley said nothing. They appeared to be confused. Hiller persisted and said, "I assume we have your promise?"

McCauley stood up. "Do any of you gentlemen read Sarkhanese?"

Carver, the assistant to Hobson, spoke up. "I read Sarkhanese." McCauley tossed a crumpled newspaper across the long table to him.

"This is the *Haidho So-Bin*, a Sarkhanese newspaper. Yesterday's edition," McCauley said. "Mister Carver, will you read for the Committee the headline on this paper and the first paragraph or two of the lead article."

Carver looked at the newspaper and then spoke in English. "North Vietnam Invades Sarkhan. General Hajn, through his press officer, General Bandhinjo, announced this morning that

Sarkhan has been invaded. On the plateau area there are about three thousand Vietnamese troops, equipped with such arms as 105-millimeter howitzers, tanks, light planes, trucks, and bulldozers. These are the advance units and they are building airstrips and logistics centers. They are not guerrillas. Across the Chinese border are some eighty thousand well-trained troops standing-by ready to carry on a full-scale invasion of Sarkhan when the monsoons stop."

McCauley said quietly, "Gentlemen, the intelligence agencies of our country receive urgent information and it is classified as top secret. Only fifteen or twenty persons know it. Yet this so-called top secret information has been published yesterday in Asian newspapers."

Hobson said, "I've had information on this situation for some time."

"Why didn't you inform other members of this Committee?" asked Dobey sharply.

"Gentlemen, perhaps, we can go into that aspect later," said Cogswell.

"May I comment?" asked Coldstream.

"Yes, Captain. Go right ahead."

"Professor McCauley and I discount this article entirely. This particular paper is highly unreliable. My company gets reports from the so-called invasion area daily. At this state of the monsoon season it is difficult even to fly over those mountains. An air drop is impossible." Coldstream turned abruptly, smiled, and rubbed his palms together. "But I'm sure you must know this, gentlemen."

"Mister Coldstream, Professor McCauley," Cogswell said, "I would like to ask a question. Is there a single American to your knowledge who claims to have seen the invading Vietnamese? Is there one American eyewitness?"

Coldstream shook his head. McCauley said nothing.

Hobson said, "I have eyewitness accounts."

"From Americans?" said Coldstream.

"No. But I have a few trusted Sarkhanese agents. Their loyalty is unquestionable." Hobson lowered his voice and, staring at Mc-

Cauley and Coldstream, added, "Perhaps more loyal and dependable than some Americans."

Cogswell said, "Jeremiah, do you have those eyewitness reports with you?"

"I do not. But I have them in my head. What would you like to know?"

Coldstream said, "Sir, do you recognize the names Qua Hai and Sku Bien?"

"I do not. Who are they?"

"Qua Hai and Sku Bien are your agents in the plateau area." Coldstream pointed to the map.

Hobson's assistant took papers from his briefcase, found a page, and showed it to Hobson. Hobson was not ruffled, but his smile was tight. Really not a smile. It was a predatory expression.

Coldstream pointed to his map again.

"You will notice red circles around some of the towns," he said. "These indicate where there are Communist agents. Mister Hobson, both of your agents up there are also employed by the Communists."

"How do you know that?"

"Sarkhanese villages are small and most everything that happens in them is known to everyone. Your two men have been seen going to the Communist camps in the hills and helping the guerrillas."

Hobson said, "Let us put the shoe on the other foot, Captain. Have you known any Americans who have been an eyewitness to my agents consorting with the Communists?"

"Yes, sir."

"Who is the witness and under what circumstances?"

"I am the witness, sir. I saw them in a Communist camp."

"How do you know that the people you saw there were Qua Hai and Sku Bien?"

Coldstream opened his briefcase. He picked up an envelope, extracted two cards. He pushed them across the table to Hobson.

"Here are their identification cards in your organization," he said.

He then took two more pieces of paper from the envelope and

slid them across the table. "And here are their Communist identification cards."

"Captain Coldstream," said Hobson. "What were you doing in a Communist camp? Can it be true that through your trading corporation you do business with the Communists?"

"I was not in that camp voluntarily."

"This is all very difficult to believe. Mister Cogswell," said Hobson, turning toward the head of the table, "we are taking evidence here from two witnesses and even though it may extend the length of a meeting and time is urgent, I would like Captain Coldstream to tell us why he was in a Communist camp and how he got the identification cards of two of my agents. These F.I.A. identification cards are authentic. I do not know about the other ones, the Communist cards."

Cogswell nodded.

Coldstream stood up nervously, pushed back his chair with his foot and walked slowly across the room. He hunched over, his hands thrust deep in his coat pockets. McCauley watched him. Coldstream was shuffling more than walking, his lips were pressed together, the muscles in his neck tense.

Hobson unbuttoned his coat and leaned back in his chair with the satisfied look of a man who is about to hear a confession.

Coldstream said, "About six weeks ago I wrote a report for Mister Cogswell and sent it from Haidho to Washington by way of courier."

Cogswell interrupted and said, "That is correct, and I received the report two days later. Captain Coldstream, you're barely whispering. Can you speak a little louder?"

"In my report," said Coldstream, speaking loud and clear, "I said that Sarkhan had become politically unstable and I had a hunch, no proof, that several highly placed persons might be betraying the government. I did not know who they were, but I volunteered to try and find out."

He rubbed his palms in what he was aware was a Shylock gesture but he could not stop. He would have welcomed an interruption.

"During the following four or five days I made strenuous efforts through my corporation to confirm my information," he said. "Later I decided to visit villages in Boa Binh district, where the Sark Cong terrorists had started. I visited Boa Binh, then Dao, where I borrowed a jeep from the chief. I was surprised to find the road had been cleared and that other cars had been on it.

"About thirty miles from Dao I saw something in the sunlight as I turned a corner . . ."

Coldstream stopped and looked at Cogswell. "Sir, I'm sorry I have to be so long-winded, but I can't tell it any other way."

"As you like," said Cogswell.

Coldstream was trembling slightly, but his voice was steady.

16

Mentado

The road curved sharply. The truck stood sideways in the road, blocking the way. It was a U.S. Army truck which had been painted over.

Four men leaned against the truck. One of them had a pistol. Two of them carried rifles. The unarmed one was not Sarkhanese. He was dark and had the features of a Vietnamese from the delta region.

Coldstream got out of his jeep.

"Hello, friends," he said pleasantly. "How is the hunting. It used to be good pig country."

"What are you doing here?" said the man with the pistol. He was a strange-looking Sarkhanese, squat, broad, and heavily muscular like a *sumo* wrestler.

"I am Buan Suang, the merchant," said Coldstream. "I have come to see if the hardwood trees are worth cutting again. A few years ago we cut here—taking out rosewood and teak."

The leader smiled. He nodded to his men.

Coldstream heard a noise behind him and felt a numbing pain along his right temple. The truck and the men dissolved, grew small and distant, then the pain became too great and he fell.

When Coldstream regained consciousness, the leader was pouring water on him. His wrists were tied.

Coldstream said, "You must have mistaken me for someone else. I am Buan Suang, the merchant. You will find my identification in my wallet."

The leader, the squat one with the pistol, kicked him and laughed. "I already have your wallet and your wristwatch also." He dangled the two objects in front of Coldstream. "And I will tell you who you are. You are a filthy spy. You are Coldstream, a filthy manure-in-your-mouth spy. Now get up, you pig." He kicked Coldstream again.

Coldstream knew the routine. He got up quietly. The leader

jerked at the line secured to his wrist and pulled him into the jungle. The others moved the truck into a glade on the other side of the road, and covered it with branches.

Coldstream was prodded uphill through a heavy forest for about a quarter of a mile. He dragged his feet to leave a trail. On the way up no one spoke.

At the top of the hill was a log house, camouflaged on three sides. Inside the open door Coldstream saw a pile of rifles. They were all U.S. Army rifles, M-14s, with the South Vietnamese Army blaze on each stock. Coldstream thought: Whenever we arm an Asian ally, we really arm the enemy.

The squat man shouted, "Captain Coldstream."

Coldstream turned. The leader hit him across the face with the flat side of his rifle butt, knocking Coldstream down. All four men kicked him, but not hard, almost disinterestedly.

Coldstream said, "What do you want?"

The squat man with the revolver pulled a knife from his sheath, and tried the edge with his thumb. "It is sharp and ready."

He leaned over and shaved the hair from Coldstream's right arm. Then he pricked the point of the blade into the wrist between the two arteries, just enough to allow a trickle of blood to ooze out.

"Now," said the small dark one in Vietnamese, "a friend of yours here wishes to ask you some questions."

"Do you understand him?" one of the others said in Sarkhanese.

Coldstream shook his head. He knew Vietnamese, but did not wish it known. The second man interpreted.

From inside the cabin came Jan Ti, his *bonze* robe torn and muddy. Coldstream knew he must have hurried over the shortcut trail which led first through the swamp and then over the mountains to get here so quickly.

Jan Ti looked at Coldstream curiously. "So you know who organized us?" he said.

Coldstream did not reply.

Jan Ti asked him again, "Who is it? Give me his name?"

Coldstream did not know how to answer. He had been bluffing

back in Boa Binh Village. Now it was clear that the *bonze* was a
Communist, but Coldstream did not know to whom the man reported. If he told the truth, he would not be believed.

The leader took his knife and held the sharp edge against Coldstream's jugular vein. "What is the name of the man?"

"I was lying in Boa Binh," said Coldstream softly. "How could
I, a foreigner, know the affairs of Jan Ti? I lost my temper and
lied."

Coldstream hoped only to delay the frightening pace of the
interrogation. If he could get these men talking, he might find
out what they knew and could give them an answer which would
satisfy them.

The Vietnamese spat in his face. Another beat his bound hands
with a stick.

"Liar. You're not dealing with bourgeois Sarkhanese now. You
told Jan Ti you know who his superior is. Do you deny that?"

"I was angry. I lied."

The leader nodded at one of the other men. He went into the
shack and came back with a junko bag, a big canvas sack with a
rubber tube at the end. The tube is designed to be put into a
man's throat and the water from the bag forced into the stomach.
When the stomach is suitably distended, the torturers punch the
victim in the stomach. The pain is among the most excruciating
known. As the water pressure increases, one internal organ after
another is destroyed.

"Captain Coldstream, do you know what this is?" the leader
asked.

Coldstream nodded.

The leader smiled. "I want you to talk. To tell us everything,
unless you want us to use the junko bag."

"I know nothing of politics or your leaders."

The squat one said, "Get the water and see if our little persuader will help the Captain's memory."

Coldstream knew his words made no impression on the leader.
He felt fear crawl down his back. This man was experienced. He
was not angry. He was professional. And he expected Coldstream
to be professional. They spoke a language of gestures and attitudes to one another. Coldstream knew he could, if he said the

wrong thing, be dead in a very few minutes. Or he could live miserably for days. Or he could live miserably for many years. It depended on the whim of the man with the cruel face and the *sumo* wrestlers' thick body.

The canvas bag was filled with water.

"We must be careful," said the Vietnamese. "He is a white man and has no stamina. A few punches and he may die without giving us the information. Should we not use the religious persuader?" he said. "*Mentado* is just as painful but it lasts longer."

The squat man laughed uproariously. "Yes," he said, "*mentado* will make him talk, and it will be amusing to hear this white pig squeal with pain."

To Coldstream's knowledge, the torture of *mentado* had not been used in six centuries, not since the end of the religious wars between the Sarkhanese Moslems and Buddhists.

"Coldstream, do you know what the *mentado* is?"

He nodded.

"Tell us the name of Jan Ti's superior," the leader said. His voice was mocking, full of understanding, enticing—the voice of the torturer.

"I do not know."

The men pulled Coldstream to his feet, untied his wrists, and pushed him over to the southeast side of the building. One went into the house and came out a few moments later with a hammer and two spikes.

They pushed Coldstream close to the building. Another man brought out two ammunition boxes and placed them in front of Coldstream. The man with the hammer climbed on top of a box and stretched Coldstream's arm up and against the wall of the log house.

"This is your last chance, Captain. Give me the name," the leader said. His voice was bored and listless. "Please."

"I don't know."

"Stand on your toes."

Coldstream did so. He was spreadeagled.

"Higher, you lying swine," the squat man said.

The man on the box jerked Coldstream's right arm. His shoulder socket ached, but Coldstream ignored it. He knew much worse was to come. Placing the sharp end of the spike in Coldstream's palm, the trooper drew the hammer back and smashed it against the flat end of the spike.

An explosion flashed through Coldstream. A terrible pain shot downward from his right palm through his arm and into his abdomen. Simultaneously he heard the crunch of metal tearing through flesh, he smelled the peculiar urine-like odor which comes with fear, and he felt the blood trickle down his arm. He concentrated on being silent. Then the same searing flash and pain and smell and blood crashed downward from his left palm.

Coldstream knew what was coming next. The foreknowledge gave him something to fasten on. With a hard, black-lined artistry his mind made pictures which broke against his closed eyes, hit the back of his eyeballs, held for a long moment, then slowly vanished as each was fulfilled. The pain did not diminish, it was simply ignored.

Someone would now cut away his clothes. Almost instantly he felt the sharp knife going through the cloth, hesitate and dig when it came to his belt, then cut through. His pants fell away. With a quick nick the elastic band of his shorts was cut and they also dropped.

Now they would cut away his shirt rather than unbutton it. But they would not cut his skin. It happened. The blade cut his collar, sliced easily down the front of his shirt, a half inch from the line of buttons. In a series of quick expert motions the shirt was cut and peeled away from his body.

Now he was naked except for his shoes.

In a few seconds there would be a terrible moment of pain. He felt hands undoing his shoe laces—and then Coldstream completely removed himself from the scene.

First, there was a chess problem. Behind his closed eyes he saw it clearly. It was beautifully simple. Black King's pawn to eight, protected by Black Knight and Black Bishop. White King left with only one move... The fat, rumpled, slovenly, sharp-tongued Professor he loved was about to fall neatly into his well-laid trap...

The shoe on his left foot was yanked away and the pain screamed down his arm. Without the shoe, he barely touched the ground. He made a neat compensation—part of the weight on his left big toe, a smaller part on his left palm.

Not perfect, but all he could do.

The new pain had destroyed the chess problem. Now he had a bright red image held fast in the center of his head—medula, res elongata, cerebella . . . He could not get the words right, they were wrong, but the bright red image was fixed, immutable in his head.

The girl was naked. She had a bright red ribbon in her hair. The color from the ribbon flowed over the rock on which they lay. He moved toward her, completely confident, delighted by the compliance in her eyes, amused by her lips ready to say "no." It was so hot that movement must be slow. He ran a finger down the curve of the girl's hips . . .

He came moaning back to reality. Someone had taken off his right shoe and removed the debris of pants and shorts. Equilibrium was ended. The pain was a rod of hot iron shoved down his right arm.

Coldstream scrabbled with his toes. His body came to an uneven balance. No alternative was anything but painful. But his crabbed posture was the best his body could work out for itself. He had no sense of control. He only knew he was completely naked.

Withdraw. Most wounded people die of shock. Withdraw. It was a command.

Once, long ago, he had floated on the ocean. It was in Pao-Pao Bay in Moorea, French Polynesia. The water was soft, very blue, and far away on some other shore he could hear the surf pound in. He was with his wife, Spring, and she laughed a great deal. They had swum a long distance and now they floated. He could smell the vanilla beans as they were cured by the three Chinese at the head of the bay. Then, at the top of the highest peak above Pao-Pao, he was startled by a glint of light just below the summit. The peak had a *hole* in it. A hole. Unbelievable. Floating on the water he eyed it carefully. (Spring had floated away somehow.) One day, not now, but one sweet and distant day, when he was unleashed, he would climb that mountain and crawl through that hole. Floating, supported by the water, he made minute calculations for his attack on the peak.

He was in the middle of a tennis game. It was in Honolulu. For doubles it was exceptional competition. He was thirsty, but if he

drank water, he and his partner would lose. The cement
court, light green and smooth, made his eyes ache, but he watched
the small white ball with an immense concentration. The sooner
they finished off the other pair the sooner he could go to the water
cooler at the end of the court and drink a gallon.

The ball bounced back and forth, back and forth, white over
green, white over green, the net a thick mesh which separated the
enemies. The water cooler was behaving like a plant. It was
growing larger and larger. Its steel legs, its ceramic top, its tempting spigot grew and grew, and Coldstream felt a sense of fear. If
it grew much larger the spigot would be beyond his reach. He
turned back to warn his enemies ...

Back in the fourteenth century some of the crucified men had
died more quickly, devoured by insects. Coldstream sucked in his
breath. The hardwood forest was where the white flesh-eating
ants lived.

The men left him, but came back every half hour and asked for
the name and spat at him. They talked to the darker man in Vietnamese. Coldstream shut his eyes so he would not disclose that he
understood. From their conversation he learned that they had not
really planned to give him *mentado*. Their orders had been to in-
tercept him, follow him, and see whom he was meeting in the
jungle. They had only wanted to frighten him into telling the
name of the person he thought to be Jan Ti's superior.

The four men had a rising sense of having made a mistake with
Coldstream. In their zeal they had given him *mentado*. They had
panicked. But now that he was pinned to the wall Coldstream was
to stay there until he confessed something. *Mentado* makes men
willing to confess—almost anything, the leader said. He told the
men to rest easy. Jan Ti, the *bonze*, had agreed. As long as the
mentado had been started, keep the white man nailed up until he
confessed.

Coldstream believed that none of them had actually seen a real
case of *mentado* before. He fainted away softly.

It rained hard the first night. Coldstream was thankful for that.
The rain would wash away the blood smell from the ground and
make him safer from the white ants.

By noon of the second day Coldstream's tongue began to swell.
The sun had sucked him dry and he had no more saliva. He re-

laxed by concentrating so hard and completely that he did not
know where he was. He no longer felt anything in his palms and
arm. Only a tingling around his ankles. He wondered if he was
dying and this was the beginning of the creeping numbness. The
tingling moved slowly up his leg to the knee, and then he felt a
soft prick on his side. He looked down but it was difficult to
focus his eyes. His eyelids were stiff and his optic nerves almost
paralyzed from continually looking into the sun, but he did
focus.

It looked as if his legs were covered with feathers slowly moving up. It was a swarm of white ants, the flesh-eating ants which
at last had found him.

Coldstream banged his heels against the building, putting weight
on his palms. The flash and the pain exploded through him again.
Blindly he kicked through the pain until all the ants were off. He
knew that they would not eat his flesh until they reached the
membrane of his mouth or nose or eyes, or found the open
wounds on his hands. All afternoon he kept kicking them off.

The men watched. Every few hours the leader asked if he
wanted to talk. When Coldstream tried to explain he had nothing
to tell they went back to their tasks of cleaning and sorting guns.

At twilight the blessed rain came again and Coldstream knew
he was free from the ants at least until midmorning of the next
day.

After dark he heard the four men talking among themselves.
Several times they mentioned names. Coldstream tried to remember them. Also he heard the four men admiring him. They had
expected that the pain, the sun, the ants, the loss of blood would
quickly break him down.

But this white man, this tall, slender enemy of the people, he
had been wrestling death with as much bravery and skill as
Ramayana, the Monkey God. Time after time he had shaken the
ants off. And his tough skin had resisted the sun. True, it had
blackened and burned, but it had not cracked. The white man
had been skillful enough to keep his muscles relaxed. The skin
had not cracked and oozed and the tensed muscles had not
ripped.

During the second evening the leader decided he needed counsel from Haidho. He said he would take the jeep and go find the

patrol near Three Mountains. The patrol had a military radio and could talk to headquarters. He would return as soon as possible. He instructed the others to leave the white man in *mentado* as long as he was conscious.

The leader walked down the hill. A few moments later Coldstream heard the noise of the coughing jeep.

By ten o'clock the next morning, Coldstream knew that he couldn't last another day. His skin was black and crusty. His legs would barely hold him, and the weight hung more and more on his torn palms. His thoughts were foggy and his eyes saw only two large sunbursts of orange. He was beyond pain and close to death.

The three guards were getting impatient. The leader should have been back by now. They went to the top of the next hill to watch for him. Jan Ti walked into the small valley beyond the cabin. He wanted to find wild honey to dab on Coldstream's face. "We will see how he likes it," he laughed, "when the wasps come."

Coldstream felt the tingling around his ankles again. He tried to bang his heels against the wall, but was too weak to move his legs. He could feel them coming up over his knees, slowly, exploring their way. Now they were on his thighs and crawling over his genitals and up his stomach. Smelling blood, the mass of ants moved more quickly. One crawled onto Coldstream's lips, and then another. He tried to mash them and take them into his mouth. Now several were going to his nostrils.

He could feel their tiny nips as they bit into the mucous flesh. Dully he was grateful that his nose and mouth were dry. Two columns of ants ignored his nose and mouth and went straight up his arms, heading for the bloodied palms.

Below on the road, Coldstream heard the sound of jeeps. He felt one of the ants bite inside his mouth. My God, he thought. If they're not up here in five minutes, they'll find a skeleton. He tried to scream, but could not. When he opened his mouth, more ants came in.

There were six jeeps at the bottom of the hill. About twenty men in Sarkanese Army uniform climbed out. The squat man led them up the hill.

The three who had been left behind ran from the hilltop to

meet the captain in charge of the Sarkhanese Army squad. They apparently knew him. He was young, slender, and had a gold tooth. They waved at him and the captain waved back. When the two groups met, the captain raised the submachine gun, aimed it at the three men, and began firing. They dropped. The man built like a *sumo* wrestler screamed, "Nam Tho, are you crazy?" and ran for the trees. The captain raised his gun, carefully aimed it, and shot the squat man down.

Two of the soldiers grabbed buckets of water and doused Coldstream. Two others pulled out the spikes.

When he was released and lay gasping on the ground, Coldstream heard the captain say quietly to another officer, "How could those fools have made such a blunder? Now it is too late."

The captain turned to Coldstream and said, "Buan Suang, were there any other bandits around?"

"Yes, about six, but I don't know where. One was dressed like a *bonze*."

The captain barked out the command to fan out and find the others. Returning to Coldstream, he said, "I will return immediately. And we will have medicine in a few minutes. Rest yourself."

When the officer had disappeared over the hill, the naked Coldstream staggered toward the men who had just been murdered. Every step took total concentration to prevent his collapsing into unconsciousness. He drove himself the fifty yards to where the bodies lay. He heard two shots on the other side of the hill, and then the voices of the men returning. So they've killed Jan Ti also. Coldstream didn't quite understand. Despite his shock and almost total physical debilitation, he had recognized Nam Tho, the captain, as the terrorist described by Xinh. He had a gold tooth. But why was he now in Sarkhanese Army uniform?

Coldstream bent painfully over the dead men and searched them. In a little waterproof container pinned inside the shirt of each, he found papers and identification cards. He made thumb prints on their cards, using his blood as ink.

He staggered back to the shack. He found his torn pants there and put them on. It was an excruciating experience to pull his trousers up, but he had to have someplace to hide the papers.

17

The Dossiers

It had taken Coldstream half an hour to tell his story. Other than his quiet voice, there was silence in the conference room. No one moved. Now Coldstream had stopped and was massaging his palms through his gloves.

Cogswell said, "Jeremiah, what do you think?"

"I'll check the fingerprints on the cards as soon as I get back to my office. It's a terrible story. But strange. We're living in the twentieth century, not the Middle Ages. Who the hell ever heard of crucifying in our time?"

Coldstream stood up, slowly unbuttoned his gloves and carefully removed them. He raised his arms to shoulder level and opened his hands. The scars were a dark purple and flamed across his palms. On the backs of his hands the scars were smaller, but still the dark purple.

"It happened six weeks ago," Coldstream said in a clear voice, "and you are right, Mister Hobson, there is something strange. For one thing, it is strange that men who work for your organization should be Communists."

"Now just a moment, Captain," Hobson said. "I don't know the specific details, but it's accepted counterespionage tactics to try and penetrate the enemy's organization. As a matter of fact, it's one of the most difficult things there is to do." Hobson made his points quickly, with the skill of an experienced debater. "In fact, Captain, penetration is the sign of a superior intelligence."

Coldstream pulled his gloves back on. He looked down at Hobson.

"And is it superior intelligence to have your people carrying identification cards which any commissar could interpret?" Coldstream asked. "And do your people usually assist in the torture of American nationals?"

The men around the table sat motionless, most of them looking at Coldstream's hands.

"Captain, those cards are not, to the ordinary eye, F.I.A. identity cards," Hobson said. "They are plastic-covered cards with the photograph of the agent on one side and the name of a Hong Kong manufacturer on the other. The identification part is the name of the manufacturer."

"It is not a very well-kept secret, Jeremiah," Cogswell said. "Not if Coldstream knew about it."

"Mister Cogswell, it's not just that I knew it, but every Communist agent in Southeast Asia knows about those cards," Coldstream said. "These two men were double agents, taking money from us, giving us information, but, in fact, working for the Communists."

"Mister Chairman, I think I can throw some light on this whole business, but I'll have to send for some papers," Hobson said. "May we have a short break?"

Cogswell hesitated. He did not want to stop now. But Hobson had spoken in a conciliatory, even ingratiating tone. He nodded his assent.

Hobson motioned to Lindquist, the Air Force General. They talked quietly for a few moments. The General walked to a phone and made a call.

A servant brought out a plate of sandwiches and more hot coffee. Coldstream and McCauley sat stiffly silent. Cogswell circulated among his guests, but quickly gave up trying to dispel the strained atmosphere. Fifteen minutes later, an Air Force courier brought a flat envelope to General Lindquist. Hobson nodded at Cogswell, and Cogswell, somewhat wearily, brought the meeting to order.

"Jeremiah, you asked for the recess. You now have your documents. Why don't you proceed?"

"Gladly. What we are really trying to determine is whether or not there is an invasion on the *Plateau des Luminaires*. These two gentlemen, amateur intelligence agents, come in and tell us there is not."

"Mister Hobson," McCauley interrupted, "we said that *on the evidence you have* there is no invasion. We are suggesting that there be no U.S. action until you have more proof of it from reliable eyewitnesses. We were deceived by this same kind of a lie in

Laos and we almost went to actual war over an invasion which was described from day to day in loving detail by the Laotian government. But, as we learned later, the invasion never occurred. It was merely a bid for more U.S. aid."

Hobson said, "Captain Coldstream, do you know General Hajn, the Minister of Defense of Sarkhan?"

"Yes, sir, for over twenty-five years."

"What is your opinion of him?"

"I think highly of him."

"Is he honest?"

"I trust him," said Coldstream.

Hobson turned to McCauley. "Professor, do you trust the General?"

"From what little dealings I have had with him, and from the history of the man, I would say yes, I trust him."

Hobson pushed the contents of the envelope across the table to Coldstream. They were photographs, about forty of them, eight by ten inches in size, taken from a plane. Although somewhat blurry, they showed troops in Vietnamese uniforms, tanks, howitzers, trucks, bulldozers, and crudely constructed barracks. The actual number of troops pictured appeared to be several thousand.

When Coldstream and McCauley had examined the pictures, Hobson handed them a letter.

"Will you read this out loud, please, Captain Coldstream?"

Coldstream picked up the letter and began reading.

"My dear Ambassador Brown, pursuant to your request for proof of the invasion—in light of my forbidding any foreigners to go to that very dangerous area—I hereby send photographs made of the Vietnamese troops and their equipment. I was flown over the plateau area for an hour during a brief period yesterday when the rains had eased off. I personally took these pictures, had them developed immediately, and rushed them to you. Should there be an opening over the plateau, I hereby invite the American military attachés in Haidho to accompany me on a flight and they can take the pictures for themselves. However, I strongly urge that we should not wait until that time comes before making preparations to repel the invasion. I request again your assistance in expediting the delivery of arms, planes, money, and men. Very respectfully, Hajn."

Coldstream studied the letter for another moment, turning it over in his hands. "It seems impossible. Frankly, I have no idea how these Vietnamese got their heavy equipment over the mountains or through what I consider the impassable swamp. There's something here I don't understand."

"Why didn't Hajn invite an American military attaché to go on the reconnaissance flight with him?" asked McCauley.

Hobson said, "Professor, war must look leisurely and orderly to the historian in his comfortable library. But the man responsible for the survival of a nation does not have such luxuries. Let me ask you, Professor, if you heard that the fog over a battle area was opening for only an hour—and it took fifty minutes to get to the scene—would you run to your plane and go, or would you telephone for witnesses?"

"I would go."

"Thank you," said Hobson.

"They're very blurred," McCauley muttered, turning a photograph in his hands.

"They just happen to be the best we have," Hobson said.

"Captain Coldstream and Professor McCauley apparently believe the invasion is a fraud," said Abbott of State, "yet they believe Sarkhan is in danger. Would they be good enough to explain that again?"

McCauley slumped a bit in his chair, making himself comfortable. His coat bunched and wrinkled. "I will be glad to explain it again," he said, with a touch of sarcasm. "In Sarkhan, the Communists are educating and brainwashing the best people in the rural areas, which is ninety per cent of Sarkhan. Almost daily, they are visiting villages which have almost no communication with the government in Haidho except when the tax collector comes or the Army requires recruits. The Communists soon will have a network of communications through Sarkhan, just as they have in Vietnam, to carry their lies and their propaganda. They are starting all kinds of disquieting rumors. They are creating religious dissension between Buddhist priests and Moslem leaders. The North Vietnamese were obviously the ones who arranged the

bombing of that old temple in the north so important to the Sarkhanese ..."

"Professor," Hobson said, "we are not interested in religion
and rumors."

"Which is, my dear Director, exactly what you should be interested in," McCauley said and pointed a professorial finger at
Hobson. "Just because a thing is intangible, like religion or
rumor, is no reason to conclude it is not important. The Communists have used the invisible everywhere around the world. By the
time they move to the visible—weapons, rifles, mortars—they
have already won the battle."

"This all has a familiar ring," Hobson said. "This talk about
morale and peasant support and ideology. Sounds like Mao and
Fidel ..."

"That's right, Mister Hobson," Coldstream said, "and Mao is
now running China and Fidel runs Cuba. And you, when you
tried to overthrow Fidel, found you had made a fatal miscalcula-
tion on one of the invisibles—the peasants were not with you."

Cogswell drew up taut. No one to his knowledge had ever
challenged the Director so directly. Coldstream and McCauley
had the valor of the innocent. If they held government positions,
Hobson would hound them out of their jobs. That was one
reason the Director had few outspoken critics and a host of
silent enemies.

"What can the United States do?" asked Cogswell, shifting the
discussion.

Hobson turned away, but McCauley's lecture went on. "Most
American diplomats and intelligence people go for the 'sure' military man. And wind up with unstable dictators in Korea, Vietnam, Formosa, the Dominican Republic, Pakistan—the list seems
endless. The only sure victory is a solid political victory,"
McCauley said. "But Americans are not prepared to travel that
harder, slower, more tedious route. The Communists are."

"What is this other route you suggest, Professor?" Cogswell
asked.

"American men must go overseas as patriots, preferably without families, willing to die, willing to learn the language and the
customs, the emotional patterns, the historical and religious back-

grounds. They must be willing as Americans to suffer and be as dedicated as saints."

"I conclude," interrupted Hobson, "that the United States should forget about the invasion and start Sarkhanese language schools on university campuses for bachelors whom we, some day in the future, will send to Sarkhan on good-will missions? And meanwhile, what about the fighting on the plateau?"

"Mister Hobson, if you were a student of mine, you would be given very low grades on the logical construction of your argument," McCauley said. "I would grade you high on experience, low on logic, high on information, low on critical analysis of that information."

Cogswell felt a wave of irritation toward McCauley. He was, after all, the youngest man present, yet in some odd way he had become the teacher. And he was appallingly unaware of the power structure of the room.

"Could you sum up your recommendations, Professor?" Cogswell said. He smiled at Jeremiah. "We can handle Mister Hobson's logical deficiencies at a later time."

Hobson did not smile back and Cogswell was disappointed. The two of them had been around so long and through so much, Hobson should not be upset by a young professor's brashness.

Asians and all of the emerging nations respected raw power, McCauley argued, but it must be used cautiously. The President's escalation of bombing military targets in North Vietnam may have been a wise use of military strength. Only time would tell. But the escalation had been slow and deliberate, the President had warned the enemy at every stage that there was greater power to come. Rushing military intervention in Sarkhan on the basis of a single report of an unlikely invasion in the north would be nonsense.

"Professor, timing is what counts," said Hobson. "Use power *early*. Make it stick. That's the lesson of all that's happened since 1945."

"I don't agree," McCauley said. "We've got the military power, we've had it for decades. But what we need right now is the political power. Example: A Peace Corps kid whom the Sarkhanese can see with their own eyes. They get to like him. He eats their food, sleeps in their hut, pays his way, brings something useful. That's politics. Contrast: The sky-raider which brings a napalm bomb to your village. That's power. It wipes out the village, blinds half the people, and leaves the rest with scars . . ."

"In short, the pacifist view," Hobson said.

McCauley laughed. Coldstream, more sensitive to what was happening within the conference room, interrupted.

"I concur with what the Professor has said," Coldstream said. "I'd add a few things. Right now we should help the Sarkhan government create a communications system with every village, to show the Sarkhanese how their own government is better than a Communist regime. Send them rice to take care of the emergency caused by two bad crops. Send doctors who will go to the villages . . ."

"Mister Chairman," Hobson interrupted, "I propose to give the Committee some information I consider relevant concerning our two guests."

Cogswell nodded.

Hobson stood up and removed from his briefcase two fat dossiers, one marked "Coldstream" and the other "McCauley," and opened the one marked "Coldstream."

"Captain Coldstream, it says here in this dossier that in 1948 you voluntarily retired from the U.S. Navy after you had received orders to be stationed in Stockholm as the naval attaché. Is that correct?"

"Yes, sir, it is."

"The record also shows that you said you did not want to be stationed in Stockholm, but that you wanted to be stationed in Sarkhan. Is that correct?"

"Yes."

"Why did you not carry out your orders as a patriotic American and member of the military service?"

"I had much experience in Asia, sir, and I speak several Asian languages fluently. I knew the chiefs of state of many Asian countries. I felt it made no sense for me to be stationed in Sweden. I did not know the language and had no knowledge of the country."

"Therefore," said Hobson, "rather than carry out the orders

from your superior, you voluntarily retired from the Navy."
Hobson looked at Coldstream and went on. "I see here a letter
from a friend in the Bureau of Personnel at the Navy Department who beseeched you to stay in the Navy and almost
guaranteed that you would become an admiral at the next selection
board. But you refused and said that you had business to do in
Sarkhan. Is that correct?"

"You are reading that a little out of context, Mister Hobson,"
said Coldstream.

"And then," continued Hobson, "you got out of the Navy,
went to Sarkhan, and established a business. I see here that some
of the capital you needed was borrowed from the Bank of
Haidho partly through the influence of your friend, General
Hajn. Is that correct?"

"Yes, sir, it is."

"Now, Captain, let me ask you one question. What would happen to your business interests in Sarkhan if the United States gave
Sarkhan full-scale help and Sarkhan went to war to repel the invaders?"

"I probably would have to pull them all out, if there was a war
up north. But I don't . . ."

Hobson said, "That's all I wanted to hear. If the United States
helps the Sarkhanese repel invaders, your business suffers. Thank
you, Captain Coldstream, and now I would like to address Professor McCauley."

Hobson closed Coldstream's dossier and slowly opened the one
on McCauley. He looked at it for a moment and then walked to
where McCauley was sitting.

"Professor McCauley, you have told us Americans should be
trained well before they go to Sarkhan. That they should be
patriotic and dedicated, but that they should be brave and zealous
and highly motivated. Is that correct?"

"It is. You said it well."

Hobson said slowly, "Professor McCauley, what did you do in
the line of military service for the United States of America, your
country, at the beginning of World War II?"

Without any hesitation, McCauley replied, "At the beginning I
was a conscientious objector."

Hobson repeated slowly and loudly, "You were a conscientious objector?"

"Yes, I was at the beginning. After that..."

Hobson addressed the Committee with a little sigh, saying, "Well gentlemen..." and with that he raised his hands and let them fall to his sides.

Cogswell drove Coldstream and McCauley to the airport in silence. It was not until the car stopped at the terminal that anyone spoke.

"For awhile," said Cogswell, as the chauffeur opened the door, "I thought you made your case. But in the end Hobson overpowered you. I'll report everything as it happened, but the President has domestic politics to fret about in addition to his international problems. It wouldn't look good, his taking the advice of two dubious characters who disagreed with the best and most trusted brains in the government. Those agencies could leak out stories that would make you two look like traitors and the President like a fool. Can you imagine the President's diplomatic and military policies being influenced by a pacifist?"

"Pacifist?" said McCauley. He drawled the word, starting in a whisper and ending with a growl.

Cogswell turned, startled.

"Let me make something clear, Mister Cogswell," McCauley said. "I am no pacifist. I have studied history too long not to know that at times force must be used to save a nation or an ideal. Further, when force is used I think it should be used fast, in overwhelming strength, ruthlessly. When the Romans moved a legion they did it for good or necessary cause, and that legion moved like a scythe against its enemy. In Vietnam I am opposed to pseudo-military thinking... all this thing of 'advisors' and 'training groups.' If something is worth fighting for, win it fast and economically and make it clear what you are trying to win."

"But what about Sarkhan..." Cogswell began.

"I am opposed to the use of military force in Sarkhan at this time for a very simple reason," McCauley said.

Coldstream had never seen him so urgent.

"That is not what is needed now in Sarkhan," said McCauley.

"What is needed is political and economic help. On the other hand, military aid right now, with its PXs and commissaries and high-living and underemployed American military men, would play right into the Communist hands. But make no mistake, Mister Cogswell. If force were needed I would want it used openly, swiftly, and with clear eyes."

Cogswell looked at McCauley appraisingly. He nodded, indicating he understood.

McCauley sank back in his seat.

"It was quite a session," Coldstream said. "Part trial, part inquisition, part Committee meeting."

"The real issues," McCauley said, "were snowed under at the end by Hobson's attacks on us. I admire the man, so skilled at the innuendo, the use of the dossier, the suggestion of subversion. No one dared raise a voice against him."

"I was chairman of that meeting and I didn't . . ."

"You didn't risk challenging him," McCauley said. He brushed ashes off his battered jacket. "And he left a very one-sided version of our backgrounds in the minds of the Committee."

"Why didn't it tell them the rest of your war record? The medic stuff?" Cogswell asked. He felt both guilt and impatience. Guilt that he had done badly by these two men, impatience that they had not pressed their own cases before the Committee.

"I was surprised. I didn't believe even a government bureaucracy could sink so low," McCauley said. "I thought university bureaucracy was bad. But these government characters are a million light years worse than campus politicians."

They stood quietly outside the car.

Something gnawed at the back of Coldstream's consciousness. "Those photos showed some yellow mango trees, I think. They never grow above two hundred feet and certainly not on the plateau." He stopped and then voiced another thought, slowly, feeling his way. "And how did they get those pictures here so quickly? The invasion supposedly began only forty-eight hours ago."

Cogswell was restless and irritable.

"I don't know. I don't know. But one thing I am sure of—the bureaucratic pressure is so strong that aid for Sarkhan will probably go through in a few days. I'll have to support it to preserve my usefulness here. But I'd like you two to find out what in hell goes on out there."

The three men stood quietly, looking out over the expanse of Dulles Airport, watching the great beetle-like buses, antennas extended, racing in from the sleek jets.

"Mister Cogswell, what do you think is the most important thing to find out about Sarkhan?" McCauley asked. He asked the question quietly.

"Find out where Prince Lin is," Cogswell said.

18

The American Build-Up

Every half hour, day and night, a broad-beamed transport roared in and bumped to a landing at Haidho International Airport. A bucket brigade of brown-skinned Sarkhanese laborers filed out lugging canned food, generals' desks, paper, typewriters, rifles, ammunition, and medical supplies.

Some of the planes brought jeeps, bulldozers, and carry-alls. Others brought personnel, and their arrival was like a carnival. Well-organized groups of Sarkhanese women and children greeted the troops, sang and hugged the soldiers, and placed leis about their necks. Army, Navy, and Air Force public information photographers jostled each other taking pictures.

The generals, the clerks, the quartermasters, the civilian sub-contractors, came off the planes in a jovial mood. But some men filed off silently, glancing quickly at the terrain, sniffing the air, listening carefully to see if they could understand the language. These men were the Marines, the Special Forces, the helicopter pilots, the captains and majors who were going to be "military advisors," the corpsmen and doctors who had been in Korea and Vietnam. These men explored Haidho quickly, made their liberties, drank their whisky, had their fist fights, then went to their bivouacs. They knew they would not be in the capital long. But they would be in the country, they said to one another, a good long time—and some of them would be buried there.

The sea-going transports arrived several days after the planes. Holds were undogged, booms swung out, winches creaked, and from the ship's cavernous bellies came the massive entrails of war. Trucks, prefabricated houses, artillery, helicopters, rockets, ammunition, tanks, hundreds of cases of liquor, food, cigarettes, and ten thousand small items to stock the shelves of the post exchange and commissary.

The face of Haidho changed quickly. A Sarkhanese student recently returned from the United States said, "Haidho now is like New York during Christmas week."

The noise of airplanes, jeeps, and clanking troops drowned out the softer native sounds of the city. The metabolic rate of the metropolis increased. Two thousand years of Sarkhanese languor was destroyed by Yankee jeeps honking through the streets. Shops stayed open late, and a dozen new industries thrived. Within one fortnight Haidho had freshly painted restaurants, whorehouses, black market stores, saloons, night clubs, garages, and two motion picture houses.

The Hotel Ritz's seventy rooms were quickly renovated and turned over to American officers. The renovation included the installation of hidden microphones which led to the offices of Sarkhanese Intelligence. This rush job had been contracted out to Hung Loo Company, Ltd., Chinese (Nationalist) specialists in "bugging." The Hung Loo Company had long experience, having installed the "bugging" equipment in American-occupied hotels in Hong Kong, Seoul, Djakarta, Taipei, and Bangkok. Hung Loo Tai, the president of the corporation, once had bragged, "There isn't an hour in the day that someplace in Asia people aren't listening to Americans over our equipment."

The Imperial Hotel, which was second-rate, had been turned over to the press. The forty-four cockroachy rooms were jammed with "war correspondents" and society writers from all over the world, but mostly from America. The society sisters had come to cover the parties and ceremonies celebrating the historic abdication of King Diad and the coronation of Prince Lin. Royalty and dignitaries from over a hundred nations were expected within a few weeks.

In the basement of the Imperial was a briefing room. Here, against a backdrop of a large "war map" complete with green pins for Sarkhanese troops and red pins for enemy troops, General Hajn's intelligence officer gave daily briefings on the progress of the fighting. Because of the monsoons, no reinforcements could be sent to the plateau, but the two thousand Sarkhanese troops regularly stationed there were fighting desperately and bravely. Once General Hajn brought in two wounded soldiers and a Vietnamese prisoner. With General Hajn acting as interpreter, they described the bloody battles.

The New York Times man had said, "If they can get out, why can't we go to the plateau and see for ourselves?"

"The trail out," said Hajn, "is dangerous. Furthermore, it is secret. We must keep it for military emergencies. When the rains stop in two months I personally will escort you to the front lines."

Then, pointing to the American general who was listening, General Hajn added, "And with his help you will be witness to a great Sarkhanese victory."

In the attic of his tiny room behind the fish-packing plant, Tuc discussed the subject with some of his National Front leaders.

"Out first step is to infiltrate. I have here a list of interpreters needed by the Americans. First, a personal interpreter for the commanding general." Tuc smiled. "Tong, you will have that position."

"Me?" Tong Chiang was the best dressed of the group. He was a middle-aged merchant trained at the Wharton School of Finance at the University of Pennsylvania. "Tuc," he said slowly, "they'll become suspicious. I am supposed to be a rich man. I entertained the General only two nights ago."

"Precisely," said Tuc. "You will receive a letter in the morning from General Hajn requesting you as a Sarkhanese patriot to accept the position. Tomorrow you will have an assistant whom you will train. General Russell is famous for his people-to-people program. He entertains and goes out a lot. He requires an interpreter who not only can be trusted, but who will be at home in the highest society." Tuc's voice took on a mock gentility. "The generous Americans are going to much trouble to help Sarkhan, and Sarkhanese patriots must go out of their way to help the Americans."

"Who will look after my business?" said Tong Chiang.

Tuc waved his hand and said bitingly, "It makes no difference. Anyway, you are a quarter Chinese and I know it is your custom to have a half-dozen relatives trained to take over every job. Your duty now is to become so indispensable to the General that you will be living at his house. He has plenty of room..."

"I know, I'm renting my house to him."

"The General," continued Tuc, "is a member of a society called John Birch. The John Birch Society is suspicious of everyone who does not hate Negroes and who does not wear an American flag in his buttonhole. You can make yourself liked by him very quickly by saying that there are rumors around Haidho that several members of the American Embassy and the President's Sarkhan Committee are Communists. Tell him that within a few months you may be able to get proof."

One of the first buildings to go up was nicknamed The Mystery Place. It was the J.U.S.P.A.L.—Joint U.S. Photographic Analysis Laboratory. It was one-story, sprawling, made of brick. Steel bars covered the windows and a high electric fence surrounded it.

Navy construction men built the place, and all went well until an Air Force general noticed that the door of the largest office had a brass plaque saying "Admiral's Quarters."

"Why, goddamn it," said the general, "the Air Force has cognizance over this project, not the Navy."

The Navy captain showed genuine surprise. "But, sir, the Navy has been doing the reconnaissance photography in this area for years. We know the terrain. And, then, under AirPac orders..."

The Air Force general sent a cable to General Lindquist in Washington. He called on Admiral Sebalius. After a few days of wrangling the matter went before the Secretary of Defense.

And he decided that J.U.S.P.A.L. would be run by a joint committee of the services headed by an "uninvolved party"—an Army general.

The story spread all over Haidho. At the Sarkhanese Officers' Club, two rooms over a noodle shop, the junior officers gave a toast. "May the Americans fight the North Vietnamese as ferociously as they fight each other."

Across the street from the Army's first temporary tent camp was Hin Boo's Herbal Shop. This was the Sarkhanese version of a drugstore. Inside there were such items as dried bats' wings, the kidneys of boa constrictors, white elephants' blood, and many other items highly prized by the Sarkhanese for medicinal purposes. The owner of the store, old Hin Boo, who was born on the same day as King Diad, had a string of herbal shops. He had made his reputation on the quality and accessibility of his dry boa constrictor livers and his excellent poppy opium. Hin Boo had other interests also, among them smuggling and the sale of stolen goods. If there was money to be made, Hin Boo could smell it many miles away. Now he sat at a table in his shop, sniffing vigorously and drinking tea with his son and two nephews. As he talked he fingered an abacus.

"Fortune is smiling upon us, friends. There, across the street, are almost two thousand American soldiers. They have only been here a few days and already they are roaming the streets looking for women. We have estimated that there will be about ten thousand here and most of them will be stationed at Haidho." He beat his left hand on the table. "When will the second shipment of girls arrive?"

His son looked at him through thick glasses and replied without hesitation, "The steamer from Hong Kong will arrive tomorrow night."

"How many girls?"

"Two hundred and sixteen, Papa."

"The usual?"

"Yes, Papa, a mixture of Chinese, French, Negro, some Germans and some Thais."

"But, of course, no Sarkhanese girls?"

"You know that Sarkhanese girls will not become prostitutes. I have arranged for forty Vietnamese from Hanoi. They will arrive on the smuggler's junk in three days."

The old man absently clicked his abacus. "The American troops will stay here at least three months. It will be at least two months before any of them can reach the plateau region and then if they depart, it will take another month to get them out of here. Let's see, we will need at least fifteen small cabarets with rooms upstairs. And a doctor to examine the girls and make out certificates. Have you arranged for a doctor?"

"Yes, Papa, the two Hindu doctors have agreed to do it on a price-per-head basis."

The old man continued, "We need dancing in the cabarets. What about the music?"

"It is too expensive to import musicians on a temporary basis. We are having record players."

"From Hong Kong?"

The son smiled for the first time. "I have made friends with an American sergeant in the recreation division. He thinks he can get us six or eight as soon as the next ship arrives. The rest we will get from Hong Kong."

"And last of all," said the old man, "we must serve good Western liquor in our houses."

"The first shipment will come from Hong Kong, Papa. And from then on I think I have a working arrangement with the officer who is in charge of the American liquor supply. Well, not exactly the officer, but his assistant."

"What arrangement?" said the old man sharply.

"Papa, there are some things you must leave to me. But I assure you it won't cost money."

Major Anthony San Carlos was an Air Force reservist. He did not have enough rank to get into the Ritz Hotel, but had been fortunate enough to get a cubbyhole at the Sarkhanese Air Officers' Club. It was almost midnight, and the Major was in his room, writing to his wife. Three floors below, in the courtyard, a noisy party blared. But the Major did not hear the noise. He concentrated on the letter.

Dear Ida,

Your letter came, Darling, and it has nourished me. Thank you, angel. It was good news to hear that the rain finally came and that the corn is green again.

I have been feeling lonely these last few days. First, I was annoyed that they called me back, me a middle-aged retread. Maybe something went wrong in the Pentagon's IBM machine? But the Personnel Officer assured me no, that I was called back because of my long experience in Asia and my skill in getting native mechanics to overhaul American equipment. Well, maybe so, but I wish I were home in Iowa with you and the children.

Being out here is like listening to an old record play over. Everything looks exactly like it did in Korea and China and Vietnam. None of us know what the score is. Why are we here? The depots are filling up with tanks and planes and ammunition. But you can't fly the planes in the monsoon and you can't drive heavy equipment in the jungles or marshes. What's more, these Sarkhanese are still in the Middle Ages. No amount of instruction can teach them to maintain the equipment. It will deteriorate and be wrecked just as it was in those other jungle places. If we want the stuff to operate, we must keep Americans out here.

The pep talks the General gives us tell us that we are here to contain Communism. Well, Ida, I guess we must live on faith. It all seems crazy, but I must assume that the big shots in Washington know their business. And if my country calls me to serve, I will try to do it cheerfully. You, too, my darling, are serving the nation. Everytime you drive the tractor or clean the stables, you are doing as much as any of us out here. Maybe more,

Love,

Tony

In Monterey, California, Delight Richards was having a tea party for her lady friends. The teapot sat on the table, steaming, and in the silver service were cream, lemon, and sugar.

The girls were drinking martinis.

Delight was the wife of Colonel Mike Richards, the Ordnance Officer with the U.S. Army in Haidho. She had called the girls together to tell them the good news.

"I'm beginning to pack," she said, squeezing a lemon rind into her martini. "Mike has written that he'll probably be allowed to bring me out next month, as soon as there's housing."

One of the women sighed.

"In Okinawa," she said, "I had two full-time maids for thirty dollars a month."

"And cheap liquor. Johnny Walker Black Label at a dollar and a quarter a fifth . . ."

"Not to mention trips. Delight, you'll be able to shop in Hong Kong, Bangkok, and Tokyo."

"Don't forget Singapore," said Delight.

"If it weren't for the fun of overseas duty," said one of the ladies, "Tom and I would have quit the Army long ago."

"As Chief of Ordnance," said Delight, "Mike will have a driver . . ."

The girl who remembered Okinawa raised her third martini on

high and sang the first stanza of "Overseas," and the others laughed and joined in.

> "The stateside army we just hate
> But overseas the duty's great
> And even with a background shady
> A girl can live it like a lady . . ."

The Commanding General, U.S. Army, made a talk at the Haidho Rotary Club. His interpreter, Tong Chiang, the patriotic merchant, did a fine job. Tong was an invaluable assistant to the General, and had, in fact, been cleared for "confidential material."

The General also had another interpreter, an American lieutenant who was fluent in Sarkhanese. He had been assigned as "Police Liaison Officer" to get any troops out of Sarkhanese jails, should the boys get into trouble.

The American build-up in Sarkhan seemed to improve Marcus Coit's disposition and even his health. His *Haidho Gazette*'s circulation had increased tenfold. Not only did almost all of the newly arrived military personnel buy the paper, but Coit had gotten the PX to sell subscriptions for the men to mail home. On the basis of increased circulation, his advertising income had almost doubled in two weeks. The many newspapers for whom he had been an inactive stringer now cabled him almost daily for stories. Sarkhan was big news, and Coit's byline appeared all over the world. *Time* magazine ran a paragraph on his scoops, with a photograph of him sitting in his wheelchair typing.

For Ambassador Brown life became faster and more complex. High-ranking officials now routed their junkets through Haidho. He spent many hours briefing them carefully until he learned they weren't listening. What most of them wanted was a photograph of themselves with King Diad or General Hajn, an evening of native dances, and an escort to help their wives shop for the fabled Haidho glass. Brown cabled requests to Washington for more personnel. He needed additional communications men, young protocol officers, extra stenographers, and at least six more people for the public relations office. Brown made a point of greeting each newcomer personally, and ordering him to enroll in the Embassy's language school.

General Hajn quickly became the official middleman in the hectic social life between the Americans in Haidho and the Sarkhanese government. There were dinners at the palace almost every day, and Hajn was in charge. He also acted as the King's interpreter. His prestige with Americans grew, but the process worried Hajn. It took all his time and he feared losing contact with the realities of Sarkhanese politics. It was almost impossible to meet with Tuc anymore.

Coldstream felt an unexpected pang of nostalgia when he saw the Navy ships moored at the Haidho docks. He visited the flagship and called on the Admiral whom he had known slightly back at Annapolis years before. The Admiral had not invited him to stay for dinner and had been blunt about it. "Eddie, we knew each other thirty years ago—so I'll level. We've had instructions to stay clear of you. F.I.A. put out a report that you may have fellow-traveler tendencies. I know it's not true—but, well, you know how it is when C.N.O. orders us to do something or not to do something."

19

By Presidential Order,
Depart Earliest

At 6:45 A.M. in Washington, D.C., the white telephone next to Cogswell's bed rang. It was more of a buzz, and Cogswell knew who was calling. The white telephone was connected to one place only. "Cogswell speaking, sir."

"Adolph, I'm sorry to awaken you so early ..."

"That's perfectly all right, Mister Pres ..."

"The press has one hell of a story on Sarkhan. They say there is a huge battle going on up north and that the Vietnamese Communists are exterminating the Sarkhanese Army. And our tanks and planes and all the big stuff still sits in Haidho. It sounds like Laos all over."

"Who filed the story, sir?"

"All the wire services. The Sarkhanese Department of Defense had a press conference. Every Communist capital denies a Vietnamese invasion. Hanoi cabled the United Nations that it will take an inspection party to the so-called battle area, monsoon or no. Peking says we have forced Sarkhan to lie so that we can get bases from which to bomb China and Russia."

"What do F.I.A. and State and Defense say?"

"They go along with the Sarkhanese reports." The voice over the white telephone became irritable. "Even now telegrams are coming in saying that the Administration is fabricating a war to keep up defense spending. The Smith-Fortly papers are running an editorial in their entire chain saying I should stop running the country with a crystal ball and start getting facts."

"But, Mister President, have you ..."

"Look, Adolph, here's why I called. I want you to get to Haidho right away. Today. Take your Committee to Sarkhan— or as many of them as you want. You will be named Minister Plenipotentiary and my direct representative. An Air Force jet

187

transport is at your disposal. A letter putting this in writing left here by messenger twenty minutes ago. Any comments?"

"What do you want us to bring back?"

"Adolph, are you deaf?" He laughed. "The facts, some kind of proof. What in the hell is happening in Sarkhan? And I want it fast. All the facts for me. Non-classified facts for the press. Do you understand me? One more thing. Find that goddamn prince. I don't know why, but it seems awfully important to the Sarkhanese."

"Yes, Mister President."

"Okay. Call me at ten and tell me the Committee is leaving by noon. If you have any trouble, I don't care what it is, call me. On this phone. Goodbye."

The White House end of the telephone hung up.

Before Cogswell had put down the receiver there was a knock on the door.

"Come in."

It was the butler, sleepy and in a dressing gown. "Mister Cogswell, there is a messenger from the White House downstairs. He has an envelope and insists on delivering it to you personally."

"Show him up."

Cogswell got out of bed. It took him a moment to straighten his back, which was stiff and hurt at the base of the spine. The dull ache of fatigue was in all his joints. In the mirror his face looked old, his eyes dull.

He was getting too old for this kind of stuff. This junket would be his last. When he returned from Sarkhan, he'd retire. Then he thought of his three sons, three daughters, eighteen grandchildren, and seven great-grandchildren. He realized he couldn't remember all their names even if he worked at it, pencil and pad in hand, for hours. It was time for others to take over. He had had more than his share of whatever all this was.

There was another knock.

The White House messenger, Cogswell's secretary, and the butler all entered at the same time.

By 9:00 A.M. the President had an unexpected caller.

"Mister President, as you know, I'm taking off with the Sar-

khan Committee at noon," Hobson said. "I think it was wise of
you to get us moving as soon as possible. Probably we would
have moved a bit sooner on our own but..."

"Adolph is a busy man," the President said. "As long as we get
you all out there by tomorrow, I'm satisfied."

The President was not giving him any openings. Even so, Hobson was determined to push ahead.

"Sir, there is just one thing I'm worried about," Hobson said.
"We couldn't have a better chairman than Cogswell. He's experienced, commands respect, has authority. But, increasingly, I'm
worried about the over-all, the global aspect of our international
strategy."

The President leaned forward. "Well, so am I, Jeremiah."

Hobson paused.

"Mister President, at some point we've got to get ourselves in a
position where we can reverse the tide," Hobson said. "Communism is going to keep moving forward aggressively until we
apply a sort of political judo—until we make it fall backwards
with a vigorous push."

"That would be a nice trick, Jeremiah. How do we do it?"

"We might start with Sarkhan," Hobson said. "It's the pivot of
Asia. We turn them back there and they lose the tungsten and tin
of Sarkhan, access to the sea and to Indonesia, and a lot of face.
The only way they can move then is backward."

Hobson waited, trying to fathom what the man across the desk
was thinking. The President remained silent.

"To start the dominoes toppling backward not only in Southeast Asia, but in Africa, the Middle East, Latin America," Hobson went on, "the first push has to be strong and emphatic."

"And you think that Cogswell might not have enough perspective to see all this?"

"He's spread pretty thin, Mister President. And he's getting
older."

"We're all getting older, Jeremiah," the President said finally.
"You, me, and Adolph." Then he leaned forward and there was a
change in his tone. "One of the things about getting older is that
you want to solve everything while you are still alive. Lots of
things take longer than that, Jeremiah."

The President knew that the wiry old man in front of him directed an agency so secret that even he, the President of the United States, could neither control nor penetrate it. This chilled him.

"Jeremiah, if you have any ideas, feel free to send them along to me," the President said. "Call me anytime. But when it comes to action, well, before you act, make *real* sure you give me a call."

Five minutes later Hobson's car was in the Washington traffic.

He doesn't see it, Hobson thought. I laid it out for him, the whole picture. He has a chance to change history and he isn't about to do it. In a way Hobson felt relief. He had always preferred working alone, running his own show.

20

The Rain Jungle

Coldstream sat with McCauley and Taja on the veranda of Coldstream's house. He stared blankly at the magnificent view of the approaches to Haidho. The monsoon had broken. But he knew it was only for a short spell. That was the character of the southwest monsoon in October, soft steady rains broken by periods of overcast for a few days.

McCauley pointed his finger at Coldstream and for a few seconds his face was cold and remote, almost expressionless. Then his eyes came alive. He spoke slowly. "If Lin is in Sarkhan, I can tell you where he is."

Coldstream looked at him, waiting for him to go on.

"What I need are The Ancient Books and my notes upstairs," continued McCauley. "Lin was going to meditate at the Temple of Buddha and Mohammed. But that was bombed. Where would he go? There are only a few places, by tradition, where royalty can meditate."

"Go on," Coldstream said.

"I've got to piece it together. From letters and conversations . . ."

McCauley left the veranda. Coldstream could hear his feet smacking the polished wood of the stairs. A door slammed. He returned minutes later with a large map of Sarkhan, and went to worked on it with a red wax crayon.

"Edward, who would want Lin out of Haidho?" Taja asked.

"Anyone who wanted the American military aid program to go ahead," Coldstream said. "Part of the problem here is that we don't know who really is running the government. But a crown prince about to succeed to the throne could stop almost anything. And Lin would seem to be a confirmed neutralist."

"I almost have it pinned down," McCauley muttered. He opened an old book bound in thick bamboo covers. The pages were of crude linen, the beautiful calligraphy dark and sweeping against the rough texture. He stopped, marked a page with a thin piece of bamboo, looked up, saw that his audience was attentive, and began his lecture.

"This book was written in 1332 when Sarkhan was threatened by an invasion of Dravidians from India. The invader could come in from any of four different approaches. Three of them were mountain passes and one of them was on the river. The King, his name was Tin Zuien, thought up an ingenious solution. His army was too small to fortify all four places, but he had to appear strong at each. He built a substantial-looking fort at each of the four approaches; rectangles of stone surrounding empty land. Within the rectangles were a labyrinth of walls, designed so that a few men could defend them even if the thick outer ramparts were breached. A handful of men patroling the parapets could appear to be legions. Inside another building a handful of men built fires which looked like cookfires for thousands of men. Occasionally a group of men would go down to the closest watering place and bring back what was obviously enough water to supply five thousand men.

"The Dravidians were patient people. This went on for over thirty years. They circled around and around Sarkhan, conquering the countries on all sides, but always hesitating to go through the four passes. King Tin, getting close to the time he must die, finally decided on an elaborate ruse to end the stalemate. He deliberately let the river fort fall into apparent disrepair, the fort called Three Mountains. It appeared to be weakly manned, almost deserted."

"I know the place," Coldstream said, "it is not too far from Boa Binh."

"Tin massed all his men in the fort he'd neglected. The Dravidians took the bait. They came down the river expecting to find almost no resistance. Instead they walked into a trap sprung from two sides. The Dravidians were massacred."

"You think Lin might be at the fort of the Three Mountains?" Coldstream asked.

"He has written often about it. Historically it pleases him because he thinks that Tin acted in the best neutralist tradition:

avoid war as long as possible, but win if it comes. Scenically it is beautiful and quiet. And then, Prince Lin made over half of the temple into a parchment library. He likes to study history between meditations. If he had a choice, he would go to the Three Mountains."

An hour later, Coldstream and McCauley were at dockside, dressed in what Coldstream called "jungle cloth," long sleeves and high shoes into which their trouser bottoms were stuffed. Coldstream smoked a cheroot. Every inch of dock space was taken by American ships, and out in the roadstead six stood at anchor, each a dull Navy gray. The docks were piled high with jeeps still covered with cosmoline, barrels of fuel, pallets of jerry cans, and the squat, unmistakable shape of tanks under huge camouflage tarps.

Coldstream said matter-of-factly, "We are being followed. Don't look around."

"How do you know?"

"It's Tuc. He doesn't know I have seen him."

A South East Asia Trading Corporation boat swung in through the pack of river craft idling just off the dock. It was no different than the others except for a red dragon's eye which peered out from each side of the bow and the slightly hunched aspect of its stern. It came easing in, a brown lateen sail limp in the wind and a small wake indicating it was moving under power.

Coldstream went down the broad stone steps to the boat landing, the steps worn smooth and slippery by centuries of fish scales, human sweat, bare feet, the ooze from copra bags, blood from freshly slaughtered goats and pigs.

The boat came alongside and they jumped in. "Keep going," Coldstream said to the man at the wheel. He wore a pair of old U.S. Navy denim trousers. "Ease out as if we're going across river. Don't use much power and put up the sail. You'll have to tack downstream before you come about. Stretch the tack as long as you can down river. When you have to come about, make it look like you're having touble with the sail and just drift with the current. Edge to the far side. I will tell you when to head upstream."

Like every other river boat McCauley had seen, this one was

dirty, smelled of copra, had a big hold amidship and a small cabin forward where the crew could sleep or keep their clothes out of the rain. The crew of three men were in their twenties. They squatted on the fo'c's'le deck, slapping cards in front of one another. At intervals, one and then another would raise his head and scan the horizon. McCauley realized they were lookouts. They seemed to have split the horizon into equal shares of 120 degrees each. They spoke in English, but with a queer inflicted lilt which fascinated McCauley and which he could not identify for a few moments. Then he realized it was the kind of English that had been taught to a few upriver tribes by young Sarkhanese teachers, who in turn had been taught by early French missionaries.

A half-hour later, the Haidho docks were well astern. They swung about and headed upstream. The water was muddy, silt-ridden by the monsoon, full of bits of debris and a few big logs uprooted and thrown into the stream. On one McCauley saw a drenched monkey turning quickly with the log, anticipating its motion and in a droll way enjoying the ride.

"Government cutter standing out from Elephant Quay," one of the men said, then slapped down another card.

Neither Coldstream nor the Captain swung his head. They went on looking over the charts. After a minute Coldstream stood up and stretched. Then he looked upriver.

"It's heading for us," he said in English so that everyone on the boat could hear it.

"Why would an employee of yours be tailing you?" McCauley asked.

"Tuc is a Communist. You know that. He's been up north a few times. I've never known how high he was in the apparatus. Maybe higher than I suspected. But if that government cutter is after us, then Tuc has telephoned someone in the Sarkhanese Defense Department. And obviously someone in the government is a Communist."

Coldstream took the helm. He maneuvered the boat close to the other side of the river, and wove in and out of the fleet of sampans and junks. After ten minutes, satisfied that he had hidden his movements, he altered course and headed for the fort of the Three Mountains.

Once in midstream, Coldstream pulled two levers under the cowling, and the character of the boat changed. It was shaken delicately by a high-powered engine, and McCauley understood the hump in the stern. The bow lifted out of the water, the frame of the ship shivered in quiet harmony of wood, metal, and high-powered engine.

"Twenty knots," said Coldstream, turning the helm over to the skipper.

For two hours they sped upriver. Coldstream showed McCauley where they were on the chart and where he planned to disembark.

"If we disembark here, I estimate it is only about a mile to the fort. However, it is all swamp. We will have to nose around for the firm ground nearest the fort.

"Captain, we are still being followed," the lookout on the stern said.

Coldstream spun the high-powered binoculars toward the stern and focused on the boat still more than a mile behind.

"Yes, it's the government cutter. And it's flying the 'heave to' flag."

"What does that mean?"

"It means they want us to stop. What the hell do you think it means?"

Coldstream was still looking through the glasses. "They are taking the canvas off the twenty-millimeter gun on the fo'c's'le. Do you want to know what that means?"

He put the glasses down, walked over to the chart. "Tad," he said, putting his finger on the chart, "a change of plans. We'll land just beyond that bend in the river. The government boat won't be able to see us. It's a hell of a hike from there to the Three Mountains area, but at least they won't know exactly where we're going. This boat will continue upriver and when the government people catch up with my crew they can say they are making a routine trip to Boa Binh."

"I agree," said McCauley.

"That's decent of you, Professor. Now put on this rucksack and try to look like a guerrilla."

A few miles upstream the helmsman edged toward the shore, bumping over a few submerged logs. He gave the boat more throttle, for now it was sliding through a mixture of weeds, slime, mud, and water.

"This is the closest," the helmsman said.

Coldstream adjusted McCauley's pack, which had been sagging low.

"Off the bow, Tad," he said.

McCauley jumped.

He came to rest as if he had leaped into a vast sponge. The water rose to his thighs. He started wading forward, Coldstream directly behind him. When they reached the protection of the first trees, they turned and flogged through the mud toward the mangroves.

The floor of the rain jungle was an ankle-deep mixture of almost liquid mulch—leaves, twigs, decayed trees, the bodies of a million insects. Beneath this yielding surface McCauley had the sensation there was nothing firm. They seemed to be walking on the barely hardened surface of a jelly-like earth.

It seemed possible to McCauley that they might sink into the earth and disappear. Then he looked at the trees and was reassured. The huge boles reached hundreds of feet into the air and were barren of leaves or branches except at the top, where they exploded into a vast green layer of leaves that almost totally blocked the sun.

McCauley felt oppressed. It had something to do with the light which was a filtered greenish gloom with a peculiar distorting quality. Trees which seemed yards away were suddenly only a few inches from his face and he jerked back from them. The air was thick and warm, and it flowed into his lungs like liquid. He had been in the jungle before, but never the low river jungle.

"We're not equipped for a long hike," Coldstream said over his shoulder.

McCauley looked down at his ripped pants already covered with slime to the waist. He could not see his shoes through the sticky layers of mud.

Coldstream took out a small compass with luminous figures.

"We're heading in the general direction of the Three Mountains. Rain jungle traveling is unnatural for most humans, like life in a submarine or a space capsule. It took me a long time to learn

not to touch a tree or a vine until I can see it clearly—a snake or a
column of red ants or a krait or a poison fungus might have
gotten there first. Sing out if you can't see me, even for a second.
If we get forty yards apart our voices will be soaked up by the
jungle foliage."

They began walking again. Sometimes Coldstream would skirt
an open space, warning McCauley it might be a mud hole. Once
he stopped beside a tree which had a gourd-like whitish plant; the
inside was full of pure water which they shared.

By two in the afternoon McCauley's lungs burned with the
exertion and the muscles in his legs ached. But the strange green
light and the silence affected him even more.

Once there was a distant sound, large and diffuse, and they
stopped. Coldstream explained that it was a rain squall, the kind
which dropped tons of water in a few moments and then moved
on, or suddenly dried up. This one came on with a hard, growl-
ing, rattling sound, like hail on a tin roof. It passed directly over
them, the noise growing to a roar for a few seconds. Not a drop
of water came through the ceiling of leaves.

Later, at a slight rise in the jungle, Coldstream called a halt.

"Tad, pull up your pants," Coldstream said. "Let's have a
look."

"At what?" McCauley said, and managed to grin.

"At your leeches."

McCauley pulled up his pants above his ankles. He glanced
down and shuddered. At the top of his socks was a cluster of slug-
like creatures, each about the size of his thumb. Coldstream told
him to loosen his belt and around his waist there was another
circle of the creatures. Their gray gelatinous bodies moved with
a heaving motion. One started up his leg, away from the stocking.
He felt absolutely no sensation of motion over his skin, only a
terrible revulsion and a desire to pluck and tear.

Coldstream tapped the ash from his cigarette and put it to one
of the slugs around McCauley's waist. The creature's head came
out of McCauley's skin, the gray mass of the thing weaved, and it
fell away. Moving quickly, Coldstream circled McCauley, applying the cigarette to one leech after another. Then he did the same
to the leeches around McCauley's stockings.

"Okay, now it's my turn," Coldstream said, pulling up his

pants and loosening his belt. McCauley, shaking a little, burned Coldstream on the first two tries. Coldstream cursed and laughed.

"If you pull them off, the sucker stays in your body," Coldstream said.

"I know." Then McCauley recited in the monotone of a schoolboy, "The sucker is a small, hook-shaped protuberance consisting of solidified calcium, much like the cartilage which rapidly decays into a highly toxic substance in the correct temperature and culture conditions of which the human body is almost ideal."

Coldstream applauded faintly.

"Bravo. A stirring lecture. I keep forgetting you patched up the troops out here during the war."

"We stayed out of places like this as much as we could. The Japanese were as afraid of rain jungle as we were. We had a gentlemen's agreement to fight along the regular tracks."

Coldstream nodded. "We're only a mile from the river that separates this peninsula from the Three Mountains. We will be there in about an hour." They began walking again. McCauley nibbled at a bar of compressed dried meat. He concentrated on attaining a kind of one-foot-after-another mindlessness. He thought of nothing, for how long he did not know.

Suddenly Coldstream vanished. McCauley moved ahead quickly, pausing before he shouted. Then, as through a microscope, he saw Coldstream had moved out of the rain jungle into another terrain. McCauley plowed ahead, anxiously keeping his friend—his leader—in sight. In a few steps he, too, was out of the rain jungle's green distorting light.

They stood in the late afternoon sun on a treeless hill which sloped away to a wide river. Across the water was the huge symmetrical form of the fort, a dull red color, almost exactly like the Red Fort of New Delhi, and out of place in the lush greenness of the jungle that surrounded it. In front of the fort was a small Buddhist temple.

"It's clever," Coldstream said. "The rear of the fort is protected by the rain jungle and swamp. See how there are only *bakal* trees there? That means quicksand. If an invader came from this side he would have to approach the river in full view. And across the river he has only one place to land: right in front of the fort, under the walls of the defenders."

McCauley was scarcely listening. He was studying the temple. "Lin wrote me once that this place had the same attraction for him as Angkor Wat. I'm sure this is where he has his library of religious documents. The interior rooms of the old fort turned out to be bone dry and perfect for a library. He once wrote me that he hoped to have as complete a library as the Buddhists have in Korea. He has all the literature of Soka Gakkai from Japan, the material on Javavarman VII who built Angkor Wat in Cambodia, the supporting arguments for the two hundred twenty-seven Theravada rules of conduct for *bonzes*."

"All right, all right, keep calm, Professor. We will have to get across the river and into the fort without getting killed. And then he might not be there."

A red-necked heron, legs dangling below the improbable body, came up the valley on the cooling airstreams of approaching night.

"The red-necked heron is everybody's victim in Sarkhan," McCauley said. "The Sarkhanese want it for plumes, the aborigines for meat. The fishermen train it to do what the cormorant does in China. And so the heron has become the most wary bird in the world. Just to survive it has to make a flying pass over a terrain before it can land to look for food. And when it comes to breeding it hides its eggs so cunningly that it defies the human mind to . . ."

Coldstream turned and looked at McCauley with admiration. The look caused McCauley to hesitate and then fall silent.

"Whatever kind of a nut you are, you're the kind we need out here," Coldstream said. "I never noticed the red-necked heron or any kind of heron before. But what you're saying is that the valley is quiet and no one is moving around. No men with guns, for instance. Right?"

McCauley nodded.

The light was fading as they started their belly-slide down the hillside to the river. They pulled themselves through taurus grass and slid over slick deserted paddies. They kept low and always they watched the red-necked heron, slowly, peacefully, easily spiraling down toward the earth.

"We have about a half-hour of light, fading light," Coldstream said, when they had reached the river. He stripped off his backpack and motioned for McCauley to do the same. "There is a CO_2 cartridge in the pack. Pull that string and the pack will be buoyant enough to keep you afloat. In effect it becomes a life jacket. Don't lose it. If we swim hard, the stream will carry us to the beach below the fort just about the time that last light fades."

Coldstream reached out and attached a thin nylon line to an aluminum catch on the straps of McCauley's pack.

They stepped into the warm water.

At least, McCauley thought, I'll wash off the jungle on the way over, then present myself to the Prince clean. And wet.

21

The Temple and
the Fort

The sun was setting. The center peak of the Three Peaks was quite incredible. Nothing McCauley had read prepared him for it. The tip of it glowed like pink jade. In the clearing below, the small red temple with its perfect proportions and its graceful cupolas was an exquisite Oriental composition. Twenty yards behind it loomed the old fort with its high lava rock walls and slate roof. The color of the roof and the rock blended with the brown-red temple.

"Observe," whispered McCauley, pointing, "how self-contained the old fort is. The tower contains the water tank. The small wing without windows is the granary. It was designed for a six-month siege."

On the other side of the lake, blue herons stood on one long slender leg near the shore. Hundreds of ducks swam and dove. A small herd of the dainty deer of Sarkhan came from the jungle to drink. A cormorant plunged beneath the lake's surface.

In front of the temple a man in a loincloth sat with his hands placed, palm upright, on his crossed knees. Three other men, fully dressed, poured water over him and scrubbed him. McCauley watched through his binoculars.

"It is the Prince," he said. "He is having his evening ablutions. I see the royal amulet around his neck." He passed the glasses to Coldstream. "We must wait until the ablutions are over. No one may disturb him at this time. It would be a violation of religious custom. Look at the Prince's face. His eyes are closed."

"How long do the ablutions last?"

"Maybe half an hour, but I don't know when he began."

A servant came from the brown house carrying towels and a

saffron-colored *bonze's* robe. He stood before the Prince, prostrated himself for a few seconds, got up, dried the Prince, and helped him put on the robe. The Prince stood up, picked up the remaining bucket of water, and poured a little on the head of each of the servants.

"That's the end of the ritual," said McCauley with relief.

The Prince and his servants were moving into the temple. McCauley and Coldstream walked to the edge of the jungle and emerged from the tall grass. They were now about two hundred yards from the graceful brown-red building.

"Strangers who interrupt the meditations of royalty—especially at night—well, it's not exactly in the best Buddhist tradition," McCauley made a wry face. "Well, here goes."

Coldstream nodded.

McCauley breathed in deeply and shouted, *"Grahnatumoko! Grahnatumoko!"* This was the old-fashioned expression for "blessing!"

A servant slammed the temple door. The low sound within the temple stopped. What looked like a rifle barrel poked through the latticework at the peak of the roof.

McCauley said to Coldstream, "Walk forward very slowly." In a sing-song manner, McCauley kept shouting, *"Grahnatumoko! Grahnatumoko! Grahnatumoko!"*

They were within forty yards of the temple. It was almost dark.

McCauley muttered to Coldstream, "Squat on your heels the way I do, but keep you hands on the ground."

They dropped to their haunches. McCauley kept up his chant, *"Grahnatumoko! Grahnatumoko! Grahnatumoko!"*

The door opened. A servant looked at them, then came out slowly. "Why do you come to the Sacred Valley? Only royalty is permitted here."

"We are friends of His Royal Highness," said McCauley in the same dialect as the servant. "I am Professor McCauley from America. I am the Prince's guest. I bring him peace and love and respect."

With tropical suddenness, night darkened everything. Simultaneously millions of fireflies rose from the banks of the

lake and flew over the water in a luminous cloud. Nearby a Sarkhanese nightingale began to trill.

The servant stood on the temple steps and talked with somebody inside. From the temple a gentle voice said, "Strangers, go
away. We will give you food and water, but then go away."

McCauley said loudly in classic Sarkhanese, "My dear friend,
His Royal Highness, gave me a Buddha amulet which I now wear
around my neck. I will take it off and give it to you. Show it to
His Highness and he will know who I am."

He heard the crunching of a man advancing. When the man
was close he switched on a flashlight, and swept it over their
faces. McCauley removed the amulet from about his neck. The
man took it, turned out the flashlight, and crunched back to the
temple.

In two or three minutes the man returned. McCauley and
Coldstream were still on their haunches with their hands on the
ground.

"It is possible you stole this from Professor McCauley," said
the servant. "Go away."

"Let me say a few words," said McCauley, "so that His Royal
Highness can hear me speak. When he hears me, he will know
who I am."

The servant flashed the light on and said, "A rifle is pointing at
you. Speak. And may the Prince recognize your voice, because
no Buddhist will kill another man except in defense of his
Prince."

"My dear friend, Prince Lin, do you not recognize my voice?"

A few moments later a soft voice within the temple recited a
poem in the ancient Sarkhanese language:

> Oh sacred Valley
> Guarded by the three tall giants
> At evening twilight thou art
> The place where all the beauties of the earth gather like little
>   children at happy play.

There was a pause, and the soft voice said, "What is it that
follows?"

"Your Highness," said McCauley, "the second verse of the poem is as follows:"

> The stars come down and dance above the lake
> The birds of night sing gaily
> And with love.
> My heart and brain unlock
> And gentle Buddha holds my hand.

From within the temple the soft voice called, "It is Professor McCauley! Bring him in."

"Rise and enter," said the servant, shining the light on the temple door.

As McCauley and Coldstream reached the door, a slight man in the saffron-colored monk's robe rushed up, carrying a small altar lamp in his hand. The light caught a lean face, sharp cheekbones, a newly shaved head, and a pair of uncertain eyes. Prince Lin was almost a perfect average in terms of Sarkhanese stature. He was five feet, two inches tall, weighed 115 pounds, and his chin, like most Asians', was beardless. Lin paused when he saw Coldstream, lifted the lamp, and there was suspicion on his face.

McCauley, still using the ancient court language, continued the poem:

> And when the golden stars
> Have tired of their dancing
> Over the sacred lake
> They return again to heaven.
> The birds, the animals, the trees,
> All go to sleep.
> And I too,
> Dreaming of truth and wisdom.

Lin brought the lamp down and swept ahead to embrace McCauley. "It is the poem I wrote for your birthday." He held McCauley at arm's length, peered at him through wet eyes. "Yes, it is you. Welcome. Welcome."

"And this is my friend, Edward Coldstream," said McCauley.

"You too are welcome."

"I have brought you a small and worthless present," said McCauley, taking a book from his bag.

"You remember our customs well."

"I learned them from you," McCauley said.

It was McCauley's latest book, *Sarkhan, A Thousand Years*. The Prince held it close to the oil lamp, inspected the binding and the title and then opened it. He read the dedication: "To my dear friend, His Royal Highness, Prince Lin Jhivonsang, the greatest living scholar on Sarkhanese history, art, and tradition, without whose library, encouragement, and generous assistance this book never could have been written."

Coldstream had been watching the Prince carefully. He had the small, almost delicate bone structure of the Malay, yet a Mongol strain was obvious in the broad face with its high cheekbones. The Prince's lips were loose when in repose, but strong and bunched with flexing muscles when speaking. His physical movements were slow, graceful, deliberate, restrained. Coldstream had the fleeting impression of a man who was delicately balanced among a number of pressures. He bent with the latest advice, was humble, but there was the suggestion of a hard, sure personality beneath his manners.

McCauley had once told Coldstream that Prince Lin resembled his ancestor Boshtunj III, the warrior priest. Boshtunj, who reigned from A.D. 561 until 597, had been a recluse, a mystic, a scholar, until the Khmer invasion of 570. He then became a brilliant general, ruthless, vigorous, and cruel. The soft body of the *bonze* had been toughened until his troops gasped as they tried to keep up with him—and were delighted.

The servants lighted eight oil lamps. The walls of the temple were lined with books and manuscripts and scrolls. Tall ladders leaned against the walls in several places, and Coldstream noted that they could be used both for reaching the high bookshelves and also for pointing rifles out of the latticework. At the far end, a bust of the Buddha smiled, but as always the eyes told nothing. Next to the Buddha was a wall of Arabic design in gold leaf and black enamel. A single shelf held a huge copy of the Koran.

In front of the religious alcove was a sleeping mat with a gold-flecked cloth on it. In the center of the cloth was the crest of Sarkhan, in royal purple.

On the right was a large librarian's desk.

In the far corner was a rifle rack and five submachine guns. Hanging on the rack was a bulletproof vest, also with the royal coat of arms painted on it. Coldstream had not realized the extent to which the Prince was protected.

The Prince led them to the library alcove, invited them to be seated. "I am eager to study your book, Professor."

"The first copy arrived as you started your meditation," McCauley said. "I was hoping to get it to you at our first meeting when you returned." McCauley paused. "But that has been long delayed."

Prince Lin looked at McCauley with the quiet, head-tilted quizzical expression which told nothing but asked a good deal. McCauley politely mocked him and Lin laughed.

"It is good to see your impudent American smile again," Lin said. "But you are tired. Was it a strenuous trip?"

Coldstream, aware of how dirty and ragged they were, said, "Yes, Your Highness."

"It was Hajn who told you I was here, so I assume you came by government boat," Lin said. "It should have been a pleasant trip on the river. And then an hour through the swamp by pirogue."

"Hajn did not tell us where you were, Your Highness," Coldstream said. "Professor McCauley deduced it from reading The Ancient Books and from his conversations with you. A government boat followed us and tried to stop us. We went ashore near Point Bodhi and walked here."

Lin's face changed. The slight smile faded and his eyes narrowed. His lower lip trembled and then steadied.

"In the maps of The Ancient Books," McCauley said, "the temple and fort are shown on the western side of the valley. But looking at some recent survey maps, I saw that the river bed had changed and you would now be far from the river which is described in the Books. We relied on the Three Peaks, which never move."

"But why did you not have the help of General Hajn? He could have made it all so easy."

Coldstream and McCauley glanced at each other but did not speak. They let the silence drag out, knowing this was a way of telling Lin something important.

The Prince closed his eyes, held his palms together in front of his chest.

"Why was it so urgent that you find me?"

Still McCauley and Coldstream said nothing. The Prince opened his eyes and said, "I know there is trouble of some kind. Tell me."

McCauley stood up, his round stomach showing through his torn, muddy shirt. He blurted, "We are foreigners, Your Majesty, and we have no right to interfere in your affairs..."

"Do not stand on ceremony."

"Your Majesty, you are two weeks overdue from your meditation. The coronation is approaching. The people are worried. There is much talk..."

"Did not my government give an explanation of my absence?"

"Yes, sir. General Hajn said you were in Haidho, ill with a cold. We made inquiries at the Royal Dispensary of the Peepul Tree."

The Prince closed his eyes again.

"So you suspected something?" Lin asked.

"Your Majesty," said Coldstream, pointing to the portable radio on the table, "have you listened to the news?"

"No, I have not," Lin said. "We have been unfortunate here. First, my battery-operated radio was crushed when it was un-loaded from the helicopter. Second, the helicopter had a break-down, so that it can neither fly nor operate its radio. The pilot has walked out of the valley and will bring back spare parts. The pirogue disappeared. So all I have received are messages which are trotted in. They said that I should stay here until the helicop-ter is repaired. At this time of the year, it is apparently too dan-gerous to walk out. What puzzled me, it is so easy to leave by pirogue and boat..."

"Your Highness, may I inspect the helicopter?" Coldstream asked. He wanted to see the helicopter, but he also wanted Mc-Cauley and Lin to have a few moments alone.

Lin did not respond.

"If it is like the one my company uses, I might be able to repair it," Coldstream said, aware he was pressing.

"It is in the small clearing behind the fort," Lin said, looking up, his eyes suddenly understanding. He made a gesture with his hand and wrist, a gesture both fey and powerful. Coldstream knew he had been given permission to leave. He bowed and departed.

"I am puzzled. I cannot put things together," Lin said to McCauley. "Things have gone well in Sarkhan. The King and I have had good advisors. Bandor the Chamberlain, General Hajn, and others. We were strangers in the Western world, but our advisors became familiar with those ways. We are not rich, but we are far from poor. But then suddenly there is a different mood, the air smells different, things seem to be tense. For some reason I do not feel I have been on a meditation. Rather, I feel I have been isolated."

Abruptly, the Prince changed the subject as if, with Professor McCauley, the eminent scholar of Sarkhan, he would gladly lose himself in the past. After dinner he would take the Professor through the library.

Coldstream returned suddenly, without knocking and out of breath. "You have been kept a prisoner, Your Highness," he said abruptly. He was wiping grease from his fingers. "That helicopter did not break down. It was sabotaged. Someone cut the wire running from the ignition key to the starter button. I repaired it with adhesive tape out of my pack."

Lin's head ducked away from Coldstream for a moment, then he brought himself erect. His face was expressionless.

"Would the pilot have known how to find the breakdown?" Lin asked.

"It was not a breakdown, Your Highness," Coldstream said again. "It was a neat snip. Any pilot who is qualified to fly a helicopter could have located it instantly."

In the silence a servant came into the room and asked about supper. Lin gave him instructions. His voice was calm.

"Captain, I am grateful," he said. He turned to McCauley. "It can mean only one thing. Someone wants to keep me out of Haidho. Why?"

McCauley took a moment to gather himself, then he went ahead.

"The Royal Council," said McCauley slowly, "has requested American aid. In fact, the King himself signed the document.

Your government said that Sarkhan had been invaded by North Vietnam on the Plateau des Luminaires. At this moment Haidho is heavy with American troops and arms. More are arriving every hour."

Prince Lin turned to see if the servants were close enough to hear. He allowed his astonishment to show on his face.

"It is incredible," he said. His face was working in small muscle spasms, but his eyes were steady. "Both my father and I are neutralists. We believe that Sarkhan must walk the middle road unless it is threatened by an external force. Our views are known to the Royal Council."

He paused and his concentration was so strong that his left hand started to tremble. He grasped it with his right hand.

"Merciful Buddha! Merciful Allah!" he sighed. "Why do all problems come at once?" He turned to McCauley. "Friend, you must know, of course, that I have the fever from time to time. The sickness comes perhaps once or twice a year . . ."

"The sickness?"

"You didn't know?" Prince Lin asked, wiping his chin. The jaw slackness had vanished now and the trembling of the left hand was slight. "It is the *tjah* fever." *

"The illness of Boshtunj, the prince who was first a priest and then a warrior," McCauley said.

"Can you tell me what happened to Boshtunj just before his coronation?" Lin asked.

"Yes, Your Highness. Boshtunj's tutor, who was acting as Regent, replaced Boshtunj's servants with spies and tried to murder him so that the regent could sign a vassal treaty with China."

"Professor, the astrologers say I am the reincarnation of Boshtunj," said Prince Lin. "I do not believe it. So far my life has not paralleled his. As for my sickness, the trembling you noticed is the first sign. Fortunately, I always receive a warning. Sometimes during the night, the sickness will come. There is a drug for the actual attack." The Prince pointed to a small box on his desk.

* *Tjah* is peculiar to certain Asian peoples. In some ways it resembles epilepsy.

Coldstream said, "But what about the permanent cure?"

"I don't understand," said the Prince.

"The permanent cure was discovered two years ago by a U.S. Navy medical team in Formosa. It is the common penicillin. I sent you the paper on this two years ago, Your Highness."

"To me?"

Coldstream hesitated. "Not directly. I gave it to General Hajn. He even wrote me a letter expressing your appreciation."

"General Hajn?" Lin asked, his voice puzzled. "Roshuro is one of the few people who know about my affliction. He should have..."

"Roshuro?" said Coldstream, tensing almost to rigidity, "who is that?"

"It is General Hajn's nickname to his intimates."

Coldstream stood up. "Your Highness, have you ever heard the word 'Konku'?"

"Of course, it is the bird who puts his head in the sand. People call scholars 'Konku.' When the palace people want to make jokes on me, they call me 'Konku.'"

Coldstream put out his hand, requesting quiet. He was trying to put together wild and fugitive fragments of the past, words he had heard, expressions. They slipped away, and then came up from some deep well of pain—and he remembered.

The words had been spoken often during the *mentado*. Then, shortly after he had been rescued, they had been spoken again by the officer in the Sarkhanese uniform riding in the jeep through the jungle back to Dao. Coldstream vaguely recalled how the officer with the gold tooth had prodded him, then said, "He's unconscious, but not dead. Well, comrades, when Roshuro takes the Konku's place, we'll nail all the white swine in *mentado*. And we'll leave them that way."

Coldstream held out his palms and told the Prince the story.

The three men stood silently in the gloom of the temple. Outside frogs began to croak and the first mosquitoes began their search for blood. Smells of hot oil and cooking vegetables came from somewhere in the fort.

"Hajn asked me to sign a blank parchment page just before I

came here," Lin said. His voice had a queer hard bite. "He said the first declaration of the coronation would be inscribed above it."

Coldstream and McCauley did not understand.

"No request to a foreign government, no communication of any kind, can be sent without the signature of my father and myself. Someone must have used that blank page to inscribe a request for American aid."

They were silent again, like men with a discovery before them but unable to understand it.

"The Royal Council would not recommend such a step unless they saw your signature of approval," McCauley said. "And King Diad would sign because your signature was on the blank parchment."

They waited again.

"The lines of logic cross and they cross over the head of one man," Prince Lin said. "General Hajn. He may be planning a *coup*. He may be a Communist. He may be an instrument of the Communists. Nothing else is possible."

"General Hajn," McCauley said slowly, "the great friend of the United States, the West Point graduate," not quite believing his own words. "But why?"

For fifteen minutes they talked over past events, trying to find a flaw in their logic. But there was no escape. They felt humiliated. They had been manipulated like puppets, misguided like children.

Prince Lin shook his head. "I won't deny it! General Hajn has been running things. I am a historian and a priest. For years I have been groomed to be a king who legally has unlimited powers, but in reality is nothing but a royal *zhavogh*." *

McCauley said, "It was the same with your illustrious ancestor, King Boshtunj."

"You are right, Professor," Lin said.

McCauley was thinking: Can he change into Boshtunj?

Coldstream was thinking of his list. It was growing. And the pieces were falling into place. Some of the nicknames still haunted him—"Mali" (the quick one), "Nuoc Tucki" (the big shrimp), "Gateg" (the crab).

* The closest this can be translated into English is "flunky" or "stooge."

22

The List

When Coldstream was at home, Taja dressed to please him—
and he liked simple, classic dresses and suits. He never had mentioned shoes, but Taja usually wore high-heeled shoes with her
Parisian dresses. With them, she also used a little lipstick and
light eyeshadow. When Coldstream was away, Taja wore slacks,
a man's shirt, and Sarkhanese sandals. She seldom wore makeup
when she was alone.

It was now 3:00 P.M. It seemed to Taja that Coldstream and Mc-
Cauley had been gone weeks. Yet not even a day had passed. She
was at her desk in the vault, running a tape on invoices. She was
not concentrating on her work because she was thinking about
Coldstream. She was certain he and McCauley would find Prince
Lin. But what would they do after they found him? Taja wondered if Coldstream had made a mistake. Despite his many years in
Sarkhan, he was still a foreigner. The affair was none of his
business.

The light on the intercom flickered, and the voice of the maid
said, "Taja, there is a man here to see you. He is from the American Embassy."

"Tell him I will be there in a few minutes. Offer him tea."

Taja left the vault and went to her bedroom upstairs. On the
way up, doubt flashed through her mind and she returned to the
vault to make certain that it was completely locked. Then she
went to her room and changed from slacks to a dress. She wondered what the caller might want, and whether the Embassy
knew that Coldstream was out of town.

A young man was waiting for her in the living room. He wore
a curious combination of clothes which indicated casualness yet
also meticulous correctness. The jacket was a light gabardine, cut
loosely, but Taja noticed that a quarter of an inch of starched
cuff showed beyond the edge of the sleeves, and the cuffs were

fastened with a conservative, yet expensive agate coupling. His necktie was a mild polka dot bow.

He stood up as Taja entered. Before Taja could speak, the young man—he was about thirty—said, "Ah, Miss Khubani, it is good to see you again."

Taja could not remember ever having met him. She extended her hand, smiled, and said, "What can I do to help you?"

The young man's face went blank for an instant. Taja knew he had planned to play the game: "Oh, you don't remember me? Well, I will remind you. We met at so-and-so's party." But Taja had not played the game back.

"I am Pierre Aubergeine," said the man, "assistant political officer at the Embassy. As you probably know, Miss Khubani, Captain Coldstream has been working with the Department of State and I have come here to get some further information on a most useful project on which he has been helping us."

"I did not know that Captain Coldstream had a project with the Department of State."

"Oh, yes, did you not know that he talked with our people in Washington?"

"I knew he had been to Washington, but I do not know with whom he did business. What information is it, Mister Aubergeine, that you wish?"

She wondered if a State Department officer would attempt to get information from a secretary without first consulting her employer.

The man opened his briefcase and took out a map of Sarkhan. Taja recognized it as one of Coldstream's maps, and from the number on it she knew that it was the one he had taken to Washington.

"Miss Khubani, Captain Coldstream left this map with us. He told us that each one of these little colored circles represents a person," he said, stopping and looking at her.

Taja looked back at him, in silence, relaxed, not offering any information.

The man continued, "You know about these colored circles and what they represent?" he said.

"Please, Mister Aubergeine, tell me what it is that you want."

"Captain Coldstream has a list of names which identify the persons represented by these colored circles on this map. It would be most helpful to the Department of State, Miss Khubani, if you would supply us that list."

"I am Captain Coldstream's secretary, but I do not know what you are talking about. I do not know of any lists that coincide with anything on any maps."

Aubergeine laughed lightly and stood up. "Well, we can solve that easily enough. Let's go down to his files and I'm sure we can find that list indexed either under maps, villages, or . . ." The man stopped because he apparently did not know how to continue.

Taja said courteously, "Mister Aubergeine, of course I cannot let you look at Captain Coldstream's papers when he is not here. I suggest that when the Captain comes home, you telephone him, make an appointment, and discuss the matter directly with him."

Taja led the young man to the door.

She returned to the vault and locked the door behind herself. She had a decision to make. How important to Edward were those lists of names? Taja knew she would have to come to a conclusion quickly. Within a short time she probably would be having additional visitors, asking for the same list.

Taja unlocked one of the filing cases, the heavy fireproofed one made of quarter-inch steel, and from it took a single sheet of paper. Written on it in Coldstream's small up-and-down handwriting were the names of the Communist agents in Sarkhan. Two or three names, recently added at the bottom of the list, startled her.

She spread the silk rag paper on the desk and memorized the list. As Taja looked at the names and then the names of the villages, she repeated them aloud. The list had fifty-one names on it.

She went over the list again and again and, a half-hour later, walked to the big wall map and, by memory, pointed to each of the villages and gave the name of the Communists associated with each area. Satisfied that she could repeat the list, she folded the special paper into a tiny wad, inserting it into a small aluminum capsule. The capsule was three-quarters of an inch long and three-eighths of an inch in diameter. It came in two halves which had minute threading at the end. In the same drawer where the capsules were stored, was a bottle of non-soluble glue. Taja took the tiny brush and coated the miniature capsule. In five minutes it was dry. Taja relaxed. She now would put the capsule in the hiding place in the garden. As she started toward the vault door, the intercom light flickered again and the maid's voice came over the loudspeaker.

"Taja, four automobiles are coming up the driveway. The first one is General Hajn's official car."

"I'll be up in a moment."

Taja began to panic. Very quickly, she took a handful of papers from the top of Coldstream's desk, crumpled them, put them in the fireplace and ignited them.

The maid's voice came over the intercom again, "Taja, General Hajn is here to see you."

"Thank you, I will be right up."

The papers in the fireplace were all burnt. She carefully broke up the ashes. Taja glanced around the vault for a place to hide the capsule.

The buzzer in the vault sounded loudly. General Hajn might be just outside the vault door. She put the capsule in her mouth, swallowed it, walked across the room. With fright she remembered the manila envelope which contained the evidence concerning the fifty-one Communists—affidavits, pictures, eyewitness accounts. Now she had no time to dispose of it. The buzzer kept sounding. Taja ran to the file and with a rubber stamp put the word INVOICES all over the envelope. She left it on top of the desk. Taja then opened the heavy steel door. Standing outside was the maid.

"Taja," said the maid excitedly, "General Hajn is waiting for you in the living room. He says you should come up right away."

"Who is with him?"

"He has with him in the living room his secretaries. Outside are four automobiles filled with soldiers."

Taja walked up the stairs slowly. She had known Hajn for a long time. She recalled twenty years ago, when she still had been the mistress of King Diad, that Hajn, an ambitious young man, was trying to pull his way upward to the realm of power. He was handsome and worldly. His years in America and at the Army college there had given him great prestige in Haidho and set him apart. She recalled how courteous, even gallant, he had been to her. She remembered the effort Hajn had made to be pleasant and helpful to everyone who might someday be of assistance to him.

Taja had not seen much of Hajn after she had gotten the small-pox and had left the palace.

Now she went into the living room. Hajn was standing up, his hands behind him, his thumbs moving around each other nerv-ously. He was angry.

He heard her footsteps and turned, and as he did so, the cor-ners of his mouth moved up into a mechanical smile.

"Taja, how good to see you."

"Ah, Panir, I know you have come to see Edward on some ur-gent matter, but I regret he is not at home."

Hajn's voice changed from one of greeting to one of authority, "Taja, we Sarkhanese understand each other's ways. Therefore let us not waste time. First, you know that I know that Cold-stream isn't here. I did not come here to see Coldstream. I came here because the American Embassy telephoned me saying that you would not cooperate with them concerning a list of names. You know what I'm talking about, do you not?"

"It is true, Panir, that a Mister Aubergeine from the American Embassy was here about a half an hour ago and he wanted a list of names which coincided with the markings on Coldstream's map of Sarkhan."

"Taja, I am surprised at you. You know that Sarkhan is in a state of emergency and that the United States is cooperating with us. For reasons which I do not wish to go into at the moment, the United States Embassy—and also, may I add, the Sarkhanese De-partment of Defense—need those names for the security and for the defense of your country."

"Panir, would your secretary let anybody go through your files?"

"I tell you, Taja," said Hajn, "the security of Sarkhan requires that we have that list."

Taja shrugged.

Hajn continued, "Give me the list."

Taja shrugged again.

Hajn said, "Taja, look outside. I have eighteen men from the engineer corps. Will it be necessary for me to bring them in to blast open the sealed door to Coldstream's office?" He pointed to the three men in civilian clothes who sat at the far end of the living room. "Those are my three secretaries. Once that door is blasted in, you know that I can find that paper. And only heaven knows what may happen to you in the meanwhile for resisting."

"Why, Panir," she said with a short laugh, "you know that is not necessary. If you wish to search Edward's office—that is as an official of the Royal Sarkhanese government—you are welcome to do so. There is nothing there but his accounts and a library of tape recordings of news broadcasts. Is that what you wish?"

"If you won't give me the list, I wish to find it for myself."

"Come, then, the vault door is open and I will unlock the filing cabinets for you. Bring your secretaries along. There are many files for them to look through."

Taja walked across the room with the four men following her. She led them down into the vault. After opening the filing cabinets, she turned to Hajn and said, "Panir, it may take you some time to look around, so if you will excuse me, I have other things to do. If you find the papers you want, you are welcome to them, but I request you show me which ones you are taking."

Hajn said, "You will not leave here. You will stay here while we search."

For an hour and ten minutes the four men went through the files. They started in the cabinets nearest the door and worked systematically to the end. When Hajn's assistants found something which might be of interest, they showed it to the General. Again and again after he had looked at some papers he shook his head and said, "No, that's not it."

In the middle drawer of the last cabinet, one of the searchers found what he wanted. He grunted as he pulled the folder out. Quickly, he showed it to Hajn. The title of the folder was *List of Communists in Sarkhan*.

Hajn took the folder to Taja and said, "This is the folder. But it is empty. What have you done to the papers?" He grabbed Taja's wrist in anger.

"Panir, all I know is that before Edward left he gave me an envelope and said if anything happens see that nobody has access to those papers."

Hajn shouted, "Where are they?"

Taja pointed to the small pile of ashes in the otherwise clean fireplace.

Hajn stared at Taja, released her wrist, and hit her on the side of the face with his open hand and sent her reeling across the room and against the wall. Hajn walked out of the room, his three secretaries following. A few moments later Taja heard the noise of automobile motors starting.

23

Battle at the Sanctuary

For dinner the three men had rice, bean sprouts, watercress, and fruit. The Prince and McCauley talked animatedly about old parchments and early rulers. Coldstream was both amused and perplexed. Amused at the detachment of the other two men, talking of parchments while a nation crumpled. Perplexed as to the next step. Radio the American Embassy? Fly back in the helicopter? Disappear in the jungle? Make a fight?

Coldstream considered their defense position. The temple was well built and could withstand a light rifle attack. The temple door was teak, eight inches thick, heavily bolted and hinged. However, an attacking party with hand grenades could throw them through the latticework at the top of the wall. There were no lights outside. It would be difficult to defend the place at night.

After dinner, the servants left the temple and went to the fort. The Prince insisted McCauley and Coldstream sleep in the temple with him, and the servants brought mats. Before departing, one of the servants placed an opium pipe and a little round box next to Lin's mat. Only one retainer, an old man, remained in the temple.

"The opium and pipe are ritual," Lin said, smiling.

"Your Highness," said Coldstream, "we are very tired and I think, with your permission, we should get some sleep."

"Of course, of course. It is selfish of me to keep you up."

"We would like to take a brief look around before retiring, sir. If you'll excuse us for a few minutes."

The two Americans were escorted to the door by the Prince, "I always lock this door from the inside. When you return, knock five times so I will know who it is."

It had turned chilly. The fireflies were no longer over the lake. The only sounds were those of the frogs and the owls. Clouds hid the stars.

"Tad, why is Lin not more excited? He is about to lose everything."

"He is a Buddhist, more inclined to meditation and less toward action. But I assure you, he is doing a hell of a lot of thinking behind that calm, scholarly manner."

"He may have to decide quickly," Coldstream said.

They turned towards the hills.

"You see the lights?" McCauley asked.

Both men concentrated their eyes on the mountain slopes.

The lights were strung together like beads on an irregular necklace, one or two disappearing from time to time, then sparkling on again.

"They're moving closer," McCauley said slowly. "We just have to assume they are a patrol of some kind. Nothing else makes sense. Neither hunters nor opium smugglers would travel at night."

"We'd better assume it's a patrol," Coldstream said. "Hajn probably had men in the hills overlooking the sanctuary. He must have sent word that we were on our way after the government boat returned to Haidho and reported us."

McCauley trembled a bit. He remembered the days of the Japanese occupation when he had crawled cautiously through sharp grass toward a wounded comrade. Always he had dreaded the moments before the first bullet cracked, when the first yellow gush of flame came flashing out of a gun barrel. And now the old, almost forgotten fear came back to him.

"We'd better move the Prince out of here," McCauley said. "Fast."

He resisted the impulse to turn and run. Just run. Run into the darkness, curl up in the deep grass, find the river and drift quietly to safety.

"No Sarkhanese would harm the Prince," Coldstream said.

"What if they aren't Sarkhanese?" McCauley said, keeping his voice steady.

"Meaning they might be North Vietnamese or Chinese?" Coldstream asked, studying the movement of the lights.

For McCauley it was suddenly too much. He felt a hard fierce rage at Coldstream.

"Coldstream, you cold bastard," he said in a low voice. "For years I've watched you and each time I look I like you less and less. You're not human. You're some crazy machine which never feels fear, always does its duty, always speaks in a calm voice, listens, but doesn't respond. If we get out of this, you'll never see me again. I'm sick of your goddamn frigid efficiency. Your competence makes me want to puke."

Coldstream did not turn his head away from the lights moving down the hill. McCauley grabbed him by the elbow and swung him around.

"Did you hear me, Coldstream?" McCauley said.

There was a moment of silence.

"I know, Tad," Coldstream said. His voice had a new sound in it, a weary sadness. "I've been told that before. Each time by someone I cared for. First, by an instructor at Annapolis who lost his temper when I corrected his solution of a trig problem. I admired him, but he was wrong, and I had to correct him. He bawled hell out of me, in front of the class, and then never spoke to me again. Later I learned he had recommended I be sent to a psychiatrist. Too much control, he said."

Later when his wife Spring had left him, she had said she was not equal to living with a flawless man. He was, she said, amiable enough, seamless. There was nothing to get your emotional fingernails under. He was too correct, too impeccable, too collected. He was a thing to admire, not a man to love.

"I can't explain it, Tad," Coldstream said. "I know that whatever it is, it irritates people. I don't excuse it and, in fact, I don't even understand it. But I can't change. I can only apologize."

Somehow McCauley felt eased. He had made a damn fool of himself. In his fear he had assailed his friend for being unassailable—and now he felt better, clear in the head, ready. Later he would figure it out, apologize to Coldstream if it seemed appropriate, and weave the incident into the fabric of his life in some meaningful way.

But right now a plan, based partly on an ancient diagram of the fort, suddenly fresh in his mind, was taking shape. It crowded everything else out.

They returned to the temple. McCauley knocked five times and Lin opened the door.

Inside, McCauley's manner changed. He put his hands, palms

together, to his forehead and bent his head. Coldstream, watching from the corner of his eye, did the same. McCauley no longer acted the part of a scholar talking to a scholar. He was a subject talking to a sovereign. But he spoke with authority. Lin's demeanor changed.

"Your Highness," McCauley said, "men are moving down the hills toward us."

"Sarkhanese," Lin said, "would not harm their Prince or friends of the royal family."

"Your Highness," McCauley said, rocking back and forth on his knees, "there is only one way to be sure."

For twenty minutes McCauley outlined his plan, using a calligrapher's brush and paper to illustrate. He sketched the fortress, outer walls and inner corridors, and spelled out a strategy. The Prince listened, palms upward on his lap, his eyes fixed on the face of the American professor, occasionally glancing down at McCauley's diagram.

"If the men come with evil intentions, we will do what you propose, Professor McCauley," Lin said. He smiled sadly. "Only an intellectual with a sense of history could devise so cruel and spare a plan."

Lin sent his retainer out to rouse the servants and instruct them. Two lamps were lighted inside the temple, and the young *bonze* who cared for the temple spread his mat outside the door and squatted. The light from behind gave his shaven head a bluish quality. His features, away from the light, were invisible in the deep shadow.

All others, following McCauley's instructions, moved into the fort. The gate was left open.

Lin, McCauley, and Coldstream went up the stairway to an aperture in the thick walls which afforded a view of the fort, the interior courts, and also the temple. The sky had cleared, and the stars provided a dim illumination. The outer wall of the fort was really a double wall, McCauley saw, with ten feet of space between the two walls. The passageway was blocked every fifty feet, and it extended into the maze of passages within the fort.

As Coldstream looked down he saw not the fort, but McCauley's plan unfolded beneath him, and he was astonished. The builder of the fort had intended that the outer wall should be breached and then the fort commander could run the enemy, like a herd of cattle, into various *cul-de-sacs*, squares, or cells.

"Men are approaching the temple," a servant said.

The patrol was made up of twenty men in Sarkhanese uniforms. A tall officer in a captain's uniform led them. They moved quietly toward the *bonze*. It was a skillful maneuver, fluid and easy, almost invisible.

Coldstream squinted. He had seen the captain before. Coldstream's palms throbbed. A lash of pain went from his palms up through his arms and shoulders. Unconsciously he stood on his tiptoes as if to relieve some obscure and strange tension. Then, he knew the captain was the same man who had cut him down from *mentado*, the man who carefully had murdered his torturers.

The captain had a handsome face, with flat angles unusual in a Malay, and a sharply defined nose. He had a gold tooth and a slash along his right chin. It looked new and raw.

"Where is the Prince?" the captain asked the *bonze*.

"The Prince is alone," the *bonze* said, his eyes looking straight ahead.

"But where is he alone?"

"He is alone within himself."

The captain shifted his feet, made a motion to his men, and they spread out, covering the entrances to the temple.

"Holy man, we are not here to do *koans* with you. There is a time for meditation and a time for action. The Prince is in danger. Tell me where he is."

"The Prince is alone."

From the top of the inner wall Lin watched. And McCauley watched Lin.

"Holy man," the captain said, unslinging his gun, "the life of our Prince is in danger. Keeping him alive is my business. It is urgent business. See this," he patted his gun. "I am going to aim it at you and count to five. If you do not tell me where the Prince is, I will pull this trigger." The captain held the gun sideways, its glistening angles giving off a smooth oily reflection.

McCauley looked at Coldstream and shrugged, asking a question. Coldstream nodded. It must be the man whom Xinh had described. McCauley felt dreamy, the euphoria which comes before combat, the desperate effort to pull away and forget where one is. Then, very deliberately, he bent back his right little finger with his left hand until the pain was shrill. His vision cleared. He watched carefully.

The *bonze* lifted his gaze and looked at the captain. He smiled and rocked gently back and forth.

"One must be ready," he said. "The first of Buddha's Four Noble Truths was 'Existence is suffering' and the first of his Five Moral Rules was 'Let no one kill any living being.' Is that not so?"

"It is so," said the captain, but his eyes were wandering about the temple, glancing toward the fort. His whole posture was a contradiction of what the *bonze* was saying. In an impatient voice he began counting, "One ... two ... three ... four ... *five*."

In a quick movement the captain went behind the *bonze* and swung his grease gun down in a savage arc. The butt of the gun against the *bonze's* head made a small sound, like a blunt ax going into hard wood.

The *bonze* collapsed forward, his arms splaying out to each side. His face rested on the stone of the steps.

"The captain meant to kill him," Lin whispered. "We will go through with the plan."

Lin turned to his closest retainer and nodded. The old man went down the stairs quietly and walked out into the loom of light from the temple. One of the patrol saw him, hissed a warning to the others, and twenty guns wheeled and pointed at the misty figure. When they saw the uniform of the royal retinue, they relaxed.

The servant said, "Captain, I'm glad you're here. The Americans arrived hours ago. They have the Prince prisoner."

The captain approached the servant slowly, his gun pointed down, but his finger still on the trigger.

"Are you the servant of His Highness?" the captain asked.

"Yes, sir, for thirty-one years. I am Tun Aung."

"I have orders from General Hajn that the servants are to assist me," the captain said.

Tun bowed.

"You must hurry, Captain," Tun said. "The Americans have persuaded Prince Lin he must move out of the fort. They said it is your intention to kill him. He believes a *coup* is taking place in Haidho. He wants to return there."

"Are they still in the fort?"

"Yes. They are preparing to leave from one of the rear exits."

"Do you know where it is?"

"Yes, sir, but we will have to move fast. The fort is a madness. There are many turnings."

"All right. Lead us," the captain said. He did not trust Tun and he was worried about leaving his rear exposed. Also he wanted to send a message to Hajn over the portable radio. But there was no time.

"The radioman and a corpsman will stay here," the captain said. "If anyone moves toward the helicopter, shoot him."

They trotted into the fort, the old servant leading.

Coldstream, McCauley, the Prince, and their small group quietly moved to the rear of the fort, where there was a command tower from which the passageways below could be seen.

It took them only a minute to reach the tower. It would take the platoon three minutes or more to reach the open area just below the tower.

"The ancient people were clever," Lin said, looking down at the maze, "clever in the ways of killing."

They heard the platoon moving through the labyrinth. Tun carried a small flashlight which made a dim orange light. The platoon ran down a staircase and into a long corridor.

"Tonight we may have to kill to survive," Coldstream said quietly.

Lin was startled. He looked quickly at Coldstream, then at McCauley. Then he reached back and took a Schmeisser machine pistol from one of the servants.

"How does it operate?" he asked Coldstream.

Coldstream showed him the safety, the trigger, the trigger guard, and how to reload. He laid two full magazines on the parapet in front of Lin.

"If it is necessary to fire, I will fire first," Lin said. He repeated, "I will fire first." He held the gun inelegantly against his robes, his posture uneasy.

The sounds came closer and then, with a clatter of shoes on stone, and clearly outlined by the servant's flashlight, the platoon came rushing into the *cul-de-sac*.

"Wait, here we must go slowly," Tun said. The soldiers stopped.

Coldstream scratched a flare against the stone of the parapet and, while it was still only sparking, lobbed it behind the platoon so that it blocked their exit. Instantly the *cul-de-sac* was brilliant with the hard light which comes from burning phosphorus. The platoon turned toward the source of light.

Coldstream watched Tun duck and disappear.

The captain turned to search the enclosure in which they were trapped. He could see little, for the light was too intense, too close, too stunning.

"Tun!" he shouted.

"Tun is gone," Lin said in a loud clear voice from above. "I am Prince Lin and I order you to put down your weapons. At once."

The captain wheeled in the direction of the voice, the gun came up in a beautiful smooth gesture and squeezed off a burst. The sound was enormous in the hard walls of the *cul-de-sac*.

The men opened their mouths, looking as if their eardrums were about to burst. They milled in confusion—away from the blinding flare, away from the walls, and finally together in a phalanx in the middle of the courtyard. Their guns searched the walls. They became a sort of primitive animal, claws raised, peering up to find its enemy.

One of the men started for the flare, but Coldstream lobbed a second toward the other side.

Lin waited. The gun burst had thrown dust and stone chips over his group on the parapet, but they were close to being invulnerable. Crouching, they had the protection of two feet of stone, and Lin could talk through one of the angled slits which had originally been designed for arrows.

"Captain, you are under my command," the Prince said. "You have sworn to obey the Crown when you were commissioned as an officer. As your Prince, I ask you to obey. But, I do not beg you to obey."

The Captain stared up into the darkness, trying to penetrate the maddening invisibility of his enemy. He muttered a few words of encouragement to his men. Then he barked out an order.

"Back the way we came," he yelled. "Jump over the flares. I'll give cover."

He crouched and his left hand was scrabbling for a second magazine. He fired bursts up toward the tower.

The first of his men broke and ran toward the flare. As they approached, the stone in front of the flare broke into tiny volcanic explosions. The troops froze, wavered for a moment, and then came back toward the middle of the *cul-de-sac*.

Lin had fired the warning shots. He had walked a few feet away from the rest of the party, easily found the safety, and then, as if trained, he shot the warning line in front of the escaping men.

Coldstream lobbed out still another flare, which landed only a few inches from the first one. The light narrowed the confines further.

"Captain, I ordered you to surrender," Lin said.

The captain turned, noticed the change in origin of Lin's voice. He was bent far over like a boxer who had been badly battered and must win with a single blow.

"How do I know that you are . . ." he started to say.

"You know I am Prince Lin because you were sent here to capture me and you have been observing me from the hills around this place for weeks," Lin cut in, his tone incisive authority. "You also know my voice."

The captain licked his lips. He glanced at the flares, at the smooth cold walls.

"Whoever you are, I am not going to surrender to you," the captain said in a voice which approached a scream.

The milling circle of men came to a slow stop, listening to the dialogue. On the far end of the group, closest to the flares, was a lean boy who could not have been more than sixteen. He raised his gun and trained it in the direction of Lin's voice.

"Just a moment, you with the raised gun, nearest the flares," Lin said. "Before you fire, tell me why you are firing."

The boy stood motionless, his face in agony. He tried to speak and stuttered.

"Comrade," the captain said in a distinct voice.

The boy's face cleared. He had an almost saintly look.

"Because you are the oppressor of the rightful aspirations of the Sarkhanese people," the boy said in a quiet voice. "You are a tool of imperialism."

"Now move out," the captain shouted. "Jump over the flares. Move. I'll shoot the first person who hesitates. You, with the big mouth, move first."

The boy did not hesitate. He jumped over one flare, started for the other and was in mid-step when Lin's burst caught him in the head and shoulders.

Instantly the *cul-de-sac* was a queer diminished battlefield. The odds were hopeless. Coldstream and McCauley fired almost straight down and it was impossible to miss. They simply hosed their bullets across the intricate exits, and the troops ran into the fire.

Men died in strange ways—in half-stride, in a crawl, in a wild jump, in a frightened cringe of retreat, wide-eyed, shouting anti-imperialistic slogans, on their knees and on their elbows. But they all died.

The captain died last. He had been hit in the thigh and the shoulder and the neck, but he could still walk. He staggered from dead soldier to dead soldier, picking up magazines and firing wildly into the sky.

At first light the Prince and the Americans inspected the carnage. There were eighteen bodies. Coldstream walked over to the one with the captain's insignia. Stooping over, he lifted the dead man's upper lip. It was stiff. Coldstream looked at the gold tooth, then straightened up.

"Two must have escaped," said Coldstream.

Prince Lin fingered the *bonze* robe he wore. "My role has changed," he said. He removed the uniform from one of the dead soldiers. The back of the shirt was stiff with dried blood. He put it on.

Prince Lin said, "At first light we will fly to the plateau to witness this invasion by the North Vietnamese—if there is an invasion."

"General Hajn says there is. That is what America believes," said Coldstream.

"I wish to see for myself. Then I will return to Haidho."

"It is dangerous," said Coldstream.

"If something happens to us," Prince Lin asked, "they will believe the lies in Haidho?"

"Yes, Your Highness. Someone should know," said Coldstream. "We can send a message to Taja. She can be trusted. But, Your Majesty, have you someone who can deliver it?"

"Write the letter," said Lin. "Describe what has happened. I will sign it, too. I have a young servant who will get it to your Taja."

A half-hour later, a royal servant jogged through the jungle with an envelope for Taja. It included a personal note from Coldstream, instructing Taja to put Hajn's name next to the nickname "Roshuro," and also to send the letter and the lists to Cogswell if anything should happen.

24

At the Plateau

"Where do we land?" the Prince shouted over the noise of the helicopter's engine and the monsoon's thunder. "How near to the plateau?"

Coldstream pointed to the map in the Prince's lap. "We go down here. With guides leading us, it is three hours of walking to the plateau."

"Who will guide us?"

"At my trading post, there are . . ."

"The are no trading posts there," interrupted the Prince. How could Coldstream have a trading post near the plateau, that wild mountain area with no people except Meo tribesmen? The Sarkhanese words for tribesmen were *Rasam Raito* which, literally, mean "thieves and marauders." Both men and women had black hair to their waists and usually wore only loincloths.

Coldstream explained: "Twelve years ago I made friends with the Meos and began bartering for herbs and furs. We cleared thirty acres and built log shelters. Now, during the monsoon, three tribes live there. About half of them stay all year and plant flax, and on handlooms they make fine linen."

Prince Lin found this hard to believe. As a boy he had climbed these mountains and he remembered the Meos. At night it had been necessary to post armed guards for protection.

"Are the Meos to be trusted as guides?"

"They are loyal friends," said Coldstream. "Also, the Meos hate the Vietnamese . . ."

The helicopter spun and dropped in an air pocket. Loose papers rose up in the aircraft. The sky became darker.

"We are in the worst part of the storm now. If we . . ." Coldstream was interrupted by a violent lurch, ". . . can get through the next hour . . ."

The Prince said, "I am tired. I will sleep for the rest of the trip." Relaxing, he shut his eyes, meditated for a few moments, then fell asleep, despite the jolting of the helicopter. He muttered and obviously dreamed. Coldstream wondered if, like a confused child, Lin was retreating from what he did not understand.

When the Prince opened his eyes, after a spine-jarring jolt, the helicopter was on the ground. Coldstream and McCauley had unsnapped their seat belts and were moving toward the hatch.

Outside the morning sky was dark. Rain was rattling on the helicopter. They were in the middle of the small circular clearing of the mountain jungle. Five people with rifles trotted toward the helicopter.

Coldstream quickly opened the hatch, and jumped down into the rain. He walked toward the men who now held their rifles waist-high. Then the man in front raised his hand and ran toward him. The two embraced. "About your son I am sorry, Apayki," Coldstream said in the Meo dialect. "More sorry than I can say. You know I talked to Bui on the radio just before they shot him?"

"He died a Meo death," Apayki said. "One must die in some manner. It is important to die well."

"Did you recover Bui's body?" Coldstream asked.

The Meos believed in ancestor worship and it was important that the body of the deceased be properly buried close to the village.

"We did," Apayki said, barely audible. "He was hard to find. And only the bones. But they are buried with his ancestors."

Lin and McCauley came toward them from the helicopter.

"Your Highness," said Coldstream, speaking in Sarkhanese, "this is Apayki, chief of the five tribes of these mountains."

The Prince saw a small skinny man barely five feet tall and naked except for a loincloth. Around his waist were two straps. One supported a pistol and cartridges, the other a long knife in a sheath. He had dark eyes in a dark, wrinkled face.

Yes, thought Prince Lin, looking at the man, he is old, but he is very much alive.

The old man stared at the Prince, then walked forward and fingered the jade amulet which hung around Prince Lin's neck.

Still holding the amulet, the man spoke in the mountain dialect. "Are you King?"

Before the Prince could reply, McCauley quickly said, "Your Highness, he is asking if you are the King."

Prince Lin, staring back at the tribal chieftain said, also in dialect, "No, leader of mountain men, I am the son of the King."

For a moment the old man bowed his head. Then he turned to McCauley. "You are a friend of Buan Suang?" Apayki asked in uncertain Sarkhanese.

"Yes, Apayki, I am a friend of Coldstream's. My name is McCauley."

Apayki showed not the slightest interest in the helicopter. The only machine which the mountain people were interested in was the gun.

"Why is the son of the King here?"

"I wish to see the battle which is taking place on the plateau," Lin said.

"The son of the King should know that his troops are not fighting. They are playing war games. Half of them make believe that they are Vietnamese. They have a good time. There are not enough Vietnamese to have battles."

"There are Vietnamese here?" said the Prince.

"A patrol of them, twenty-one men in all."

"What do they do?" Lin asked.

"They live in a cave about five miles up the mountain. Sometimes they go down and watch your troops playing at their battles."

Another tribesman, much lighter-skinned and six inches taller than the chief, stepped forward and shook Coldstream's hand.

Coldstream turned to the Prince. "Your Majesty, this is Pattejmoda, who is the manager of my trading post here."

"There is much to do," said Apayki, "if you want to get to the plateau in time to see the games."

He jogged ahead of them the few hundred yards to his village, several very large log huts. Women and children peered out the doors. They stopped in front of one hut and Bui's widow came out. She was a tiny woman, less than five feet tall, and she carried a baby on her hip. She avoided meeting their eyes, but she moved in front of Coldstream and in a very low voice told him that Bui's remains were safely home and his spirit would live on.

Apayki took them to the largest hut in the village. At one end was a raised fireplace with the hindquarters of a deer cooking on a spit. With quick swipes of his knife, Apayki cut off chunks of meat and handed them to his guests.

"In three hours the rain will stop on the plateau and the make-believe war will begin," he said. "It only happens when the rain stops. And then the plane comes overhead. If we go quickly, we can get there in two and a half hours." He looked into the Prince's face. "There is trouble."

"Apayki, what makes you believe there is trouble?" asked the Prince.

"Son of the King, at the trading post there is a little shiny box which brings us words and music," said Apayki. "For a full day the shiny box has not spoken from Haidho. But this morning we learned that there is to be an important announcement to all Sarkhanese. It is to be spoken at two o'clock by General Hajn, the Minister of Defense. If it is for all Sarkhanese, then why is it not the son of the King who speaks? If it is an announcement to all people, it should be made by the Prince. Therefore, I believe there is trouble."

The Prince did not reply.

"We will start immediately," said Apayki.

The Prince was glad that the trip had been strenuous. For an hour and a half the hard walking had kept him from thinking. He wondered what had become of his father in Haidho. He knew himself to be in exile.

He should not have trusted anyone. Being a scholar for so long had corrupted and paralyzed him, and removed him from reality. He, Prince Lin, was the only son of King Diad and his official queen. It was the Prince's duty to stay close to reality. The Prince remembered back over the last ten years. General Hajn had been one who had encouraged him to build a library and to write.

The Prince looked sharply at Coldstream and McCauley. A great suspicion jolted through him. Whom could he trust? Were these two foreigners part of a plot, perhaps, with General

Hajn? Captain Coldstream had been a friend of Hajn's for years.

Within an hour they reached the rolling hills. Apayki stopped. His mouth puckered and he made the call of a mountain dove. Seconds later, a similar call came from ahead.

Apayki began trotting again, now to the left and toward a wooded section. Soon the flat cleared part of the plateau came into view. On the northern half, scattered about in various camps, were some fifteen hundred troops in black North Vietnamese uniforms, and beyond them was an airplane. Its two propellers were turning slowly.

Apayki said, "The make-believe fight will begin soon. The sky should clear in a few minutes."

McCauley looked at his watch. It was 1:20.

Coldstream took out his binoculars from the knapsack and raised them to his eyes. He looked for a few moments, then handed the glasses to the Prince.

First the Prince examined the northern camps. It was true, most of the men there were in Vietnamese uniform. A few still were putting their black clothes over Sarkhanese uniforms. Some officers were putting North Vietnamese flags on sticks. He moved the glasses to the south. There, in the other camp, men in Sarkhanese uniforms were picking up their rifles. He looked at the airplane, a DC-3 with the markings of the North Vietnamese Air Force. It was beginning to taxi along the field. It increased speed, heading directly into the north wind, and soon it was airborne, disappearing quickly into the fog bank on the south edge of the plateau.

Apayki said, "It is always this way. The plane disappears until the make-believe begins, then it comes back."

One of the men in North Vietnamese uniform, an officer, blew a whistle and abruptly everyone began moving. Tarpaulins were yanked off equipment. Heavy machine guns were swiveled so that their barrels pointed south toward the Sarkhanese troops. Mortars were dragged into place, also pointing to the south. All covers now had been removed from a line of what had looked like covered haystacks. Through the binoculars Prince Lin saw there were twelve Russian heavy "Stalin" tanks. They too had North Vietnamese markings. He looked again and saw that they were not tanks. They were replicas of tanks made from wood—and appeared to be real. Underneath each a wagon was pushed by several men.

The officer who had blown the whistle was pointing almost directly overhead. Whatever he saw was important. Another officer blew a whistle and the plateau erupted in noise and spurts of flame. The Prince was startled by the sudden explosion of sound and action. On both sides, machine gun tracers made an intricate pattern in the air. Crews jammed projectiles into mortars and the projectiles came out with a hollow belch. The masquerading tanks on wagon wheels ponderously moved over the terrain toward the troops in Sarkhanese uniforms, and from the slight elevation where the Prince stood, even the treads looked massive and real. As the North Vietnamese tanks approached, a squad of Sarkhanese ran to blow up the tanks. The men appeared to be shot down, the whole squad reeling and staggering and dying slowly along the side of the road. Patches of explosion brought the black-uniformed men out of trenches and some of them also died. The whole area where the two small armies met was feverish, blazing—and staged.

The black-uniformed troops were pushing back the Sarkhanese, who had nothing but rifles and a few light mortars.

Out of the fog bank, flying at about two thousand feet came the DC-3 with the North Vietnamese markings. When it was over the field the door opened and parachutists jumped and floated down, landing behind the North Vietnamese lines.

A second plane, at a considerably higher altitude, was flying back and forth across the plateau.

Coldstream reached for the binoculars, "That is a U.S. Navy photographic plane," he said.

For about fifteen minutes the action, which appeared to be a ferocious battle, continued. Prince Lin watched the sham violence without expression, missing nothing. There were explosions and bullets and flames, but no one was shot. The desired effect was clear: to make it look as if the North Vietnamese with superior equipment and arms were driving back a brave, ill-equipped Sarkhanese Army.

The wind changed and the fog drifted back in. Almost as

abruptly as the weather had cleared, the skies became dark gray. A heavy drizzle fell on the plateau once more.

The officer blew his whistle three times, and the battle stopped.

The Prince watched the stage put back into order. The make-believe Russian tanks were pushed back into place and covered. The North Vietnamese removed their black uniforms. Yellow-tan clothes of the Sarkhanese Army showed underneath. Some of the troops were laughing. The DC-3 landed and taxied back to its former place on the flat ground of the airfield.

"Make-believe is over until the sky clears again. Maybe in several days," said Apayki. He put his hand on Coldstream's shoulder and said, "The important news broadcast."

They walked away from the troops, farther into the woods. The fog had moved in heavily, giving the trees a ghostly appearance. The group stopped and Coldstream took the small radio from his knapsack. It was almost two o'clock.

The Prince felt his heart beating quickly. A dozen terrible things raced through his mind. They might have murdered his father. Perhaps China had declared war against Sarkhan because of the American troops.

The radio announcer said, "We now play the national anthem. Sarkhanese, stand in reverence."

The Sarkhanese national anthem was played for twenty seconds and then the announcer cut in: "The news is of such importance that it is being announced personally by His Excellency, General Panir Hajn, the Minister of the Royal Department of Defense. General Hajn."

The deep, well-modulated voice came immediately over the loudspeaker. "Fellow Sarkhanese citizens, today I am the bearer of sad and tragic news." He paused for fully five seconds, then continued. "Our beloved Prince Lin, who was to be crowned the forty-second monarch of Sarkhan in a few weeks, has been kidnapped. We do not know where our Prince is. We do not know if he is dead or if he is alive. This foul deed was done by two American spies. A Captain Coldstream, to whom we have given hospitality for fifteen years, and a Professor McCauley. This traitorous deed was done yesterday. The two American criminals entered the temple where our beloved Prince was meditating.

"Members of a Royal Sarkhanese Army patrol came to rescue the Prince. Coldstream and McCauley murdered most of them. The next morning, shortly after dawn, they ordered the Prince at pistol point into the helicopter and flew toward the north. Our beloved Prince is either dead or in the hands of these murderers.

"It is the duty of every Sarkhanese to be on the lookout for Prince Lin. His Majesty, King Diad, has offered a reward of one million rupees to anyone whose action brings the Prince back to Haidho. A description of the two Americans will follow this announcement. They are dangerous and should be killed on sight. Long Live Sarkhan!"

The broadcast ended.

Everyone looked at Prince Lin.

Apayki said, "Son of the King, is it true? Is it true that these two Americans murdered your guards and kidnapped you?"

Prince Lin walked slowly to Coldstream and McCauley. He put one arm around each and then touched his cheek to the cheek of each. Apayki smiled. Lin told Apayki that they must get back to the helicopter.

Apayki nodded and took his hand off his knife.

Prince Lin said, "What General Hajn said is as false as this battle we just saw take place."

"Son of the King, I and my people will help you."

Prince Lin raised his hand in graceful acknowledgement of the the offer. He said, "In the morning, I must return to Haidho."

Apayki stiffened. He had heard something. He gave the dove whistle, and the answer came back, slightly from the north. Apayki repeated his signal and a minute later two mountain men arrived, out of breath. One of them spoke immediately.

"The North Vietnamese who live in the cave in the mountain have discovered the iron bird in which the Son of the King flew."

25

Ambush of the Ambushers

The interior of the cave was relatively dry. In any case it was the best shelter Senior Gunner Vat, Company A, 4th Regiment, 316th Division of the People's Army of North Vietnam had enjoyed in several years.

Twenty yards back in the cave someone was cooking rice and salted fish. They would eat soon, but not until they had gotten their tactical instructions for the ambush of the helicopter. And, Gunner Vat thought, the usual harangue from Captain Hien, the political officer.

Gunner Vat looked at the twenty other men in the cave. Only four of them were, like himself, veterans of the battles against the French and the siege of Dien Bien Phu. Most of them were younger men, some not more than seventeen. Even so, thought Gunner Vat, they are trained for jungle fighting, physically tough and well disciplined.

"All right, comrades, this is how we will fight this ambush," Captain Nguyen Trat said, putting the radio earphones down. Nguyen was a small dark man who had seen much action to the south of Hanoi, where he led the People's Revolutionary Party against the Americans. He talked little, but he fought well, and he was careful of his men. "We are going to kill three men. Two of them are white. The other is a Sarkhanese. It makes no difference if he is a Prince or not. Headquarters wants them all killed. And killed close to the helicopter. This means we must make sure that all three are in position before we fire. Do not touch the bodies. A photographer is being sent from the plateau to take pictures of the dead men. The three enemies will be along in several hours, but I want us emplaced long before they come. We will go after eating."

He squatted near the rice pot and raised his hand in recognition of the political officer, Captain Hien. The men squirmed lest

Hien begin lecturing again. He would harangue for a half-hour, telling the men that Vietnam would never be safe as long as Sarkhan was occupied by white imperialists. Gunner Vat had long ago stopped listening to these speeches. He was tired of being told that he was "the vanguard of revolutionary Asia." He wanted only to win the next fight and hoped always it would be the last.

But Captain Hien kept quiet. He was wise enough to know that before combat operations he should not harangue the troops.

When they had eaten, Captain Nguyen lined the men up along the wall of the cave, their weapons forward for inspection. No one made the mistake of having a dirty gun when Nguyen was in charge. He nodded and led them out of the cave. The men quickly tore new foliage for camouflage, stuck it in helmets and belts, and held a piece of greenery along their guns to dull their glint.

They moved in a diamond-shaped formation. If the forward men contacted an enemy, they fired, then dropped to the ground, and the rest of the men shot over their heads. Then the diamond changed into a crescent to start an enveloping movement. Gunner Vat had seen French, American, and South Vietnamese patrols completely destroyed by this simple maneuver.

They reached the clearing where the helicopter was secured. The men fanned out into a half-circle facing the opening where the path from the plateau came into the clearing. Working quietly with their entrenching tools, they dug shallow foxholes, slipped into them, and pulled camouflage over themselves. Three men guarded the rear.

In a few minutes the platoon was dug in and the clearing was silent except for the normal sounds of the jungle. Gunner Vat dozed. He knew that when the enemy approached they would make enough sound to wake him up.

When he awoke he immediately looked to both sides. The men flanking him were almost invisible. The average American, Gunner Vat knew from experience, could walk within a foot and be unaware of them.

The ants and insects had, by now, found him. He felt the familiar small crawling sensation. He was used to it and did not stir. Too often he had seen a soldier reach to scratch an ant and wind up with hand or head blown off.

Gunner Vat heard sounds down near the trail. He knew now why he had awakened. They were the sounds of men talking in loud conversational voices, men unaware they were walking into an ambush. He was astounded at the noise they made. The Americans must be fools to move so carelessly.

The voices stopped just short of the clearing. Someone laughed. Gunner Vat looked along the half-circle of Vietnamese troops. Nothing moved. This one was going to be easy.

A tall white man walked into the clearing. He went toward the helicopter, looked inside the cockpit, checked the rotor mechanism. He was whistling.

Gunner Vat carefully moved the foliage from his gun barrel so he could see the sights.

Suddenly, with a terrifying roar, the ground all around Gunner Vat exploded. He sat up, wheeled instinctively to the rear from whence the bullets were coming. He brought his rifle up. There was a sting in his hands and a blur across his eyes. When he could focus again, he saw his rifle had been hit in the stock and was useless.

Accurate rifle fire poured into the half-circle of ambushers. Gunner Vat saw Captain Nguyen stagger forward in a great dying spasm, blood pouring from a throat wound. In some of the foxholes the foliage heaved, but the men never made it out. A half-dozen were cut down as they emerged. Gunner Vat sat quietly, waiting for the final bullet. He had always known it would come one day and he was ready for it.

"Two prisoners, remember two prisoners," a voice shouted. An old Meo bounded toward the half-circle. "Stop firing. We have our two."

The other man still alive was Captain Hien. Meos flocked out from behind trees, from beneath foliage, from under great clots of moss. Gunner Vat knew that the ambushers had been ambushed. At the last moment before an ambush one is vulnerable from the rear, for everyone looks ahead at the target. That is what the three rearguard men had done, duped by the white man who had approached the helicopter alone and noisily. He had been the decoy. And the Meo mountain men had the moment they needed for the silent, final approach.

Moving quickly the Meos pulled Gunner Vat to his feet and bound his hands behind his back with a thin copper wire. They did it quickly, with hard jerks, the way one would truss a pig. It hurt, but Gunner Vat knew that the long pain that must end only in death was just beginning.

He was marched into the clearing. The first white man had been joined by another and a brown man, probably a Sarkhanese. The Meos crowded around and suddenly Gunner Vat was ashamed, ashamed because so many people had been able to surround them without being detected.

"Say nothing," Captain Hien said to Gunner Vat.

"Bind their ankles and put them in the helicopter," the Sarkhanese said.

The small powerful hands of the Meo threw him to the ground. The wire bit into his ankles. And then they were carrying him toward the big bird.

Senior Gunner Vat was not frightened. He had been frightened the first moment when the Meos had fired from behind. Then he had been preoccupied with the pain in his twisted fingers as the rifle tore at them.

Vat had seen death before. It was no great shock to him. Usually it was followed by the dreary digging of graves. He had been fighting since he was fourteen and he had been twenty years old when his artillery company had rained fire down on Dien Bien Phu.

Gunner Vat examined the helicopter with interest as he was placed aboard it. He had fired often at them, had inspected the carcasses of ones shot down, but had never been inside. He couldn't see much from the floor where he lay, but he was surprised at how it shook in the wind, even on the ground. Suddenly the motor roared, the helicopter vibrated violently, and Vat felt the swaying as the craft became airborne.

He looked over at Captain Hien. Hien trembled like a man in a fever. He had always been a political officer and he had not been in many fights. Gunner Vat felt no pity for Hien. Political officers were always disliked by the fighting men, but Hien was one who especially deserved to be. He had cashiered three men in the battalion when they had drifted into a brothel in Saigon a year before. Hien was certain they had gone for reasons of espionage.

"Captain Hien, who is the combat officer in charge of your unit?" the short fat white man shouted over the engine's roar, glancing up from the papers he had taken from the Captain.

The helicopter was vibrating savagely and, although Gunner Vat was frightened by the strange motion, he was even more surprised to hear the white man speak Vietnamese so well.

Captain Hien stared back at the white man, his face flat and expressionless.

"You really are no use to us if you cannot speak," the white man yelled above the noise. "We must get rid of you, for there is no reason in taking you to Haidho. We will get some distance in the air and then I will roll you out of the hatch."

Gunner Vat did not believe the white man. Neither did Captain Hien, he could tell. The white man was soft to look at, clumsy in his movements.

The white man turned to the tall one who was the pilot and gave a punch upward with his thumb. The helicopter shuddered, then, with a sickening swoop, went straight up. Gunner Vat was more frightened than he had been since his first combat moment. His fingers clawed at the smooth metal surface. It was unnatural to be moving through the air at all, but to be moving straight up was even worse. After ten minutes the helicopter stopped climbing, moving only up, down, and sideways in the wind.

The fat white man, breathing hard, first opened the hatch, then rolled Hien toward it. The third man, a Sarkhanese, sat toward the rear, his face impassive.

The white man had rolled Hien over twice before the political officer sensed that he might be serious. He arched his body backward, strained against the wires, writhed away from the open hatch. His eyes bulged.

"You wouldn't dare," Hien hissed at the white man. "It's against the Geneva Convention."

Geneva Convention? Gunner thought. What was that?

The white man laughed. He grabbed Hien by the collar and pulled him to the hatch, then pushed him half-way out, head first.

"Friend, you never signed the Geneva Convention," the white man panted. "Remember what old Uncle Ho and Uncle Mao told you about the Convention? Murder in the service of the revolution is good. So you went out and murdered women in front of their husbands and killed Catholic priests and Buddhist *bonzes* and everyone that got in your way. Don't tell me about the Geneva Convention."

The white man laughed again and it occurred to Gunner Vat that he must be insane. No one could laugh while slowly pushing a man out of a helicopter, hundreds of meters in the air, unless he was insane. Gunner Vat wished he had been killed in the ambush.

The short white man spoke to the larger man in a strange language. Then the short man grabbed Gunner Vat by the neck and pulled him to the hatch, face first. He was close to Hien. Gunner Vat's head was over the edge and he was staring down through empty space. He could see the river far below and the huts of the Meos. He looked sideways at Hien. Hien was rigid with fear. His eyes were expanding, turning red in the corners, almost bursting out of his skull, and he was screaming.

"Now watch your political officer go, Gunner Vat," the fat white man said.

Then, unbelievably, he gave Hien the final push. For a moment Hien was hanging in the air below him, his contorted face staring up directly at Gunner Vat. Then he was the size of a doll, growing smaller each second.

"Take a very good look," the white man yelled in Gunner Vat's ear. "Watch him all the way. You're next."

Gunner Vat stared. Hien's figure was now tiny, a dot, and then he hit the ground. He landed on the bank of a stream. Mud flew in the air. He could see Hien's figure for a moment, flattened on the bank. Then the mud seemed to roll back and Hien's tiny body vanished.

He had seen many men die, but this was a new way to die, Gunner Vat thought. His body cringed at the awful seconds ahead of him when he would hit the ground and explode inside and die. He ached to die in a familiar way.

The hand on his collar pulled him back into the helicopter. He was yanked across the compartment and wedged against a seat just behind the pilot. The other white man had shut the hatch. He knocked on the window of the cockpit and yelled something. Instantly the helicopter swayed with forward movement.

The fat one grinned into his face.

"All right, comrade," the man said. "Tell us what company you belong to."

Gunner Vat paused. Not because he was trying to hide anything from the crazy white man, but because his company had been given a special designation for this assignment. Did the white man want the special designation or the regular one?

"Tell us the truth and you will not be dropped from the helicopter," the white man said.

Gunner Vat scarcely heard him. He did not expect to live past sunset, but he would do anything rather than be pushed from the place. His stomach convulsed at the thought.

"Company of People's Liberation," Gunner Vat said, his mind made up.

"Louder, talk louder," said the white man.

Vat shouted, repeating his answer.

The tall white man at the controls turned, his face hard.

"There is no such company in any battalion in North Vietnam," the tall man said.

"I know that," Gunner Vat said. "We are put together for this single operation, to observe the false battle and spy, and are given a new name, but they promised we would be returned to our old companies when this mission was over."

"False battle?"

"Captain Hien said it is a new type of strategy."

The Sarkhanese bent forward and spoke for the first time.

"Gunner, if you are truthful with us, I will personally guarantee your security," the brown man said. He spoke flawless Vietnamese. "What is your permanent company?"

"Company A, 4th Regiment, 316th Division," Gunner Vat said.

"What does your company do?" the Sarkhanese asked.

"We are an artillery company," Gunner Vat said. The fear was still there, the awesome black fear, but it was overlaid with a slight flush of pride. "We fought at Dien Bien Phu. For the last four years we have been training cadres to go south to support our comrades against the imperialists."

"What sort of weapon did you man at Dien Bien Phu?" the Sarkhanese asked.

"We brought in and fired 105-millimeter cannons," Gunner Vat said. He wondered at the recollection.

"It takes a regiment to move a single 105-millimeter cannon," the tall white man said.

The Sarkhanese held up his hand, raised his voice to be heard over the noise of the helicopter.

"Later we will get to that," the Sarkhanese said. "Tell me when you started to fight for the liberation forces."

Gunner Vat told him the story, quickly and without exaggerating. The Sarkhanese seemed surprised that Gunner Vat had been a fighter at the age of fourteen. They talked about the campaigns which had ranged up and down the length of Indochina. The Sarkhanese knew much about the fighting of the last twenty years.

"Why did you join the army?" the Sarkhanese said finally.

"I joined a People's Liberation Front. To fight the French, and later the Americans and the traitors in Saigon."

"But the liberation fronts are Communist organizations," the Sarkhanese said. "Do you not understand that?"

Gunner Vat shook his head and his jaw set. He explained that he had heard it said many times over the Saigon radio that the liberation fronts were Communist, but he had only laughed. Not once in the years he had been soldiering had anyone told him he was fighting for communism. In fact, he did not know what communism was. He had sat through hundreds of lectures, but no one ever spoke about communism.

"Have you ever heard of democracy?" the tall white man said.

Gunner Vat shook his head with irritation.

"Yes. I have heard the word, but I do not know what it means," Gunner Vat said. Even though these men might end his life in minutes, he could not resist the old irritation he and most of his comrades felt when they were given political talks or asked political questions. "I only want to drive the white man out of Vietnam, have our own free elections, and return to my village."

"What are you doing in Sarkhan then?" the fat man asked.

Abruptly Gunner Vat felt fear rise up in his throat. He was frightened of this fat one who laughed crazily. He knew he must speak truthfully or he would go out the hatch the way of Hien. The little man was mad, and madmen had a special way of detecting the truth.

"We were told that we were threatened by Sarkhan because of the arrival of American troops and equipment," Gunner Vat said slowly, very deliberately. "We were sent to the border, which is the big river, and told first to observe the false battle and then to be prepared to instruct Sarkhanese comrades in the use of arms they would capture from the Americans. That, truthfully, is all I know."

"So you believe that the defense of your country is advanced by invading another?" the Sarkhanese asked.

Gunner Vat shook his head. This kind of talk confused him. The whole thing had sounded reasonable when Captain Hien had explained it. Now it was somewhat fuzzy in his mind.

"Tell us about the battle of Dien Bien Phu," the tall white man said. "It is very difficult to move a 105-millimeter cannon through a jungle."

"That is what the French thought," Gunner Vat said, "but we carried the cannon in."

"But it takes an entire regiment," the tall white man said, never removing his hands from the controls of the helicopter. "The truth now. You are not talking to fools."

"I am telling the truth," Gunner Vat said. "Yes, sometimes, it took a regiment. We carried the gun through more than one hundred kilometers of jungle. We were patient. We had peasants who volunteered to help us. We knew the French would never suspect us of being able to do it and that gave us determination. And when we fired down on them, they were caught by surprise. Complete surprise. My gun was firing at Doc Lap, the position the French called Gabrielle. Later the captured French told me that they did not know of the existence of my gun until it fired.

When it did fire, they expected it to fire only a half-dozen rounds. How could the ammunition be hauled for hundreds of kilometers through jungle which had no roads?"

"They came on the backs of thousands of coolies?" the tall man suggested.

"They came on the backs of *hundreds of thousands* of patriots," Gunner Vat said. Talking to this white man was reassuring. He was a soldier of some kind. He understood.

"The French laughed at us, called us ants, and we accepted the name. Like ants, we crawled through the jungle and built slowly, but every ant worked hard, and there were many of us."

The tall white man turned to the Sarkhanese and spoke to him in Vietnamese.

"This is a well-trained man, sir," the white man said. "He uses political slogans because he has been exposed to nothing else for over twenty years. But he tells the truth. Now, Senior Gunner, tell us why you fought so hard at Dien Bien Phu."

Gunner Vat had listened carefully to the conversation. He realized that the Sarkhanese was the superior person, but he could not conceive of how this was possible. He had never heard a white man say "sir" to an Asian in his life.

The helicopter dipped and swayed violently in the wind, but Gunner Vat forced the fear out of his mind. Outside, the monsoon had closed in, gray and scudding, and the helicopter seemed very fragile.

"If you are an ant and you are told on the French radio that you are an ant, you wish in a terrible way to destroy the people who call you an ant," Gunner Vat said, thinking very carefully. "But you want to do it as an ant. So we did."

For fifteen minutes he told them how they had wrestled the cannons across the slimy mountains, gelatinous rocks, and spongy hills above Dien Bien Phu. The Sarkhanese asked many many questions.

"When we emplaced our gun above Dien Bien Phu, we looked through a pair of captured French binoculars," Gunner Vat went on. "We could see the whores flown in from Hanoi and Saigon to serve the brothels of the French. And we thought the French must be both insane and contemptuous of us. We had not touched women for months, even though many of them worked beside us. We saw planes land and unload champagne. And we drank the water from the buffalo wallows and took our dysentery. But we thought the French were mocking us. And so we fought very hard."

Gunner Vat stopped speaking. The three men looked at him in silence. The helicopter giddily swayed its way through the monsoon, falling hundreds of meters, recovering, then soaring uncontrollably into the air. Gunner Vat was glad he had not eaten much or he would have been sick in front of his captors.

The short white man reached down and loosened the wire bindings about Gunner Vat's ankles. But he did not remove them. Gunner Vat did not smile. He also was careful to move his legs slowly. He did not wish to alarm the madman.

"You came here to train Sarkhanese comrades in foreign weapons," the short white man said. "How would you use a tank?"

Gunner Vat laughed.

"We would not use a tank," he said. "We do not care about tanks. When Sarkhan faces its Dien Bien Phu, the tanks will long ago have sunk into the mud or have been destroyed by patriotic sappers. Put a handful of *plastique* against a tread, insert a detonator, break a fuse, and walk away. The tank is useless."

"Then what would you have the Sarkhanese patriots use?"

"Artillery, machine guns, rifles, grenades, mortars, *plastique*, mines," Gunner Vat said, and then looked slyly at Coldstream. "The kinds of weapons that ants use. Even your American jets at ground level must fly slowly, and then one slug from a machine gun into such a beautiful machine and it is ruined and comes spinning down."

"To shoot down such a plane calls for great amounts of ammunition," the Sarkhanese said. "How will you move it into my country?"

"By bicycle," Gunner Vat said. He was pleased with the look of surprise that went over the Sarkhanese's face. "You find that hard to believe. But before Dien Bien Phu we bought two thousand Peugeot bicycles in Hanoi. Then we strengthened them with struts and wire and bits of iron. Each of them could carry five hundred pounds of material. That is as much as an elephant can carry. Five bicycles, each pushed by a single man walking, can carry as much as one of your trucks. And the bicycles do not need fuel or roads. Just pushers—ants."

The tall white man turned to the Sarkhanese and spoke in English.

"That is how they fought in Korea and Vietnam and China, Your Highness," he said. "Ants against the tanks and the fighter planes and the heavy artillery of the West. Napalm kills a few hundred, but that only makes the other ants angrier. And now the ants are turning their attention to Sarkhan."

"There is about this man something to admire," the Sarkhanese said slowly. "He is sure. He believes in something and that belief gives him a steadiness. In a way this man is admirable. But I would not like my people to be admirable in this way. This man has cut a part of his mind out, he has thrown away judgment and he has substituted faith. I would like to question him."

Gunner Vat listened carefully. The Sarkhanese was, beyond question, the senior person.

"What do you think of the Americans as soldiers?" the Sarkhanese asked. "Have you ever fought or talked to one?"

Gunner Vat thought a moment. He began slowly. "It was in the second year of the Korean War, caused by the imperialist invasion." He rubbed his forehead, trying to remember. "These are hard things to recall. I was very young. I had been sent to a school where we were instructed in the use of the American 37-millimeter anti-aircraft gun. The Chinese had captured many of these and they were being sent to help us in Vietnam. Our instructor was an American prisoner. We were surprised. We had never seen an American before. He was older than I, but not much, although it is hard for me to guess the ages of white men. He knew the gun very well. He was a good technician. He talked and one of our officers translated. The American had a very peculiar look. He looked like a child who is going to be punished. Do you understand this?"

"Yes, I understand," the Sarkhanese said.

"I would talk to the American after our classes, using a non-commissioned officer who could speak English as an interpreter," Gunner Vat went on. "Once I asked the American what he would like from the war in Korea. His face worked tears almost. He said he would like to go home and drive his automobile. He called it a 'car.' He said its top came down and it could go over one hundred kilometers an hour. That was all he saw in the war—an ending and then he could go back to his automobile."

"What did you want from the war for yourself?" the Sarkhanese asked.

"A chance for ants to build a new society," Gunner Vat said. He held up his hand. "I do not know what the new society will be like, but it will be ours. We will make it with our own hands. In one of the battles, I will be an ant that gets stepped on. I will die. But the revolution will go on and I will have had a part in it."

His three interrogators settled back now. The questioning was over. There would be no more yelling above the noise of the helicopter. Gunner Vat was tired and he was no longer afraid. He closed his eyes and went to sleep.

26

The Briefing

The meeting of the President's Special Sarkhan Committee in the American Embassy at Haidho had been in session for over three hours. Bandor, the Minister of Finance, came before them first. Very neatly, he summed up the economic situation, outlining fiscal requirements for the present emergency and also for possible all-out war. Bandor pointed out that, based on the experience of South Korea and Vietnam, an ally of America in an anti-Communist campaign could be debilitated. He concluded by presenting a rehabilitation program to be financed by the Americans after they moved out. All equipment would remain in Sarkhan and there would be a minimum of fifty million dollars in aid a year for five years, and a most-favored-nation agreement. Bandor did his task well. The Committee judged his requests to be reasonable.

General Hajn was next. He began a conservative, well-organized, and vigorous presentation of the military situation. He gave his estimate of what equipment and manpower would be required both now and when the monsoon lifted. He described the North Vietnamese invasion by using on-the-spot radio reports from his commander and reconnaissance pictures recently taken.

The Marine, General Patrick, asked a few questions about conditions on the plateau, but the rest of the military people were obviously satisfied.

Marcus Coit, publisher of the *Haidho Gazette*, had been chosen by the Ambassador to be the single journalist to report the conference on a pool basis. More than a hundred other newspaper men and women who had rushed to Sarkhan to cover the fighting agreed reluctantly on the choice.

Cogswell admired General Hajn's cool performance, knowing how outraged Hajn must be over the kidnapping of Prince Lin by two Americans. But Cogswell was puzzled. Something was distorted here. Coldstream and McCauley might be oddballs, but they would not kidnap Prince Lin. How much of the story is true? Every member of the Committee was aware that Cogswell had been working with Coldstream and McCauley. He had told the Committee after the Washington meeting that he had encouraged Coldstream and the Professor to find Lin. He had been noticing a change of attitude toward him by some of the Committee members. The kidnapping had hurt his position as chairman.

At that moment General Lindquist, the Air Force's eloquent spokesman, had the floor. The debonair middle-aged officer was persuasive.

"General Hajn brought up the question of techniques for repulsing the invasion, gentlemen. The new version of the F-105 is being rapidly adapted for jungle warfare. We will need six-thousand-foot strips placed in strategic places around the country-side ..."

"General Hajn has stated," interrupted Cogswell, "that there are few flat places in Sarkhan which can support a six-thousand-foot all-weather strip. The soil is too swampy. But, General, thank you for your views."

Cogswell turned to the entire Committee. "I would like your final views on how to handle the Coldstream-McCauley-Prince Lin affair."

He looked at Hobson, but Hobson merely stared back at him. No help there. Only a glint of satisfaction.

No one else responded.

"General Hajn, you have been most cooperative," Cogswell said, "and we appreciate your attitude. But it is still difficult to believe in this bizarre kidnapping of Prince Lin by two Americans. Why would they do it? What did they hope to profit? Coldstream has a substantial economic enterprise throughout Southeast Asia. If he has kidnapped Prince Lin, Coldstream will lose everything. Professor McCauley is a specialist in Sarkhan, a respected scholar, not a left-wing extremist or a political activist of any kind."

"It is not a question of belief, Mister Chairman, it is a fact," said Hobson. "They *did* murder the guards and kidnap the Prince."

"I would not like to be unfair to the two men," Hajn said slowly. "I considered Captain Coldstream a friend. But the evidence is unmistakable. Would you agree?"

Most of the men at the table nodded. Earlier in the meeting Hajn had brought in two survivors of the massacre at the Fort of the Three Mountains. They both testified to having seen Coldstream and McCauley march Prince Lin to the helicopter with a gun at his back. They also brought back photographs, authentic beyond dispute, of the Sarkhanese soldiers who had been slaughtered—a pile of tangled bodies.

"But what were Coldstream's and McCauley's motives?" Cogswell said.

"Mister Cogswell, there have been a number of defections from England and the United States to the Soviet Union," Hajn said in his careful voice. "Usually they were, like Burgess and McLean, men leaving in pairs."

"Meaning that homosexuals commit treason in pairs?" Cogswell said.

Hobson moved forward in his chair a bit and then sank back with a bored look on his face.

"Mister Cogswell, I just do not know," Hajn said. "The only other explanation I can think of is that the two of them are committed Communists who wanted to make a great offense to the Western people. Can you think of anything else?"

No one spoke. Cogswell had feelings of guilt and low-pitched anxiety. If he had not suggested it, Coldstream and McCauley might not have gone in search of the Prince.

"Of course, I can, General Hajn," Cogswell said, breaking the silence. "Politics around here is confusing. Maybe *they* did not kidnap Prince Lin. Maybe someone else wants to give that impression."

"No one in Sarkhan would kidnap or give the impression of kidnapping Prince Lin except Communists," Hobson said testily. "Unless they have the delusions that often go with the sort of sexual deviation General Hajn mentioned." He paused, then added wearily, "I read from their dossiers at our last meeting in

Washington. I tried to alert everyone to their character and background."

Something about the whole thing angered Cogswell. Sarkhan was misty, slippery, hard to grasp. But Hobson's intention was not. He was trying hard to make up the minds of the others. He was changing the value of information by emphasis or downgrading.

The door behind Cogswell opened and an Embassy official entered quietly. He put a folded piece of paper in front of Cogswell. Cogswell read it and sat still for a moment.

"Let's take a break," he said.

He went directly to the Communications Center, where the communications officer was waiting.

"I'll take the call in your office, on the scrambler, and no monitors," Cogswell said.

The officer nodded.

It took ten minutes to re-clear the circuit. When finally it came through, the voice on the other end was firm and clear. "Adolph, I got the full story. Those two so-called informants of yours have kidnapped a head of state. They are being called traitors, maybe homosexuals, and God knows what else.

"Adolph, I know things are complicated out there. But this sensational kind of thing gives everyone a chance to make it simple—dirty and sensational. And they're doing it. Anti-Administration newspapers are already linking these two men with your mission and with me."

"Sir, there is no proof . . ."

"Listen, Adolph, straighten it out. Fast. Unless this is cleared up, and cleared up completely, I'm going to have to make a statement. I'll have to call the shots just as I see them from here. When I do that your usefulness is ended. Understand?"

"I understand, sir."

Cogswell slowly put the phone in its cradle. The President's toughness was no surprise to him. Oddly enough, although he now knew he was in the most exposed and vulnerable position of his life, he felt a curious buoyancy.

The communications officer was waiting for him outside the room. He was nervous, blinking. "Mister Cogswell, we just had a voice transmission that Prince Lin's helicopter is going to land here at the Embassy in half an hour. Prince Lin and the two Americans are aboard. Coldstream is the pilot and personally sent the message. I know his voice. Also they have a North Vietnamese prisoner. Here is the transcript, sir."

Cogswell's face wore a tough, tired smile.

"I will give the message about Prince Lin to the Ambassador."

He walked quietly back down the corridor to the conference room. The conferees were in their seats. Cogswell went to the end of the table, looked at everyone before speaking.

"Gentlemen, I have news. Prince Lin and Captain Coldstream and Professor McCauley are on their way back to Haidho by helicopter. Coldstream is the pilot. They have a North Vietnamese prisoner with them. They are landing here at the Embassy in thirty minutes."

For fifteen seconds no one spoke.

That, thought Cogswell, is a strange reaction.

"Thank God!" said Hajn.

"I hope the Prince is alive," said Hobson.

"I request we adjourn," Ambassador Brown said. "There are some arrangements to be made."

"We are adjourned," said Cogswell. "But gentlemen, I propose to have Prince Lin, Captain Coldstream, and Professor McCauley in here. It may solve some . . ."

"Did Coldstream say the Prince was alive?" Hobson asked.

"They did not say he was dead, Jeremiah."

"Coldstream and McCauley will be under arrest," said Hajn.

"I will handle that, General," said Brown, going out the door. "As long as they land on Embassy grounds, I will handle that."

General Hajn knew he must get Lin out of the Embassy as soon as he landed—and McCauley and Coldstream out of Sarkhan. He started out to find a telephone. There was one in the anteroom, several down the hall. He heard his name called sharply. Marcus Coit wheeled across the room.

"General," said Coit softly, "right now I am the only journanlist who will witness this event. It would be wise to keep it that way."

Hajn touched the cripple's shoulder, walked out, and went to the nearest telephone, asked the operator for a number. He wondered if the telephone was bugged.

The phone rang in the fish-packing plant of the South East Asia Trading Corporation. A boatload of shrimp had arrived only five minutes before and there was confusion.

Tuc walked toward the phone, wiping his hands, giving directions to his assistant.

"The fish is going to spoil if we wait much longer," he said. "We can't process both the shellfish and the fish at the same time. Use the fish to make *nuoc man*. Process the shellfish."

The assistant nodded and trotted away. *Nuoc man* was a rich, salty sauce, with decomposed fish as its base, and is used throughout all of Indochina to flavor rice and whatever other cereal food was eaten. It is not as profitable as shellfish.

Tuc picked up the phone with his cleaned hand and said hello.

"I am calling for the fish-gutter," he heard the General say softly.

"This is he."

Tuc knew something was wrong. He listened carefully.

"That's enough," Tuc broke in. "It is clear. The ambush of the helicopter failed. We have to assume that our three friends got to the plateau and saw what is going on. You must block them from telling what they saw. If you don't, you will no longer be effective."

Tuc's mind raced back over his own career, seeking precedents for guidance. He thought about the tactics of countless revolutions that he had read about. He also thought, with a numbing pain, of the reception he would get in Hanoi if he failed.

"General, I'll take care of things outside," Tuc said, harshly but calmly. "You get the Prince out of the Embassy and back to the palace. Then get the other two onto the street. The people will gather outside to welcome the Prince—they will be angry at the two Americans. Call me in thirty minutes. I'll be in the office across from the Embassy."

Tuc put the phone down. Trotting to the wharfside, where a

foreman was supervising the unloading of green shrimp, he said he would be back in a few hours.

From a public booth he telephoned the Sunrise Hotel. The phone operator there was a member of the Sarkhanese Liberation Front, a patriot who had never heard the word Marxism. He put Tuc through to room 201.

"Have the others arrived in Haidho?" Tuc asked. The provincial leaders had been called in by Tuc the moment he heard of the slaughter at the sanctuary. They had instructions to stay away from Tuc and to contact room 201 and then remain in different hotels.

"Today is crucial," Tuc said. "The imperialists are trying a *coup*. The only sure force we can rely on is the force of the people."

Tuc gave the nineteen-year-old boy in room 201 detailed instructions on what he must do within the next hour.

From his seat at the conference table, from which he had not moved, Jeremiah Hobson watched General Hajn stride purposefully back into the room. Hajn's commanding height and confident bearing reassured Hobson. So long as Hajn remained strong and the country under U.S. military control, Hobson's plan would succeed. But now the return of that neutralist Lin might unbalance a beautiful and intricate plan—to turn this neutral country into a bastion of anti-Communism.

If Prince Lin has the facts, Hobson thought, he'll fire Hajn. If he has *all* the facts, he could execute Hajn by sundown. America's future in Southeast Asia could be made or broken within the next hour. Three men—a weak neutralist prince and a couple of American crackpots—might destroy U.S. foreign policy for Asia, the one Hobson had planned alone, independent of the President or the Department of State. Hobson knew it was the right plan. And it was in danger.

Ambassador Brown sat in his office, preparing for the helicopter's arrival. He instructed the Marine captain where the honor guard would stand, and how to handle Coldstream and Mc-

Cauley, and what to do with the North Vietnamese prisoner.

He had the Embassy front gates closed, told his chauffeur to put the Sarkhanese flag on the Embassy limousine and stand by to drive the Prince to the palace.

Assistant Secretary of State Abbott watched him and was pleased by his efficiency.

"Suppose," Brown said to Abbott, "that the Prince is wounded or dead? Why else would they land here? Do we give them asylum?"

Abbott said, "We're in one hell of a ticklish situation. Anything can happen in the next hour. Just remember this: the last thing the President wants is a revolution or a second Vietnam. All you should do is listen and keep calm. Make no commitments. Start nothing. If the Prince is dead, then listen to Hajn. As to the other two, get them out of Sarkhan as quickly as possible. Smooth everything over. Understand?"

Brown nodded.

A communications messenger brought a note to Brown.

The Ambassador read it and said, "They'll be landing in ten minutes."

The Committee went to the lawn where the helicopter would land. Cogswell noticed a crowd gathering in the square in front of the Embassy. He wondered how the populace had learned the news so quickly. Hajn, standing nearby, stared at the crowd, his eyes narrowed, his neck muscles tense.

27

Haidho Confrontation

As the helicopter circled over Haidho, Coldstream looked down at the city. There was no one near the palace, but small groups of people were gathering in front of the American Embassy. The Royal Square was gray and wet. The sun broke through occasionally and patches of the square steamed.

When Coldstream had radioed to the Embassy frequency ten minutes earlier, the controller's Arkansas accent came through clear and unruffled but with an undercurrent of urgency.

"The President's Committee on Sarkhan is meeting at the Embassy with General Hajn. They request you to land. General Hajn will escort the Prince to the palace."

When Coldstream had relayed the message Lin shook his head.

"Sir, you are going to have to face Hajn and have a showdown with him," Coldstream said. "Are you sure the Embassy is where you want to do that?"

Lin smiled, a slow tough smile, an expression Coldstream had never seen before.

"That is where it counts," he shouted into Coldstream's ear.

Coldstream put the helicopter into a long sliding dip toward the Embassy. The earth came into hard fast detail, faces swam into focus. He saw Cogswell, Brown, Hobson, Hajn, the military people from Washington, and the Marine honor guard. The helicopter hovered a few feet off the ground, shuddered, then dropped softly to the lawn.

The rotors stopped. Coldstream opened the hatch and nodded at the Prince. Prince Lin, caked with mud, his uniform torn, his royal medallion showing against his chest, stepped down the small metal ladder. Coldstream and McCauley followed, carrying Senior Gunner Vat feet first. Before they even straightened up from where they laid him on the grass, they were surrounded by Marines.

"We'll take care of him," the Marine captain said, pointing to the tied-up prisoner.

"He is the only living member of a twenty-one-man North Vietnamese patrol," Coldstream said. "'He's worth a great deal to an intelligence officer. Take care of him, Captain.'"

He turned and watched Hajn. The General bowed to the ground, apparently greatly relieved to see his Prince. Lin responded quietly and it seemed to Coldstream his eyes lingered overlong on Hajn's handsome face.

Prince Lin was introduced by Hajn to the Embassy officials and the Sarkhan Committee, who stood in a long formal line. The General managed it smoothly, remembering the names of the Committee members perfectly and introducing them in order of rank, Cogswell first, then Hobson. No one looked at the helicopter or toward Coldstream and McCauley, who were still surrounded by Marines.

A Sarkhanese Army officer came from the Embassy. Discreetly skirting the group of dignitaries, he walked toward the Marine captain.

"I am Major Phong of General Hajn's staff, and I will take custody of the prisoner," he said, touching the North Vietnamese with his foot.

The Marine eyed the Sarkhanese carefully. He glanced at Coldstream and then back at Phong. "Major, that will have to be decided by someone other than me. I take orders from the Ambassador."

The Sarkhanese major raised his eyebrows. "It is urgent that we have a chance to interrogate him at the earliest moment to determine what is happening on the *Plateau des Luminaires.*"

"I see your point, Major, but I have custody of the prisoner until the Ambassador orders otherwise."

"Men are dying," said the Major, his voice low and imperative. "It is urgent! Ask your Ambassador. I have orders, tell him, from General Hajn."

The Marine captain looked over and saw that the Ambassador was with the Prince.

"All right," he said. "I'll ask."

Coldstream and McCauley started to follow, but the other Marines closed in on them, forming a barrier.

"We have orders to keep you here," said a sergeant.

The Marine captain spoke a few words to the Ambassador.

Ambassador Brown excused himself from the Prince and strode over, as prim as a nineteenth-century missionary.

The Marine captain said, "Mister Ambassador, this is Major Phong, the one who wants custody of the prisoner."

"Major Phong, you're going to have to wait," Brown said, ignoring Coldstream and McCauley.

"Mister Ambassador, I fully understand that these Embassy grounds are considered American territory," the Sarkhanese major said, "but what this prisoner has to say is crucial, urgent, for the military situation of Sarkhan. He is the first prisoner we have had in weeks who can tell us how many North Vietnamese are committed on the plateau, their order of battle, their equipment."

Brown hesitated. He looked down at the prisoner. "Very well," he said. "You may interrogate him but within the Embassy. I cannot permit his removal."

The Ambassador turned to the Marine captain. "Have one of your men take the Major and the prisoner to the empty office two doors from the conference room. They are not to leave there without orders from me."

The captain saluted.

"Thank you, sir," said the Sarkhanese major.

"Mister Ambassador, don't you want an American intelligence officer at that interrogation?" Coldstream asked.

The Major halted, turned, and looked at the Ambassador.

"Captain Coldstream, you are hardly one to give me advice," Ambassador Brown said.

Major Phong directed one of the Marines to untie Gunner Vat's feet. He nodded toward the Embassy.

Coldstream shrugged, his eyes following Gunner Vat into the building.

"Hajn and I had a moment with Prince Lin," the Ambassador said after they had left. The anger went out of his voice. Coldstream thought he detected honest confusion. "The Prince said you two did not kidnap him, that in fact you saved his life, and he wishes to give you some sort of decoration. Frankly, I do not know how to evaluate this. We have information about Prince Lin's physical and psychological condition not known to you. In any case, the public mood is such that for your own protection the Sarkhanese government has withdrawn your visas and you are to leave the country within twenty-four hours."

"If the Prince has said we have done him no harm, you have no legal basis on which to withdraw our visas," McCauley said.

"Professor, *I* have not withdrawn your visas. The Sarkhanese government has done that. I happen to think they are correct. You don't seem to understand the amount of public indignation and hatred which has built up against the two of you. You have almost caused a break in diplomatic relations."

"The indignation was manufactured," Coldstream said. "It was not based on what we did."

Prince Lin broke away from the group of Committee members. Brown saw him approaching.

"Let me tell you right now," Brown said quickly, "that even if Prince Lin persuades his government to change its mind on your visas, I will pick up your passports. It is not in the interests of the United States to have the two of you meddling about out here."

The Prince approached, and Brown bowed.

"Mister Ambassador, your Mister Cogswell tells me that approximately six thousand United States troops have landed at Haidho," Lin said. "And a military aid agreement has been signed. Under normal circumstances I would prefer to return immediately to the palace. Now I shall meet with the members of this extraordinary Committee here in your Embassy. I wish to include Captain Coldstream and Professor McCauley."

"We will be honored with your presence," said Brown. "Let me inform Mister Cogswell."

Prince Lin came close to Coldstream and McCauley. Turning to the Marines, he forcefully waved his hand and they backed off a few paces.

"Hajn is resisting a meeting, but I have ordered it," Lin said quickly. "He keeps hinting about 'Your Highness' condition' and he obviously wants me out of your Embassy. He knows we have been to the plateau. You will come with me. But I will do the questioning."

Over the Prince's shoulder, Coldstream saw Hajn hurrying alone toward the Embassy building. He felt a stab of helplessness. He knew Hajn was moving fast to protect himself, but the Marine guard made it impossible to follow the general. He's going to telephone someone, Coldstream thought.

After one ring, Hajn heard Tuc's voice say, "Yes?"

"Hajn here."

"You're five minutes late."

"Listen," said Hajn, whispering, and he described what had happened.

"Hajn," replied Tuc. "The objective is exactly as before. Only the tactical situation is in danger of disintegrating. Do not allow it. Discredit Lin and the two Americans. If you are unable to do that, signal me through the window. Within fifteen minutes I will be close enough to the Embassy to see you." Tuc hung up.

The conference table was long and surfboard-shaped. Ash trays had just been emptied but the rancid odor of butts remained. There were scraps of paper on the table and large circles of condensed moisture where glasses had rested. A single pencil had been broken in two and lay on the table, an exclamation of surprise or anger.

Cogswell and the Ambassador led Prince Lin to the conference table, Committee members following. Cogswell pointed to a seat saying, "Your Highness."

Lin stood unmoving. The Ambassador hesitated, then stepped to the doorway and beckoned to Coldstream and McCauley. Lin sat down and so did the others. Coldstream and McCauley stood behind Lin. The Ambassador gestured to his assistant, who went for chairs.

"We are on American territory, Mister Cogswell," Lin said. "You should act as chairman."

"If that is your wish, I would be honored," Cogswell said.

"I would, of course, like to ask questions and this group deserves one explanation immediately," Lin said. "I was not kidnapped by Captain Coldstream and Professor McCauley. Quite the contrary, I was helped by them. In fact, they probably saved my life. The action at the Fort of the Three Mountains was in self-defense against what I believe was an attempted assassination." He paused. "I fired the first shots into men wearing Sarkhanese uniforms."

"The circumstances are somewhat unusual," Cogswell said.

"Quite," Lin said. His voice had a sharp quality. Half the men at the table looked up and stared at the Prince.

The single word hung in the air, changing the ambience. Hobson made a single slashing mark on his pad.

A thin harsh voice cut into the group. "Prince Lin, I suggest that the actions of these two individuals might not be exactly what they appear." It was Marcus Coit. He was seated beside Brown, his shrunken form deep and twisted in the wheelchair. "It is easy for zealots or mercenaries to put on a performance which might be quite convincing to you, but is still only a performance. Remember the Potemkin villages, the Trojan horse, the rehearsed performance."

"Your name, sir?" Lin asked.

"Coit, Marcus Coit."

"Thank you, Mister Coit," Lin said abruptly. "Now may I ask the chairman what is the view of this committee concerning the invasion on the *Plateau des Luminaires?*"

"We have been persuaded by considerable evidence," said Cogswell, "that there is an invasion by North Vietnamese troops on the plateau. Mister Hobson, you might like to show His Highness the evidence."

Hobson reached under the table and pulled out an attaché case, slim, custom-made of handsome Italian leather. The lock came open with a satisfying thump.

He passed the Prince a sheaf of photos. Lin nodded toward Coldstream and McCauley. They looked over his shoulder.

They recognized the scenes, but gave no sign. Hobson made a running commentary on the pictures as Lin turned them over.

"Number 1 shows a Soviet-made tank approaching a Sarkhanese roadblock," he said. "Number 2 is a picture of Molotov-trucks. Number 3 shows a regiment of North Vietnamese troops moving toward a roadblock . . ."

Lin came to the last picture. Sarkhanese troops littered the road, their bodies limp in death, machine-gun emplacements with the machine guns blown yards away and the soldiers' black bodies scattered as if by a bomb or heavy artillery shell.

"Charming," Prince Lin said in the same final voice he had used since he had entered the room.

The men at the table looked at him wonderingly. Perhaps the young Prince had taken leave of his senses.

"Charming as a composition," Lin said. "What Mister Coit would call a rehearsed performance. Ten minutes after these pictures were taken all these 'dead' men were walking about. The Russian tank is a camouflaged truck which was pushed by coolies onto the plateau."

"How can you know that?" Hobson said. His face was composed. He did not use Lin's title, and spoke with the voice used to subordinates.

"Hobson, I was there," Lin said slowly.

Hobson leaned back. The springs and the heavy leather swivel chair squeaked under the tension. Coit's breathing was audible.

"Hobson, who took those pictures?" asked Lin quietly, one finger tapping the photos. "And has one of your experts, a photo-intelligence officer, examined them?"

"Your Highness, it doesn't take an expert to understand those pictures," Coit said, his voice tight. He moved crab-like in his chair and it was an oddly aggressive movement.

Cogswell said, "Mister Coit, I must remind you, you are here as an observer only. Please do not speak again."

The Prince repeated his question. "Who took those pictures?"

"What difference does it make?" Hobson said, his voice sharp and condescending. "Evidence is evidence."

Coldstream glanced at Cogswell. The old man's eyes studied Hobson. Coldstream felt a sense of relief: Cogswell no longer trusted Hobson. It showed in his eyes and in the tightening of his mouth. Hobson's rudeness to Lin and his too-obvious effort to pass over critical information solidified a feeling which had been tentative and inchoate.

Cogswell said, "Answer the question, Jeremiah."

"The pictures came from General Hajn."

Cogswell jerked his head up and said, "What?"

"That's not what I understood from the earlier briefing," said General Patrick, the Marine, surprised. "I thought these photos were made by reconnaissance planes from the Seventh Fleet."

"Yes?" said Lin.

"I don't mean to question Sarkhanese competence," said the Marine, embarrassed but stubborn. "But, Your Highness, everything depends upon the level of professionalism, and we just don't know about Sarkhanese reconnaissance capability."

"A U.S. Navy plane was up there . . ." Hobson said.

"We saw it," interrupted Lin.

"But," Hobson continued, "it was too high and there was too much haze. The Navy pictures lack detail, they were indistinct. These pictures were made at a thousand feet by General Hajn's photo men."

"Did our photo interpreters look at the Navy pictures?" Cogswell asked.

"No. They were too blurred."

General Hajn remained impassive. He had been scribbling on a pad. Hajn quietly pushed the pad toward Hobson, who sat at his right.

First, His Highness is ill [the note said], *hallucinations, and also stress of abduction. He may even be drugged. Second, thousands of Sarkhanese will come here when they learn Prince Lin returned. Already assembling. Unless I take Prince to palace I cannot guarantee the security of the Embassy.*

Hobson stood up and spoke directly to Cogswell. "Mister Cogswell, may I request a two-minute recess. It is imperative that I speak with you."

Cogswell looked toward the Prince. Lin turned his palms upward in a gesture of both consent and resignation. General Hajn and Hobson joined Cogswell at the window and out of earshot of the conference table.

"General Hajn, repeat for Mister Cogswell what you just wrote for me."

Hajn did, quietly, indicating profound sympathy for his ailing Prince.

Cogswell said, "I suggest you bring this up so that Prince Lin can reply."

"In front of Coldstream and McCauley?" asked Hobson.

"Hobson," said Cogswell, "for God's sake drop your cloak-and-dagger game, whatever it is. There was no kidnapping and you know it." He turned and went back to the table.

On the opposite side of the room, Assistant Secretary Abbott cautioned Brown. "Remember, if there's a fight, keep it between Hajn and Lin. Make it an all-Sarkhan thing and keep Coit quiet. My God!" he said, pointing out the window. "Look at the crowd outside the gates."

Coldstream, too, was looking out the window. The crowd in the square was considerable and growing. It was the largest crowd Coldstream had ever seen in Haidho.

Tuc's assistants had spread the word over Haidho. They did it by telephone and messengers. Each had a dozen students belonging to the Sarkhanese National Youth Front at his disposal. The messengers were equipped with bicycles. They were patriotic students, so patriotic that they never dreamed of opening the messages they carried.

It happened, therefore, that many a Buddhist student took a message to a Moslem leader. The reverse also, and all in the name of patriotism.

In room 201 the assistant hung on the phone, making calls asking how many "crystals" had been contacted, how many placards had been assembled, what the Sarkhanese police were doing, how large the crowd was in the square.

Some of the "crystals" had been hard to locate. Most of them had jobs in schools or government bureaus or factories. Room 201 called up an additional two platoons of the Youth Front to carry messages to the "crystal" elements. The Youth Front people were already excited. They had heard of the kidnapping of Prince Lin and they thought the messages they carried were part of a plan to rescue Prince Lin from the American oppressors.

In the Embassy conference room, the Committee members heard the murmur of voices in the square outside grow louder. Brown commented that the citizens of Sarkhan were anxious to see their heir apparent after the kidnap stories and the radio broadcast. Prince Lin was again pressing Hobson concerning the Navy photographs.

"Perhaps the negatives are at J.U.S.P.A.L.," said Coldstream. "The Ambassador could telephone for them."

"By all means," said Hobson.

Brown nodded to his assistant, who went to the telephone in the anteroom.

Lin continued. "As I said before, I was on the plateau. I saw the fake Russian tanks. I saw the men fall dead and then get up when the plane disappeared. They fired machine-gun rounds over one another's heads."

"It is within the realm of reality that the invasion might be a misunderstanding," Cogswell said, carefully choosing his words.

Lin interrupted, "Hajn, what do you think?"

Hajn spoke humbly. "Is it not possible, Your Highness, that you were misled in what you perceived?"

"Anything is possible," Lin said. "But in an imperfect world, I am inclined to rely on my own eyes and my own judgment."

"Your Highness, on a matter of such extreme importance to our country, I believe you should acknowledge that in the past you have had certain difficulties in perception," Hajn suggested. "Your illness . . ."

Lin turned and looked steadily at Hajn for a moment. Then he half-smiled.

"It is true I had the *tjah* fever. Recently I discovered that penicillin cures it permanently, a fact with which you are familiar. You can rely on my perceptions, General Hajn. Can I rely on yours?"

Coldstream sensed the heightening tension. Then Hobson broke it with a question. "You brought back a North Vietnamese prisoner? Doesn't that mean there are Communists in the country?"

"There are Communists in Sarkhan," Lin said. "Some of them are masquerading as patriotic Sarkhanese here in Haidho."

"I suggest we bring the prisoner in," Hajn said, rising from his chair.

At that moment the Ambassador's assistant returned from the anteroom. He whispered to the Ambassador.

"The J.U.S.P.A.L. photo lab," said Brown, "cannot find the negatives."

"They can't find the negatives?" the Air Force general said. "That's ridiculous."

"They were not usable anyway," said Hobson gently. "It's no loss."

The small office near the conference room was hot. Gunner Vat was confused. He could not understand why this ax-face told him strange things. He expected to be tortured and eventually killed. That had been the way of the war for the last twenty years.

"Remember, Vat, if you are asked by anyone, you are to say just one simple thing," the Major said. "Repeat it to me."

Gunner Vat, who seldom perspired in the jungle or even in combat, was drenched with moisture in the confines of the little room.

"I am to say that I belong to a battalion of the 316th Division," Gunner Vat said, "and we have been engaged with an enemy on the plateau for the last four days." He paused. "No one will believe that. The 316th is around Hanoi. And your scouts would have seen a battalion-sized group."

"Vat, do not concern yourself with these things," the Major interrupted. Gunner Vat watched the Major and knew this man could be cruel, cruel just like Captain Hien. It was the nature of political officers, Gunner Vat thought. It was a cruelty of the mind and Gunner Vat did not understand it.

"What is the last thing you say?" the Major asked, leaning close.

"That we were detached from the battalion to capture the helicopter and to take whatever passengers were alive. We were to take them to Hanoi."

"Say just those things. No more. If you do well, you will find your way back to Hanoi. Understand?"

Gunner Vat nodded. He did not believe the Major.

It was so much like other committees Cogswell had chaired. *No one knew for sure what was happening.* Yet each man wanted to advance his own position, his own agency, his own budget. Each man believed only the evidence which supported his position. But two other things were unmistakable: Hobson knew what he wanted, and there was something bizarre, something hysterical, about this man Coit's fanaticism. Cogswell made a note to tell Brown to check carefully everything Coit wrote for the papers.

General Patrick raised his hand. Cogswell nodded.

"Mister Cogswell, I've had some experience with aerial photography. In Korea they told me that photographic intelligence indicated there were no Chinese moving above the Yalu. I was a colonel then. I lost almost a thousand men. Earlier, at Iwo Jima, they told me that aerial reconnaissance indicated that the Japanese were 'knocked out' before we went in. I was a captain in my battalion. We had twenty survivors. In Vietnam I saw the difference between aerial reconnaissance and reality. All of this stuff about being able to detect human bodies when they are moving through the jungle, ducking under bushes at the first sound of a plane, is a dream. There is no substitute for the guy who walks into enemy territory, knocking off the mosquitoes and leeches, and has a hard direct look."

General Lindquist looked at Cogswell and shook his head in embarrassment for the Marine. "General, we've got cameras that can fly over a golf course at seventy thousand feet, snap two thousand pictures a second and show a golf ball from the moment it leaves the tee until it lands on the green. We've got..."

"I know, you've got a lot of things," the Marine said bleakly. "But you don't have anything that will push aside the leafy cover of a rain jungle and tell me if a line of Communists are moving down a trail carrying a disassembled 105. Someone has to walk in to do that. And it's usually the Marines or the Special Forces who walk in, and just hope they come walking out."

Cogswell felt that now he must go beyond his usual firmness. Harshness might be required. It hadn't happened to him often in his long career and it was a strange experience. There were in the room too many divergent views, opposing positions, conflicting ambitions, contradictory experiences, gray ambiguities. The President had told him to go out there and get the facts. He had gone.

He had gotten the facts, he was sure, or most of them. But he didn't know how to put them together, how to use them. He had to hammer and scrape now.

The streams of people pouring out into the square had thickened. Tuc estimated about four thousand, and the crowd was getting larger all the time.

"I am going inside the gate, into the Embassy grounds," Tuc said to the "crystal" leader who carried his binoculars. "Keep your eyes on me." He turned to Chan, who stood next to him.

"We're here and dispersed," Chan said. "Everyone is ready."

"You remember the signals?" Tuc asked.

Chan pointed his thumb up.

Tuc pushed his way through the crowd. The people, densely packed around the Embassy gate, were discussing Prince Lin. Was he safe? Why did he not come out? Tuc reached the edge of the crowd, then ran to the side of the Embassy compound. He climbed the fence under a protecting tree, dropped to the lawn and went to the rear. Tuc walked close to the Embassy, to the right of the entrance. He found a walkway with hedges on both sides and sat down. Here he would not be noticed, but he could observe both the conference room and the crowd.

He took a banana leaf out of his pocket, unwrapped it, and picked at the dried fish and rice.

28

The Ants and the Elephant

"This morning, I spoke to one of the nameless ants who helped haul a big gun . . ." Lin said.

"Ants, Your Highness?" Hobson did not try to keep the sarcasm out of his voice.

"Yes, Mister Hobson, ants. What the French colonials called coolies. The gun was a . . . ." Searching for the right words, he turned to Coldstream.

"A 105-millimeter cannon."

"A 105-millimeter can-non," said Lin pronouncing the unfamiliar word oddly, "which the ant carried from Son La to Dien Bien Phu. Sometimes the ants with their big guns crawled only one kilometer a day. When the hills were like quicksand, they used logs as levers and moved only a few millimeters at a time. They were primitive ants. Hungry ants. Dedicated ants. It was only at night that they moved across the open spaces. Many of them burst their hearts in the effort, Mister Hobson. But they delivered cannons to General Giap . . ."

"Impossible in the Sarkhanese terrain," said Dobey. Then he added, "Your Highness."

"Impossible, hell!" said Patrick, the Marine General. "Just before every Communist victory I've heard the word 'impossible.' The Bay of Pigs, the shooting down of the F-105s by ancient Migs, the arming of fourteen thousand rebels in Santo Domingo —always impossible."

"And when the ants opened fire with their cannon," the Prince went on, "the French colonel in charge of artillery listened, climbed into a bunker, and pulled the pin on a hand grenade and blew his chest open."

Hobson said, "Gentlemen, this is supposed to be a life-and-death discussion of a nation in peril—not a biology discussion. Can we drop the ants?"

"Perhaps it would be an error if we did," Prince Lin answered.

"There is clarity in parables, even as your Jesus found. The nation you say is in peril is *my* nation. And the future of my nation will be determined by the ants." He turned to McCauley. "This American professor wrote the parable of the ants and the elephant so well in his book, *The History of Sarkhan's Survival*. It is very pertinent. May I request you to tell it here?"

"It is an old story," McCauley said quickly. "There was a time when the ants envied the elephant for the broad trails the elephant herds had smashed through the jungle. The ants were forced to live among the dense *mai-hok* and the *mai-rai-krua*, the impenetrable bamboo of the jungle. They wanted space. And so the tiny ants decided to challenge the elephant for his trails."

Cogswell shifted in his chair. He must bring the discussion to a point. But McCauley continued with the storyteller's confidence.

"The ants moved out of the bamboo and into the broad highway of the jungle. Waving their tiny feelers, they attacked the elephant, sure of their ability to overwhelm him. But there they were wrong. The elephant did not even see them. He thundered down the trail, stepping on the ants as if they were not there, and eating their bamboo leaves as he went."

Hobson yawned. The Marine General was rapt. "But an ant generation later, they lured the elephant into the dense foliage of the *mai-hok*. Here the ants were in their element. From the dirt they swarmed over the elephant's feet and up his legs and into his eyes. In the dense bamboo he could not move easily. He could not see. He was confused, maddened. Thousands of the insects crawled up the soft pink flesh inside his trunk, into his mouth. In the end the huge elephant was a pile of whitened bones."

"What does all this have to do with Sarkhan?"

Coldstream answered. "Mister Hobson, the ants of Asia contrive to attract the powerful elephantine armies of the West into the dense bamboo. America, with its Western mind and massive equipment, is only able to fight on broad highways. America is the elephant. The fraudulent invasion, the fraudulent mobilization, the fake pictures are the lures which duped the United States into the bamboo."

"Mister Hobson," said Prince Lin, leaning forward, "do you now understand what this has to do with my country?"

Hobson shrugged.

The civilian head of the Defense Intelligence Agency spoke. "With all due respect, Your Highness, there is no conflict between us. We've all read Mao Tse-tung and his theories of guerrilla fighting. But when you get down to brass tacks, modern war is between elephants. That is why we are helping you. In other countries of Southeast Asia modern methods came too late. But here, Your Highness, we're on time. You're going to have first-rate aircraft—supersonic 104s, the F-111 if you need it. Lots of firepower. Each of your men will be as powerful as a whole platoon of Sark Cong."

McCauley said, "Sun-tze wrote that the best battle victory is that which is won without fighting. He meant winning by deception, cunning, trickery exactly as . . ."

"Professor," Hobson interrupted, "Sun-tze lived centuries ago. The Chinese Communists won in 1949 because the Russians gave them massive aid. They gave them all the Japanese weapons."

"And we equipped Chiang's people up to the teeth with more and better weapons than Mao had," Coldstream replied. "But Mao did the long hard job of political indoctrination before he gave peasants guns. Mao's ants had not only guns, they also had belief."

"You're not suggesting that communism is a superior cause to ours?" Coit asked. "Or are you?"

Brown turned and spoke in a sharp low voice to Coit. The cripple coiled back in his chair, his eyes fixed on Coldstream. Coldstream looked at him curiously. There was more here than just the rabid anti-Communist, the fanatic reactionary. Coit was motivated by a common mixture—hate and the desire for power. With power, he could smash those he hated, the tall ones, the ones with whole bodies.

"I think we can now take Captain Coldstream's patriotism for granted," Cogswell said calmly.

"Mister Chairman, we are merely rehashing the Mao Tse-tung theory of guerrilla warfare," Hobson said impatiently. "It's an antiquated myth. These techniques don't work anymore. Warfare today is simply a careful calculus of guns, planes, firepower, supply lines. You Asians have bit on the Mao theory and you're hypnotized by it."

Cogswell bent forward to stop Hobson's insult, but Prince Lin was already speaking, forcefully but without anger.

"I am a neutralist. I object to foreign troops. But if I saw one company of U.S. soldiers who—besides being skilled warriors—could help peasants build houses, make compost heaps, teach literacy to my people, give medical help in the villages, clean out old water wells, then I would abandon my neutralism. For then the soldiers would be building a belief more powerful than any gun."

Coldstream looked around the table. Only Hajn and Hobson knew they were at the edge of a defeat. The rest were listening attentively to Lin. Cogswell moved his eyes occasionally from Lin's face and studied Hobson and Hajn. Coldstream felt a sense of relief. Cogswell understood and that was the important thing.

Tuc was tense. He was tense because of vanity, just as a concert conductor nervously preens himself before a concert. Tuc wished that he could tear out his vanity, as he tore the guts from a fish. Years before he had been told at Communist self-criticism meeting that this vanity was due to his early bourgeois experiences.

Tuc made a signal to the observers for the "crystals" to begin a low rhythmic chanting. It was an essential part of crowd manipulation, something like the warming up exercises which athletes do before a contest. It drew the crowd together, gave them a sense of unity, increased their plasticity.

A single "crystal" caught the signal from the observer and started to chant in a pleasant neutral voice, "Prince Lin Ho, our Honored Prince, we want to see him." There was the inevitable moment of crowd embarrassment, but other "crystals" took up the chant, and in a few moments the whole crowd was murmuring in unison. They had received their first order, unobtrusive and subtle, but they were responding. They were unknowingly preparing themselves to take stronger orders.

Then Tuc saw Hajn at the window. Hajn stared at the crowd and without looking for Tuc, ran his finger inside his collar.

Tuc was certain of the signal but uncertain of Hajn's judgment. If only he could be in the conference room to hear what was being said. He suspected that Hajn was always waiting for the moment when he could trap Tuc and eliminate him. But the General was boxed in tightly, he could not betray the Party now. The long intricate game of entrapment had taken years. Hajn's weakness, it developed, was a fierce ambition to hold a titled position and permanent power. Tuc had decided that, because Hajn would make the best man, the General should achieve his ambitions. At least he would have the semblance of permanent power.

But now Tuc must control events. At this present moment his judgment alone mattered, and he had to make decisions without knowing exactly what was happening within the Embassy.

Tuc stood up, raised one arm high, fist clenched. He held it for five seconds, then dropped his arm and crouched among the bushes again.

His assistants, watching with binoculars, saw the gesture. Pahi, the son of a prosperous importer who hated his father and the Western world, knew it was his responsibility to originate the slogan which would mold and move the crowd toward anger.

There was a lapse of two or three moments and then a single voice cut sharply out of the crowd. "Americans, let our Prince go," the voice said. The rhythmic chanting stopped. The crowd, puzzled by the change in mood, was for a moment fractured again into individuals, waiting for some sort of leadership.

A second "crystal" sang out the phrase. Many voices picked it up. Men breathed faster, gestures and body motions became more aggressive. Acting from a primordial instinct, women with children began moving outward toward the edge of the crowd, sensing that violence might be close at hand.

"It is almost night," another "crystal" shouted. "We must go home soon. Why cannot the Prince come out?"

The people became aware of the hour. Women particularly grew restless, knowing they had to go home and prepare dinner for their families.

It took only two minutes for the idea to spread through the crowd. The original shout was reduced to a simple easily repeated slogan: "Lin before night." Everyone chanted now. There was a trace of belligerence in their collective voice.

Tuc was not surprised. Like Lenin's masterful phrase, "Peace,

Bread, Land," the crowd often selected slogans that were short and rhythmic. The crowd was child-like, and the simplicity and repetition of the sound was reassuring. There would come the moment when everyone would be shouting, no one holding back, and then the crowd would be a mob.

Tuc would hear these transformations with the appreciation of a conductor passing over difficult points in the score.

"Soon the Moslem must make evening prayer to Mecca," a "crystal" shouted.

The crowd hesitated, a ripple of confusion spreading through it. The Moslems fell silent while the Buddhists kept up their chant. The crowd was momentarily split. Tuc knew they would come back together.

"Lin before dark," the Buddhists shouted.

"Lin before prayers," the Moslems shouted.

For a few moments there had been a hard suspicion between the Moslem and Buddhist segments of the crowd. But the instant each segment had its own slogan, the split, the seismic crack of suspicion, was gone. They chanted two different slogans, but in unison. Now there was a new strength in their unity.

What was necessary was a sense of controlled movement. Tuc gave the sign.

"He's coming out," a "crystal" shouted, surging toward the gate. The other "crystals" moved with him. They did not carry all of the crowd but most of it.

In front of the Embassy the Marine guards snapped to attention and took a step forward. The crowd, like a blind groping crab sensing hostile action, drew back a few feet.

Now they have had their first instruction in movement. Later they will think they have moved out of their own volition and their own courage and to accomplish some undefined task, Tuc thought. The next time it will be easier.

Tuc, confident of the crowd in the square, worried only about Hajn's judgment in the conference room.

29

The Testimony of Gunner Vat

The conference room was quiet.

"Do you mean to say, Your Highness, that Sarkhanese statesmen are luring, enticing, and provoking America to come into your country?" Hobson asked. He did not wait for an answer. "Your Highness, America has no interest in spending its money and lives in Sarkhan if there is no real Communist threat."

"I understand."

"Do you also understand that if what you saw on the plateau is the truth, some of your trusted colleagues are traitors or Communists or both?" Hobson pressed on.

Coldstream saw that Hobson, because he was unsure of himself, was pressing hard, probing for a break in Lin's argument.

"Of course, Mister Hobson. I also know some of the traitors. They are not practicing *coup* politics. They want to deliver the country to the Communists."

Hobson hesitated. He caught Cogswell's eye. The old man at the head of the table was composed. His look was cold and unbending. Hobson knew he must move ahead, but he felt a sense of confusion. He started to swing his head to look at Hajn, then his years of experience told him not to.

"Your Highness, it is easy to get misled in such intricate matters," Hobson said, and his voice was gentle, cajoling, confiding. "I know. I'm in the intelligence business. If there were Communists in Sarkhan, my organization would know about them."

"I believe I have proof, Mister Hobson," Lin said. "It was supplied by Captain Coldstream. He also told me about your one hundred and seven F.I.A. agents in my country. I am curious why they have not been able to assemble a list of the real Communist agitators and organizers, as I believe Captain Coldstream has done."

"Is that true, Jeremiah?" Cogswell asked. "Do you have one hundred and seven people here? The last time we met you said you had fifteen."

"I'll have to check. We've upped our number of agents, for obvious reasons, in the past few weeks." Hobson knew it was not convincing.

"Where is your list, Captain?" Cogswell asked.

"It's at my home, Mister Cogswell, in the possession of Taja, my secretary."

"Captain, I'd like you to telephone your home and have the documents brought here," Cogswell said.

"Mister Cogswell," Lin spoke up. Then he paused and his voice fell. "May I ask you to order that no American leave this room or use the telephone until the list arrives. I hereby issue that same order for all Sarkhanese present."

Cogswell sighed. Now it was out in the room.

Hajn turned slowly. He held up his hand.

"Mister Chairman, I am sure that no reflection on the intelligence-gathering resources or the integrity of the Sarkhanese armed forces is intended here." His tone was sober, his face pinched.

"General Hajn," Cogswell answered, "this is a fact-finding committee. The competence and loyalty of our allies is a factual matter. Between honest allies there is no need for subterfuge. Consider the situation. The military people in this room have not seen first-hand what is happening on the plateau. These three men say they have, and they say it is a sham battle. Unless we doubt their integrity, or there is contrary evidence of a concrete nature, we must take their accounts as the most reliable we possess. And their accounts wipe out the grounds on which the United States came to the aid of Sarkhan."

Ambassador Brown rubbed his cheek and wished he were elsewhere. Cogswell was complicating things. The argument should be between Lin and Hajn. Brown looked across at Assistant Secretary Abbott. Their eyes met. Each read worry in the face of the other. Abbott saw it slightly differently, however. Cogswell's unrelenting candor could make future diplomatic negotiations difficult.

"Mister Cogswell," Hajn said. "I was about to bring in first-hand evidence." Hajn did not ask permission now. He stood up, walked to the door, and gestured down the hall. A moment later a Sarkhanese major appeared escorting the North Vietnamese prisoner.

Gunner Vat blinked as his eyes became accustomed to the brightness of the conference room. He saw Lin, Coldstream, and McCauley, and grinned.

It was a peculiar grin, the kind that can come only out of Asia. It was the grin of the man who is genuinely friendly, who does not know if he will live out the day, who is satisfied with the shape of his past life, and is prepared to meet whatever comes. It was a tough grin.

"Major Phong, ask the prisoner where he is from," said Hajn abruptly. Turning to the rest of the room, Hajn said, "Major Phong is an officer of the Sarkhan Intelligence Service, which, apparently, is held in disrepute by some people around the table. He speaks Vietnamese fluently."

The Major turned away from Gunner Vat, who had been speaking to him.

"He says he is from North Vietnam," the Major said in impeccable English.

"What was he doing on the plateau?" Hajn asked.

The Major asked Gunner Vat the question and relayed the answer.

"He was a part of an artillery regiment which was ordered to support the 316th Division, which has the nickname of 'People's Fist.' "

"Their objective, Major Phong?" Hajn asked.

Gunner Vat paused, looked innocently around the table, and asked the Major to repeat his question.

Coldstream whispered to Lin, "Phong is one of the names on my list."

Gunner Vat was talking fast, making firm gestures with his hands. He spoke in a low voice, but whatever he said appeared to excite Phong.

"He said his regiment set up 51-millimeter mortars just below the plateau to support the general assault by North Vietnamese troops."

"Had he fired any rounds before he was captured?" the Marine General asked.

The Major answered the question.

"Yes, fifteen hundred rounds in the two days before he was captured."

General Patrick got up and walked toward the prisoner. Gunner Vat looked up, his face unafraid, but serious. He jumped to his feet and snapped to attention.

"I will be the General's interpreter," McCauley said casually.

"The prisoner is more relaxed with me," said Phong, "and I know his dialect."

"I also know it."

"Do you think the Professor really speaks it?" Dobey, the Assistant Secretary of Defense, asked Hobson.

Hobson did not reply. He looked at Cogswell.

Cogswell sat quietly.

The tension, gradually allowed to increase, was clarifying some things. Cogswell glanced at Lin. Lin nodded as if they had been communicating.

"This is largely an American meeting," Lin said. "Let Professor McCauley interpret. Don't worry, Major Phong. If the white man makes a mistake, you and I can correct. True?"

Phong looked at Lin and then, uncertain, shot a glance at Hajn. Hajn ignored him.

"Your hands. Turn them palm up, please," General Patrick ordered. McCauley repeated the order in Vietnamese and Gunner Vat did not hesitate. He put his hands out.

"If any rounds were fired this man did not fire them," the General said. "Their shells are covered with a Vaseline-like lubricant and then a layer of cosmoline to protect them from the dampness. The oily covering sticks on their hands for days. This man's hands are dry."

"He is a senior gunner," Phong said, "not a coolie. He directs placement and firing, but he does not handle rounds. Not any more."

"That's possible," Patrick said, "but not plausible. Everyone in jungle artillery handles rounds."

"General, has it ever occurred to you that Asian armies operate on the mandarin basis? Coolies load, but mandarins aim," Hobson said. "This man has no reason to lie to us."

"Mister Cogswell, my intelligence people would like to continue the interrogation of the prisoner," Hajn said. "Have we finished with him?"

Phong turned to lead the prisoner from the room, but Coldstream's voice stopped Phong at the door.

"Major Phong, how are things in the Northeast Province?"

Phong stopped.

"I do not know," Phong said. "I live in Haidho."

"Sorry. Some of my people report a Phong, built very much like you, who has been organizing youth groups in the northeast."

"You are mistaken," said Phong, continuing toward the door.

"Major Phong," Lin called sharply. "Have you forgotten that no one is to leave the room?"

"I'd like to question the prisoner further, Your Highness," said McCauley.

"You may proceed, Professor McCauley."

"Senior Gunner Vat, do you remember what I did to Captain Hien?" McCauley asked.

"Yes, sir."

"Now tell me, how many men—total, officers and men—were with you in Sarkhan?"

Hajn interrupted. "He is threatening the prisoner."

"How many men?" repeated McCauley.

"*Phori!*" commanded Phong softly.

"The Major said '*Phori*' to the prisoner," Lin said. "General Hajn, what does *phori* mean?"

"It means 'keep quiet,' " said McCauley.

"That is correct," said Prince Lin. "Phong told the prisoner not to speak."

"Gunner Vat, this man is the Prince of Sarkhan," McCauley said, pointing at Lin. "Whatever you were told by Major Phong, let me assure you that I have control of your person. Speak the truth and you will be returned to the border. Lie and we will continue the questioning in the helicopter."

Gunner Vat stared. Major Phong looked at him in bafflement.

"Yes, sir," Gunner Vat said.

"Now again, how many men—officers and men—were there with you in Sarkhan?" McCauley said.

"Twenty-one, sir."

"That was all?"

"Only twenty-one, sir."

Hajn got up and walked to the window. He looked out at the growing crowd. It was getting dark. He made the final signal.

"What were you doing in Sarkhan?" McCauley said.

"We are there to observe the false battle and spy and later to infiltrate south and capture American arms when the monsoon stopped," Gunner Vat said.

From outside, the noise of the mob changed abruptly, as if a switch had been pulled. A new slogan came from the crowd, and its belligerence was unmistakable.

Ambassador Brown nervously repeated it.

"Amerik Augai Lin! Amerik Augai Lin!"

At the student riot in front of the Embassy there had been only several hundred people. Now there must be five thousand. Brown did not want *his* Embassy sacked or burned.

"Mister Chairman, we must do something to quiet the people!" Brown blurted.

"They will only be satisfied," said Hajn, "if they can see His Highness."

"I suggest that General Hajn go out and tell the people the Prince is safe," Coldstream said.

"Mister Cogswell, I assure you the crowd will not be satisfied unless it sees His Highness," Hajn said.

Prince Lin looked appraisingly at Hajn. "All right," he said, "I will go." He started for the door and turned. "I desire Ambassador Brown and my two friends here," he said, "to come with me. And I request that everyone else remain. We have more to discuss."

Lin walked out slowly, with Brown, Coldstream, and McCauley behind him. In the hall he said, "Mister Ambassador, please instruct your Marine sentries to let no one leave the room."

Brown hesitated. He could hardly keep the Assistant Secretary of State and Hobson prisoners. But then he heard the rhythmic screaming of the mob—*"Amerik Augai Lin!"*—and he did what the Prince requested.

When they reached the rotunda and opened the front doors of the Embassy, the enormity of the crowd swept over them in a wave of sound and motion.

The Prince walked down the steps, his hand on his hips, in the traditional position of royalty. The crowd stopped screaming. For a moment there was silence, then a great roar—"the Prince!"

Thank God, they recognize him, Coldstream thought.

In stately, measured gait, the man in the torn, muddy uniform walked toward the crowd. On his chest the royal medallion swung from side to side. The Prince glanced at Coldstream and McCauley, and beckoned them to follow. He nodded at Brown to stay on the steps.

The crowd pushed against the Embassy fence, not because they wished to get close, but because of the mounting pressure from behind.

This is his real coronation, thought Coldstream. He wondered that such a thought could come to his mind. All three of them were filthy, bedraggled, exhausted. There was no pomp, no ceremony, no crown, no priest or music. There was only Lin and his people. Then he recalled the last strange astrological prediction made for the Prince: "On the twenty-sixth day of October Prince Lin's life will change. He will make history and gain fame. His father will still be the king, but the Prince will wear a crown, and it will be adorned by the sun, moon, and the stars."

Within the conference room, Hajn addressed the group. "My Prince," he said, "is terribly ill. You saw his blank stare, the enormity of his pupils. I have seen him this way before. It is almost as if he were in a trance. He is easily influenced and can recall almost nothing."

"Why did you insist he go out to the people if he is so sick?" said Cogswell.

"He had to go out. Could you not hear the crowd? They are ready to attack the Embassy. Also, his exposure to so many people may shock him out of his trance."

"He sounded rational to me," said General Patrick. "For a man in a trance he certainly described events on the plateau in detail."

"General Patrick," said Hajn, "Prince Lin did not visit the plateau. He was talking a hysterical hallucination induced by those other two. To the plateau? Impossible. It is difficult for our heavy planes to get there through the monsoon. How could they have made it in a flimsy helicopter?"

"Then where did the prisoner come from?" asked the Marine General.

"We have a camp near Boa Binh where we keep prisoners. That's close to where the Prince was meditating. That's probably where they went . . ."

He was interrupted by the roar of the crowd.

Hajn moved quickly to the single window overlooking the front of the Embassy grounds. Cogswell also crowded into the narrow window space. There was room for no one else.

They watched the Prince, closely followed by Coldstream and McCauley, approach the fence. Behind the fence the crowd seemed enormous, alive. Ambassador Brown had not followed the other three toward the crowd, but stood uncertainly by the Embassy steps.

The sun had almost set. There was no wind and it was hot. The women with children now ringed the edge of the crowd. Those behind heard the cries of "the Prince!" They shoved and strained and clamored for a view of Prince Lin. The moment was approaching, Tuc saw, when the crowd would become a mob.

Then another movement at the edge of the crowd caught Tuc's eye. It was Coldstream's jeep, and Taja was driving it slowly through the crowd toward the side entrance of the Embassy.

30

The Mob

The two Americans followed the Prince. He walked slowly with
dignity and certitude, head high, back straight, his pace cadenced.
Coldstream and McCauley, five feet behind the Prince, kept step
with him.

It is almost as if we are bridesmaids, Coldstream thought. We
have been lucky. It is ending well. Everyone at the conference
must now know how the United States has been duped and by
whom. Even Hobson must see it.

How slowly the Prince was walking. Ahead, Coldstream saw
thousands of Sarkhanese pressed against the fence. Those in front
grasped the bars, pushing backwards to relieve the pressure.

The Prince might have denounced Hajn immediately. But
Coldstream thought him wise not to. He had managed the conference so that the evidence came out slowly, logically. The Prince
had wanted the Committee to make up its own mind and take action. The United States should have the opportunity to withdraw
troops voluntarily, without humiliation.

A feeling of triumph surged through Coldstream. Washington
will learn much, he thought. They will learn that Communists
make many mistakes, that they are not ten feet tall, that they can
be defeated in the early stages by intelligence and planning more
easily than later by blind military panicking.

Coldstream glanced at McCauley. The Professor looked dis-
tinctly uncomfortable in this unaccustomed public role. In a few
minutes the story of their kidnapping the Prince would be discredited. Taja would be relieved. He wondered what Hajn would
do back in the conference room.

Crouching low, Tuc ran along the thick hedge that flanked the
Embassy walk. He must stay close to the Prince. He had seen Lin
smile at the two Americans. They were friends. The Prince's

very first words would tell the fish-gutter what he had to do. The Prince stopped. The two Americans moved up behind him.

Lin held up his hands. Thousands of brown bodies pushed forward expectantly. A few fainted in the crowd, but were too closely packed to fall. Their heads lolled with the movement of the mass. The silence, considering the number of people, was extraordinary.

"My people, I am made joyful by your welcome," Lin said. His voice carried well. "This is a critical time for our country. We are torn by rumors that I have been kidnapped. We are torn by rumors of an invasion on the *Plateau des Luminaires*. We are torn by religious suspicions which we buried centuries ago."

Lin paused, his control over the crowd almost complete. "Now I shall tell you the truth."

Tuc felt a deep envy, a pulse of rage, something close to pain. This soft, soft little man, this sheltered Prince, had by inheritance a grip on the people which Tuc, with all his skill, would never achieve. He moved closer. Still behind the hedge, he was within fifteen feet of the soft man.

"We are in danger from a high and unsuspected source," Prince Lin said.

Tuc took a pistol from inside his shirt, aimed through the hedge, and fired three times. Each shot hit the Prince in the back.

Lin's face took on a look of surprise, then fearful realization, finally a smile of embarrassment. Then came the first hardening grimace of physical shock which would deepen quickly and, if not arrested, end in death.

Lurching forward, Prince Lin turned to Coldstream and reached for support, missed and fell. His royal medallion hit the pavement, its 2000-year-old jade shattering into a dozen pieces.

Coldstream and McCauley turned toward the hedge, but there was nothing. Then they bent over the Prince, not noticing that Tuc had pushed through the hedge and was running toward them.

With the flat of his gun Tuc smashed McCauley on the temple. It appeared to have been done with his fist. In the same rolling motion he jolted Coldstream, knocking him over, and dropped the gun to the pavement.

"They have murdered our Prince!" Tuc screamed, beating

Coldstream's head against the concrete. "The white men have murdered our Prince!"

The crowd was quiet. The shout and the sound of the shots had suddenly rendered them individuals again. They were leaderless, stunned by an unbelieveable act. Then a dozen voices shouted, "The white men have killed the Prince, the white men ...!"

The crowd sighed and moved together again, massive and menacing, taking up the cry.

Coldstream smelled the sweat, the fish, the rage-stench of the man. Staggering to his feet, he kicked out at Tuc and then smashed him back toward the hedge. He bent over the Prince, who lay on his stomach, one arm reaching crookedly ahead, the fingers opening and closing spasmodically. He lifted Lin's limp body.

The front ranks of the crowd saw three patches of blood on their Prince's chest become a single splash. They gasped and surged backward, then forward, and in that gesture were reunited and became a mob.

"This white man is the murderer," Tuc screamed, grabbing again at Coldstream.

In a rage Coldstream freed his right hand and slashed it across the fish-gutter's neck. Tuc dropped to the pavement.

"Murderer," screamed the mob and, like a strange organisim, it surged against the Embassy gate.

Lin looked at Coldstream with bright startled unseeing eyes, his hands unconsciously searching his bloody chest.

The mob howled, "He is killing the Prince," and made another vengeful, rolling undulation forward.

The gate of the American Embassy was made of rods of iron, each topped by a small bronze American eagle, and joined by horizontal bands of steel. As the pressure against it increased, a thin woman of about thirty was squeezed between the rods. She was held outside only by her head and buttocks. Then her buttocks narrowed and there was a cracking noise as the full weight of the crowd popped her head through the fence. She was dead as she landed inside, her head oddly elongated.

On the Embassy steps, Brown shouted, "General Hajn! Get

General Hajn." Without waiting to see if anyone were carrying out his orders, he turned and ran for the conference room.

The mob sensed its first casualty, felt wounded in some part of its huge organism, and gave off a sound of revenge. There was a ripple along the fence as the hinges on the gate broke and it crashed forward. The first ranks fell to the ground and those behind, pushed by the crazed triangle of human bodies, poured over them, running, stumbling on to the Embassy grounds.

A shock of animal heat and odor preceded the horde. Coldstream knew he must get Lin to the Embassy, fifty yards away. He saw McCauley nearby, still sprawled openmouthed and unconscious. Coldstream hesitated. Could he drag both men? In a swift brutal decision of survival, he knew he must abandon McCauley. With a jerk he hoisted Lin up, carrying him like a heavy child, and started for the Embassy. He calculated he could reach the steps in thirty seconds, the front door in forty-five. Why didn't someone from the Embassy come out to help him? Where in hell was Brown and his Marines?

Lin suddenly uncoiled in an unexpected spasm of movement, falling from Coldstream's arms to the ground. Coldstream saw the blood smeared all over his own shirt and pants. He lifted Lin up, supporting him with a hand across his chest, and dragged the inert Prince toward the Embassy.

A thousand people undulated and rolled toward Coldstream and the Prince and two wings of the mob had already by-passed them, like great encircling arms. Coldstream saw their faces, dark and sweating, gasping for air. He heard the stamping of bare feet becoming louder every second, and the sound of hysterical screaming, "Murderer! He is murdering our Prince."

Tuc slowly got up from the ground. He appraised the situation, grunted with satisfaction, pushed back through the hedge and disappeared.

Coldstream moved awkwardly with his heavy burden. The Embassy steps now were only ten yards distant. But the horde was exploding across the grounds with increasing speed.

The mob reached McCauley, hesitated a moment, then trampled over the professor's rumpled form.

Close to Lin and Coldstream, the first wave of moving people tried to stop. They bent over as if bowing to their Prince. But the people in front could not resist the momentum from the rear. They were knocked to their knees, screaming, grunting, flailing their arms and protesting. The second wave of bodies attempted to jump over the fallen ones; and they also tumbled. The third wave flowed over everyone, knocking the fallen ones to their faces and stamping over them.

As he stumbled ahead, Coldstream turned his eyes from the mob to the Embassy. Twenty feet away the front door of the Embassy opened and some people were starting out. "'Thank God," said Coldstream, tightening his grip on the Prince and trying desperately to move more quickly.

Hands from the mob grabbed him, scratched his skin, tore his clothes. Behind, he glimpsed a mass of wet faces, contorted mouths open, shouting, full of teeth.

The Prince was ripped from his grasp. A violent vortex engulfed Coldstream, lifting him off his feet, slamming him down hard on his back. A herd of bodies pounded over him and Prince Lin. A bare foot was the last thing Coldstream saw, the blackened sole becoming enormous in its downward thrust and bringing with it a last surge of light. Coldstream heard a violent crunching sound, and for a moment the image of Taja flashed through his consciousness. Then came total blackness.

The thousands surged ahead. Some fell and were trampled. Those in front knew that if they did not move forward they would die. They stampeded over the fallen. The Prince and the two Americans were forgotten. There were other bodies now, just as dead.

The mob spread out on the Embassy lawn, the pressure eased, the passions drained, the screams died, fear was replaced by a dull anger. The animals became human again, stood uncertainly in small groups and then stumbled back over the bodies of those who had fallen at the gate.

The tall commanding figure of General Hajn appeared among

them. He spoke quietly, he herded stragglers away from the Embassy. His very presence seemed to induce calm and re-establish order.

He bent over the body of the Prince, then straightened. Tears were in his eyes, grief distorted his face. He motioned to a group of men. They picked up the Prince gently and, holding him high, bore him reverently into the square, back to the palace.

The bodies of Coldstream and McCauley were dragged into the park and the mob separated enough so that those who wanted could spit on them.

Men with hammers and nails appeared in the square and the bodies of Coldstream and McCauley were spreadeagled against two *doba* trees and spikes were driven through their palms to hold their bodies upright.

When the last hammer stroke sounded and the hammerer stood back to view his work, a strange silence fell over the mob. People stared at one another and at the bodies of the Americans. Astonishment flowed over them, surprise at their sudden, savage power. Then came guilt, and in that moment the mob no longer existed.

The people left the square, walking more quickly than usual, their eyes straight ahead, anxious not to recognize anyone, anxious not to be recognized.

31

The Traitors

HAIDHO, Sarkhan. Oct. 27, by MARCUS COIT

[Editor's Note: Marcus Coit, veteran Sarkhan correspondent, and one of the world's acknowledged experts on Asia and Asian politics, was the sole journalist eyewitness to the death of Prince Lin. This newspaper considers that report, printed in this space yesterday, one of the classics of modern journalism. Coit's account of the event, done on a pool basis, was printed in over 1200 newspapers. Today's story is a follow-up.]

Yesterday, I gave you an exclusive eyewitness account of the brutal murder of Prince Lin. He was killed exactly three weeks before being crowned the forty-second monarch of Sarkhan. The event was bloody and tragic. It would have been worse had it not been for the cool leadership and courageous action of America's professional diplomats and General Hajn of Sarkhan.

Today, history continues to be made. This reporter is privileged to give you another eyewitness account.

Evidence now indicates that Prince Lin was assassinated by Captain Edward Coldstream, U.S.N. (Retired), and Professor Thaddeus McCauley. The murder weapon, found near the scene, in front of the entrance of the United States Embassy, positively has been identified as Edward Coldstream's. Tuc Hung, an employee of Coldstream's for nine years, identified the gun as belonging to his former employer. At the investigation held by the Sarkhanese Royal Council, Tuc swore he often had seen Coldstream use this weapon at target practice.

Jeremiah Hobson, Director of the F.I.A., disclosed that there is considerable information indicating that Coldstream and McCauley had subversive tendencies. McCauley was a conscientious objector during World War II, an authority on Sarkhan and on Communism.

Coldstream, Hobson disclosed, retired from the Navy under strange circumstances. He became a businessman in Sarkhan, but it was well known that he occasionally sent commercial agents into Red China. In the basement of Coldstream's house was a steel and concrete vault with extensive communication equipment. In the vault was unmistakable evidence that Coldstream tuned in regularly on the Communist broadcasts, according to General Hajn.

Another mystery was cleared up when Sung, servant to Prince Lin since childhood, testified that the Prince occasionally had *tjah* fever, a strange illness. General Hajn says this explains the Prince's unusual behavior in allowing himself to be taken north by Coldstream and McCauley in the Prince's helicopter.

The next point of inquiry in the investigation will concern the motives of Coldstream and McCauley in slaughtering a detachment of Prince Lin's Sarkhanese Army guards. What did they hope to gain? Also what caused them to return to the United States Embassy in Haidho?

The investigation will be delayed five days until after His Royal Highness, Prince Lin, has been cremated. The nation will be in mourning. So great is the grief of the Sarkhanese that a five-day period of fasting and silence has been decreed.

[This exclusive series will be continued tomorrow.]

HAIDHO, Sarkhan. Oct. 28, by MARCUS COIT

King Diad of Sarkhan said he will abdicate on the 15th of November as scheduled. The date of abdication was established by astrologers in 1890, when the King was born.

His Majesty also announced this morning that General Hajn, the anti-Communist Minister of Defense, has been appointed the regent of Sarkhan. In this capacity he will be the acting chief of state for two years. At the end of that time, there will be a plebiscite. The people will then decide what form of government Sarkhan will have for the future.

General Hajn is a living legend. His courage and popularity were demonstrated three days ago when, unarmed and alone, the General went into the beserk mob and raised his hand for silence. In a matter of moments thousands of screaming Sarkhanese, who had been behaving like animals, were calmed. Had it not been for this courageous action, according to Ambassador Brown, the mob in its vengeful mood would have sacked the Embassy.

White House sources indicate the President may recommend Ambassador Brown, Jeremiah Hobson, and General Hajn for high awards.

They deserve them.

HAIDHO, Sarkhan. Oct. 29, by MARCUS COIT

The inquiry concerning the death of His Royal Highness, Prince Lin, discloses one bizarre fact after another. Today it was learned that Adolph Cogswell, multi-millionaire, advisor to many Presidents, and chairman of the President's Committee on Sarkhan, has long been involved with the Prince's murderers, Coldstream and McCauley.

Cogswell admitted he had known Coldstream for fifteen years, and for five years he had received intelligence reports from both men. These reports reached the highest official ears, *even though the reports usually were contrary in content and opinion* to the evaluations of the Department of State, the Pentagon, and the F.I.A.

The Pan Am flight would be leaving Haidho in two hours. Adolph Cogswell did not wish to return to Washington on the official plane. Furthermore, he was not certain he would be permitted aboard. Awaiting departure, he had moved from the Embassy residence to the Ritz Hotel. Now he looked around at the shabby furnishings. They were symbolic.

He did not know what to do with the bulky envelope in the inside pocket of his coat. It was the one Taja had given him when she finally reached him in the Embassy on the day of the riot, shortly after the mob had receded from the Embassy compound, taking the bodies of Coldstream and McCauley with them. He had watched unbelievingly as these people, normally so gentle, had savagely hammered the two dead bodies to trees.

Taja had touched his elbow and introduced herself. She was calm and her eyes were dry. She gave the impression of deep, sad, resigned control.

"It was Tuc who shot the Prince," she had told him on that tragic day. "I was coming from the parking place in the rear of the Embassy to deliver this envelope, and I saw him. A dozen other people hanging on the west wall must have seen him also, but you will never find those people. In Asia one does not step forward to bear witness."

She said she could not talk long to Cogswell. It was important that he remember everything. Most of what she said concerned the manila envelope and its contents: affadavits, pictures, lists, pamphlets.

"What can I do for you?" asked Cogswell.

"Nothing." She had smiled slightly, in appreciation. "You must help yourself. You are vulnerable. And when one is vulnerable, the carrion-eaters move quickly."

She had been right, thought Cogswell.

The next day Ambassador Brown, apparently full of regret, had brought him a radiogram from the White House. "YOUR ASSOCI-

ATION WITH COLDSTREAM AND MC CAULEY HAS ENDED YOUR USE-
FULNESS. YOU ARE HEREBY RELIEVED . . ."

Like some aged and strangely wounded animal, he had moved
to this shabby hotel room with its stuffy air and slowly turning
fly-specked fan. He had wept for Coldstream and McCauley and,
yes, for himself. Later he had wept for Taja. Her body had been
found in the Sekong River where, Radio Hanoi said, "an angry
crowd had thrown her because of her association with the assassin,
Coldstream."

Adolph Cogswell had not slept. He dared not even remove his
coat. In his indignation he determined to publish the documents
in one of his own magazines as soon as he got home. He would
blast the story wide open. But the chances were against anyone
believing him. He had been so thoroughly discredited.

He had known the truth when he left the Embassy. He had
gone directly to the United States photo lab in Haidho, known as
J.U.S.P.A.L. The Navy reconnaissance photos made at the plateau had turned out, but had been accidently ruined, negatives
and all, by the F.I.A. representative who came to claim them. He
had stumbled and dropped them into the acid vat. But the en-
listed man who developed them had found two rough prints in
the trash basket for Cogswell. They showed clear details of the
fake invasion. These two pictures were in the envelope now.

Cogswell knew he could not publish them. He had received the
information while he was the official chairman of the Committee.
Now that he had no position, he had no right to the information.
Furthermore, if they were published, the entire U.S. government
would be humiliated in the eyes of the world. President Johnson
was almost impeached in 1866 for far less an offense.

Adolph Cogswell knew what he could not do: use his privileged position to attack his own government. And all other evidence had been destroyed. Taja was dead. The Vietnamese prisoner, Gunner Vat, had been shot while trying to escape immediately after the riot. During a two-day break in the monsoon, the
plateau had received saturation bombing, square foot by square
foot. Quick action, the press said, had nipped the invasion in the
bud. Even the troops on the plateau were dead.

Cogswell had tried to telephone the President from Haidho,

but had never reached him. He knew that after he got back to Washington and called in person at the White House, the President would not see him. Cogswell was too firmly linked with the murderers and traitors. A few papers already had compared him to Alger Hiss. There were rumors of a Congressional investigation, but the President, the papers said, had squashed that by reminding the Majority Leader of Cogswell's age and past good service.

If, thought Cogswell, I give this evidence to anyone else in the government except the President, it will disappear.

Cogswell looked around the hotel room and made sure he had not left anything. The telephone rang. It was the clerk reporting that the limousine was ready to take him to the airport.

At the airport, Cogswell, numb and unthinking, stood in line at customs. When the inspector saw his special passport, he waved him through. Cogswell shuffled. The fatigue and the shock finally had caught up with him.

He was sitting wearily in the waiting room when a high strident voice spoke his name. He looked up. It was Jeremiah Hobson.

"Adolph," he said easing himself to the bench, and putting his hand on Cogswell's arm. "I'm sorry this had to happen to you . . ."

"Nothing's happened to me. It's the United States something has happened to."

"That's why I'm here, Adolph—to explain. You got in the way of the inevitable. It's either America or communism. One of them must live and one of them must die. They cannot both exist. Some of us have spent our lives trying to strangle communism. We are about to succeed. We will roll it back, snuff it out. Why couldn't you see this?"

Cogswell shook his head, but said nothing.

"Adolph, action against communism must take place simultaneously all over the world. But first we must get strong friends in power . . ."

"Like Chiang Kai-shek, Syngman Rhee, General Hajn, and Fulgencio Batista?"

"Precisely. And Sarkhan is the springboard in Asia. We need Hajn in power. It is crucial."

"Do you know he is a Communist?"

Hobson hesitated. He had not known. Cogswell saw it.

"It makes no difference what he is. He is strong and he is the head of state, and we control him. A crazy neutralist like the Prince—one couldn't predict his decisions."

"Jeremiah, those Navy pictures were destroyed on purpose, weren't they? They showed too much."

"Too much what?"

"You've known from the beginning there wasn't any invasion on the plateau." Cogswell's voice went flat with conviction. "You're a conspirator with the rest of them, Jeremiah. Conspiring for power under the name of patriotism.

Hobson shook his head mournfully as if to indicate that his friend should be committed to a home for the senile.

The loudspeaker announced Cogswell's plane. He stood up.

"It won't work," he said. "A lot of people before you have tried it and failed—Hitler, Napoleon, Caesar. There is always another devil, stronger and smarter. No, Jeremiah, it is against chicanery and exploitation that these Asian nations are revolting. If we want them to join us, we will first have to convince the people that we will help them build their nation *the way they want it*."

"Adolph, you'll never learn, will you?"

"You will go down in history, Jeremiah, as the man who turned Sarkhan over to the Communists. I pity you. Years ago you started as a patriot, but your desire for power has blinded you."

Hobson's face hardened. He said, "Adolph, Coldstream sent for a list . . ."

"Yes. It had the names of the Communists in Sarkhan—both Sarkhanese and American. Also evidence."

"Where is it?"

"I have it."

"Give it to me," said Hobson. "I am in a position to make use of it. You are not."

"It's not handy," said Cogswell, moving forward toward the ramp. He had spoken the truth. The manila envelope Taja had delivered to him was sewn into the lining of his coat.

"What do you intend to do with it?"

Cogswell shrugged.

"I can get that list, you know. I have the means."

"Then do it. It's also in my head. Can you get that too?"

"Don't be an old fool," said Hobson. "Please."

"I *am* an old fool. And I'm going home to try to remember the names of my grandchildren and great-grandchildren. To sit quietly. Even to think. But at least I am an honorable fool."

The two old men stared at each other. Cogswell turned and walked out of the wooden terminal building with the pagoda roof and toward the plane.

A half-hour later, Adolph Cogswell was airborne, en route to Hong Kong. He was unshaven and his suit was rumpled. The inside pocket of his coat bulged. The stewardess said, "May I hang your coat up for you, sir?"

"No, thank you," Cogswell said.

"You'll be much more comfortable, I believe, sir, without that coat. It must be heavy."

"Very heavy," said Cogswell.

Now he adjusted his seat for sleep and wondered idly if he could. His coat was folded in his lap and the envelope pressed against his thigh. Countless times he had fingered its contents during the past few days and each time he felt the shock all over again. The documents told him so much—that General Hajn was somehow a part of the Communist apparatus, that the hunchback reporter Coit was similarly involved and that he printed much of the Communist propaganda in Southeast Asia, that the fish-gutter named Tuc, employed by Coldstream, was probably the leader of the apparatus in Haidho, that Major Phong, Hajn's translator at the meeting, was the Communist in charge of the Northeast Province . . .

He still had a page of notes to add to the envelope's contents and he wrote it in longhand now under the heading, "Conclusions about Jeremiah Hobson."

Confused at first about Hobson's intent, method, and *modus operandi*. Like the Pope, he had no troops—or so I thought. Now clear. His intent is sincere patriotism: save world from Communism. His method is simply to gather power to himself, he is self-appointed Savior. His *modus operandi* in Sarkhan: first, find strong man (Hajn—perfect record, impeccable background, national hero), capture him for F.I.A., and promote him in Washington. Second, after Communist crisis (real or fancied) American troops are committed, country occupied, crisis "solved." Third, American troops pull out, leaving strong man as head of government. Who controls (or thinks he controls) strong man from Washington? Hobson. The error: it has never worked. The strong men capitulate to or are broken by the Communist organization. The real ultimate power is with the people. It is the people we must support.

The document in the envelope that had affected Cogswell the most was the message in Coldstream's neat handwriting that he had sent Taja from the sanctuary, with its list of names and the Prince's signature, along with Coldstream's, at the bottom of the royal stationery. Cogswell had stared long and hard at the signatures of the two dead men as if by concentration he might bring them back to life.

Fourteen hours after easing himself wearily into his plane seat in Haidho, he was at Dulles International Airport. There his bags were nowhere to be found. The customs and baggage people were honestly perplexed. The bags showed up three days later—"Misplaced in the terminal, sir"—with nothing missing.

In Washington, Cogswell tried many times to see the President. The President was either not in or he was busy.

Cogswell felt he was another person, one of the defeated. The telephone calls and invitations which he had learned to expect for so many years were no more. Ambassadors, congressmen, cabinet members pretended they did not know him. The stigma and disgrace of the Coldstream and McCauley affair had stained him.

Cogswell thought often of Coldstream and McCauley. He wondered where they had been buried. No one knew. He felt in some ways responsible for their deaths, but was helpless. He made half-hearted attempts to get in touch with their families, but McCauley had only distant cousins and it could be assumed that Coldstream's ex-wife would not be interested. It was then

that Cogswell realized how completely Coldstream and Mc-
Cauley were gone. For a few years they would be remembered
vaguely as traitors or Communists, and then the names would disappear except for an occasional library file that still had a card for
Sarkhan: A Thousand Years, by McCauley, Thaddeus.

Something had to be done with the manila envelope. It worried
and nagged at him. He never let it out of his sight. He carried the
papers in his coat pocket. At night they were under his pillow.

Finally he telephoned Wally DeVoto, the special assistant to
the President.

"Wally, don't hang up until you hear me through. I have some
documents which are terribly important to the future of the
United States. It is imperative that the President see them. I am
the only person alive who knows what is in the documents. If the
President reads them, my responsibility will be over. I need have
no acknowledgment. I want you to take these papers to the
President."

"Mister Cogswell, the President is very busy."

"Not as a favor to me, Wally," said Cogswell, "but as a duty to
America, I ask you to accept the documents and look at them."

"Okay. Mail them."

"I don't dare. If they got into the wrong hands . . . I'll be glad
to bring them to your apartment any time you say."

"Seven-thirty tonight."

At seven-thirty that night Cogswell rang DeVoto's doorbell.
When the door opened, he gave the envelope to DeVoto.

Without a word, he turned and left.

Two nights later, at ten minutes to eleven, Cogswell was in
his study. He was examining a copy of one of his newer magazines without, he realized, a great deal of interest.

His butler entered.

"Sir, there is someone to see you."

"At this time of night? I don't want to be disturbed. Not by
anyone."

"It is Mister DeVoto from the White House."

Cogswell pushed the copy away.

"Show him in."

Wally DeVoto entered briskly. All the Presidential assistants he'd ever known, Cogswell thought, did things briskly.

"Mister Cogswell, I was told to hand-carry this to you," DeVoto said, handing over an envelope. "It is for your eyes only."

Cogswell took it, turned it over, and was aware his fingers trembled. He was prepared for another blow. He looked at DeVoto, but the young man was studiously examining the spines of books on the library shelves.

Cogswell opened the envelope. The letter was handwritten, undated, but on White House stationery.

Dear Adolph:

I would have come to you personally. But I am sure you understand that this would not be wise.

The documents you sent me I have read carefully. It was a painful experience but I learned from them.

I cannot honor your two friends. I can do nothing to repair your reputation. This I regret.

The Communists can be beaten—but only with new instruments and fresh ideas such as those suggested by your two friends and yourself.

I shall ask for your anonymous help in the future, Adolph. And I know I can trust your discretion.

With thanks.

Cogswell sat back in his chair and sighed as he stared at the President's scrawly signature. He heard the riffle of pages and remembered that DeVoto was still in the room.

"Wally," Cogswell asked harshly, the old strength and assurance back in his voice, "are you waiting to see if I am going to burn this letter?"

"No sir. The President did not instruct me to wait." He hesitated a moment. "But I thought there might be a reply."

"No reply, Wally."

DeVoto walked slowly, with obvious reluctance, to the door. He looked once more at the letter in the old man's hand.

"Good night, sir." He left.

Cogswell read the letter again. He paused over the last sentence. "I know I can trust your discretion."

He went to the fireplace, took a big wooden match from a pewter cup, struck it, and bent forward. He lit the note and let it burn until the flames were close to his fingers. Then he dropped the charred paper on the grate.

About the Authors

Both William Lederer and Eugene Burdick have traveled widely in, and written extensively about, Southeast Asia. Together they are celebrated as the co-authors of *The Ugly American*.

William Lederer, a retired Navy captain, is a novelist, a writer for many national magazines, a lecturer, and author of *A Nation of Sheep*, *All the Ships at Sea*, and others.

Eugene Burdick, who died on July 26th, 1965, was an associate professor of Political Science at the University of California (Berkeley), wrote many articles and short stories, was the co-author of *Fail-Safe*, and the author of *The 480*, *The Ninth Wave*, and other books.